"This superb book explores the intersections between walking and ethnography, narrative and biographic methods, visual and participatory methods. The authors' enthusiasm is infectious and will surely inspire researchers to get walking!"

Jennifer Fleetwood, Senior Lecturer in Criminology, Goldsmiths College, UK

"*Walking Methods* is an important contribution to the field of walking studies through a critical new method – the Walking Interview as a Biographical Method (WIBM). The book is comprehensive in scope, detailing the history and current iterations of 'methods on the move' across the arts and social sciences. WIBM is significant because it considers how people's biographies and life stories are shaped through perambulation that takes place through various durations and movements. Rich in examples, exercises, and (auto)biographical reflections this book makes a unique contribution to walking methods."

Stephanie Springgay, Associate Professor, Ontario Institute for Studies in Education, The University of Toronto, Canada

"A learned, revealing and absorbing route one guide to the sociology of walking and using the self as a sociological resource. Essential."

Chris Rojek, Professor of Sociology, City University of London, UK

"This book is the first complex composition of theoretical and empirical approaches to the different aspects of 'research on the move'. Deeply inspiring for sociologists, anthropologists, psychologists, and researchers of cultural studies. The high quality pedagogue supports qualitative researchers, especially those working and representing biographical studies."

Prof. Kaja Kaźmierska, Director of the Institute of Sociology, and Chair of the ESA Research Network 3 on Biographical Perspectives on European Societies, University of Lodz, Poland

WALKING METHODS

This book introduces and critically explores walking as an innovative method for doing social research, showing how its sensate and kinaesthetic attributes facilitate connections with lived experiences, journeys and memories, communities and identities. The book situates walking methods historically, sociologically, and in relation to biographical and arts-based research, as well as new work on mobilities, the digital, spatial, and the sensory.

The book is organised into three sections: theorising; experiencing; and imagining walking as a new method for doing biographical research. There is a key focus upon the Walking Interview as a Biographical Method (WIBM) on the move to usefully explore migration, memory, and urban landscapes, as part of participatory, visual, and ethnographic research with marginalised communities and artists and as re-formative and transgressive. The book concludes with autobiographical walks taken by the authors and a discussion about the future of the Walking Interview as a Biographical Method.

Walking Methods combines theory with a series of original ethnographic and participatory research examples. Practical exercises and a guide to using walking as a method help to make this a rich resource for social science researchers, students, walking artists, and biographical researchers.

Maggie O'Neill is Professor in Sociology at the University of Cork. She has a long history of doing critical theory/feminist research and conducting walking, participatory, and biographical methods with communities and artists, as well as marginalised groups on topics such as sex work, migration, and participatory, creative, and arts-based methodologies.

Brian Roberts taught and researched at several UK universities and was a visiting academic at institutions in a number of countries. He was closely associated with the early work of the Centre for Contemporary Cultural Studies, University of Birmingham, UK. He has written widely on biographical research, social theory, and research practice.

WALKING METHODS

Research on the Move

Maggie O'Neill and Brian Roberts

Routledge
Taylor & Francis Group

LONDON AND NEW YORK

First published 2020
by Routledge
2 Park Square, Milton Park, Abingdon, Oxon OX14 4RN

and by Routledge
52 Vanderbilt Avenue, New York, NY 10017

Routledge is an imprint of the Taylor & Francis Group, an Informa business

British Library Cataloguing-in-Publication Data
A catalogue record for this book is available from the British Library

Library of Congress Cataloging-in-Publication Data
A catalog record has been requested for this book

ISBN: 978-1-138-18247-9 (hbk)
ISBN: 978-1-138-18248-6 (pbk)
ISBN: 978-1-315-64644-2 (ebk)

Typeset in Bembo
by Deanta Global Publishing Services, Chennai, India

CONTENTS

FIGURES

INTRODUCTION

Maggie O'Neill and Brian Roberts

Walking Methods: Research on the Move is a text which is very opportune – coming at a time of increasing emphasis on methodologies at the boundaries of the arts and social sciences, including explorations of the role of space, movement, and the senses in research practice, and associated social intervention or 'policy impact'. 'Walking', in particular, is the focus for the authors' innovatory research practices within biographical research, utilising 'life story', ethnographic, visual, and participatory approaches in exploring lived experiences ('lived lives') within the broader social structures, contexts, and processes of our social worlds (cf. Mills 1970). This monograph combines biographical study and the 'walking interview', supported with stimulating examples from our primary research, and our long history in the field of both biographical research and artsbased methods.

Walking is something we do every day and yet we reflect little upon it – as an experience, source of knowledge, personal sharing, and memory. Beyond the few histories of walking and its use as part of artistic practice, there has been little application of the 'walking interview' until recently in the social sciences. The long tradition of walking in arts practice (Morris 2017; Hind and Qualmann 2015; Heddon 2007; Long 1984; Fulton 2010 – see Chapters 3 and 9), is now being complemented by increasing work in ethnographic and anthropological research (Ingold 2007; Ingold and Vergunst 2008; Pink et al. 2010; Irving 2010; Edensor 2010), but in areas such as biographical sociology and criminology, there is still relatively little contribution (see O'Neill 2015, O'Neill 2017; O'Neill 2018, Roberts 2015).

This text will seek to develop the walking interview for biographical sociology, by: raising awareness of the researcher and the 'researched' 'within the world' as moving, interacting, experiencing beings; contributing a new approach – the Walking Interview as a Biographical Method (WIBM). Meanwhile, the text will critically reflect upon the theoretical, experiential, and imaginative application of the act of 'walking' as part of biographical research. 'Walking', although an 'ordinary', familiar activity and relatively novel form of research practice, is beginning to gain 'momentum' within social sciences as an attractive and exciting form of sociological, criminological, and other exploration.

This text will also contribute to the emerging diverse range of texts on 'walking' as a field of experience (see e.g., Horvath and Szakolczai 2018; Gros 2015; Springgay and Truman 2018), and to biographical and other areas of sociological investigation, such as the expanding field of 'mobilities' research (Urry 2007; Büscher et al. 2010; Smith and Hall 2016).

Social science research is increasingly 'on the move' – technological advances in video and cameras, tablets, smartphones, and digital recorders are enabling researchers to record, share, and transmit materials and reports in a wider variety of means across time and space. For instance, this development, as in the employment of cameras, ranges from such research as Whyte's (1988) application (alongside direct observation) to study the public spaces of the city and how people use them, to the time delay photography of Matos Wunderlich, who studied the phenomenology of walking in city spaces, and how its rhythmic quality 'forms an integrated and supportive part of place-rhythms and contributes to the temporal continuity and distinctiveness of urban places' (Matos Wunderlich 2008: 136; see Lyon 2016). In general, digital technology has very important implications for contemporary and future biographical research practice, since it allows the investigation of everyday routines, spaces, personal and group life, and researcher experience – an 'interactivity' with participants and others – in 'present time' and 'on the move'.

Overview of the field: Why this book and why now?

This book introduces, theorises, and shares walking as a method for doing social exploration, specifically within biographical research.

Biographical research seeks to investigate individuals' daily life experiences and their past and future perspectives, using a variety of materials and interpretive approaches (Roberts 2002: 2; Bertaux 1981). Biographical research methods are 'an umbrella term for an assembly of loosely related, variously titled activities: narrative, life history, oral history, autobiography, biographical interpretative methods, storytelling, auto/biography, ethnography, reminiscence' (Bornat 2008: 344). The many approaches to conducting biographical research are rooted in a long and diverse genealogy from a focus upon one or more 'personal documents' – 'life stories', diaries, letters, autobiography, to archival and (increasingly) multimedia and arts-based research using creative and performative methods (Chamberlayne et al. 2000; Roberts 2002; O'Neill et al. 2015).

Walking is not to be privileged as a way of 'knowing', but it has certain sensate, kinaesthetic, and performative attributes that make it particularly 'insightful' for means for biographical, ethnographic, phenomenological, and psycho-social research – in accessing the 'routes' and movement, and the use and interpretation of spaces by individuals, as well as for sharing research findings with various publics (O'Neill and Hubbard 2010).

Innovations in research methods, especially artistic, sensory, digital, and multi-modal methods are gaining ground in the social sciences, building upon the various 'turns' in sociology, including the 'narrative' (Bruner 1987; Riessman 2008), 'visual and sensory' (Pink 2007, Pink 2008), 'biographic' (Roberts 2002), and 'performative' (O'Neill et al. 2015). There are also important connections in our approach, including with long and deeply embedded ways of doing sociological research with marginalised peoples, as in urban sociology (cf. the Chicago School); with urban geographers (cf. Massey 1994); critical theory (Benjamin 1992); and participatory methodologies (increasingly utilising art-based practices, including the work of walking artists).

Ethnographic studies are particularly important for the development of the WIBM. Contemporary approaches to ethnographic research commonly highlight, not merely a concern with 'movement' and spatial flows, but also visual and sensory dimensions of ethnographic practice. New technologies are increasingly relevant here: for instance, Evans and Jones (2011) used devices to track people's location, speed, and speech content and the timing of what participants said, finding that environmental features were important in forming discussion, and created a typology according to whether a setting was known to the interviewer or respondent.

As biographical sociologists, we are both inspired by walking ethnographies as well as walking histories as linking 'the imagination and culture' or the 'rhythm of walking' as it 'generates a kind of rhythm of thinking' (Solnit 2001: 4–5). The pursuit of walking as constitutive of the history of imagination and culture can be variously captured in the study of pilgrimage and settlement (Horvath and Szakolczai 2018) and protest, as so clearly evidenced in such events as the early 20th century women's suffrage marches; the Annual Miners' Gala and march in Durham, UK; the annual march in honour of missing and murdered women in Vancouver, Canada; and the global women's marches in solidarity with the women's march in Washington, 2017. It can be shown in examining walking as carnival; as creative, 'meditative, contemplative and educative'; as connected to experience of the natural world (cf. Wordsworth) (Coverley 2012: 23; Evans 2012). The history and philosophy of walking reveals how we conceive the interconnections between our bodily movement, our consciousness, and our surrounding environment – how knowledge and responses of each these are related (Solnit 2001: 27, 29).

The history of walking as an activity is deeply embedded in broader social contexts, social relations, and social structural differences: for example, class politics and inequalities in the work of Engels, Mayhew, and Orwell; gender politics in the writings of Virginia Woolf and Mary Wollstonecraft; the history of suffrage marches and the figure of the flâneuse (in contrast to the flâneur); and the politics of race in the migratory movements from South to North, and the slave trade. In the UK, social movement, social mobility, migration, and race relations are inextricably connected in immigration law and the governance of migration and social space (O'Neill 2010). The Vagrancy Acts (for instance, the Act of 1824) and the formation of the modern police in London (1829) to 'oversee the street' were designed to eradicate or deter the poor from walking in certain urban areas, while the subsequent Contagious Diseases Acts (1864, 1866, and 1869) were aimed not merely to protect men's health from the perceived risk from street 'prostitutes', but served also to sanction and 'police' poor women and the urban 'underclasses' (see Walkowitz 1980).

The gendered and racialised aspects of walking are important to consider in the development and application of walking methods in biographical research. Female walkers feature relatively little in the histories of walking – a lack of recognition that is now being addressed in accounts of work by women artists (see Heddon and Turner 2010) and the 'recovery' of 'walking women'; for instance, Virginia Woolf (like others) undertook a great deal of her creative work as she walked, drawing on her memories, and shaping her thoughts (Coverley 2012: 170).

The recent work within ethnography emphasising the visual and other sensory 'realms' and their relations, the growing attention to the history and forms of walking and its experiential importance, and how walking is regulated or constrained, all give a focus to how we live our daily lives – its context and its movement. For our purposes, all these concerns point to how we form a sense of who we are, our past, present, and future – how we create our 'biography/biographies', shaped through and within our ongoing social and other circumstances. It is in this sense – the attention to 'daily biographical formation' – in using the WIBM, which makes this book timely as a contribution to a rapidly developing biographical sociology.

Biographical Research: Walking – thinking, experiencing and imagining

The use of the Walking Interview as a Biographical Method (WIBM) is a powerful means for understanding the lives and experiences of others. Walking is not just what we do to get from 'A' to 'B', but is integral to our perception of an environment. Taking a walk with someone is a significant way of communicating about experiences: one can become 'attuned' to another (Scheff 2006), connecting in a 'lived' (embodied, related) way with the feelings and corporeal presence of someone else. Walking with another opens up a space for dialogue where embodied knowledge, experience, and memories can be shared (O'Neill and Hubbard 2010; Pink et al. 2010; O'Neill and Stenning 2013; O'Neill and McHugh 2017; Roy 2016). Interviewing while walking has particular benefits for understanding another's life and experience, otherwise one 'cannot effectively capture the momentary impressions confronted, the peculiar evanescent atmospheres, the rhythms, immanent sensations and physical effects of walking' (Edensor 2008: 136; see also Myers 2010, Heddon and Turner 2010).

There are interesting parallels to be drawn between walking and 'telling a story' – how we give an account of our past in 'retracing our steps' that others can follow while composing their own. In this way, a story is also a journey between locations and subjects, and our knowledge gained is part of that movement (Ingold 2007: 90). A walk can therefore be given as an oral story or written by a writer; in fact, walkers as tellers can take many 'forms', from philosophers to vagrants, 'flâneurs' to pilgrims (Coverley 2012: 16, 21; see Chapter 5).

Walking, in summary, has strong 'experiential dimension': for instance, Rousseau described walking as an 'escape mechanism', as well as a philosophical and melancholic practice – he declared that unlike being tied to place, it 'stimulates and enlivens my thoughts' (Coverley 2012: 25, 28; see Chapter 1). There can also be an 'experimental aspect' in our relation to how we walk in given contexts, as in the practices of Dada and Situationism to more recent psychogeography (Coverley 2012; Richardson 2015). Hence, we develop here an innovative method for conducting biographical research that extends our earlier work on participatory, visual and performative biographies (O'Neill et al. 2015) by introducing and examining walking as a research method engaged in multi-sensory ways of knowing; a means to elicit phenomenological, sensory (e.g., visual) and biographical understanding through time, space, and place.

Examination and discussion of the intersection of biographical research, ethnographic walking methods, and arts practice is a key contribution of this text, to form a research practice that shows the lived/living individual in movement, as embodied, as well as related to sensory experiences and within a material world, and in communication with others in forming their (and our) biographical account(s) of life. The content of the book is influenced by walking as an 'art practice', due to the attention that field gives to embodiment and sensory experience in our interpretation of our social world. Again, such areas of experience are of importance in the development of walking as a method within biographical research to give a wider portrait of individual biography as 'lived/living' and produced in 'the everyday'.

Although we are both influenced by and engage with walking as an art practice, the main focus of this book is to deliver a social science approach to walking as a research method, as part of the 'turn to movement' in social research methodology, and specifically what this means for biographical sociology. We have developed what we have designated the Walking Interview as a Biographical Method (WIBM).

The Walking Interview as a Biographical Method (WIBM)

The walking interview method is being used increasingly widely and innovatively, but this may induce 'pressure' to formalise procedures and principles, including the forms of interview and recording. Types of concept formation and interpretation necessary may well come under increasing debate as the variety of 'data' collected (from across the social sciences, the arts, digital, and other fields) becomes more apparent, eliciting the need to have strategies to encompass the range of material sought and methods applied, and then the choice of related forms of interpretation of the diverse data. 'Walking research' can, in fact, be used in a number of broad ways: as an area to research (i.e., how, why, amount, and so on); as a methodology to gain materials (via recording an interview and 'subject's' relation with surrounding environment); and walking can also be used for dissemination of 'findings' (e.g., through a 'performance event').

As a relatively new methodology in social science, the 'walking method' needs to make clear its assumptions on the 'social' and its interpretive basis. For example, 'To what extent is the method actually 'new' – innovative, creative?'; 'What does it get to that other methodologies may not?' In the employment of the interview walking method, various 'practical' questions arise: 'What skills are needed and how might they be facilitated?' and, again, 'Are the skills needed "new"?'; 'Is the methodology more appropriate to some respondents and topics than others?'; 'What are its main techniques and materials gathered?'; 'What are its advantages or disadvantages over other approaches (i.e., in terms of cost, time, access)?'; 'In what ways may it link with other methods?'; 'Is it 'better' than other methods in making such links – in "mixing methods"?'; 'Are there particular difficulties in mixing methods which include the walking interview as a biographical method?'; 'How close to "informal" interviews within "traditional" ethnographic practice is it? For example, such interviews could also be considered to be "on the move" from "scene to scene"?' In short, 'What are the "unique claim(s)" for the walking interview as a biographical method?' We attempt to respond to some of these questions in the following chapters.

There is the possibility that a rather restrictive notion of the WIBM may be assumed – that it is taken as merely an interview conducted while 'on the move'; in that sense, it could be conceived, again, as little different from the 'informal' interviews – the passing conversations – within ethnographic research (where traditionally notes are usually compiled later, rather than by an audio recording and then transcribed). What we have found is that the WIBM puts to the fore that the interview and its recording is based 'within the present', while recognising that memories emerge, re-emerge, and are re-viewed, and re-interpreted within the current 'passing' of time. As will be described, the method, as based on research 'in the present' and the 'settings' of the 'researched', emphasises how perceptions and feelings, memories and understandings become apparent, are organised and meaning re-cast, by individuals within and moving through various environments, in material culture, and daily time and space.

While it could be argued that the method is merely and traditionally part of ethnography, which maybe 'on the move' within and between locations – for instance, the work of Irving (2010) and Edensor (2010) exemplify walking as part of the practice of the ethnographer – it should be noted, that the *walking* method concentrates on the experience as within movement: it gives attention to contextual 'moves' from scene to scene and in changing time perspectives; we are beings in shifting place and time; memory is not fixed; our consciousness 'moves' across these dimensions. A strength of the 'walking interview' is that the social conditions are laid bare and their relevance in the research process: the orality, landscape, the sense-scape (sound, smell, touch, visual), perceptions, and emotions are based within context, within which both interviewer and interviewee interact.

The WIBM brings new perspectives to biographical narrative research, asking 'What are our imaginative spaces, our sensory scapes?' and 'How biographically do we relate to our 'present', our immediate environment, our past(s) and future(s)?' These dimensions require a variety of interpretive theories, materials, and schemas, which can include narrative; phenomenology; textual and image analysis; artistic approaches; and their relations (and possible 'mixings') (Roberts 2015; O'Neill et al. 2015).

The WIBM could be described by critics as based on an inclusive, 'holistic', 'utopian', or 'romantic' assumption about social life and walking in an attempt to construct a 'complete' individual within 'everyday' social contexts through undertaking a biographical interview 'on the move'. But in 'capturing' a person within a series of scenes, the WIBM can 'tap into' a multitude of dimensions of individual experiences and their interpretation, and so enable a 'fuller', rather than 'full', portrait of the individual and their life. This attempt points to the 'storied' (Bruner 1987) nature of our lives, while recognising that there are multiple ways to conduct a biographical analysis, and that there is no such thing as 'raw experience' – what we recount is mediated in various ways, according to how we understand or 'define' situations in the present and past (and future). This is because the 'stories' we tell of our lives are reflexive and recursive, and involve memory and self-construction over time. As Jackson makes clear, the narrated and narratable self is temporally and socially located: both the narration and the events recounted position the teller in a social landscape (Jackson 2010: 123).

While the 'stories' each of us tells about ourselves typically invoke a past (distant or recent), implicitly or explicitly linked to a present and to a possible future, the act of giving a personal account not only takes place within the flow of time but is situated within a sequence of social interactions between narrator and audience and in relation to socio-environmental contexts. We are not simply determined by our pasts, we re-form our complex histories, to situate them within our contemporary life – our perspectives, experiences, tasks, and 'ongoing' biography.

For us, the objective of biographical work using the WIBM is not to attempt the impossible of a 'complete individual', but rather to view the individual as evolving and moving in time and place, *and* stress the participatory nature of the relationship between respondent and the researcher, the co-productive nature of life accounts. Here, we need to be clear on the extent and form of this participation – different applications of the walking interview method will necessarily have different 'degrees' or forms of relationship – in walking practice, diverse means of relating 'findings and interpretation', and in the dissemination of the research (see Chapter 6).

The challenge to the WIBM is to establish and confirm its 'innovative status', rather than merely, at base, giving new names to old practices, or simply taking from other disciplines; to not only avoid the criticism as being 'not that new', as merely using existing techniques and dimensions – the oral (the interview), visual practices (video/photographic images), etc. – but to go beyond the limitations of the traditional informal interview (see Wiles et al. 2011). Even so, in pursuing a 'new' practice (WIBM), we are concerned not to jettison concepts, perspectives, or methodologies, but to re-form them, so that they may aid the understanding of how we construct our biography. In the combination of arts-based walking and biographical methods, something innovative and insightful in perspective comes into being – the individual 'on the move'.

In adopting 'perambulation' in research, we must not assume a singular exclusive conception of individual experience (for both the 'researched' and 'researcher' or as combined) of 'to walk'. The approach must also include recognition of those who require technical help in terms of movement (cf. walking or mobility aids), or for the variability of the senses (i.e., in abilities to hear or see, etc.). Walking can be a solitary occupation (perhaps, paradoxically, especially so within a crowd), as related to others, or with another person (or in group), and may include being physically helped or guided by someone (or by technology). As in any research, individuals, including both researchers and researched, have differing physical and mental capabilities, previous experiences, and knowledge (see Young and Temple 2014).

We must bear in mind that a walking interview is also circumscribed in various ways – as urban and rural spaces are subject (sometimes increasingly) to layers of regulation and private/commercial/state policing (national and local official laws, land/building owners' stipulations, entrance fees, security measures and vetting, gated communities, etc.) covering rights of access, terms of use, opening and closing times, permitted behaviours, numbers and so on, as well as 'informal' customs and practices (see Ingold and Vergunst 2008). Walking, of course, is often within the ubiquity of personal cameras, especially on mobile phones or other devices, the pervasiveness of 'social media', texting, and video blogs, including the proliferation of 'citizen news', and often undertaken under the watching eye of the technologies of the 'surveillance culture' (e.g., CCTV). In short, walking must be contextualised in terms of social institutions and (historical) shaping processes and practices which relate to inequalities of law and power, to how social hierarchies are formed, maintained, and overlaid, including how class, national/regional/city, ethnic and race, age, gender, and sexual identities are positioned within the definition and regulation of public/private spaces (see Shortell and Brown 2014; Beaumont 2015).

The WIBM enables researchers to get in touch with 'realities' that demand critical reflection through mobile ways of knowing and 'understanding'. In advocating 'research on the move', we reflect on the need to experience and value the importance of innovative ways of working with research participants, to advance dialogue and understanding by attention to the performative and sensing body in biographical research. As we will outline, it is here that arts-based walking methods are relevant, due to their embodied, relational, sensory, and use of multi-modality. In this book, we introduce, explore, interpret, and apply the walking interview as a method in order to advance understanding of biographical formation, and as conception of research 'on the move'. We do so in three parts.

Part I, *Theorising/observing/thinking*, sets out the inter-disciplinary, theoretical, and historical underpinnings to our perspective on walking as a biographical research method. Chapter 1, *Methods on the move: Moving methods*, is a foundational chapter that deals with key questions of definition regarding walking as a 'method' and the embodied, cognitive, sensual, relational, visual, communicative dimensions and possibilities. It also situates walking as a method in relation to contemporary work on mobilities, the sensory, digital, and visual/arts. Chapter 2, *Theorising walking in the sociological imagination: Walking in context*, extends our discussion on the importance of the sociological imagination and histories and theories of walking to biographical research, especially the pioneering investigations of the Chicago School sociologists in their work on the city, migration, and urban experience, the critical theory of Walter Benjamin, and Situationism, as well as the 'everyday' walking of de Certeau. We also discuss the social documentary tradition of text/photography (e.g., the photo book) and street photography. Chapter 3, *Walking, art-making, and biographical research*, extends the discussion in the previous chapter by consolidating the development of our practices of thinking, observing, and theorising walking in biographical research, by focusing upon the important interrelationships between walking, biographical research, and arts practice, which underpins our development of the WIBM.

Part II, *Experiencing*, focuses upon the experience of doing and undertaking WIBM and draws upon our research projects to demonstrate the theoretical and methodological basis for the method. Using ethnographic, arts-based, and participatory approaches, a phenomenological, dialogic, sensory conception of biographical research emerges across the three chapters. Chapter 4, takes a walk with biographical sociologist Robert Miller to examine *Migration, memory, and place: Connecting with memory and place in urban landscapes*. Chapter 5, examines forms and motivations of and for walking in relation to *Walking as re-formative and transgressive: Health, pilgrimage, trespass, marching*. Chapter 6, *Walking in the Downtown Eastside: Experiencing the WIBM as participatory, visual, and ethnographic*, discusses walking biographical interviews undertaken with marginalised residents of the Downtown Eastside, Vancouver, and the extent to which the experience and application of the WIBM can contribute to community-based, participatory research.

Part III, *Imagining*, focuses upon the role of the imagination in developing and using the WIBM across four chapters. Chapter 7, *Walking, sex work, and community: Towards a radical democratic and imaginative space for addressing sexual and social inequalities*, extends the central theme of the WIBM as an imaginative method for doing biographical research by discussing four walks undertaken around the common theme of sex work in London, Liverpool, a northern UK city, and Vancouver. Chapter 8, *The phenomenology of walking in a garden*, examines the way that emotions, memories, and the senses are attached to place, as in gardens, and in turn can shape our biographies. Chapter 9, *Walking artists: Critical dialogues and imaginaries*, extends the central theme of arts-based imaginative research and walking biographies of place by discussing walks undertaken with two walking artists, and in Chapter 10, *Auto/biographical encounters in time and space: Roots and routes*, the authors recount and reflect on walks they have taken in their childhood home village and town – Scrooby and Consett – and outline how our 'root(s)' and the 'routes' form and shape the most important aspects of who we are.

In the *Conclusion*, we discuss the future of the Walking Interview as a Biographical Method, and we summarise the ways in which the WIBM brings a new approach to biographical research and look forward to future developments and applications of the WIBM.

We include an Exercise at the end of each Part and Conclusion for the reader to become sensitised to and try out the method, and some guidance in the form of 'Principles and Practice' towards a framework for those taking forward the WIBM.

References

Beaumont, M. (2015) *Nightwalking*. London: Verso.
Benjamin, W. (1992) The storyteller. In: *Illuminations*. (Tr. H. Zohn). London: Fontana Press.
Bertaux, D. (ed.) (1981) *Biography and Society. The Life History Approach in the Social Sciences*. London: Sage.
Bornat, J. (2008) Biographical methods. In: P. Alasuutari, L. Bickman, and J. Brannen (eds.) *The Sage Handbook of Social Research Methods*. London: Sage.
Bruner, J. (1987) Life as narrative, *Social Research*, 54(1): 11–32.
Büscher, M., Urry, J., and Witchger, K. (eds.) (2010) *Mobile Methods*. London: Routledge.
Chamberlayne, P., Bornat, J., and Wengraf, T. (eds.) (2000) *The Turn to Biographical Methods in Social Science*. London: Routledge.
Coverley, M. (2012) *The Art of Wandering: The Writer as Walker*. Harpenden, UK: Oldcastle Books.
Edensor, T. (2008) Walking through ruins. In: T. Ingold, and J. L. Vergunst (eds.) *Ways of Walking: Ethnography and Practice on Foot*. Aldershot, UK: Ashgate.
Edensor, T. (2010) Walking in rhythms: Place, regulation, style and the flow of experience, *Visual Studies*, 25(1): 69–79.
Evans, D. (ed.) (2012) *The Art of Walking: A Field Guide*. London: Black Dog Publishing.
Evans, J. and Jones, P. (2011) The walking interview: Methodology, mobility and place, *Applied Geography*, 31(2): 849–858.
Fulton, H. (2010) Walk, *Visual Studies*, 25(1): 8–14.
Gros, F. (2015) *The Philosophy of Walking*. London: Verso.
Heddon, D. (2007) *Autobiography and Performance*. Basingstoke, UK: Palgrave Macmillan.
Heddon, D. and Turner, C. (2010) Walking women: Interviews with artists on the move, *Performance Research*, 15(4): 14–22.
Hind, C. and Qualmann, C. (2015) *Ways to Wander*. Axminster, UK: Triarchy Press.

Horvath, A. and Szakolczai, A. (2018) *Walking into the Void: A Historical Sociology and Political Anthropology of Walking*. London: Routledge.

Ingold, T. (2007) *Lines: A Brief History*. London: Routledge.

Ingold, T. and Vergunst, J. L. (eds.) (2008) *Ways of Walking: Ethnography and Practice on Foot*. London: Routledge.

Irving, A. (2010) Dangerous substances and visible evidence: Tears, blood, alcohol, pills, *Visual Studies*, 25(1): 24–35.

Jackson, S. (2010) Self, time and narrative: Re-thinking the contribution of G. H. Mead, *Life Writing*, 7(2): 123–136.

Long, R. (1984) One hour. A sixty minute walk circle on Dartmoor. Available at www.richardlong.org/Textworks/2011textworks/41.html (Accessed 21 September 2018).

Lyon, D. (2016) Doing audio-visual montage to explore time and space: The everyday rhythms of Billingsgate Fish Market, *Sociological Research Online*, 21(3): 1–12. Available at www.socresonline.org.uk/21/3/12.html (Accessed 21 September 2018).

Massey, D. (1994) *Space, Place and Gender*. Cambridge, UK: Polity.

Matos Wunderlich, F. (2008) Walking and rhythmicity: Sensing urban space, *Journal of Urban Design*, 13(1): 125–139.

Mills, C. W. (1970) *The Sociological Imagination*. Harmondsworth, UK: Penguin.

Morris, B. (2017) *Walking Networks: The Development of an Artistic Medium*. PhD Thesis submitted in partial fulfilment of the requirements of the University of East London, for the degree of Doctor of Philosophy, July 2017 (From personal communication with the author).

Myers, M. (2010) Walk with me, talk with me: The art of conversive wayfinding, *Visual Studies*, 26(1): 50–68.

O'Neill, M. (2010) *Asylum, Migration and Community*. Bristol: Policy Press.

O'Neill, M. (2015) Participatory biographies: Walking, sensing, belonging. In: M. O'Neill, B. Roberts, and A. Sparkes (eds.) *Advances in Biographical Research: Creative Applications*. Abingdon, UK: Routledge.

O'Neill, M. (2017) Studying the marginalised with mixed methods. In: S. Walklate, and M. Hviid Jacobsen (eds.) *Liquid Criminology: Doing Imaginative Criminological Research*. London and New York: Routledge.

O'Neill, M. and Hubbard, P. (2010) Walking, sensing, belonging: Ethno-mimesis as performative praxis, *Visual Studies*, 25(1): 46–58.

O'Neill, M. and McHugh, C. (2017) Walking with Faye from a direct access hostel to her special place in the city: Walking, body and image space. A visual essay, *Journal of Social Work Practice*, 31(2): 207–223.

O'Neill, M., Roberts, B., and Sparkes, S. (eds.) (2015) *Advances in Biographical Methods; Creative Applications*. Abingdon, UK: Routledge.

O'Neill, M. and Stenning, P. (2013) Walking biographies and innovations in visual and participatory methods: Community, politics and resistance in downtown east side Vancouver. In: C. Heinz and G. Hornung (eds.) *The Medialization of Auto/Biographies: Different Forms and Their Communicative Contexts*. Hamburg: UVK.

Pink, S. (2007) Walking with video, *Visual Studies*, 22(3): 240–252.

Pink, S. (ed.) (2008) *Doing Sensory Ethnography*. London: Sage.

Pink, S., Hubbard, P., O'Neill, M., and Radley, A. (2010) Walking across disciplines: from ethnography to arts practice, *Visual Studies*, 25(1): 1–7.

Richardson, T. (2015) *Walking Inside Out: Contemporary British Psychogeography*. London and New York: Rowman and Littlefield.

Riessman, C. K. (2008) *Narrative Methods for the Human Sciences*. London: Sage.

Roberts, B. (2002) *Biographical Research*. Buckingham: Open University Press.

Roberts, B. (2015) Biographical research: Past, present, future. In: M. O'Neill, B. Roberts, and A. Sparkes (eds.) *Advances in Biographical Methods: Creative Applications.* Abingdon, UK: Routledge.

Roy, A. (2016) Learning on the move: Exploring work with vulnerable young men through the lens of movement, *Applied Mobilities*, 1(2): 207–218.

Scheff, T. (2006) Mobilization and Silence: Emotional/relational Dynamics. Available at www.soc.ucsb.edu/faculty/scheff/main.php?id=44.html (Accessed 21 September 2018).

Shortell, T. and Brown, E. (eds.) (2014) *Walking in the European City. Quotidian Mobility and Urban Ethnography.* London: Routledge.

Smith, R. J. and Hall, T. (2016) Pedestrian circulations: Urban ethnography, the mobilities paradigm and outreach work, *Mobilities*, 11(4): 498–508.

Solnit, R. (2001) *Wanderlust: A History of Walking.* London: Verso.

Springgay, S. and Truman, S. E. (2018) *Walking Methodologies in a More-Than-Human World: WalkingLab.* London: Routledge.

Urry, J. (2007) *Mobilities.* Cambridge: Polity.

Walkowitz, J. (1980) *Prostitution and Victorian Society.* Cambridge, UK: Cambridge University Press.

Whyte, W. H. (1988) *City: Rediscovering the Center.* Philadelphia, PA: University of Pennsylvania Press.

Wiles, R., Crow, G., and Pain, H. (2011) Innovation in qualitative research methods: A narrative review, *Qualitative Research*, 11(5): 587–604.

Young, A. and Temple, B. (2014) *Approaches to Social Research: The Case of Deaf Studies.* Oxford: Oxford University Press.

PART I

Theorising/observing/ thinking

This Part comprises three chapters and informs Parts II and III by connecting and exploring the work of social and cultural theorists and commentators, and noting the importance of walking and the walking interview to sociology and wider interdisciplinary research, in terms of observing, thinking, and theorising. *Chapter 1: Methods on the move* discusses issues relating to the definition and practice of the Walking Interview as a Biographical Method (WIBM) and the sensual, relational, situational, and other dimensions of the experience of walking. It describes how the method 'opens' the biographical perspectives of others in the act of walking with others – in movement – in an interactive, 'attuned' manner. *Chapter 2: Theorising walking in the sociological imagination*: Walking in context grounds the act of walking, observing, relating to others in the socioenvironment in the history of social explorers, commentators, and social scientists from 19th century urban walkers, through the work of the 1920s–30s Chicagoan researchers, social documentary work, and more recent writers and practitioners (e.g. urban explorers) who seek to observe, understand, and 'connect' with their surroundings. *Chapter 3: Walking, art-making and biographical research* takes forward the discussion of observation and understanding in the earlier chapters to examine walking as experienced within contemporary city urban spaces. It examines the work of the mobilities perspective, Benjamin and C. W. Mills, and walking artists in constructing a biographical research practice employing walking as a relational, imaginative, and aesthetic experience, and gives an example of WIBM research.

At the end of each Part, we include an exercise for readers to theorise (Part I), experience (Part II), imagine (Part III) and apply the WIBM (Conclusion).

1

METHODS ON THE MOVE

Moving methods

Introduction

This chapter addresses key questions of definition regarding walking as a 'method' (in contrast to 'mere' movement or routine experience) – operating with an awareness of everyday action as embodied, cognitive, sensual, relational, visual, communicative dimensions and possibilities. It also situates walking as a method in relation to contemporary work on mobilities, the senses (e.g., the visual), and digital methodologies. We introduce the process of theorising methods 'on the move' by connecting the activity and conceptions of walking with art, philosophy, politics, and the psychosocial. It is argued that walking is an excellent method for entering into the biographical routes, mobilities, and experiences of others in a deeply engaged and 'attuned' way.

Walking

'Walking' is commonly apprehended as a routine activity, which we usually engage in with little thought. But, perhaps due to its ordinariness, we usually do not (or do not have to) consider that it encompasses a range of activities with differing styles, demands, abilities, characteristics, and motivations. 'Walking' can also be associated with numerous terms, reflecting its diversity: to promenade, saunter, step, or trudge; as a gait, a march, or stride; or to 'dally', dither, ramble, roam, traverse, stalk, and wander. It can be for many purposes: utilitarian (such as commuting for work); as a pleasure in itself; to fulfil domestic and family tasks (shopping, picking up children from school); or to meet some other objective (as a protest, for health, etc. see Chapter 5). Walking, of course, is both an embodied physical and mental experience – involving an awareness of the motion of the body, of its aches and pains, impact on the ground, or in raising the sheer exhilaration of movement. Therefore, the act of walking engages the senses: looking, hearing, the feeling of being touched by air, rain, or other elements of the environmental atmosphere, and contact with changing aromas.

As walking is undertaken under particular conditions, according to the elements, and during the day or night, questions arise as to the possible effects of 'choice' of when to walk, in terms of weather (e.g., rain: see Harrison 2016), time, route, and the impact of circumstance on an individual's mood, outlook, and relation with others (e.g., in conversation). In short, when examining walking activity or undertaking walking research, the physical (and social) conditions may have an influence and should be considered – and may even be an important 'topic thread' in the walking dialogue itself. Walking can be metaphoric of life as a biographical journey, a path, and often articulated as linear – 'walking a (fine) line' between 'travails' along the way, with dangers on each side. We also say we have 'walked in a circle' – someone may see their life as 'circular', or even as a 'return', as 'up' ('life on the up'), 'down' ('life has been downhill'), or some combination of such trajectories, as a 'life graph', with an evaluation of 'success' or 'failure' (see Brockmeier 2002; Gergen and Gergen 1984). To take 'firm steps' (in life) is to enact definite plans, whilst to 'toe the line' is to conform or follow another's lead.

Methods on the move: The Walking Interview as a Biographical Method (WIBM)

The academic (and popular) interest in walking as a topic and research practice has grown rapidly during the last few years, cutting across a wide range of disciplines and practices – sociology, history, geography, anthropology, education, architecture, traditional and 'new' arts (e.g., drawing, performance, video/film), and also in terms of association with cultural environments (museums, schools, urban spaces, rural settings) and in differing and national/regional locations (e.g., Vergunst and Ingold 2008; Bates and Rhys-Taylor 2017). The rise of interest in 'walking' is worth examining both in itself and in its intellectual context. Over the last 30 years in social science, a whole range of ideas have gained currency – often defined as instigating a 'turn' in theoretical and methodological orientation – 'time', 'space', 'culture', 'body', 'emotion', 'senses', including a 'biographical turn'. The Walking Interview as a Biographical Method (WIBM) is introduced at a time when new approaches are being described as 'creative' or 'innovative' in gaining new materials and insights in the furtherance of social science endeavours to examine current rapid social and technological shifts (e.g., migration flows, information/social media developments) (see Wiles et al. 2011).

In considering the WIBM, an initial question arises whether it is 'unique' or part of something broader in methodological approach? Initially, it can be placed within ethnography – where an interview may be carried out 'in the field' within a wide variety of circumstances – so it can be put (roughly) on a continuum between informal (conversational, unstructured) and formal (with a more organised set of questions) procedures. But, while the walking interview may also vary in the degree of pre-organisation and the 'set' format, its central feature is that it is 'on the move' – within processual experience (in time and space) – as participants traverse through social settings, or 'scenes'. The method is based on recognition that we have changing sensual, cognitive, and relational feelings; complex social and environmental relations; and a conviction that social research methods have not always fully taken account of the diversity, depth, and shifting character of social life. So, it takes from ethnography the cultural multiplicity of meanings in the social world and the necessity of understanding how values, interpretations, and attachments can change over time, and vary from social arena to arena. When used in biographical research – the central aspect of this book – methodologically, the walking interview brings an ethnographic orientation to study individuals as socially located, but also as 'mobile': individuals as embodied in 'moving' in time, space, and in mental life (cf. Simmel 1950).

The concern of the WIBM is not simply that people are in 'motion', but rather that they are involved subjectively in 'passing' through social and material circumstances (buildings, streets, trees, and gardens, people met and left behind). Also, that a particular perambulation, no matter how many times it has been undertaken (e.g., a repeated walk to or from school, work, shops, etc.) is never exactly the same in its context(s), experience, current mental and physical state, and memory. A locale may have altered to some degree – a new street sign or changed billboard advertisement – various sounds from a building now undergoing renovation or some new aroma from street food may be noticed; different 'facets' of light (cf. Wroe 2016), such as due to the weather, or streaming through trees and between housing blocks etc., may affect perception of surroundings, all impinging on the experience of a contemporary walk. A walk takes place within various kinds of time duration; for instance, the particular day or season can have an importance, having resonance in meaning for a participant. It also involves time in regard to the age or ability of the individual; for instance, the depth of memory a person has accumulated or influencing the length of an intended journey due to the physical effort required. Of course, the reason or objective for the walk may be dissimilar and its tempo rather different from other occasions. Walking is often solitary, but even when walking with others, there is a 'conversation' with the self – monitoring action, moving in thought and time. The walking interview can be expanded here to include a research interview before and/or after a 'respondent's' lone walk ('reviewing' and 'talking through' any recording that the respondent has made), or the interviewer and respondent may repeat the actual walk that the individual made.

To engage in a walking interview is to 'follow' someone ethnographically – a walk on their 'daily round' (a routine activity) or one that they have chosen, perhaps due to some special meaning for them (e.g., similar to a past situation or, say, revisiting a childhood home environ) (see Chapter 10). Researchers, here, relate to others in their 'natural environment' – how they live in giving meaning to their lives, in everyday exchanges with others and their surroundings.

The research procedure to be employed may be pre-set (e.g., questions and areas to be covered, route to be taken outlined in detail), or emerge more during the walk (e.g., questions/comment as issues, observations, and situations arise), or be (mainly) after the event (e.g., the respondent writing a post-account). Particular methods or procedures can be used within these 'stages'. A walking interview may use a wide range of 'additional' methods – 'reportage' drawing or sketching, which can make a participant (and researcher) observe closely; audio, photographic, and visual recording; internet-based resources; and formal maps and map-drawing (see Chapters 3 and 4) – in short, utilising and combining methods from the social sciences and across the arts (and elsewhere).

To walk obviously requires a person to be in movement – in 'ordinary' routines, as well as in a research project, a walk may vary in pace, and is likely to have stops where participants 'dwell' at a particular site. The WIBM, as with other research, has basic practical decisions – how long, who with, what to ask/talk about, when and where to take place – and for each of these, why? Again, not all of these practicalities will be decided (by researcher, participant, or in collaboration) beforehand. So, in the course of walking: how are the 'practicalities' of the walk and issues chosen? There can be participant or researcher choice, or mutual decision, emerging during the walk which could be fairly 'aimless' in route taken: the route may be altered or emerge during its course. In setting the length in time of the walking interview, how is the timelength determined, and how do the pace, rhythm, and pauses take place? The length, time, and tempo for a walk may depend on the type of informal or formal questions asked and the depth of discussion that ensues. An interviewee could be presented with a single question asking for an account of their life or an aspect of it, for their account to then proceed during a walk (Schütze 1992; Wengraf 2009).

Who sets the pace in walking can be subject to ability: walking can be a physically demanding activity for any individual, in part due to the weather, and the physical energy required (hence the need for rests and refreshments) should be borne in mind. In fact, the degree of bodily (and mental) effort often demanded in ethnographic research often tends to be overlooked in discussion of research practices. In short, a walk is subject to the mobility of participants (including the researcher) and other variations in personal attributes. So the WIBM (as any research) should not presume a type or ideal of the 'researcher' and 'researched' – and must not exclude those who are helped to move by mobility aids or are slower due to injury or disability (O'Neill 2015: 78) Similarly, it must also recognise that not everyone will have the same degree of sensory ability (in hearing, sight, smell, touch) and may be assisted by devices and technologies (see Young and Temple 2014; Heddon 2017; see Chapter 9). Some respondents may simply choose to walk at their own (slow, fast, or varying) pace. The method should be inclusive and participatory – an open, interactive, dialogical, processual method recognising, for example, that the voices of the disabled have been commonly missing in research – and that this interviewing approach takes account of their presence, lived experience, relations, and purposive action in their surrounding world (O'Neill 2015; Heddon 2017). Finally, it must be remembered, of course, that research participants (and researchers) bring cultural assumptions about 'biography' and 'interview' gained from 'nonacademic' contexts (media, employment, etc.) and in experiences of 'walking'.

A central feature of qualitative research has been the 'interrogation' of the researcher–'subject' relation, especially the degree to which it is a 'conversation' or 'dialogical', and the actual experience of the relation (i.e., the interview) on both sides – a recognition that two personal biographies are implicated in the relation, the 'subject's' and the 'researcher's'. The 'auto-ethnography' of the researcher in practice should be made apparent. Interestingly, this 'two-way flow' of experience and feeling can sometimes be made clear by the 'researched' – as Stuart found when an interviewee asked at the end of an interview, 'And how was it for you Mary?' (Stuart 1993). In walking research, the interviewer is a 'companion' for the journey. The WIBM brings into sharp relief the researcher and participant as being embodied, having a living presence in the social world as physically and mentally engaging with each other and with their environment. It also forefronts the sharing of 'moments' and rapport – in the act of walking and conversing, serving to put both at ease, with the participant (perhaps) feeling more in 'control' of the circumstance in this method, as more of an equal in the 'exercise', and commonly choosing the walk to be accomplished (A walker may also be accompanied by an animal – a dog, donkey, mule, etc. cf. R.L. Stevenson, *Travels with a Donkey in the Cevennes*, 1879; Thomson 2017). A researcher can learn from the 'story' a person has to tell and through their experience in locations (see Horowitz 2013). The researcher may be made aware of unappreciated physical, aesthetic, and sensual elements of even a regular walk they make from 'informal' or 'expert' knowledge (say of art, architecture, or local history) of the participant.

Practitioners and commentators have described a number of key features or claims for the walking interview. Kusenbach (2003) gives the merits of what she describes as the 'go-along' method with its basis in 'street phenomenology'. The walking interview enables the researcher to meet respondents within their 'natural' surroundings and in taking part in their routine activities (shopping, leisure, going to formal appointments and informal meetings with friends, etc.). While the interview is 'on the move', it will not simply stop when there is a pause in walking; such a hesitation may have significance, the respondent may wish to emphasise something in their account, or may specifically comment on a feature in the scene. In any event, there is the opportunity by the method to gain information on the respondent's relationship with their environment that would not arise or be only separately described in the 'traditional' 'static' interview. A walk may take place in the respondent's 'normal' circumstances, but could be in an unfamiliar locale. Importantly, information perhaps otherwise missed is obtained or 'elicited' in more 'depth', thereby gaining more insight into the 'present' daily experience of the researched (Kusenbach 2003, 2012; Clark and Emmel 2010). Information on lived experience can be enhanced further by respondents being able to record their experiences (by video, photographs, oral recording), and in some degree, gaining an influence or participation on what 'data' is collected, in a proactive rather than reactive manner. Here, there are the advantages of ethnographic practice with similarities with 'conversations' as they arise with 'key informants' and others 'in the field'. Of course, there are limitations as in wider ethnographic research: for example, 'external' access and dissemination for research materials is restricted according to ethical considerations (e.g., consent, privacy, and assessments of forms of risk to participants).

The walking interview is embedded in the daily life of individuals – giving insights into how people 'frame' and respond to their social and natural environments through the creation of meanings, conceptual 'tools', and practices. It also has the possibilities of undertaking a sequence of scenes to gain a view of the wider patterning of an individual life, how they 'put together' experiences and understandings across settings – it therefore, can draw out how individuals understand past and future, within current present time and setting (see Kusenbach 2012: 199; Clark and Emmel 2010). It can show how individuals consciously 'move' between settings, their reflections, evaluations, adjustments and plans in daily practice. Thus, the walking interview has considerable merit for biographical research since it 'enables us to *connect with stories,* to see and feel the experiences of another in an *embodied way* ... and opens up a *dialogue and a space* where embodied knowledge, experience and memories can be shared' (O'Neill 2015: 86–7). Such research is both situated and on the move, employing a biographical view of the respondent as reflective, as creating meanings in action – relating to their social and physical environments, organising practices, assessing information, and decision-making within emotional and sensual relations. Individual biography can thereby be studied 'in the present', in the 'flow' of the complexities of daily experience, in the 'routine' scenes through which individuals live.

The walking 'interview' can combine very productively with a number of other means of gathering 'data', but such connections necessitate careful consideration. The discussion of how 'methods' can be 'mixed' has increased recently, reflecting broadly how quantitative and qualitative methods (although 'mixing' can actually be within either) can be put together, and perhaps in response to the growing innovation in the use of 'artistic' and other sources/procedures in the latter (e.g., in adopting the 'visual', i.e., drawing, photographic, video, performative, fictive/poetic, participatory, documentary, 'found' materials, and artefacts, and so on) and the application of 'computer-aided' 'data' techniques. This is a complex area with questions concerning the degree that differing 'materials' can be 'mixed' and how – and the issues of conceptual precision, epistemological bases, and language or paradigm to be applied (see Cresswell 2002; Cresswell 2011; Tashakkori and Teddlie 2010; Tashakkori and Teddlie 2011). In short, methods can be 'mixed' in numerous ways, depending on degree or type of integration (see Mason 2006).

Importantly, a walking 'interview' for biographical research purposes is a dialogue with the 'participant' that can also include a whole range of other materials and artefacts in elicitation (provided or made by the respondent) and information from various sources – and, in doing so, applying/adapting methodologies and practices from social science and other fields. It could include 'quantitative' longitudinal or cohort survey data, statistical census materials, as well as visual and other recording through digital devices and artistic practices. Biographical research, in adopting the interview walking method, must be clear on why and how certain methods are to be used in understanding an individual (or group), their life and context – what conceptual and interpretive 'apparatus' is to be employed, and how the 'outcomes' are to be represented, disseminated, and what form of participatory approach is conducted (see Chapter 3).

In terms of interpretative and representational practice, WIBM 'outcomes' must be regarded as 'provisional': allowance should be made for alternative 'understandings'; 'research on the move' recognises that research always remains to some extent unfinished. It also, has at its centre (again), a 'mix of methods', not merely the participatory interview itself, which can employ differing biographical research approaches. Such mixing necessitates a number of techniques to relate the various kinds of materials (text, image, and secondary 'data' from recording, transcription, and wider sources e.g., on the Web): some clarity is required on whether, say images, are 'descriptive' supports to text, have an 'independence', or in a deeper 'integration'. Here, some strong cues can be taken from artistic, video, and digital practices that relate very diverse materials. Such techniques as 'mosaic' and 'layering' – 'making' and 'connecting' of 'materials by 'cutting out', 'affixing', 'layering' (cf. Matisse's 'cut-outs'; see Buchberg et al. 2014) and offering the means and opportunities of re-ordering and re-working materials. Thus, research becomes 'provisional' – subject to revision as analysis and interpretation proceeds, new materials added, and as with the social world itself, changes. Indeed, a new insight may be gained years after the field research (e.g., a comment from a presentation audience). Techniques such as bricolage, collage, montage, frottage, collé, épingle, erasure, pentiment etc. from cubism and surrealism and other artistic 'currents' may be adapted, along with (other) 'language(s)' of film/video (cf. Russell 1999; Bate 2004), and newer digital screen 'techniques' and forms of 'linking' (cf. screen icons, hypertext, etc.; gaming and virtual lives environments, augmented realities; image/sound manipulation software, and so on). For example, through procedures of collage, the means of 'juxtaposition' and 'assemblage' (i.e., of research materials) can remain apparent in showing contrast/opposition and fragmentation/disruption in mixing meanings and objects (Roberts 2015: 24).

Methodologically, for instance, one notion, 'faceting' (a term used for the refraction of light by cutting gemstones) has been adopted in social science and used due to a recognition that lived experience is multi-dimensional and different insights can be pursued using mixed research, taking multiple lines of inquiry and ways of seeing, with the researcher using creativity, invention and imagination (Mason 2011; Denzin 2012). The notion of 'faceting' was famously earlier used in cubism (e.g., Picasso, Braque) as part of its radical approach to give fragmented, multiple perspectives, the effects of differing light sources, and to bring objects 'closer' to the viewer (Richardson 2009). Here, O'Neill (2017) argues for a 'constellational' approach (rather than fractal or triangular), using the concept that Adorno borrowed from Benjamin. In the practice of the WIBM, there is the intent to 'capture' the 'being-in-the world' using new methodologies and data, not simply in a traditional linear research model by, for example, linking to input and dissemination through internet resources and communication (Roberts 2016:163). This more complex model reflects the movement and diversity of the social world, its disrupted meetings and the crossing of social trajectories, and it is thereby a challenge to hierarchical, binary, generic, and 'holistic' cultural explanations (Roberts 2015: 24; Clifford 1981, Clifford 1997).

The walking method shares ethical concerns that govern social science research in gaining approval from relevant institutional and professional bodies, and legal requirements regarding consent (e.g., safeguards in the use and access of 'data'; secure storage; the relationship between the researcher and the interviewee; and in relation to the 'public' nature of the research: Kazmierska 2018). Digital recording of personal data intensifies ethical issues (e.g., consent, access) due to its intrusiveness and ease of collection and dissemination. Personal health and safety risks require assessment (as in other research): for instance, when or where to take a walk on the street or other setting and (again), restriction of public access, and keeping to local bylaws, and wider legislation. Pre-planning and taking into account the physical abilities of the researcher and participants is necessary.

The WIBM draws on a number of influences and parallels, including: senses, emotions, and communicating; mobilities; art and walking; new mobile technologies; philosophy, literature, and walking; the psycho-spatial, time, and walking.

Senses, emotions, and communicating

There can be something quite 'enigmatic' about walking – both in taking a walk and also in observing others' movement. It seems walking can both 'clear the head' and bring new thoughts, taking us 'on a new journey' in the mind without a clear end point. We may also 'perceive' the act of walking in ways of which we are not aware: for example, do we unconsciously 'see' walking to the left or right differently – one as slower than the other? In seeing others walk, we may often wonder about 'their business' – where are they going and why? It seems we are drawn to observing others walking (cf. 'people-watching' passers-by outside cafes); in doing so, we may make a whole range of assumptions about them according to their gender, age, clothes, gait, voices, demeanour, and so on, about their social position, 'taste' and manners, purpose. We may 'detect' in their movement and posture (body language) a mood, an infirmity, a character (Goffman 1971). Perhaps also the act of walking itself may culturally change:

for example, are we now walking faster as the 'pace' of modern life in general (e.g., in travel, digital information transfers) speeds up, becomes more complex, or as more streets are pedestrianised, and, of course, walking today is often 'set to music' (soundtracked) in shopping malls, and emitting from bars, shops, and train stations.

It has become common to point out, in academic discussion and social research, that the 'visual' has been dominant in Western society, with other senses having unduly little attention. This elevation of the visual, it can be argued, has been reflected in intellectual study and research, as in ethnography, for example, which has only latterly been more joined with the conceptualisation of the body and other senses (Sparkes 2009; see Classen 1993; Classen 2005; Falk 1994; Howes 2003; Howes 2005). As Pink argues, referring to the 'visual' and visual anthropology, a fuller account of 'experience' has a dual relevance, because how senses are conceived influences methodologies to be applied, while the prominence of the 'visual' (as in visual anthropology) is put into doubt by a broader sensory approach, which relates the visual within the wider patterning of senses (Pink 2006: 41).

In the Enlightenment, concern for the visual, it is held, was associated with the rise of new 'disciplinary techniques', bringing the surveillance of populations and a 'micro physics of power' spreading through social institutions – prisons, factories, asylums, hospitals, etc. (cf. Bentham's 'panopticon') – and the increasing influence of scientific observation and measurement (Foucault 1991). As Buchan and Ellison argue, there was been a 'sensory hierarchy' associated with modernity, a notion of the dominance of the eye and its relation to 'power', while 'sound', for instance, became a secondary consideration to 'vision' in terms of the creation of 'civility' and 'politeness' (Buchan and Ellison 2012: 4–5). Nevertheless, how the senses are culturally organised and prioritised is socially and historically variable; there is growing work which addresses smell, touch, and hearing in our experience of daily life as a 'multi-sensorial' environment (Sparkes 2009; Vannini et al. 2012). How we experience and interconnect our various senses informs our interpretation of the everyday world, our identity formation, and communications with others (Pink 2006: 45; see Bathurst 2017).

There are a number of issues with regard to restoring the fuller sensorial range – it is not simply a matter of 'adding' other senses to the focus on the visual (the gaze, the image) in research and considering them individually – a danger is of new priorities or a rather indiscriminate, loose notion of the 'multi-sensorial' (Sparkes 2009: Pink 2006). A debate is needed on biological – social and individual – society relations in the formation and relative influence on senses and their enactment, and on the degree to which the senses can be considered separately or interrelated (even synaesthesically), so enhancing understanding how they occur in experiential practice, in space, and in social relations over time (see Howes 2005; Ingold 2000). Importantly, included here must be a consideration of what the 'senses' actually are – whether others apart from the 'traditional' ones should be recognised (e.g., 'agency', as in activities such as walking) and, significantly, how they 'conspire' (or fail) to give a 'sense' of self (in time, space, relationships) (see Vannini et al. 2012).

The 'visual' and other senses must be conceptualised in relation both to each other and in a wider exploration of embodiment, relational experience, and action – within cultural formation and representation. The importance of music, for example, in peoples' lives (cf. in their adolescence) has generally been overlooked – how music can express feelings (a deep 'resonance') through ceremonies (weddings, funerals), or how individuals may describe their lives (e.g., lines taken from songs) and identity (Roberts 2010a) – or certain smells may have important associations, say, with memories of family meals, the seaside, or country holiday walks, romantic moments, etc. (cf. Proust's 'madeleine' in *Remembrance of Things Past*, 1913–27) (see also Benjamin 1992; Classen et al. 1994). Finally, for research including the walking interview, how the senses can be studied in practice and relayed in/through research via forms of dissemination, are crucial issues.

The biographical text or 'tape' can, thereby, be retained, but also extended by interrelating it with other audio and visual materials within digital media or even more 'traditional' graphic forms – 'found' or the respondent's own drawing, diagrams, images, maps, etc. Sparkes (2009) considers newer representational means from traditional writing, such as fictional, poetic, and performative expression. In this way, the neglect of how we experience, its nature and representation, can be addressed in research and theorisation, including how sensory experiences relate to interviewees' lives and location (Sparkes 2009; see Pink 2006: 42–4; Roberts 2008, Roberts 2011; Ingold 2000; O'Neill and Perivolaris 2014). The ethnographic orientation of the WIBM is one entry into this enterprise to 'reveal' the senses and embodiments of understanding the shaping of everyday life experience.

In summary, difficulties will remain in how research can represent (and 'transmit') sensual experience to others – a recognition that has led, in part, to the upsurge of artistic procedures in qualitative research, including walking interview research. Here, we need a new approach to the conception of senses and research procedures – one that understands the senses as connected, even interpenetrating, or substituting (Jones 2006: 215, 231–2). It seems, for instance, the loss or impairment of one sense may lead to other senses being enhanced or creatively used.

The senses must be seen alongside another area that was previously rather neglected in social science – emotions – now increasingly seen as important area for understanding action and identity within sociological research (Roberts 2006:139–42; see Hochschild 1983; Barbalet 2001; Bendelow and Williams 1998; Layder 2004; Williams 2001). Emotions have commonly been regarded as involving 'feelings' and the more 'irrational' springs to action, while social behavioural study has been biased towards 'cognitive' or 'calculative' and rational aspects of motivation. A fuller understanding of action must include the senses and emotions, as part of a complex pattern of elements informing motivation

(Roberts 2006: 139–40). Similar conceptual issues are found in the study of emotions that are raised in the examination of the senses: the degree to which they are socially, psychologically, or organically formed – and how these dimensions interrelate. How the emotions are connected to self expression and identity, and are part of immediate and wider socio-cultural contexts remain central questions, including for biographical research (see Williams 1998)

In developing new approaches to the emotions in social science research, their interconnection with the senses and perception should be considered in how we shape and interpret our surroundings (e.g., a certain piece of music may – and may be used to – induce a mood and memories). Here, perhaps there is a necessity to form new conceptions around the interplay of the senses and emotions. They seem more interconnected than has been assumed; 'synaesthesic' perspectives are of interest here in understanding such associations within particular contexts, how we may associate a sound with a colour, a feeling, a taste, etc. (cf. Jones 2006: 215, 231–2; Roberts 2015: 25–6). This investigation is necessary to understand the formation and reshaping of the self, our daily experience, memories, and anticipated future. 'Walking', of course, takes place physically, but also in the imagination as we plan, carry out, and look forward in the mind – and also in writing, reading, and in the arts, as well as 'on the ground'; again, the capacities of expression and 'knowing' involving emotion, senses, perception are not separate entities, but are intimately interrelated (Ingold 2010).

We need to consider the senses and emotion as interrelated within the broader 'communicative' apparatus of individuals, not merely adding senses and emotions as experiential frames to communicative means and action. A new sensual–emotional conception is required, not just taking terms or including 'missing' items, a new 'sensibility' (cf. 'sensoriality': Pink 2008), an 'acuity' with the emotions and senses as 'dimensions' of the cognitive and the visual. This would involve a reflexive awareness on the part of the sociologist – a re-visit to the 'sociological imagination' of the interpenetration of biography/culture/structure/history (Mills 1970). Such an imagination would produce a more sophisticated model of action formed from an awareness of the range and parameters of human communication:

> … there is no wall between the many visual practices of human beings – graphic, pictorial, scriptal, even gestural, interact and blend. So too with other human arts. Gestural movements merge into graphic signs … into played sounds, into tactile systems. Pictorial images mingle in with danced, musical and material symbols and the movements and touches of human bodies … This unending chain of multiple connections is an essential feature of human communication, not to be dismissed as a mere secondary or contextual matter.
>
> *(Finnegan 2002: 242)*

We must not merely deal with 'experience' as a collection of related areas but also how we 'move' in 'consciousness' – shifting between forms of action in everyday life, employing-receiving or 'encoding' and 'decoding' (adapting Hall 1980) sensual–emotional–cognitive communications and experiences. Of central importance here is how we form and shape notions of time, and use of memory within consciousness (see *New Scientist* 2013). In walking, as in other everyday activities, we shift in forms of consciousness according to time – in memory and contemporary experience, and in future anticipation and plans.

Mobilities

The walking method could be said to have some affinity with the idea of 'mobilities' – one of the many shifts or 'turns' in social science over the past thirty years or so (see Adey et al. 2014a; Büscher and Urry 2009; Büscher et al. 2010; Fincham et al. 2010; *Mobilities* (2006-) journal n.d.; Sheller and Urry 2006; Urry 2001; Urry 2007; Vergunst and Ingold 2008). The notion of 'mobilities' as a social 'paradigm' is a response to the upsurge of mobile personal communication, mobile media practices, mobile data collection and its visualisation and analysis, and global shifts in population in migration and tourism. The task, according to mobilities researchers, is to understand a moving 'subject' – the everchanging social world – in areas such as social media involvement, the use of digital devices, areas of transport transition (e.g., train stations) and the journeys themselves, mass population flows, etc. (see Adey et al. 2014b; Sheller and Urry 2006).

The 'mobilities paradigm' envisages social institutions and social relations as being crucially altered by forms of mobility. Society should be conceived as being dynamic, rather than a static entity, with 'mobilities' shaping leisure and work, family patterns, health, political involvement, migration and its effects, and so on; as changing, but not as some formless world: individuals are not simply 'rooted' in institutional or other spaces, and neither are they free-floating (see Adey et al. 2014a; Cresswell and Merriman 2011; Sheller and Urry 2006). 'Mobilities' writers cite influences from many perspectives: for example, cultural studies, transport and logistics, anthropology, and gender and postcolonial approaches (see Sheller and Urry 2006). The perspective's emphasis on social diversity and its provisional or constructed perspective on knowledge, rather than following 'grand theories', has parallels with poststructural or postmodern concerns. It also claims connections with a number of previous 'turns' in social science, including 'space', 'time', 'performance', and 'body' to account for the dimensions of mobility – the degrees and forms of mobility in differing locations, amongst individuals and groups. The intent is to provide new theorisation and methodologies, including 'mobile ethnography', employing 'multi-media', locational tracking, computer techniques, etc., to take account of the changing experiences of everyday life and emerging empirical data on societal changes, i.e., statistics on the mobility of people, 'new' knowledge (data, images), and rising movement of 'things' (trade, logistics) (see Sheller and Urry 2006; Urry 2001; Urry 2007; Adey et al. 2014a). However, the mobilities approach faces similar issues to other perspectives and research – how to 'merge' or 'mix' different kinds of methodologies and 'data' – interpretive, quantitative, and newer digital, artistic, etc. procedures, and so on.

'Mobilities', from one view, is more like a theme or dimension in social research, rather than a separate field – a certain perspective to try to understand the social world. It could also be argued that its 'object' is to a large degree an extension of forms of 'mobility' that have been very much part of the sociological tradition in terms of migration, social movements, industrialisation, technological development, urbanisation, and modernisation, which theoretically connect with many existing macro and micro perspectives on social process, personal and social change, and social conflict (see Martindale 1961; Roberts 2006).

'Walking' activity as an area of study can be set to a degree within a 'mobilities paradigm', with analysis resting on an emphasis on 'micro theories' and everyday experience of change (e.g., performance, network, exchange, interaction, see Roberts 2006) in considering how mobilities are mentally and bodily experienced, as in relation to new mobile technologies, migration, family connectedness, civic duties and rights (Adey et al. 2014a). The mobilities perspective is a reminder that in the study of 'walking activity' and in walking interview research, a recognition of the societal dimension must be given, that today individuals are 'connected', e.g., via social media, as well as being 'scanned' by 'surveillance' and monitored by CCTV cameras, and part of broad social or transnational processes. For the WIBM, the idea of 'movement' – the experience of space, embodiment, time (and tempo) in motion (and in stasis), and communication and interaction, is centrally important (see the *Principles and practice* guide at the end of the book).

In biographical study, 'moving stories' evoking empathy and insight from the reader for the experience and impact of 'mobilities' on the 'subject's' life and outlook, have long been a key area, as in oral history (Thomson 1999), life history in urban and migration sociology (Thomas and Znaniecki 1958; see Roberts 2010b), and in social documentary (e.g., 1930s 'photo books' on the US Depression) and photo-journalism, The use of the portable audio tape recorder (post-World War II) gave an impetus to oral history, while earlier changes in camera technology and printing advances in the 1930s allowed the rise of the photo-essay in photo magazines. For example, in America, Dorothea Lange, Walker Evans, and other photographers employed by the Farm Security Administration, travelling hundreds of miles by car, made it possible to record the experiences of farmers and others during the Great Depression and the subsequent migration West (Cohen 2009; Mora and Brannan 2006). Some of this work reflected tensions between the perspective of a static ethnographic 'particularism' of the photographed and studied community, and a practice of movement in research study due to the cultural and social mobility brought by the automobile (both for documentarian and 'subjects') (see Allred 2010). These 'methods on the move' came at a time of expansion of 'mobile' and other technologies in the 1920s–30s – not only increasing mobility by car, the ocean passenger liner, and aircraft, but also the growing influence of radio, films, and gramophone, and the telegraph. Social documentary was responding and recording lives undergoing these economic, social, and technological upheavals (see Stott 1973). More widely, within early 20th century art (painting, cinema, literature, etc.) – while not forgetting earlier artistic depictions of human and other 'movement' – there were also important specific responses to technological advances in power, speed, and movement (by aeroplane, car, subway, train, ocean liners etc.) (cf. Futurism; Vorticism), work which has a continuing legacy (see Miller 2010).

Today, we can say that 'interviews' can take place 'on the move' in the 'enclosed' spaces of vehicles, on a train, bus, or car (Ferguson 2016). The notion of 'mobilities' can remind us that walking takes place and is experienced in time/ space – in many varied contexts, and within the diverse constraints and expectations of when and where to walk (Edensor 2010). The 'mobilities paradigm' is relevant to the WIBM, as it draws attention to the 'movement' of the researched 'subject' (person, group, knowledge, object) – and researcher, from space to space, the tempos and temporalities of change, and the related pursuit of new methods and theorisation (see Chapters 3, 4).

Arts and walking

Qualitative research has increasingly looked towards the arts in terms of the use or production of art as research materials, for new means (not only digital) of representation and dissemination of social research, and for ways of accessing and representing the sensory, emotional experiences of lived lives. O'Neill, for example, argues that the combination of art and ethnography as 'ethno-mimesis' enables a more sensuous understanding of social relations and lived experience with the inclusion of visual, poetic, and performance texts in the research process – collaborating with artists to conduct research at the borders of art and ethnography (O'Neill et al. 2002; O'Neill 2008).

Since the 1960s–70s, artists have interrogated the common act of walking as a form of artistic practice in numerous contexts; often it has taken an existing walking event – visiting a gallery, going on a guided city tour, a group ramble, and so on – and 'redefined' it into an 'artistic performance'. Of course, art, performance, and walking have been associated in numerous ways (cf. in dance, examples such as the 'Lambeth Walk' etc.; see Harrisson and Madge 1986: 139–84), but a distinction could be made between where art depicts walking (in a painting, sculpture, photograph, graphic, etc.) and as (or part of) a gallery (or other building) or street performance. It is worth remembering here the attempts to understand the physiology of walking by use of photographs in the pioneering work of Muybridge (cf. Tate Britain, Exhibition, September 2010–January 2011, see Brookman 2010). Journeys through cityscapes, rural settings, or remote areas have been employed by artists using a very wide set of perspectives and modes of collection and representation, applying drawing and painting, found objects, and photography and film (documentary, textual and photojournals, performance, landscape art, etc.). Walking tours may be undertaken to 'walk in the footsteps' of artists (cf. Turner, Constable) or literary figures (cf. Austen, Hardy) to 'trace' their lives and see where they gained 'inspiration'. The artist's position as living and working in the landscape can also situate them as part of the art itself. Common contemporary social themes such as migration experience, history and memory, borders and power, inequality, and the environment are addressed in these works.

The recent 'art of walking' can be placed within a longer historical arc, as the studio became extended to the outside world. Evans argues that all avant-garde movements at the beginning of the 20th century saw walking on the street as a creative venture, as combining a mundane daily activity with art (Evans 2012a). However, with the 'institutionalisation' of these movements, their creative works were narrowed to those that could be readily shown in exhibitions. Thus, sculpture and painting remained, whereas walking art was overlooked until its revival during the 1960s (Evans 2012a: 13). Evans provides a 'guide' to the 'art' of walking and outlines a series of walks along a number of connected themes, including walking with dogs, marches, museums, drifters, philosophy and walking, and so on (Evans 2012b).

Writers and theatre companies have sought to place types of performance in both densely urban and rural (or wild) contexts – from cityscape to deserted seashore, moor, or woodland settings – the audience may not know the detail of the route and destination, the information given may be factual or fictional or both (see Gardner 2010). There may be elements of play, politics, myth, personal story, or historical event. The audience may be asked for degrees of participation, and to record observations (by various means – written, audio, video, photographs) or give verbal responses, provided with a sound or textual commentary, or give later 'feedback'. For some artists, when an audience gives up mobile phones and other devices, it enhances a deeper connection in walking within the landscape – as an 'immersive journey' (cf. Robert Wilson, see Lawson 2012). In recent years, walking as 'promenade' or 'immersive' theatre has become prominent, although there are examples at least going back to the 1980s.

Walking as artistic involvement (i.e., including audience, viewer) can be rather more than shifting from one situation or position to another, say to gaze (briefly) at a series of paintings, tableaux, or acted scenes. Rather than merely drawing attention to actual walking in viewing art or theatre, Trueman argues that in 'walking theatre' the audience can become more part of the performance itself – not merely as moving from scene to scene, but perhaps in a shared procession with the actors, as 'fully' involved in the event (Trueman 2014). For Field (2009), the 'joy' needs to be sponsored in 'promenading', walking as part of the 'show', rather than merely a transition from place to place. He argues that artists (e.g., Janet Cardiff's work in London) have employed walking as a kind of memory in connecting with the past. Walking, it seems, is a simple activity, but it contains much politics, narrative, and great potential for new theatrical experiences (Field 2009). Walking theatre need not be out of doors – it may be indoors, or in some combination. There are recent examples of the use of various kinds of empty premises (e.g., warehouses) to 'stage' theatrical experiences – via maze, labyrinth, or other routes with video and other installations, and performance through which the audience walks/participates (Lawson 2012).

By the 1960s, the 'art object' was being questioned (by 'conceptual art', 'live art', 'living sculpture', 'body art', 'actions', etc.) and placed within a socio-cultural context that was wider than the object and immediate (institutional) setting (see Wood 2016: 58; Goldberg 2001). Today, artists use 'performance' within a range of artistic practices employing both older and new media, and informed by a realisation that a social world – the context of art – is relevant and should be questioned. Performative practices in their 'fluidity' of movement both inherently show and contest a notion of a dominant societal 'status quo' (see Wood 2016: 59). Lambert, for instance, discusses such 'political possibilities for aesthetic disruption of urban space and time' within the context of the 'neo liberal city' with a description of 'live art' walks, as 'urban praxis' disrupting 'normative spatial patterns and rhythms of urban life' through play and experimentation (Lambert 2013).

A major form of 'observation' of walkers can be found in 'street photography', which developed during the 1960s–70s (especially in New York) in the work of Meyerowitz, Shore, Davidson, and others (including Ray-Jones, Steele-Perkins, Sykes, and Parr in the UK). It has a longer history in the more social documentary work of Atget, Brassai, Cartier-Bresson, Doisneau, and the later (quite different) 1950s work of Frank (2008) and Klein (2010) in the US, while Brandt, Hardy, Mayne, and others in the UK explored cultural changes, especially in working class areas (see Seaborne and Sparham 2011: 57–87). Street photography commonly seeks to capture moments of ordinary life of people in the busy urbanscape (or desolate post-industrial territories) – often individuals inhabiting their own world and thoughts while (usually 'caught') in the presence of others (cf. Goffman's 'civil inattention') – recording the banal or the odd circumstance, the individual diversity, the vitality of life, even it seems, the 'sounds' within the hard cityscape (Killip 2016; Konttinen 1988; Pardo and Parr 2016; Stanton 2015).

Walking appears to aid conceptual thinking: while walking, an artist may create in the mind a painting, a composer form a melody, a writer plan a book. We all may 'play' music in our head, hum a tune, or sing a song to accompany our walk, which has some personal significance or 'matches' the moment. Walking itself can be likened to following a song or musical piece – the percussion of the feet, the rhythm of the body's movement, our inner or outer voice following a melody – and also as a means of describing, relating to, and immersion in the landscape (cf. Chatwin 1987).

In summary, walking as an artistic pursuit can take a wide variety of forms, using/creating photographs, text, and maps, or even leaving a trace on the environment – perhaps a mark (e.g., a footprint) or a sculpture of found objects (stones or wood) in some arrangement (e.g., a geometric design – circles, squares, lines) (cf. Richard Long and his extensive walks, often in less accessible regions) (see O'Rourke 2013). The artistic practices that engage with walking may involve the 'performance' of walking (e.g., through a gallery, or through urban/ rural areas) to the appreciation of a location or installations in the landscape – land-art and site-specific sculpture (see, e.g., Myers 2010; Heddon 2007; Mock 2009; Heddon and Myers 2014). Sculptures and other artworks can be situated 'formally', as in commemorations or major 'monuments' (e.g., 'The Angel of the North', UK, and older figures cut in chalk hillsides) and viewed in passing or 'informally', as items left to be 'discovered' (e.g., items such as 'yarn-bombing' or 'knitted art') by walking. 'Sculpture parks' allow works to be set landscapes and also in galleries (cf. Yorkshire Sculpture Park, UK). 'Art and Walking' as an artistic practice is now well established – as witnessed in the title of an exhibition held at the Northern Gallery for Contemporary Art (UK) in 2013: 'Walk on – 40 years of art walking from Richard Long to Janet Cardiff' (Northern Gallery for Contemporary Art 2013) – and in the existence of groups, for example, the Walking Artists Network (WAN) which was formed in 2007 by Clare Qualmann and artists from a wide variety of backgrounds to share the practice (WAN 2017; see Chapter 9).

'Art' can be part of the WIBM in a number of ways: for example, migrants may bring artworks with them that have personal significance, may produce art after arrival which represents and interprets their previous lives, or they may choose (or construct) art that they feel summarises their current life, routines (e.g., walks), and possible future. This art may be on their person or carried on a walk, providing a subject for narrative elicitation in the walking interview.

New mobile technologies and the future

The practice of the walking interview method can be recorded in a variety of ways – for instance, by (paper) notes taken at the time or later, or visual and audio recording of participants and surroundings on digital devices (tablets, smartphones, etc.) and perhaps sent via internet links (cf. Pink 2007; Pink 2012; Pink et al. 2010; Roberts 2015: 17–22). 'Digital technology' has very important implications for contemporary and future research practice, since it permits the investigation of everyday routines, spaces, personal and group life, and researcher experience, 'interactively' with participants and others, while 'on the move'. Communication by mobile phones, tablets, and other devices via social media voice, text, image, and video, adopting locational and other informational tools, will lead to new methodologies and conceptual development (see de Souza e Silva and Sheller 2014; Roberts et al. 2016). The ease of digital audio and imaging allows greater possibilities of 'video diaries', 'photo voice', and artworks in biographical/narrative study, including walking research (before, during, and after the walk), and the use of 'blogs' interconnection – 'narratives' formed across a range of 'modalities' (Alleyne 2014).

Visual imagery and audio recording can provide for detailed description, and elicit emotional or other responses (e.g., aiding emancipatory discourses), but in doing so, it raises ethical issues (cf. the depth of personal data collected) and interpretive complexities (e.g., realism, representation, authenticity, image–text relation: see Price and Wells 2004; Riessman 2008: 141–82). Walking with another can be considered as a face-to-face interconnection, but with increasing and varied use of digital technologies, this personal detail of embodied co-presence has to be used carefully with safeguards (again on safe storage, consent, access regulation, etc.), especially due to the ease of digital communication.

Mobile phones, email, and social media allow for text and speech interaction. Information can be uploaded and stored from an individual, while others can be invited to participate and follow through locative media – which itself is developing as a means of artistic, fictive, performative, game, and narrative expression, as well as making available a wealth of information about locations (on a walk), such as on sports grounds, buildings, parks, markets, services, and so on. Locative technology can be used to trace distance, speed etc. covered and note what is said at what points in the walk (Evans and Jones 2011; Jones et al. 2008).

Someone could be interviewed while doing a walk 'physically alone', via phone/video/web, but this raises interesting methodological issues, including the extent to which this approach may limit interactive and participatory possibilities within the research. For walking research, there is the possibility that these technologies could have a 'third walker' – a potential 'participant' (or audience) via digital services. A walk shown by real time videolink can enable others to take some part. The 'on-going' walk can be continuously related to information being collected via the Web (e.g., locative technologies, socio-historical data on the setting). There are other technical developments that can be experienced on computer or special headset glasses – for example, in augmented reality by which the existing reality is overplayed with other information; these 'embedded' images, graphics and so on, can provide further possibilities. A walk can be 're-created' later (with further possible augmentation) on computer, device, or headset. 'Data' may be 'performed' in various ways (see O'Neill et al. 2015; Roberts 2008) including 'walked': a recorded walking interview can be 'viewed' and 'heard', as well as retaken in virtual reality. Through 'virtual reality', the creation of other worlds as walks can be experienced on digital devices or a via a 'social science lab' environment using multiple video-screen projection.

The WIBM can make use of video as an interactive experiential procedure that attempts to outline an ethnographic sensorial experience of place (cf. Pink, 2007). Through use of video in walking, research participants can relate their personal meanings about their environment and their sensual interaction. Pink points to a phenomenological method, which enables an empathetic, ethnographic understanding of participants' lives and the dissemination of their worldview (Pink 2007). Participants can be given video or photographic cameras or other recording devices to make their own record of their experiences. In O'Neill's participatory research with women seeking asylum in Teesside, the participants shared their experience of living in the area by taking her, and a film-maker, Jan Haaken, on a series of walks (Haaken and O'Neill 2014). The women took photographs, shared the use of a flip video recorder, and had conversations along the way that were digitally recorded. The spoken voice of a woman reading her poetry was also recorded. An exhibition of the women's photographs toured the North-East (UK), and Haaken made a film, *Searching for Asylum*, with input from the women.

A third party (e.g., a film-maker) could take recordings, and perhaps a walk could be repeated after a given period by the researcher (and researched), depending on the objectives of the research (e.g., to show any shift in biographical outlook, reflections, etc.). Digital developments in hand-held devices are taking place to include interaction with the environment and experiencing data across the senses and emotion (e.g., on touch). Also, 360 degree photography, 3D, and holographics (and 'personal sensors' on mobile devices for detecting/recording 'smells' and other environmental conditions and effects) are creating further recording and representational means, while interestingly, at the same time, 'old technology' (such as film cameras and processing) are undergoing a revival – and researchers are using 'traditional' drawing reportage, postcard communication, flip books, etc., in innovative ways which can be applied to walking interviews. Finally, an area of rapid development is 'artificial intelligence', which takes many forms, and is relevant to walking research: systems that can readily translate languages, can connect with the mind to move objects or parts of the body, or aid perception (tactile, visual etc.) of the environment by sensors on hand-held devices.

The methods employed in biographical walking research are intended to record the experiences in the 'real world', including our contemporary relations with digital technologies, and how we interpret social contexts and adjust ('move') between them. In applying a number of devices and methods to 'capture' a walk, the question of their purpose and how they relate is important – some 'materials' gathered might be used more descriptively, while the 'results' of others analysed and interpreted more systematically. Thus, some clarity on how methods are employed to gather materials needs to be addressed. Digital technologies give new possibilities on how materials can be connected – by 'layering', 'linking', and selection of information in different levels which allows for multiple 'readings' of the materials – to understand experiences, emotions, and senses. How these materials (text, sound, photographs, video, etc.) are to be analysed and connected ('mixed') is crucial; a wide number of differing analytic and theoretical perspectives are possible to an understanding of experience: senses, emotions, decision-making, identity, and relation with social environment. For example, 'multimodality' or 'hypermodality' perspectives are being explored, as the technologies associated with the 'traditional' academic 'end products' (often the published book, chapter, or article) are being questioned by newer ones that are 'on the move'; again, such as smart phones, tablets, video, etc. (see Jewitt 2013). In short, new digital devices have brought new, easily available and usable modes of gathering text and images and disseminating them – combining with possible contributions from wider audiences and sources (e.g., via the Web) (see Kaufmann and Holbrook 2016; Price et al. 2013; Jewitt 2013, 2014; NCRM n.d.).

How do we assemble and connect these very different forms of data? Also, to what extent does communicative technology (use of smartphones and watches, hands-free, or headphones) affect how we respond to the surrounding environment and other people we are with, and how we walk (gestures, pace, oral and physical regard to companions and other walkers); for instance, there is the common observation of inattention to walking 'etiquette' by users of hand-held technology (smartphones, etc.). There are wider contextual dimensions here which should not be overlooked: the relation between new data technologies and how 'spaces' (urban and rural) are defined and 'managed' – the collection, use, and ownership of data in the regulation of environments (services, cultural and material production, social identity, etc.) – and the degree and form of the participation of citizens.

The possibilities of these technologies and (presumably) their successors will have profound implications for the research and 'publication' process – with new forms of data giving new 'mixtures' of image and sound, immersive environments, routes of access, and 'revision' (by other researchers) – as the formal timeline model stipulated by traditional research is disrupted, its 'stages' of construction ('problem' identification, data collection, analysis, interpretation, writing up, dissemination) are now no longer to be accepted as simply linear. Research becomes more a 'distributed accomplishment' and 'remediated', enabling greater participation and critical intervention (see Marres 2013).

Some caution should be mentioned in using digital methods (platforms, blogs, social media, information, etc.): a 'sociological imagination' must look beyond the ('ahistorical') 'plastic present' of 'digitalised surfaces', and remember the role of time and temporality, and pre-existing sociocultural context, in forming our conceptions of the social world (Uprichard 2013). In addition, as new digital (and later) technologies are developed, the interrelation between the senses, emotions, and intentions will become more intertwined as devices respond to our bodies and mind. Here, there are possibilities of synaesthesic procedures, as we increasingly understand and employ these dimensions of being as interrelated (see Jones 2006; Roberts 2015).

Philosophy, literature, and walking

Walking can be regarded as a 'performance' – even a lyrical, poetic movement – to oneself and subject often to 'audiences'. Walking features in song and literature as an inspiration for poetry and prose (cf. Wordsworth), or as described in Dr Johnson and Savage's nocturnal perambulations, or in the description (reverie) of scenery and reportage of travellers (18th and 19th century explorers' accounts and contemporary books written or Web travelogues) of their experiences i.e., people met, hills climbed, hardships endured, wonders beheld. In literature, walking is often associated with 'romance', seeking fortune, or taking pleasure or adventure. There is a long history of popular travel writing and guides (Fodor, Michelin, etc.); in the 20th century, some of the well-known travellers' accounts (often walking) by Gertrude Bell, Freya Stark, Laurie Lee (2014), Patrick Leigh Fermor (2014), Patrick Thesiger, Eric Newby, and more recently Rory Stewart, have been very popular. Many major novelists have written about their travels, as well their trips influencing their fiction (cf. Mary Wollstonecraft, Graham Greene, Lawrence Durrell). Of course, the genre boundaries between travel fiction and non-fiction are extremely porous. Today, contemporary travel guides (e.g., Rough Guides, Lonely Planet, etc.) containing reviews, descriptions, walks and sightseeing, and histories are very popular, and specialist walking holiday companies' brochures describe itineraries and walks of varying levels of hiking difficulty.

While walking has its mundane quality, it remains rather mysterious; it is bound up in utilitarian matters, and yet can be a contemplative activity, even a philosophical pursuit. It is possible to give an account of walking as a philosophical and literary history. Recent 'academic' writing on this topic has received a great deal of attention, often drawing on philosophical themes, alongside environmental and political issues, as well as referring to art, history, biography, and including personal story telling (Solnit 2006; Solnit 2014; see also Amato 2004; Gros 2015; Minshull 2000; Horvath and Szakolczai 2018). In philosophy, there is little to suggest that walking was a key topic to classical Greek thought, although 'contemplative' or 'discursive' walking apparently took place (Solnit 2014: 15). For Coverley, it is during the Middle Ages that a 'more spiritual' contemplation had a part in walking in the cloistered monastic world – quite unlike 'the unbounded, and less structured excursions favoured by the Romantics, to whom the walk and the walker were to become symbolic not of systematic thought, but of intellectual freedom and solitary creativity' (Coverley 2012: 22, 23, 24; see Solnit 2014: 14). Coverley says that for Rousseau, the walker is placed beyond society, in a natural state where the individual is really free; his own walks seemed to 'attempt to replicate the purity of this experience', sharing with Nietzsche and Kierkegaard a notion of 'solitude and alienation' (Coverley 2012: 26, 31; see Solnit 2014: 17–22). Gros argues that while walking is a mundane activity, it has various 'freedoms', including placing the demands of daily life behind, or a long walk bringing release from time, a motive, or an end point (Gros 2015: 3–9). Other types of transport appear to be 'lacking': in walking, we are not merely getting closer to objects, the surroundings (colours, smells, flowers, wind, trees) become more pressing and intrusive to our body (Gros 2015: 38). Finally, Gros observes that while certain great writers (Thoreau, Rousseau, Nietzsche) argued that a walk alone let an individual set their own pace (although the walker may be 'interrupted' by greetings from passers-by and other distractions), interestingly, an internal conversation emerges, between 'body and soul' in contemplation and solitude, and a commentary on how a walk is going (Gros 2015: 53, 56, see also Solnit 20014: 16–26). Some work on walking and its 'human meaning' has taken a longer span: Horvath and Szakolczai (2018) have written an historical sociology and political anthropology of walking in their study on contemporary liminality. Drawing attention to the mundane, liminal genealogy of walking in early human history, the entering into caves during the late Palaeolithic age as a pilgrimage, they define as two turning points in the history of walking the rise of 'cave art sanctuaries' and the pilgrimage as a long distance 'cultural practice'.

Methodologically, we suggest that the WIBM is the injunction to render the 'meaning' of walking or a particular route for the individual (or group), its 'function(s)' for them in daily life; even while a utility (e.g., to shop, visit social services) may be apparent, (through the interview) other deeper 'philosophical' life meanings can emerge, in the 'story' that is told.

The psycho-spatial, time, and walking

Walking takes place in time: this is not only in 'clock time', as in the actual duration of the walk. In walking, 'time' can be 'suspended' as we are engrossed in movement and thought: we are in an 'ongoing moment' (Dyer 2007). A walk may be on our own or even with others, having a conversation or merely temporarily 'sharing a moment' with another. In our imagination, we may also move backwards and forwards in time to events gone or to come. 'Passing' through an environment (rural, urban, 'wild', seascape, etc.) brings 'cues' – elements that stimulate our imagination, which we 'fit' within our previous remembered experience. We meet a gamut of sensory 'stimuli', we may seek out or are affected by sensual elements (feel, smell, etc.), we are engaged in 'realisation' in space and time – an interactive awareness of our environment through which we construct and reconstruct our 'sensual-emotional-communicative' 'registers' (see Finnegan 2002: 244–63).

One perspective that has a focus on time and walking is 'psychogeography' in its concern with seeing the present through the lens (archaeology) of the past (Coverley 2010: 14). Psychogeography is difficult to define, because it contains many diverse elements, drawing on a number of themes from longer traditions: its 'urban wandering' may include 'political radicalism' and a 'playful subversion' overlaid with an inquiring approach to change our connection with the urban environment (Coverley 2010: 14). Psychogeography, for Debord in 1955, was the attempt at an interpretation of the meanings of city areas – the study of particular 'laws' relevant to how environments influenced emotions and action, even if individuals were unaware (Solnit 2014: 212; see Nicholson 2011: 48; O'Rourke 2013). The mix of playfulness, 'following your own walking steps' by wandering or 'drift', and an inquiry, shows its affinity to 'Situationism' (cf. Debord, and Dadaism; see Plant 1992), although practitioners, while usually making literary connections, appear to vary in the political nature of approach. For Situationists, the physical constraints on traversing through the urban environment were a challenge – resulting in experiments in city space to attempt new sensual experiences, as a response to the 'given' paths and hardness of the buildings and spaces of the cityscape. 'Playfulness' was intended to alter consciousness in the mundanity and conformity of the existing environment – an acknowledgement of the determinations of the city while exploring new experiences or alternatives (Coverley 2010: 14).

Contemporary psychogeography, while not necessarily indicating the conceptual language of Situationists, has been has been associated with a number of writers and novelists (although not all would subscribe to the term) such as Iain Sinclair, Peter Ackroyd, Will Self – and connections are made with a longer history as in the works of Blake, de Quincey, and others (Coverley 2010: 31–56; Nicholson 2011: 40–2; Self 2007; Self 2009). The writer and film-maker Iain Sinclair links personal concern with walking in the marginal, unloved, or 'darker' areas of the city (London) with layers of historical, literary, criminal, even mystical, traditions, and along the way, raising a series of historical and literary characters and other figures (e.g., Defoe, Blake, etc.) (Sinclair 2003; Nicholson 2011: 46–7). Sinclair (2017) has documented subsequent changes in London that brought a deep sense of impermanence or being ungrounded in his experience of city walking. Earlier, Wright's (2009) 'journey' through London's East End's poor neighbourhoods depicted how these areas were being transformed by Thatcherite property development and welfare policy, gentrification, and the 'heritage industry'.

Psychogeography has been linked with artists whose lives and work connect with the environment: for example, Richard Long makes art associated with walking in often physically demanding landscapes walks; 'textworks' leaving traces (footprints, artworks) in the openness of the environment (Nicholson, 2011: 96–9; see Evans 2012b: 112–3). Another artist, Phil Smith (cofounder of Wrights and Sites) draws on a very eclectic range of psychogeography, Situationism, performance, architecture, cinema, and geology in retracing W. G. Sebald's walk through East Anglian villages, for a deeper 'sensitised' walking – a ramble, going further than historical and other features in tourist or heritage guides to demonstrate a walk can be art, pilgrimage, and a radical change in how the world is seen (see Smith 2014). His 'mythogeography' is intended as a 'subversive' approach which entails choosing to walk in unfamiliar places, celebrating the multiple meanings of sites, rather than the homogenous interpretations of official and other literature (see Smith 2009, Smith 2010, Smith 2015).

In psychogeography, there is the initial observation that city districts shift in 'psychic' feel or 'ambience', even within a short space, and instead of conforming to the usual paths that are laid down, to 'drift', even to take one's own line and goal (Nicholson 2011: 48–9). This may be developed, not merely as a resort to simple chance, but by making a radical questioning of the urban distinctions that are made – as not shaped by common reasons for walking (work, leisure), and letting the mind drift and be attracted by what is experienced. Of some relevance here is the notion of 'Guerrilla Geography' (by Raven-Ellison), to make people examine 'preconceptions' about places, and also secure 'social and environmental justice', and establish 'active community connections' (*National Geographic* 2012).

Some 'enthusiasts' for London regard themselves as sensitive to the 'detail' of the city, 'animate' its varied 'time spaces', and so, give a personality to the city (Reed 2002). The moving feet can be described as an 'exercise in mapping', joining up seemingly differing and separate local environs of the city, seeing how they relate (Elkin 2017: 21). In 'mapping' and 'sensing' the city, we must not forget the centrality of voices (cf. Mayhew): two recent accounts of London have included oral reportage which gives insightful varied portraits of lives, communities, migratory experience, and wide social divisions in a rapidly changing 'global city' (Judah 2016; Taylor 2012).

The idea of 'drift' (dérivé) can have a great deal of relevance for types of the WIBM. A walking interview may not have a set plan, map, itinerary – it may be more of a 'drift', albeit around a particular locale – but that also may in itself be a 'strategy', a conscious, investigative slant and intent as a more open-ended interview – still with a purpose: to understand the thoughts, identity, and outlook of an individual and their relationship with their current environment, relationships, and circumstances. For the WIBM, we can see how we are the observer of the observed, but are observed ourselves; while seeking to understand others, we are asking to be 'understood'; in observing (commenting, interpreting), we are 'observing' our inner selves.

Biographical research 'on the move': 'Moving' research

The rise of the walking interview is a reflection of the search for innovative methods that relate to everyday experience – a 'life' perhaps made more complex by shifting social relations and new technologies – an idea that research should be grounded in the daily lives and activities of those to whom the researcher seeks to relate and understand more fully. This does not merely require the 'adding on' of new techniques, methods, or practices to an existing array of research procedures and problems – there is an inherent challenge to existing modes of research (including research relations and dissemination). The initial task is for the researcher, as Mills described: 'to trust yet to be sceptical of experience ... thus developing self-reflective habits, you learn how to keep your inner world awake ... you are loosening your imagination' (Mills 1970: 217, 221). Here, imagination can be associated across a number of dimensions: engrossment, attunement, immersion, and acuity, which can sensitise us to new areas for exploring the everyday world of the (walking) 'subject' and produce observation, thinking and theorising (Roberts 2016: 156–8).

Biographical research can 'disrupt' assumptions that we have regarding the social world and produce new insights and 'appreciations' of the complexities and connections in lives. It brings a notion of 'the life' as passing within and between forms of consciousness – in retrospection, in the moments of living and in anticipation, of prospection, or what may possibly occur, as shaping our narrative connections between our individual past, present, and future (see Roberts 2011).

'Walking and artsbased research' can 're-invigorate biographical methods'; walk-ing 'extends its relational and connective aspects' – 'the importance of affective understanding, psycho-social experiences and prioritises the situational authority of participants' (O'Neill 2015: 87). Thus, the walking interview method is also connected to current 'trends' in biographical research

> containing multi-methods, multi-media, and multi-sites; as multi-sensual, multi-temporal, multi-conscious; as critical, participatory and socially engaged; and theoretical and theorizing
>
> *(Roberts 2016: 164)*

There is a further and profound challenge for biographical research. The WIBM as a development is touching on something deeper – the need for qualitative research not merely to re-assess previous methodologies, but to avoid still being 'caught' ('imbricated') by their assumptions; an apparent 'critique' of a practice can fail to go beyond its limits (see Townsend 2006: 66, for an example in photo-graphic approaches). The need is to transform existing qualitative methodologies from an interior debate to a new stance, to create new procedures, and foster a new critical awareness of changes in the social and natural world as a basis for interpretive incisions. Having outlined a case for the WIBM, Chapter 2 further develops its theoretical context.

References

Adey, P., Bissell, D., Hannam, K., Merriman, P. and Sheller, M. (2014a) Introduction. In: P. Adey, D. Bissell, K. Hannam, P. Merriman, and M. Sheller (eds.) *The Routledge Handbook of Mobilities*. London: Routledge.

Adey, P., Bissell, D., Hannam, K., Merriman, P. and Sheller, M. (eds.) (2014b) *The Routledge Handbook of Mobilities*. London: Routledge.

Alleyne, B. (2014) *Narrative Networks: Storied Approaches in the Digital Age*. London: Sage.

Allred, J. (2010) *American Modernism and Depression Documentary*. Oxford: Oxford University Press.

Amato, J. A. (2004) *On Foot: A History of Walking*. New York: New York University Press.

Barbalet, J. M. (2001) *Emotion, Social Theory and Social Structure*. Cambridge, UK: Cambridge University Press.

Bate, D. (2004) *Photography and Surrealism*. London: I.B. Tauris.

Bates, C. and Rhys-Taylor, A. (eds.) (2017) *Walking through Social Research*. Abingdon, UK: Routledge.

Bathurst, B. (2017) *Sound: Stories of Hearing Lost and Found*. London: Profile Books.

Bendelow, G. and Williams, S. J. (eds.) (1998) *Emotions in Social Life*. London: Routledge.

Benjamin, W. (1992) *Illuminations* (Tr. H. Zohn). London: Fontana Press.

Brockmeier, J. (2002) Possible lives, *Narrative Inquiry*, 12(2): 455–466.

Brookman, P. (ed.) (2010) *Eadweard Muybridge*. London: Tate Publishing.

Buchan, B. and Ellison, D. (2012) Introduction: Speaking to the eye, *Cultural Studies Review*, 18(3): 4–12.

Buchberg, K., Cullinan, N., Hauptman, J. and Serota, N. (eds.) (2014) *Matisse: The Cut Outs*. London: Tate Publishing.

Büscher, M. and Urry, J. (2009) Mobile methods and the empirical, *European Journal of Social Theory*, 12(1): 99–116.

Büscher, M., Urry, J., and Witchger, K. (eds.) (2010) *Mobile Methods*. London: Routledge.

Chatwin, B. (1987) *The Songlines*. London: Jonathan Cape.

Clark, A. and Emmel, N. (2010) *Using Walking Interviews, ESRC RM Realities Toolkit #13*. Manchester: The University of Manchester, Morgan Centre for Research into Everyday Lives.

Classen, C. (1993) *Worlds of Sense: Exploring the Senses in History and Across Cultures*. London: Routledge.

Classen, C. (ed.) (2005) *Fingerprints: Writing about Touch*. Oxford: Berg.

Classen, C., Howes, D., and Synnott, A. (1994) *Aroma: The Cultural History of Smell*. London: Routledge.

Clifford, J. (1981) On ethnographic surrealism, *Comparative Studies in Society and History*, 23(4): 539–564.

Clifford, J. (1997) *Routes: Travel and Translation in the Late Twentieth Century*. Cambridge, MA: Harvard University Press.

Cohen, S. (2009) *The Likes of US: America in the Eyes of the Farm Security Administration*. Boston, MA: David R. Godine.

Coverley, M. (2010) *Psychogeography*. Harpenden, UK: Pocket Essentials.

Coverley, M. (2012) *The Art of Wandering: The Writer as Walker*. Harpenden, UK: Oldcastle Books.

Cresswell, J. W. (2002) *Research Design: Qualitative, Quantitative, and Mixed Methods Approaches*, 2nd edn. London: Sage.

Cresswell, J. W. (2011) Controversies in mixed methods research. In: N. K. Denzin, and Y. S. Lincoln (eds.) *The SAGE Handbook of Qualitative Research*, 4th edn. London: Sage.

Cresswell, T. and Merriman, P. (eds.) (2011) *Geographies of Mobilities: Practices, Spaces, Subjects*. London: Routledge.

Denzin, N. K. (2012) Triangulation 2.0, *Journal of Mixed Methods Research*, 6(2): 80–88.

Dyer, G. (2007) *The Ongoing Moment*. London: Abacus.

Edensor, T. (2010) Walking in rhythms: Place, regulation, style and the flow of experience, *Visual Studies*, 25(1): 69–79.

Elkin, L. (2017) *Flâneuse: Women Walk the City in Paris, New York, Tokyo, Venice and London*. London: Vintage.

Evans, D. (2012a) Introduction. In: D. Evans (ed.) *The Art of Walking: A Field Guide*. London: Black Dog Publishing.

Evans, D. (ed.) (2012b) *The Art of Walking: A Field Guide*. London: Black Dog Publishing.

Evans, J. and Jones, P. (2011) The walking interview: Methodology, mobility and place, *Applied Geography*, 31(2): 849–858.

Falk, P. (1994) *The Consuming Body*. London: Sage.

Ferguson, H. (2016) Professional helping as negotiation in motion: Social work as work on the move, *Applied Mobilities*, 1(2): 193–206.

Fermor, P. L. (2014) *The Broken Road*. London: John Murray.

Field, A. (2009) Promenade shows must step up and put the joy back into walking, *The Guardian*, 26 March Available at: https://www.guardian.com.stage/theatre.blog/2 009/mar/26/promenade-shows-walking (Accessed 30 May 2019)

Fincham, B., McGuinness, M., and Murray, L. (eds.) (2010) *Mobile Methodologies*. Basingstoke: Palgrave Macmillan.

Finnegan, R. (2002) *Communicating: The Multiple Modes of Human Interconnection*. London: Routledge.

Foucault, M. (1991) *Discipline and Punish*. Harmondsworth, UK: Penguin.

Frank, R. (2008) *The Americans*. Göttingen: Steidl.

Gardner, L. (2010) Walking theatre must look where it's going, *The Guardian*, 20 September (Available at: https://www.theguardian.com/stage/theatreblog/.../walki ng-theatre-accomplice-en-route (Accessed 1 May 2019)

Gergen, M. M. and Gergen, K. J. (1984) The social construction of narrative accounts. In: K. Gergen, and M. Gergen (eds.) *Historical Social Psychology*. Hillsdale, NJ: Erlbaum.

Goffman, E. (1971) *The Presentation of Self in Everyday Life*. Harmondsworth: Penguin.

Goldberg, R. (2001) *Performance Art*. London: Thames & Hudson.

Gros, F. (2015) *The Philosophy of Walking*. London: Verso.

Haaken, J. K. and O'Neill, M. (2014) Moving images: Psychoanalytically informed visual methods in documenting the lives of women migrants and asylum seekers, *Journal of Health Psychology*, 19(1): 79–89.

Hall, S. (1980) Encoding/Decoding. In: S. Hall, D. Hobson, A. Lowe, and P. Willis (eds.) *Culture, Media, Language, 1972–9*. London: Hutchinson.

Harrison, M. (2016) *Rain: Four Walks in English Weather*. London: Faber and Faber.

Harrisson, T. and Madge, C. (1986) *Britain by Mass Observation*. London: The Cresset Library.

Heddon, D. (2007) *Autobiography and Performance: Performing Selves*. Basingstoke, UK: Palgrave Macmillan.

Heddon, D. (2017) Going for a walk: An audio-verbatim play. Available at http://wal kinginterconnections.com/audio-play-going-for-a-walk/ (Accessed 21 September 2018).

Heddon, D. and Myers, M. (2014) Stories from the walking library, *Cultural Geographies*, 21(4): 639–655.

Hochschild, A. R. (1983) *The Managed Heart: The Commercialization of Human Feeling*. Berkeley, CA: University of California Press.

Horowitz, A. (2013) *On Looking*. New York: Simon Schuster.

Horvath, A. and Szakolczai, A. (2018) *Walking into the Void: A Historical Sociology and Political Anthropology of Walking*. London: Routledge.

Howes, D. (2003) *Sensual Relations*. Ann Arbor, MI: The University of Michigan Press.

Howes, D. (ed.) (2005) *Empire of the Senses: The Sensual Culture Reader*. Oxford: Berg.

Ingold, T. (2000) *The Perception of the Environment*. London: Routledge.

Ingold, T. (2010) Ways of mind-walking: Reading, writing, painting, *Visual Studies*, 25(1): 15–23.

Jewitt, C. (2013) Multimodal methods for researching digital technologies. In: S. Price, C. Jewitt, and B. Brown (eds.) *The SAGE Handbook of Digital Technology Research*. London: Sage.

Jewitt, C. (ed.) (2014) *The Routledge Handbook of Multimodal Analysis*, 2nd edn. London: Routledge.

Jones, A. (2006) *Self/Image*. London: Routledge.

Jones, P., Bunce, G., Evans, J., Gibbs, H., and Hein, J. R. (2008) Exploring space and place with walking interviews, *Journal of Research Practice*, 4(2): 1–9.

Judah, B. (2016) *This is London: Life and Death in the World City*. London: Picador.

Kaufmann, J. and Holbrook, T. (eds.) (2016) Special issue: Hypermodal inquiry, *Qualitative Inquiry*, 22/3, March. 159–60.

Kazmierska, K. (2018) Doing biographical research-ethical concerns in changing social contexts, *Polish Sociological Review*, 3(203): 393–411.

Killip, C. (2016) *In Flagrante Two*. Göttingen: Steidl.

Klein, W. (2010) *Life Is Good and Good for You in New York*. New York: Errata Editions.

Konttinen, S.-L. (1988) *Byker*. Newcastle: Bloodaxe Books.

Kusenbach, M. (2003) Street phenomenology: The go-along ethnographic research tool, Special Issue: Phenomenology in Ethnography, *Ethnography*, 4(3): 455–485.

Kusenbach, M. (2012) 'Go-Alongs'. In: S. Delamont (ed.) *Handbook of Qualitative Research in Education*. London: Edward Elgar.

Lambert, C. (2013) Live art as Urban Praxis: The political aesthetics of the city, *Sociological Research Online*, 18(3): 1–17. Available at: www.socresonline.org.uk/18/3/12.html (Accessed 21 September 2018).

Lawson, M. (2012) How I learned to love immersive theatre, *The Guardian*, Sept. 25. 2012.

Layder, D. (2004) *Understanding Social Theory*. London: Sage.

Lee, L. (2014) *As I Walked Out One Midsummer Morning*. London: Penguin.

Marres, N. (2013) The redistribution of methods: On intervention in digital social research, broadly conceived. In: L. Back, and N. Puwar (eds.) *Live Methods*. Oxford: Blackwell.

Martindale, D. (1961) *The Nature and Types of Sociological Theory*. London: Routledge and Kegan Paul.

Mason, J. (2006) Six strategies for mixing methods and linking data in social science research. NCRM Working Paper, 4/06, Real Life Methods. Manchester: University of Manchester. Available at http://eprints.ncrm.ac.uk/482/1/0406_six%2520strat egies%2520for%2520mixing%2520methods.pdf (Accessed 21 September 2018).

Mason, J. (2011) Facet methodology: The case for an inventive research orientation, *Methodological Innovations Online*, 6(3): 75–92.

Miller, J. (2010) *On the Move: Visualising Action*. London: Estorick Foundation.

Mills, C. W. (1970) *The Sociological Imagination*. Harmondsworth: Penguin.

Minshull, D. (2000) *The Vintage Book of Walking*. New York: Vintage.

Mobilities (journal) (2006–) London: Taylor & Francis.

Mock, R. (ed.) (2009) *Walking, Writing and Performance: Autobiographical Texts by Deirdre Heddon, Carl Lavery and Phil Smith*. Bristol: Intellect Books.

Mora, G. and Brannan, B. W. (2006) *FSA: The American Vision*. New York: Abrams.

NCRM (n.d.) *Multimodal Methodologies*. NCRM (National Centre for Research Methods, UK).

Myers, M. (2010) 'Walk with me, talk with me': The art of conversive wayfinding, *Visual Studies*, 25(1): 59–68.

National Geographic. (2012) Explorers bio: Daniel Raven-Ellison – Guerrilla Geographer. (online). https://www.nationalgeographic.org/find-explorers/daniel-j-raven-ellison (Accessed 24 April 2018).

New Scientist. (2013), Special Issue, Consciousness, 218(2917), 18 May 2013.

Nicholson, G. (2011) *The Lost Art of Walking*. Chelmsford, Essex: Habour Pub.

Northern Gallery for Contemporary Art. (2013). 'Walk on – 40 years of art walking from Richard Long to Janet Cardiff', Exhibition, Sunderland, UK.

O'Neill, M. in association with Giddens, S., Breatnach, P., Bagley, C., Bourne, D., and Judge, T. (2002) Renewed methodologies for social research: Ethno-mimesis as performative praxis, *The Sociological Review*, 50(1): 69–88.

O'Neill, M. (2008) Transnational refugees: The transformative role of art? *Forum Qualitative Sozialforschung, Forum: Qualitative Social Research*, 9(2) Available at www. qualitative-research.net/index.php/fqs/article/view/403 (Accessed 21 September 2018).

O'Neill, M. (2015) Participatory biographies: Walking, sensing, belonging. In: M. O'Neill, B. Roberts, and A. Sparkes (eds.) *Advances in Biographical Methods: Creative Applications*. Abingdon, UK: Routledge.

O'Neill, M. (2017) Studying the marginalised with mixed methods. In: S. Walklate, and M. Hviid Jacobsen (eds.) *Liquid Criminology: Doing Imaginative Criminological Research*. London and New York: Routledge.

O'Neill, M. and Perivolaris, J. (2014) A sense of belonging: Walking with Thaer through migration memories and space, *Crossings: Journal of Migration and Culture*, 5(2): 327–338.

O'Neill, M., Roberts, B. and Sparkes, S. (eds.) (2015) *Advances in Biographical Methods*. Abingdon, UK: Routledge.

O'Rourke, K. (2013) *Walking and Mapping: Artists as Cartographers*. Cambridge, MA: MIT Press.

Pardo, A. and Parr, M. (eds.) (2016) *Strange and Familiar: Britain as Revealed by International Photographers*. London: Prestel.

Pink, S. (2006) *The Future of Visual Anthropology: Engaging the Senses*. London: Routledge.

Pink, S. (2007) Walking with video, *Visual Studies*, 22(3): 240–252.

Pink, S. (2008) *Doing Sensory Ethnography*. London: Sage.

Pink, S. (2012) *Advances in Visual Methodology*. London: Sage.

Pink, S., Hubbard, P., O'Neill, M., and Radley, A. (2010) Walking across disciplines: From ethnography to arts practice, *Visual Studies*, 25(1): 1–7.

Plant, S. (1992) *The Most Radical Gesture: The Situationist International in a Postmodern Age*. London: Routledge.

Price, D. and Wells, L. (2004) Thinking about photography: Debates, historically and now. In: L. Wells (ed.) *Photography: A Critical Introduction*. London: Routledge.

Price, S., Jewitt, C., and Brown, B. (eds.) (2013) *The SAGE Handbook of Digital Technology Research*. London: Sage.

Reed, A. (2002) City of details: Interpreting the personality of London, *Journal of the Royal Anthropological Institute*, 8(1): 127–141.

Richardson, J. (2009) *A Life of Picasso*, Vol. II. London: Jonathan Cape.

Riessman, C. K. (2008) *Narrative Methods for the Human Sciences*. London: Sage.

Roberts, B. (2006) *Micro-Social Theory*. London: Palgrave Macmillan.

Roberts, B. (2008) Performative social science: A consideration of skills, purpose and context, *Forum: Qualitative Sozialforschung/Forum: Qualitative Social Research*, Art. 58. Available at http://nbn-resolving.de/urn:nbn:de:0114-fqs0802588. (Accessed 21 September 2018).

Roberts, B. (2010a) Rock and pop music and identity in wales. In: B. Horgby, and F. Nilsson (eds.) *Rockin' the Borders: Rock Music and Social, Cultural and Political Change*. Newcastle-Upon-Tyne: Cambridge Scholars Publishing.

Roberts, B. (2010b) 'Ahead of its time': The legacy and relevance of W. I. Thomas and F. Znaniecki, 1918–20. The Polish Peasant in Europe and America. In: C. Hart (ed.), *The Legacy of the Chicago School of Sociology*. Poynton, Cheshire, UK: Midrash.

Roberts, B. (2011) Interpreting photographic portraits: Autobiography, time perspectives, and two school photographs, *Forum: Qualitative Sozialforschung/Forum: Qualitative Social Research*, 12(2): Art. 25. Available at www.qualitative-research.net/index.php/fqs/article/view/1687 (Accessed 21 September 2018).

Roberts, B. (2015) Biographical research: Past, present, future. In: M. O'Neill, B. Roberts, and A. Sparkes (eds.) *Advances in Biographical Methods*. Abingdon, UK: Routledge.

Roberts, B. (2016) Reflections on a life in social science. In: M. Greiff och R. Johansson (Redaktörer) *I ständig rörelse: Mellan Arbete, Kultur och Didaktik – En vänbok till Lars Berggren*, Malmö: Mezzo Media.

Roberts, S., Snee, H., Hine, C., Morey, Y., and Watson, H. (eds.) (2016) *Digital Methods for Social Science*. Basingstoke, UK: Palgrave Macmillan.

Russell, C. (1999) *Experimental Ethnography*. London: Duke University Press.

Schütze, F. (1992) Pressure and guilt: War experiences of a young German soldier and their biographical implications. Part 1, *International Sociology*, 7(2): 187–208.

Seaborne, M. and Sparham, A. (eds.) (2011) *London Street Photography, 1860–2010* (Museum of London Exhibition). Stockport: Dewi Lewis Publishing.

Self, W. (2007) *Psychogeography*. London: Bloomsbury.

Self, W. (2009) *Psycho Too*. London: Bloomsbury.

Sheller, M. and Urry, J. (2006) The new mobilities paradigm, *Environment and Planning A: Economy and Space*, 38(2): 207–226.

Simmel, G. (1950) Metropolis and mental life. In: K. Wolff (ed.) *The Sociology of Georg Simmel*. New York: The Free Press.

Sinclair, I. (2003) *London Orbital*. London: Penguin.

Sinclair, I. (2017) *The Last London: True Fictions from an Unreal City*. London: Oneworld Pub.

Smith, P. (2009) Crab walking and mythogeography. In: R. Mock (ed.) *Walking, Writing and Performance*. London: Intellect.

Smith, P. (2010) *Mythogeography*. Axminister, UK: Triarchy Press.

Smith, P. (2014) *On Walking: And Stalking Sebald*. Axminster, UK: Triarchy Press.

Smith, P. (2015) *Walking's New Movement*. Axminster, UK: Triarchy Press.

Solnit, R. (2006) *A Field Guide to Getting Lost*. London: Penguin.

Solnit, R. (2014) *Wanderlust: A History of Walking*. London: Granta.

de Souza e Silva, A. and Sheller, M. (eds.) (2014) *Mobility and Locative Mobile Communication in Hybrid Spaces*. London: Routledge.

Sparkes, A. C. (2009) Ethnography and the senses: Challenges and possibilities, *Qualitative Research in Sport and Exercise*, 1(1): 21–35.

Stanton, B. (2015) *Humans of New York: Stories*. New York: St Martin's Press.

Stott, W. (1973) *Documentary Expression and Thirties America*. Oxford: OUP.

Stuart, M. (1993) 'And how was it for you Mary?' Self, identity and meaning for oral historians, *Oral History*, 21(2): 80–84.

Tashakkori, A. and Teddlie, C. (eds.) (2010) *Sage Handbook of Mixed Methods in Social and Behavioral Research*, 2nd edn. London: Sage.

Tashakkori, A. and Teddlie, C. (2011) Mixed methods research: Contemporary issues in an emerging field. In: N. K. Denzin, and Y. S. Lincoln (eds.) *The SAGE Handbook of Qualitative Research*, 4th edn. London: Sage.

Taylor, C. (2012) *Londoners: The Days and Nights of London Now*. London: Granta.

Thomas, W. I. and Znaniecki, F. (1958) *The Polish Peasant in Europe and America*, 2 vols. New York: Dover Press (First pub. 1918–20).

Thomson, A. (1999) Moving stories: Oral history and migration studies, *Oral History*, 27(1): 24–37.

Thomson, H. (2017) *One Man and a Mule*. London: Preface.

Townsend, C. (2006) *Francesca Woodman*. London: Phaedon.

Trueman, M. (2014) Theatre goes walkabout: These shows really move audiences, theatre, *The Guardian*, 19 June 2014.

Uprichard, E. (2013) Being stuck in (live) time: The sticky sociological imagination. In: L. Back, and N. Puwar (eds.) *Live Methods*. Oxford: Blackwell.

Urry, J. (2001) *Sociology beyond Societies: Mobilities for the Twenty-First Century*. London: Routledge.

Urry, J. (2007) *Mobilities*. Cambridge, UK: Polity Press.

Vannini, P., Waskul, D., and Gottschalk, S. (2012) *The Senses in Self, Society and Culture.* Abingdon, UK: Routledge.

Vergunst, J. L. and Ingold, T. (eds.) (2008) *Ways of Walking: Ethnography and Practice on Foot.* London: Routledge.

WAN (Walking Artists Network). (2017) Available at www.walkingartistsnetwork.org. (Accessed 21 September 2018).

Wengraf, T. (2009) *Qualitative Research Interviewing.* London: Sage.

Wiles, R., Crow, G., and Pain, H. (2011) Innovation in qualitative research methods: A narrative review, *Qualitative Research*, 11(5): 587–604.

Williams, S. J. (1998) 'Capitalising' on Emotions?: Corporeal reflections on the (Ir)rational, *Sociology*, 32(4): 747–769.

Williams, S. J. (2001) *Emotion and Social Theory.* London: Sage.

Wood, C. (2016) What is performance art now? *Tate Etc*, 38(Autumn): 54–59.

Wright, P. (2009) *A Journey Through Ruins.* Oxford: OUP.

Wroe, A. (2016) *Six Facets of Light.* London: Jonathan Cape.

Young, A. and Temple, B. (2014) *Approaches to Social Research: The Case of Deaf Studies.* Oxford: Oxford University Press.

2

THEORISING WALKING IN THE SOCIOLOGICAL IMAGINATION

Walking in context

Introduction

This chapter is an historical 'engagement' with 19th century city 'social explorers', taking in the 'flânerie' of Baudelaire and the later idea of Benjamin, Situationism, and walking in the 'everyday' with de Certeau, along with the social documentary tradition of text/photography (e.g., the photo book) and street photography. Included here also are the pioneering works on the city and urban experience by the 1920s–30s Chicagoan sociologists (R. E. Park, W. I. Thomas) on marginality, migration, personal and social disorganisation, and formulating life history and ethnographic practices. This discussion (and that in Chapter 1 on mobilities, senses/visual, performative, digital developments in terms of defining the field) will inform Chapter 3, *Walking, art-making, and biographical research*, on theorising walking, art, and ethnography. It also provides part of the foundation for chapters in Parts II–III, and our *Principles and practice: A framework* guide to WIBM, at the end of the book, which gives a number of dimensions for practice.

Walking and the sociological imagination

Very occasionally it may cross our mind – while walking – just how many people have similarly passed over this route, this spot, across decades, and even hundreds of years. Through its space, the wider terrain, and its views, although altered often dramatically, even unrecognisable from years ago, of course, others will follow the route, replacing our predecessors and us, as 'ghosts' of the past, figures in the future. In current time, meeting people by chance or appointment is also a feature of walking – people come into view, may 'ignore' or greet us, sometimes even appearing suddenly and cause us to physically 'start', express surprise, often followed by (mutual) apology. Walking is, in fact, a criss-crossing of lines of travel and at times we intersect with others at those 'meeting points'. To walk is to 'experience' and 'imagine'. We walk through and within 'places' moving in time, space, and with others (in a sense) from the past and in the present. In walking, we 'move' through differing states of individual consciousness. Our environment informs our outlooks and perceptions – how our social, material changes are to be interpreted and understood. Here, we also are bringing the discussion of walking within a 'sociological imagination' (Mills 1970) – a tradition, 'a social consciousness' arising in the 19th century (in the work of Marx, Durkheim, Weber, and others, including social reformers and urban commentators) with new conceptions of the city, social change, and social life.

Nineteenth century walking and 'social exploring'

Humphrey Jennings, in *Pandaemonium* (1985), compiled a collection of writings by writers, poets, scientists, and travellers during the changes brought by industrialism in Britain. Jennings' compendium shows how the consciousness of society was undergoing profound change as the impact of new technologies affected everyday patterns of cultural and social life. Given the changes to the 'traditional' rural order, due to the emerging industrial system and its massive mills, the glow and pollution of the ironworks, the coalmines, and slag-heaps, the growth of the urban poor and working classes, health and poverty problems (see Keating 1976), a variety of attempts emerged to measure (via social statistics and census), chart, photograph, report, and record observations on the impact of work and social conditions in the new social world. One well-known researcher and commentator on the social intricacies of city and work life was Henry Mayhew. Despite Mayhew's intimate social observations on the 'workers, poor, lumpenproletariat, criminals', and so on, these groups were 'often ill-distinguished in the middle-class mind' as 'the Other' (Price 2004: 79). In his *London Labour and the London Poor* (Mayhew 1851), his 'street folk' included the street performer and trader, actor, sweatshop worker, beggar, scavenger, flower girl, and others who were given a portrait and a voice (see Quennell n.d.).

Of particular interest in Mayhew's investigative journalism and his street interviews, especially today, given the discussion of mixed methods in social science, was his pioneering use of an eclectic range of means and materials. He employed in his observations and 'typologies' of the labouring poor, 'a mixture of interviews, statistics and descriptive writing'; the result was that his accounts were 'to be one of the dominant modes through which working people were surveyed' in the period (Price 2004: 79; see also Tolson 2005; Yeo 1984). Interestingly, his research contained engravings based on photographs – an early 'documentation' using photographic images to establish 'authenticity' of observation (Price and Wells 2004: 58). A major feature of Mayhew's work was that it exhibited an attempt to reproduce the 'voices' of the London 'soundscape'. He said his reportage was from the 'lips of the people themselves', a 'literal description' of their 'labour' and 'sufferings', in 'their own "unvarnished" language', providing a picture of their circumstances through 'personal observation' and 'direct communion' with individuals (Mayhew 1851, in Quennell n.d.: xvii). It was a 'documentary impulse' to relate street imagery and printed text at a particular instance using 'new media' (Buchan and Ellison 2012). It can be argued, following Groth (2012), that Mayhew's research is part of an expanding 'multimedia archive' (book, newspaper, performance), as his texts moved between genres and audiences to make readers aware of (and appreciate) the captured 'voices' rather than simply the general 'noise' of the street, and so anticipating the invention of sound recording machines.

Mayhew, of course, was one of very many 'observers' of the poor and their work, housing, and street conditions – novelists, social reformers, compilers of official reports, journalists, and other commentators, such as Dickens, Mearns (1883), Morrison (1896), W. T. Stead, and General Booth, who described the 'submerged tenth', the 'sunken', or those on the 'edge of the abyss' (Booth, 1890; see Stedman-Jones 1976; Keating 1976). The 'city' – London, New York, Paris – became a fascination and fertile resource for writers' and commentators' imagination (see Miller 2014). Dickens, as is commonly noted, gained much creative stimulation through his wanderings in the city 'soundscape' and general life of London. In his early life, he became very accomplished in shorthand and so was very alert to the accurate reproduction of word sounds, a gifted 'dexterity' in relaying everyday speech he retained in his novels (Ackroyd 1991: 133). In his letters when travelling abroad, Dickens often commented that he missed the sounds of the streets of London that he found to be the necessary stimulus for his writing.

Dickens's novels (which included illustrations) and other writings can be regarded in a parallel way to Mayhew's investigations, in their anticipation of future media or recording technologies. Indeed, Smith argues that in Dickens, there is a 'dream' of the cinema that came into being after his death in 1870 (Smith 2003; Groth 2012). Dickens's immersion in street life, his interest in railway travel, keen awareness of photography and entertainments such as the panorama and diorama, and the language and form of his writing, are elements that reflected and shaped a wider consciousness of 'movement' underlying the development of film (Smith 2003). The oldest surviving pieces of film, by Le Prince, are of a suburban garden group and city traffic on a bridge, both in Leeds (UK) in 1888.

This discussion of Mayhew and Dickens raises a number of issues regarding the degree to which they were perceiving the city (experiencing, imagining, 'dreaming') in both pictorial and aural ways – and seeking to record those experiences across a variety of writing genres, rendering urban life 'realistically'. In their 'portraits' of urban life relayed in multiple modes of dissemination, Mayhew's 'characters', images, and descriptions and Dickens's rich ('heightened') mix of literary genres (and journalism) and figures, 'anticipating' technological developments, perhaps there is a lesson for current social science study. Given the 'dramatic' emergence of mobile devices, HD, 3D, holography,

360 degree photography, virtual and augmented reality, voice activation, sensing applications, locative media, big data, AI, etc., it can be asked: 'Are these "anticipations" of techniques and devices still to come, some perhaps "already" fundamentally reshaping our conceptions and means of (biographical) research and its dissemination?'

Many commentators have remarked that Dickens was a prodigious and rapid walker; his journeys on foot appear to have been a central, and compulsive, part of his life – even a 'walking toward death' (Bodenheimer 2007: 180, 203). For him the city, London, was a dark 'labyrinth' which he had to explore, but which also 'held' him (Smith, 2003: 62–81). Other writers made similar comparisons between the city and the labyrinth (Aubrey, de Quincey, Southey, Wells): the city was not only seen to be growing, but also enveloping and confusing its inhabitants (Ackroyd 2000: 584). Walking, of course, can take place in (nearly all) weathers and differing seasons (see Somerville 2017), as well by time of day or night. What impressed 19th century observers was the vastness of London at night, its silence, and form, like a 'darkened theatre' and prison; it appeared to be a city that felt the 'presence of the dead' and was filled with shadows (Ackroyd 2000: 452). Ackroyd says that 'night life' held a keen interest for 19th century figures; while they were appalled by the urban darkness, night walking began to have popularity – the marvel of the city 'awake' through the night drew out walkers to witness its nocturnal life (cf. Charles Lamb, in Jennings 1985: 115). Artists began 'night painting', poets drew upon its imagery, and it became a feature of theatrical melodramas (Ackroyd 2000: 451). In the case of Dickens, it can be said that he was not only using his London (night) walking to release the tensions and exhilaration of writing and mentally 'review' recent work, but also in a 'rewriting' of his life – he was 're-walking' his past, his self (Bodenheimer 2007; see Ackroyd 1991; Frank 1984). Here, the notion of the 'shadow' was a strong theme in Dickens's writings – as a memory of a former self, or even as a possible journalistic persona as someone who would delve into, and report on, the intimate workings of the city and its ills by night or day: as a 'restless shadow' (Charles Dickens Museum 2017; see Jennings 1985: 243–4). Smith says: 'these themes – the city as dream and nightmare, its sounds and movements, its oscillations between light and dark, its prefiguring of cinema – are present everywhere in Dickens's work' (Smith 2003: 70). He adds,

> the city, that is London, was at least initially a primary source of his imaginative energy, affecting his work at the level of form as well as subject matter. Both are encapsulated in one of Dickens's key words, 'labyrinth', to which he recurs continuously in his attempts to capture the essence of the metropolis.
>
> *(Smith 2003: 68)*

The 'novel' itself can be labyrinthine in 'content and form', as can the 'maze-like' 'mysteries of social and personal life' (Smith 2003: 74, 76).

In the history of discussions of walking, nightwalking, in fact, features a great deal. Beaumont extensively investigates 'nightwalking', pointing to the 'alien' character of London (even after the introduction of street lights), and the possibilities of becoming 'disorientated' in 'roaming' tiredly in the 'dead of night' – what had seemed recognisable now appears as a strangely different city (Beaumont 2015: 1– 3). He argues that the growth of urban centres and the rise of 'capitalist modernity' brought a new nightlife – writers such as Johnson, Savage, Goldsmith, and others began to walk in the 'phantasmagoria' of the night; nightwalking became a 'countercultural form', although moral opprobrium for the poor out at night remained (Beaumont 2015: 8–13). Walking at night in a city has a parallel underground; many writers have traced and commented on the journeying of London from below – its dark network of rooms and routes (n.b. Victor Hugo's Paris sewers in *Les Miserables*). For example, recently Ackroyd (2012) has described the layered worlds beneath London, the catacombs and vaults, forgotten streams and sewers, buried history, canals, tunnels, and utility pipes, and its underground train stations (current and abandoned) (Ackroyd 2012; see also Ackroyd 2000: 561–69). He gives the atmosphere of this 'under the pavement domain' – the oppressive reality of dirt and smell, the secrets, mysteries, dangers, fears, fantasies and dreams, memories and myths, and includes its residents – rats, ghosts, and disturbing creatures – and notes those who built and maintain the subterranean tunnels, scavenged and sought refuge, and tourists who have trod its dark byways. 'Darkened London' beneath the streets in the Underground has been an inspiration for artists, commentators, and investigators (such as Mass Observation); for example, Bill Brandt's and George Rodger's photography and Henry Moore's drawings of the people sheltering on the platforms in World War II and, more recently, Wallinger's labyrinth pictures at stations (see Field 2002; Rodger 1994; Harrisson 1990; Higgins 2018: 147–8). These 'bowels' of the city give rise to another notion. In his book *London: The Biography* (2000), Ackroyd gives an account of the city as if a being, an organism, in a description of its growth and features – its noises, diseases, weather, stink, rivers, and also silence and light. Thus, it is London – the urban environment – as a body, with its senses, its organic byways, inner vessels and functions.

Nightwalking has fascinated photographers for the difference it brings in light, texture, and atmosphere of the streets and nightlife. From the inter-war period, Brassai's book *Paris de Nuit* (1933) is particularly well-known; also Robert Doisneau is famed for his pictures, not only of ordinary working class daily street life in the Paris suburbs (from the late 1930s onwards), but also pictures of night scenes (clubs, cafes) (Gautrand 2003: 8, 15). In England, 1930s London became the subject of 'photo-essays' by Francis Sandwith (*London by Night*, 1935), Bill Brandt (*A Night in London*, 1938), and Morrison and Budekin (*London Night*, 1934), while earlier, the popular travel writer H. V. Morton had described *The Nights of London* (1926). Such books often included images of the night from dusk to dawn. Wasson outlines the work of writers (e.g., Greene) in World War II and describes an 'urban' that 'subverted' the dominant wartime narrative of community and resilience, giving disruptive narratives with haunting, doubling, and a depiction of marginal and shadowy figures (Wasson 2010). These writers are reminiscent of Poe's description of London at night in following the 'man of the crowd' and the despair, doom, and sadness of the walker in James Thomson's *The City of Dreadful Night* (1880). The wandering in the Victorian city brought a new fraught 'urban' sensibility – a reflection on and projection of the self, and a musing on the lives of others. The 'crowding of the city' was a major feature of its 'mystery' – what was going on, Wordsworth wondered in *The Prelude*, behind the 'sea' of many faces in the crowd (see Minshull 2000: Ch. 6).

Walking in the dark (or semi-darkness) can have a number of effects on the senses – disorientation of place, and fears (for safety from physical attack) real and imagined. Such walks can give a different perspective – as the 'uncanny' in its silence, strangeness, or it can be a very vivid and seemingly an 'alternative reality', as in the pulsating ('timeless') nightlife of the club and bar. Today, there is a renewed interest in photography at night (aside from that of wildlife) and its history; it can be regarded as a popular sub-genre, with images of buildings, bridges, tunnels, and other architectural features – often to emphasise an eerie or 'gothic' feel, or the geometric, contrasting features of buildings (Sparham 2018). Various contemporary walking artists and others have sought to resist the perceived and real 'gendered risks' that walking at night may bring (see Burton et al. 2017; see Chapter 9).

While London appeared to be a 'labyrinth', particularly at night, an unknowable organism – it was also being 'mapped'. Reformers, for example, were beginning to calculate and 'map' social issues (cf. Morrison's 'sketch plan' of the fictionalised, 'The Old Jago', Morrison 1896). To the 'darkness' of crime, disease, 'moral degeneration', and want in London, reformers and campaigners, such as General Booth of the Salvation Army, offered what they regarded as a 'way out' (for a 'submerged tenth', and so for society as a whole) by a myriad of help schemes in housing and work. In General Booth's schema of social and moral intervention, he also set a clear path by a coloured, pull-out illustration of London, the surroundings to the sea, with signposts for the poor to the Colonies (Booth 1890; cf. Stanley 1890). John Snow, pioneer of epidemiology, famously produced his mapping of cholera outbreaks in the 1850s (Johnson 2008), Charles Booth with a team of researchers compiled his well-known residential street mapping of poverty in the 1880s, resulting from his inquiry into *Life and Labour of the People of London* (1889–1903) (see Booth 1968). London streets were colour-coded according the circumstances of residents and depicting the changes of populations (n.b. Booth's maps were used recently in a TV series to show how some London streets had changed since his surveys of 1880s: Bullman et al. 2013). Finally, British pioneering investigative journalist, W. T. Stead (who died on the *Titanic*) plotted the saloons, pawnbrokers, and brothels of Chicago (*If Christ Came to Chicago*, 1894).

The consideration of 'social explorers' of the 19th century city draws attention to the multiple methods and written genres employed and raises the important question of not only how we 'see' our surroundings, but also the importance of other 'sense-scapes' through which we experience, record, and communicate, and the overall 'conceptions' of urban social life that are interpretively employed.

Chicago School of sociology

The Chicago 'School' of sociology has been described as the first Department of Sociology (at the University of Chicago) in the world. It was founded in the 1880s. At the time, Chicago was a rapidly expanding city with a great range of social problems and conflicts (Roberts 2006: 13–14). The city pioneered a number of social projects and initiatives, such as by Jane Addams and her co-workers at the Hull House settlement, to meet the demands of immigration, the impact of crime and poverty, and other effects of urban growth and change. The new University sought a close connection with its urban context, and in its early years, its sociologists were closely involved in the civic life of the city and social intervention. By the 1920s and 1930s, the Department had a wide variety of research interests on urban life – crime and delinquency, communication, migration and immigration, race relations, and other issues (see Madge 1963; Smith 1988; Washington 1984). Robert Park, who became its leading member, cited a range of influences on his thoughts on the city – the social survey movement (e.g., *The Pittsburgh Survey*, 1907–8), Henry Mayhew and Charles Booth, and commercial firms who were planning for city expansion (real estate, utilities). He set out a research programme in his early article, 'The City: Suggestions for the Investigation of Human Behavior in the Urban Environment' (1915) (Roberts 2006: 17–18). Park gradually built a range of concepts to understand urban processes (e.g., 'natural history', 'natural area', 'symbiosis', 'accommodation') as part of a 'human ecological' view of the city as a 'social organism' (Short 1971) and the department collected a large body of data on urban life. In Park's view, the city was not merely a physical collection of streets, buildings, and institutions, but a 'state of mind', part of the transmission of customs and traditions by its inhabitants. Students were encouraged to go out into the streets to observe and understand the city at first hand. The results of the Chicago interest in urban life were numerous pioneering studies across a wide subject range, including studies of the homeless, delinquents, the 'taxi dance hall', organised crime, family and race relations, the press, immigrant groups, suicide, the slum, and 'vice'.

Before becoming an academic, Park had a career in journalism in various cities (e.g., Minneapolis, Detroit). As a journalist, Park said he had 'tramped' the streets in many cities, examining and reporting on social ills, but he began to realise the need for a deeper analysis of urban problems – a 'scientific reporting' (see Park, in Baker 1973). Chicagoan studies on a whole gamut of urban phenomena produced a number of important methodological developments – the use of the 'life story/history', ethnographic research, the drawing of maps, collection and analysis of statistics – to bring *multiple* forms of data to account for the individual lives and groups within cultural diversity and structuring of urban neighbourhoods (cf. Shaw and McKay: see Burgess and Bogue 1964) Although Chicago sociology in the 1920s–30s is particularly associated with ethnographic study and the life history to uncover 'situated meanings', it has often been overlooked that it also pioneered the collection of statistics and statistical techniques (Roberts 2006: 28–9; Angell 1945). Here, Charles Booth's residential area maps, the *Pittsburgh Survey*, and the work of Hull House in Chicago informed Chicagoan's urban studies (e.g., the mapping of delinquency areas: Short 1971; Shaw and McKay 1972).

Following Small, Park regarded the city as 'social laboratory' (Smith 1988: 119). Park was invited in 1914 to the Chicago Department of Sociology by W.I. Thomas, and was influenced by his anthropological work and interest in immigrant ethnic groups. They also shared some personal similarities in coming from rural backgrounds: Thomas was raised in Virginia, whereas Park was brought up in Pennsylvania and Minnesota. Both had moved from rural life to experience the modern, urban city (and had studied in Germany) and were interested in how city life affected individual mental outlook, and how groups adapted to new urban conditions, as shown in Thomas's and Znaniecki's *The Polish Peasant in Europe and America* (1958) (see Roberts 2010). Park's notion of the 'marginal man', drawing on Simmel's (1950a) work on 'The Stranger', addressed immigrant experience as 'old habits' are replaced with new ones and a 'moral dichotomy and conflict' arises between two patterns of life.

Park's 'marginal man' can be said to differ from Simmel's 'stranger' – the former individual 'resents his marginality and aspires to the full group membership from which he is excluded', whereas the latter 'is a wanderer who still relishes or yearns for the freedom of coming and going as he pleases' (Smith 1988: 121–2). For the 'marginal man', the 'period of crisis' becomes more permanent – with 'spiritual instability, intensified self-consciousness, and *malaise*' (Park in Roberts 2006: 16). The origin of the conceptual difference seems to lie in Park's concern with 'social adaptation' – how individuals and groups go through a process of adjustment to a new environment through consensus, conflict, accommodation, and assimilation (see Braude 1970: 3–4; Schuetz 1944: 507). For Park, the city had created a plethora of 'neighbourhoods', as a 'segregated' 'mosaic of little worlds', but was associated with disruptions to personal relations (Park 2005: 31). What is of particular interest, in Park and the work of other Chicagoans, such as Wirth, is the formation of 'personality types' in the 'metropolis' (cf. Simmel 1950b) – for Park the 'marginal man' (and 'new and divergent individual types') (Park 2005: 32; Smith 1988: 163), for Thomas (and Znaniecki) the 'philistine', 'bohemian', and 'creative individual', to understand responses to social transition to city life (Roberts 2006: 25). Chicagoan sociologists, while constructing these 'types', were reflecting on their own personal life transitions and associated research concerns. Thomas declared that he felt in his 'sociological history' a 'dominant interest has been new experience of concrete types'; he observed he was 'an extrovert leading an introvert life'. Park reflected that until he worked at the Tuskegee Institute (prior to joining the Chicago School), he had been in 'intellectual vagabondage' as a 'muckraking' reporter in various cities and then studying in Germany (Thomas and Park, in Baker 1973). The pursuit to understand their own life histories and intellectual concerns possibly played a part in Park's and Burgess's encouragement of students to enter the 'field' to pursue their own interests, to engage in what became known as 'participant observation' in the streets and areas of Chicago, and to uncover personal meanings through use of life history materials, as found in a range of key studies (cf. Angell 1945).

The work of the Chicago School has been placed within a liberal intellectual and political stance (e.g., Pragmatism, Progressivism, cf. Mills 1970), and has been charged with ecological determinism and its 'construction' of subjects' life stories as comparable with 'romantic', 'fictional' film heroes (Plummer 2001: 115). Chicagoan work may be seen as part of a wider social documentary milieu in the 1920–40s across a whole range of social inquiry and arts (novels, photography, art); for example, there was wide publication of 'informant narratives', particularly in radical journalism, dealing with social problems (rather than in 'pulp confessionals') (Stott 1973: 190–210). In fact, the 'documentary movement' exhibited various political and aesthetic tendencies. Chicagoan sociology itself was perhaps a mix of approaches: it has been described as exhibiting a 'liberal practicality' (Mills 1970) or even creating a 'sociology noir' reflecting a modernist sensibility to the 'darker' side of life (in marginality, estrangement) (Salerno 2007; Salerno 2010). It can be broadly distinguished from other 1930s social documentary currents. For instance, Entin identifies 'left-leaning, Depression-era' artists and photographers who attempted to counter dominant 'representational and aesthetic modes' – those including 'sentimentalism, realism, naturalism', having (as in some photographic documentary) rather romanticised or passive portrayals of the unemployed and poor (Entin 2007: 2). He argues a 'sensational modernism' (of writers, photographers) gave an alternative view with images of 'pain, prejudice, crime, and violence' that challenged moral authority and cultural control – to 'shock' the 'higher' classes into an urgent 'new way of seeing' the dispossessed (slum inhabitants, criminals, immigrants) often taking cues from pulp magazines, tabloids, and cinema: the depiction of 'disfigured' or 'sick' bodies summarised a 'social crisis and cultural critique' (Entin 2007; 2–3). Further 'documentary' portraits of urban life in the 1920s and 1930s were 'city films' or 'City Symphonies' by Vertov, Strand, Cavalcanti (the latter came to Britain to work on documentaries), and others who brought the rhythms of music in their visual and sound portraits (using montage and other techniques) of the changing daily routines of inhabitants and cityscape). The poetic aesthetics of 'city films' and the 'ethnography' of the Surrealist *Documents* had some commonality in their usage of montage and mixing of documentary and art (Russell 1999: 28). Baudelaire was perhaps an anticipation of this 'vision', just as Dickens's portrayals of the 'sound and vision' (panorama) of the city was also a precursor to the cinema (Smith 2003).

An issue for the Walking Interview as a Biographical Method (WIBM) (and wider research) here is an awareness of the kinds of genre or writing style (cf.

Bruyn 1966) and *sensibility* being employed – how description, speech, comment, analysis, political assumptions, 'aesthetic view', personal orientation, etc. are being used (adopted, connected, mixed) within ethnographic documentation (cf. Atkinson, 1990) i.e., whether 'styles' of melodrama, sensationalism, romanticism, feminist, realist, empathetic, objective, etc. are central or part, mixed in, or the general stance and 'tone' of the 'report'. An application of the 'walking method' must be continuously reflective on the collaborative form and the authorial 'voice', tone, or view and theoretical orientation adopted – and the degree and type of personal and intellectual (autoethnographic) awareness that is included in the research process. We 'document' the street or other environments, and our act of walking, relationships and 'life' itself in our particular ways, but are influenced by wider modes of 'documenting' (by institutions, groups, forms of media) which provide the resources and viewpoint for narrations of 'reality'.

Mass Observation

The WIBM has a focus on the 'everyday', and a form of ethnographic dialogue and exploration, a 'documentary' approach to using a range of means of information collection and reportage (visual, verbal narrative, and commentary). Mass Observation, working in the late 1930s and 1940s Britain, combined many of these concerns, with an overall intent to reveal the 'human element' in social study – in particular, the ordinary lives and thoughts of those in who had not been given sufficient 'voice' and consideration during the Depression and its aftermath.

The founders of Mass Observation were Tom Harrisson, an anthropologist, Charles Madge, a poet and journalist, and Humphrey Jennings, a writer, filmmaker, and artist, who combined to study social life, particularly from the Depression's 'forgotten' areas', and during wartime, the daily concerns and morale of people in the factories and at home (Calder and Sheridan 1984; Cross 1990b). Its work can be seen, not only as part of a documentary 'impulse' (see Stott 1973), but as part of a broad educational and political movement in the UK and elsewhere (cf. the *Penguin Specials, The Left Book Club*). For example, in 1934, J. B. Priestley reported on his *English Journey*, which was followed by George Orwell's visit to Northern England (*The Road to Wigan Pier*, 1937), who vividly described the dark (as if 'subterranean') living conditions and slag-heaps, smoke, and filth of industrial areas, arguing that it was a 'duty' occasionally to view and smell the 'labyrinthe slums' so this experience was not lost in memory: in fact, it seems descriptions of odours and scents – 'smell narratives' – were an important element of Orwell's social commentary in fiction and non-fiction writings (Orwell 1989: 14, 141–2; Sutherland 2016).

Mass Observation employed a number of documentary means – not only observation of street and institutional activities and informal 'voices' (including reporting on the Blitz and shelters: see Harrisson 1990), but also a range of other materials, including questionnaires, interviews, monthly diaries, and 'directive replies' to a 'panel' of respondents to give a contemporary report on social and political issues and a 'vision' of life during the aftermath of the Depression in the 1930s and the pressing daily conditions of World War II. Prior to World War II, Mass Observation observed crowds assembled to celebrate the Coronation on 12 May 1937 of George VI (Jennings and Madge 1987). Initially, Mass Observation's work was carried out in London and on the large Worktown (Bolton) project (see Hall 2015; Cross 1990; Spender 1982; Calder and Sheridan 1984). Tom Harrisson led research in Worktown from a small house where many observers (and artists) stayed for varying periods. The researchers were unusually, there-fore, living and studying within the centre of working class culture, compiling information on pub life, sporting events, shopping, cinema-going, religion, and politics (Hall 2015: 44–5; Sheridan et al. 2000: 27–8). Mass Observation even followed the 'Worktowners' on holiday in Blackpool to document their enjoy-ment (on the promenade, the beach, etc.) (Cross 1990). Humphrey Spender took photographs of holidaymaking and Worktown life (Spender 1982; Harrisson and Madge 1986). The Worktown project was concerned with the 'anthropology' of the 'everyday' – the recording of (to other classes) an unfamiliar culture and its concerns in its mundane daily round.

Mass Observation had some influence from Surrealism, but the degree of that effect and its nature is rather difficult to estimate. Jennings had taken part in a major Surrealist exhibition in London, but any Surrealism must be placed alongside Madge's broad approach in assessing the 'aesthetic tendencies' of Mass Observation research (Marcus 2001: 16). For Marcus, Mass Observation's 'radical positivism' was different from Surrealism due to the amassing of ordinary 'facts' – a 'mass project'. However, she adds that 'its status as "surrealist ethnography" [cf. Clifford 1981] could be said to emerge in its project of exploring familiar aspects of everyday life as if they were part of an unfamiliar culture, and as a way of revealing cultural meanings' (Marcus 2001:16). Interestingly, Humphrey Jennings' book *Pandaemonium* (1985) in 'amassing' quotations and recording opinions and observations in essays, reports, novels, letters, etc. diverse writings, by wide range of writers, artists, scientists, and others over 200 years, shows a shift in 'conscious-ness' with the rise of industrialism – it gives an 'imaginative history', looking back to understand the present. *Pandaemonium* is a *montage* of documents (cf. Benjamin 2002); a kind of ethnographic retrieval to *reveal* the *imagination* brought with the coming of the machine and the rise of the industrial city.

Nineteenth century walking and exploring, the Chicago School, and the Mass Observation project contribute to a sociological history and imagination for the development of the WIBM. When we walk and interview in ethno-graphic research, what is the social world we see, how do we 'apprehend', frame, and report it to others and ourselves? If social research can be an 'anthropology of ourselves', how do we 'structure' the 'sensual scenes' we pass through – in naturalism, realism, romanticism, or surrealism, etc. – or as Bruyn described, in ethnographic 'styles' – 'romantic', 'realistic', 'poetic', 'factual', 'analytic', 'satiric', 'journalistic', and 'existential' (Bruyn 1966: 245)? How can we construct ethnographic accounts that 'represent' time and place, and contain the dialogue of the walking interview? Can we 'create', 'employ', a form of 'realism' that goes further than the 'limits of representation' to 'other realities of experience, desire, memory, and fantasy … [that] are historical and produce real effects' (Russell 1999: 25), a practice that can range backwards and forwards in time, content, and critique? The WIBM must begin with attempts to show how we form and apply our 'maps of meaning', our intellectual, aesthetic, and other frames of the social world (Jackson 1989).

Baudelaire, Benjamin, and the flâneur

The growth of the modern city brought a fascination to observers, leading to attempts to understand its nature and evolution. One starting point for Benjamin's influential account of city life in the *Arcades Project* is Engels, who stated that a place like London was a 'strange' thing, since someone could 'wander for hours' without the 'slightest hint' that the 'open country' was near. The 'colossal centralization', he said, of two and half million people has created the world's commercial centre and the thousands of vessels in massive Thames docks (Engels in Benjamin 2002: 427). But this growth with its 'marvels' had come at a cost that was apparent in 'roaming' the London streets, which is that Londoners have had to give up the higher aspects of human nature for these new features of civilisation (Engels, in Benjamin 2002: 427). For Engels, there is a rather disturbing feeling brought by the chaos of the street. He asks whether these masses from differing classes pushing by share a common commitment to happiness and its means. But they crowd together on the street indifferent to each other, without a glance, as if they have disparate lives. It seems the more individuals are put in proximity in the city, the more they show indifference and isolation and self-interest (Engels, in Benjamin 2002: 427–8).

Benjamin's well-known commentaries on the city, on Paris – and more specifically, the character of the 'flâneur' (in relation to the crowd, and observing and recording the urban) drawing on Baudelaire (cf. *The Painter of Modern Life*, 1863) and many others – are attempts to understand its development in terms of its commercialism and the shopping arcades, the crowd, and its past. For Benjamin, the flâneur is 'the observer' of market relations, an idling in opposition to the organisation of work, someone waiting without resolve (Benjamin 2002: 425, 427). It is in Paris that the flâneur's life and his vista is formed (Benjamin 2002: 416–7). Echoing others, Benjamin argues that the city brings to fruition the long anticipation or dream of the labyrinth, an entity to which the flâneur does not realize he is committed. The mass, for Benjamin, is the latest labyrinth (Benjamin 2002: 429–30, 446). He also makes close comparisons between the flâneur and aspects of the detective, journalist, and literary individual. The flâneur walking the street, he concludes, descends steeply in time into the past (Benjamin 2002: 416, 442, 446).

The flâneur appears to be a detached character – dislocated from his class background, embedded (but separate) in the crowds, and loitering within the 19th century arcades (which preceded the large departmental shopping stores of the early 20th century). He is set on discovering the elements of the past – metaphors and signs of previous existence – but (for Benjamin), such 'traces' are not to be set in a linear historical frame. Instead they are perceived disparate historical elements that can be re-discovered and joined in differing historical accounts (Milburn 2009: 5). Within Benjamin's strolling flâneur (from Baudelaire), three main themes can be identified: concerning the city, the crowd, and capitalism (Gros 2015: 175). First, unlike the rural rambler or the loafer, the flâneur walks with regard to the attraction of the shop displays in the new expanse of the cityscape whose density was like a forest or jungle – (i.e. a labyrinth) (Gros 2015: 176). Second, there was the teeming nature of the crowd, the relentlessly moving, anonymous mass of the industrial city. Third was the consumerism of capitalism where everything becomes a product – the crowd itself appears to 'consume individuals'. Even so, the 'stroller' is subversive of the crowd and commerce, observing the multitude of things surrounding him, with his slowness differing from the bustle of commerce and enabling a recording of city experience, challenging the alienating effects and conditions of the urban by an ambiguous emphasis on the poetic and mythic of the experience (Gros 2015: 178–80). The flâneur is an observer, chronicler, and wanderer who is gathering, interpreting, and retrieving signs and disjunctive elements of the 'cultural world' of the modern city (McCabe 2004:161), and so, at least shares some characteristics of the separateness of the 'marginal man and the 'stranger'. Finally, in Benjamin, the figure can be related to the author's own collecting, organising, and commenting in *The Arcades Project* (cf. Jennings 1985 in *Pandaemonium*) as a means of using or composing the selections, in 'producing' the past and re-forming it within the shifting present (McCabe 2004: 161–2). The flâneur, at least in one reading, appears to be an isolated figure that surveys 'a bleak, nocturnal world' that 'thrives after dark' (Wrigley 2014: 10).

Traditionally, there has been no place for the 'flâneuse' – the recognition of the gendered nature of space (and particularly at night), gendered social regulation and male gaze (Milburn 2009: 6). But feminist writers have sought to re-inscribe the female stroller, and overcome the failure to acknowledge her presence. The notion of the male flâneur fails to account for women's experience of modernity, one who is not only 'present', but active in exploring and enjoying the city, as engaged in self-discovery, but still within an ambiguous presence, the dominance of the male in the public sphere, and the continuance of varying anxieties about women's social place and access to 'space' (Wolff 1985; Wilson, 1995). However, it can be argued that there are various possible histories of walking that can be constructed – not simply the 'trajectory' ('Baudelaire to Benjamin' and on to Situationism and Psychogeography) of the male flâneur. For instance, Elkin (2017) uses Virginia Woolf and George Sand to mark out a rather different literary trajectory, one that makes clear the role of women walkers and their experience, by describing the 'flâneuse': women did walk the 19th century city, its (often less desirable) streets and parks, and shopped (and worked) in the arcades and emerging department stores – despite spatially gendered conventions and restrictions – and some wrote on their urban experience (Elkin 2017: 7–20; see D'Souza and McDonough 2008). On a wider scale, it is worth noting that women journeyed afar (and often alone) as shown in the major contributions of 18th–20th century women to travel writing, journalism, and photography (e.g., Wollstonecraft's accounts of European travels, and women's reportage in the Spanish Civil War and World War II, Elkin 2017: 250). This 'reinstatement' of women in the 19th century city should remind us of alternative perspectives or 'histories' that are possible on the experience of the city and walking in the urban environs (see Chapter 3 and Chapter 9).

Key postmodern writers (e.g., Baudrillard) have commented extensively on late capitalism and the 'post-industrial urbanscape'. Los Angeles has been the key reference point for writers on the 'postmodern condition', often described as producing an 'experience of disorientation' and 'fragmentation' (see Jones 2006: 89). For Jones, such feelings are to be expected if we take from particular visitors to the downtown city who are seen as exemplifying postmodernist experience. She points to the 'constructive' nature of such a perspective coming from of dominant parts of 'Euro-American society' – and that the 'disorientation' of city walking and observation may not be so prevalent as stated (Jones 2006: 89–90). Nicholson (2011), a confirmed walker in Los Angeles, questions the 'legend' or 'myths' of walking in the city – as though no one expects to walk, or that walking is seen as a social threat (as in Baudrillard) (see Amato 2004). Although the city layout and distances militate against pedestrianism, even so residents are increasingly walking (and jogging) – with a passion, for pleasure, health, or to maintain sanity – so not everyone believes in the legends (Nicholson 2011: 89–90). Further, he points out that there is a strong history of walking, as political (for social justice), a literary or artistic tradition, and for recreation (Nicholson 2011: 89; see Chapter 5). Jones (2006) attempts to reshape the understanding of urban experience. She describes the work of a range of urban artists in Los Angeles, using performance and digital photography to construct a very different city to the anxious and disorienting image in postmodernism. It is one that is 'experienced in and through the body as a new kind of social space' as 'multivalent and never fixed in terms of ethnic, class, gender, and sexual experience' allowing for different 'versions of postmodern posturban subjectivity' – Los Angeles as both 'virtual' ('represented or imaginary') and 'lived' (meaningful material experience). Thus, these artists are indicating a possibility of reforming urban areas and creating new kinds of subjectivity (Jones 2006: 91, 103).

The notion of the flâneur, despite its difficulties in conception, does raise issues on the walker's demeanour, and activity in the 'everyday' of the street, the living relation with modern life, the social dynamics of the crowd, and the distractions of commercialism. While postmodernism pointed to the fragmentation and disorientation of the modern city on the individual, the work of artists can enable us to 'key in' to the actual experience of walking and its cultural context. One approach here would be to examine 'thinking and feeling' as 'embodied' in walking. For example, Ingold and Vergunst (2008) discuss the relationship between the walking body and the context of social relations and surroundings. They note that Mauss (in 1934) described the techniques of the body (hands, arms) in walking and the various associated cultural customs. Following from Mauss's neglected ideas, they point out that Bourdieu, in using 'habitus' in the 1970s, wished to conceive walking not simply as representative of 'collective representations', but the walking body in 'active engagement in its surroundings' undertaking its daily tasks, and as a 'way of thinking and feeling'. But they argue that this 'proposition' could be 'reversed' by arguing that 'thinking and feeling are ways of walking'. In walking, we are 'social beings', but as social beings, we are walkers, and so we can understand our sociality – and subjectivity – more deeply if we study our walking 'routines' (Ingold and Vergunst 2008: 1–2).

Social documentary photography

The practice of walking interviews can include photographs – by the researched or the researcher – during its course. In doing so, there is a clear overlap with social documentary photography. Following its invention, photography expanded rapidly, for example, in portraiture and carte visite, but also in recording urban scenes. Early in its history, the photographer was compared with the flâneur as an observer and recorder of the modern city streets. Photography soon found official and reform use to 'observe' and 'survey' populations for social policy and control purposes (government, charities, medical intervention, etc.), and lay bare social conditions and perceived 'threats' (the 'unknown', 'mysterious', 'outcast', and 'threatening') for the middle classes (Price 2004: 75–6). Photography was also part of early anthropology (and travel and exploration) and urban sociology (e.g., the Chicago School and in social surveys): the original edition of Thrasher's classic *The Gang* (1927) had photographs, and Lewis Hine (working for charities) photographed the lives of new immigrants to America, their jobs and locales and, in particular, the exploitation of children, contributing to the famous sociological *The Pittsburgh Survey* (1907–9) (which influenced Robert Park) (Jeffrey 2008: 70). *The Pittsburgh Survey* (1907–9) also contained art by Joseph Stella. Early photography brings attention to the connections between the photographer, social explorer, and artist, and the practice of the flâneur, all as observers of city life. Unfortunately, the use of photography went into decline in social science usage, until the rise of an interest in the 'visual' in 1980s ethnography.

In the history of photography, a number of forms (styles, method, procedures, genres, etc.) have developed, although distinctions between them are difficult to fully sustain. Social documentary, photojournalism, street photography, and social landscape photography (even portrait photography) commonly overlap, and terms are often used interchangeably (see Price 2004: 69). As Price argues, in the case of social documentary and photojournalism, they share a 'claim' to the 'real' – the 'accurate' and 'authentic' reflection of the social circumstance, despite the intervention of the photographer in the choice and production of the image, and later editing for publication (Price 2004: 71).

A pioneer of street photography was Eugène Atget who began, in the late 19th century, to take pictures of 'interiors' and how they connect with Parisian pavements and streets – shops and displays, brasseries, vehicles, vendors, and occupations of all kinds (Jeffery 2008: 30, 34). Earlier photographic recorders of the streets and social conditions were John Thompson in London in the 1870s, while in the 1880s–90s, investigative journalist and reformer Jacob Riis photographed the slums of New York for magazines and books (cf. Riis 1890, *How the other half lives*, see Marien 2006: 204-5; Price 2004: 77-8).

During the 1920s and 1930s, a number of related changes took place in social documentary photography: first, technological advances made cameras easier to use and new printing reproduction allowed for the rise of photo-magazines (e.g., *Vue* in France); second, war photography (cf. the Civil War in Spain), imagery of street scenes, and fashion photography expanded; and finally, the Depression brought a reportage of the conditions of the workless, marginalised, struggling farming communities and others to the fore, for example, in the work of photographers for the Farm Security Administration (FSA) in the US (e.g., Dorothea Lange, Walker Evans) and in 'photobooks'. Much of the work on the poor in this era has been criticised for its 'hierarchal' view – as reformism and romanticism or having a sentimental appeal, with the subjects as 'uni-dimensional' victims. However, much debate recently has focused on whether this is a rather simple characterisation of the complexity and range of 1930s social documentary work (see Price 2004: 94–7; Allred 2010; Entin 2007). The 1930s also saw radical workers' photography and film groups across US, Europe, and elsewhere (e.g., The Photo League, NY) recording the lives and struggles of the working class.

'Street photography' emerged strongly in the 1950s, but its origins can be found in the earliest days of photography (Seaborne and Sparham 2011). Similarly, early film in the 1880s featured street activity, as seen in Le Prince's recording of a busy bridge in central Leeds. Marien argues that the endless images of the throng of city streets can have a deeper import that 'expressed the photographer's inner feelings or evinced the seedy materialism of postwar American culture' (Marien 2006: 340). She describes the post-World War II work of Harry Callahan that included 'brooding street photographs' showing the 'city as tense and inhospitable' and Weegee, who took 'sensational images of crime and violent death', as a 'place of barely submerged brutality, fear, and confusion' for magazines (Marien 2006: 342–4; see Entin 2007). However, while a more 'humanistic', 'empathetic', or 'observational' street photography continued during the 1950s (for instance, Helen Levitt, Berenice Abbott, Vivian Maier), two photographers brought a different, more disruptive 'style': William Klein (2010) presented a rather stark view of New York with strong contrasts of dark and light, blur, and unusual angles which gave an alternative to conventional image-making. Robert Frank, in *The Americans* (2008), again with some challenge to the rigours of photographic conventions, produced a cross-USA road trip that was a rather downbeat portrait of American life and symbols in contrast to the contemporary 1950s aspirational 'good life' of advertising (Marien 2006: 339–40).

The idea of capturing the 'mundane' or banality of life (say, 'the bustling street') with a degree of detachment became common during the 1960s and 1970s, from photographers often based in New York, but many of whom also undertook 'road trips' (of course, there were also 1950s–60s writers, like Kerouac, Steinbeck) echoing the earlier work of Frank (cf. Winogrand, Eggleston, Friedlander, Shore, Ray-Jones) and writers and photographers of the 1930s. Such work varied in its 'rawness', dynamic, and humour (and later in use of colour) (see Westerbeck 2005). Some photographers began to focus on marginalised and vulnerable groups and subcultures (including their friends), giving very intimate images of their lives, others providing some critique of contemporary media, entertainment, and advertising in popular image construction (cf. Cindy Sherman). In the UK during the 1960s–70s, there was also 'street photography' in London (cf. Roger Mayne) and also a tradition of 'social documentary' work from the 1940s–50s *Picture Post* (Bert Hardy and others) to the studies of working class communities and de-industrialisation (see Konttinen 1988; Bulmer 2012; Killip 2016).

Today, social documentary and street photography (and portraiture), as in the 'photobook', are prominent cultural practices (cf. Howarth and MacLaren 2011; Meyerowitz and Westerbeck 2001; the Urban Photographers Association), with a range of attendant social and political issues for 'visual storytelling' and questions arising from digital advances, including contributions by non-professionals through social media, etc. (see Ritchen 2015). These should be seen as broad genres which overlap – street photography can vary from fashion, portraiture, social record, and protest; social documentary includes reporting on international and local issues concerning human rights, political events, and social action, but topics are not exclusive to either form. The walking method can connect with these photographic genres through its concern to report and understand individual and group experiences through 'moving stories' of daily lives. Even so, in using photography (by researcher, 'subjects', or in collaboration), there are various important questions for the 'walking method' in how images are taken, processed, and presented (e.g., placed together, and in relation to text) and sociopolitical context. In short, there is a complex process of composition that sets out to define (and respond) to the social world, rather than merely reflect it (Price 2004: 73–4; see Roberts 2011).

The notion of the 'flâneur' has an appeal to some photographers within documentary or street practice – the photographer as a lone 'voyeur', or as a 'casual observer', or stroller within the urban scene, 'catching' the passing scene. One international, collaborative project – 'Flâneur: New Urban Narratives' – takes the idea as an inspiration for artistic, engaged practice, sharing its work (with outside installations), and open to chance opportunities rather than follow a set path (Padley 2017: 83–5). The idea has also had influence on wider artistic practice (e.g., the impact of Baudelaire's *The Painter of Modern Life*, 1863 on Picasso: see Richardson 2009).

Walking research methods should not simply 'add' the use of the camera to existing methodologies as merely another means to record but, instead take it as 'carrying'/'conveying' (in its use of form, perspective, arrangement) meaning as a process in which decisions are being made on what, when, where and how (the relation of 'background' context to the portrait, how the image of the street, building are being composed, etc.), and why the photograph(s) or film are being taken. In addition, there should be an awareness of how the images are going to be placed, the degree and manner to which they will be connected etc. to other materials (voice, text – as a descriptive addition, as a separate and different 'record', as in some dynamic relation, etc.) and ethical concerns (e.g., the consent and individual and communal impact of research on those involved). For example, O'Neill's research used photographs taken by women (seeking asylum) along a route they have chosen, and which are then discussed and placed or 'curated' back in the workshop setting to express and represent the process, experience, and meaning shared, in what she describes as a 'constellational analysis' (O'Neill 2017a; O'Neill 2017b).

Finally, the use of the camera must be 'open to opportunities' (by respondent and researcher), which matches the WIBM's approach to being within the 'ongoing present', but even if the route has been set, 'things happen' in our daily lives with differing levels of, or no, anticipation.

Situationism

The current artistic (and social science) exploration of walking as a method, source, and mode of representation can be traced not only back to the 1960s and 1970s, but also further to the artistic and literary explorations of the early 20th century. As Evans describes, the notion of 'drifter' connected with work of Debord and Situationists of the middle years of the 20th century, was clearly traceable to Baudelaire's earlier figure, the 'flâneur' – both sought to 'defy' the commercial imperatives of the modern cityscape while intent on 'new experiences' (Evans 2012: 14). The Situationists 'tended to document their performative forays in the streets of Paris through whimsical "maps" (uniting fragments of actual maps with arrows indicating the propulsive trajectory of the various "*derives*", or wanderings, of the group' – more recently, work by video artists and photographers uses technology to allow subjects to 'navigate' ('open out') the experiences of 'highly disorientating, posturban spaces' of the turn of the 21st century (Jones 2006: 107, 110). There were also 'affinities' between the drifter and 1920s Surrealism in Paris which moved art out of the confines of the studio to pursue an 'avant-garde dream' of combining 'everyday life' and art, while also taking in later urban perspectives as associated with Lefebvre (Evans 2012: 14). Surrealism attempted to re-align 'the everyday' through disruption and 'shock', and introduced 'hybridity' and 'pluralism' to ethnography, but (for Benjamin) its potential for 'revolt' was limited (see Russell 1999: 39). It is worth noting here the possible differences in 'city experience' between locations. Smith suggests that the idea of 'spectacle' can be applied differently to London and Paris: the former, with its commodification of life, is similar to Debord and the Situationists' usage, whereas the latter has the theatricality of the urban parade – a difference indicated in Dickens's images of the city as the dark labyrinth or exhibiting the light of panorama (Smith 2003: 76). Alternatively, it is worth remarking that Charles Lamb interestingly described London as a pantomime and masquerade (Jennings 1985: 115).

Michel de Certeau also understands walking within a city by examining the activities of inhabitants by reference to how walking can have a subversive aspect. He draws on a range of writers (Lefebvre, Freud, Vaneigem, Lacan, Foucault, and others) to uncover the neglected everyday practices, and the need to account for the actual street patterns that individuals take rather than from a 'totalising' voyeuristic gaze from above that does not allow for particular individual identities and given localities (Coverley 2012: 31–3). Part of de Certeau's concern is how individual walkers navigate the streets unconsciously, and create their own complex, urban paths, different from those of administrative, governmental routes, texts that they 're-write' and 're-read' (Collie 2013: 5). An interesting contrast is made between the ideas of tactics and strategy – the 'consumer' acting according to tactics in places that are defined by the strategies of institutions and power. Collie says 'the speaking body' can be introduced, at this point, since 'stories about place' give a different 'metaphorical geography' (of 'legends, memories, and dreams') and 'spatial practices' that allow a different 'possibility' of the city (Collie 2013: 7).

There is a 'conversation' between de Certeau and Foucault – perhaps whereas the latter's concern is with the various 'micro-physics' or techniques of power that shape the body, in de Certeau, there is a focus on detailed unconscious resistance. While de Certeau raises the different ways that spaces and movement within the city can be undertaken, rather than merely prescribed from above, there remain some difficulties or lack of clarity in both accounts – there is an abstract quality that tends to reduce the diversity and specificity of the exercise of power and forms of resistance, and often the subtleties of their inter-connection. The notion of the 'everyday', the actual lives and 'making out' of differing groups (and intra-group relations), rather than merely being subject to 'disciplinary technologies' requires elaboration – how individuals actually, reflect, experience, and 'resist', and create narratives (see Collie 2013: 9, 32). An interesting project here on urban experience, lives 'as lived', is by Helmreich, who in his book *The New York Nobody Knows: Walking 6,000 miles in the City*, describes the outcome of the idea to walk 'systematically, block by block' – a 'transformative journey' to understand the 'soul' or inner life of the city, and to 'comprehend' the lives of the people and its 'villages' 'up close' with 'spontaneous' interviews (Helmreich 2013: 1–4).

In summary, 'Baudelairean sauntering' gave rise to various strands, such as the Surrealist (Aragon and Breton) focus on 'chance and night' and the Situationists' (Debord) 'exploration of differences', but does the development of uniformity (e.g., shops chains), the proliferation and dominance of motor vehicles (cf. traffic lanes), the contemporary cityscape, restrict 'urban strolling' and its pleasures (Gros 2015: 180)? Perhaps the gentleness and mystical aspects of the 'romantic walker' (cf. Rousseau and Wordsworth) can be contrasted with the 'urban stroller' who is subject to a myriad of pressing or violent stimuli (Gros 2015: 181; see Amato 2004: 101–12). For the WIBM, a main interest here, in relation to the Situationist 'drifter', is a concern with the 'stance' (political, aesthetic, investigative, etc.) that is being adopted in relation to others, the wider social and physical environment, and oneself.

Conclusion: Theorising walking in the sociological imagination

Walking is seemingly so mundane that it deserves little scrutiny, and yet it is full of 'possibilities'. So what is the 'special nature', the inherent aspects of walking? Moving in 'space' is physical – experiential – and a shift between forms of consciousness and conceptions of 'multiple realities': past, present, future. Walking experience can now be supplemented: informed and intertwined – by new digital technologies, giving connection to social media, sources of socio-historical information (i.e., on the locale – statistics, text, imagery), location and movement-tracking, even augmented reality, and forms of recording of what is being 'sensed', conversation, and video during the walk. A 'walk' can become multi-modal in terms of techniques of recording, 'external' sources, and shifts between forms of experience.

The social scientist is often a walker in research, moving and communicating with others – not simply asking questions and in dialogue with 'respondents' – but also both actors are relating with the surroundings. The experience of the walking 'situation' cannot be the same for both, the sharing has limitations – individuals have their own sensual feelings, memories, and meanings; however, each can express much of what they are experiencing – what the surrounding environment evokes, and elements of their life histories. As we 'pass' through 'scenes' in walking, we are 'editing' – both adding, fashioning, interlinking, 'building' – and subtracting, simplifying, essentialising, 'excavating', our experiences – making it 'our walk' (cf. Stott 1973: 266; Nicholson 2011: 41–2). We are sensing, pre-sensing, sorting, pre-meaning, and making new meaning – 'perceiving' and understanding our 'passing', applying the 'resources' of memory within the complexities of our present 'everyday' and what we are anticipating: we are observing, thinking about our ongoing situation.

The flâneur or flâneuse is more than an observer, but is also a recorder or is even using means of delving into the urban scene and its pre-history, but the figure is alongside and overlaps with other city observers – inquirers, detectives, journalists, photographers, reformers, radicals, novelists, and artists – and, of course, urban dwellers themselves are providers of narratives (to themselves and others) from their 'passing' through their daily urban journeys. In this chapter, the 'review' of some Victorian social explorers, Chicago Sociology, Mass Observation, social documentary photography, the flâneur, Situationism, etc. reveals that varying perspectives on the 'urban' have been conceived – imagined, 'dreamed' – observed, studied, and *theorised*. It alerts us to forms of consciousness or awareness in observation and conception, e.g., the 'urban' as gothic, noir, modern, postmodern, etc. concerning how the elements or 'fragments' of social reality are interrelated. The work of urban artists and commentators also enable us to focus on another important theme: how the city is owned, organised, and controlled – 'whose city?' and 'right to the city' (cf. Lefebvre) – or questions including access and space, political and social participation (micro and macro activism), use of new technologies, and the spatial bases of civil society.

In the WIBM, the researcher is both participant and an observer – as in the traditional ethnographic distinction – an informal 'interactive' interviewer sensitive to the 'conversation', but also to the 'scene'. The walking researcher may well share aspects of the above 'characters' from reformer to film-maker in employing a range of methods and with various intent. But, centrally, there should be 'reflexivity' (monitoring) and a theoretical orientation on how the 'scene' is being (will be, may be) 'constructed' (via 'genre' cf. 'realism', 'naturalism'), and in 'emotional form' or stance (cf. 'sentimentalism', 'detachment', 'objective', etc.). In WIBM, we are in a walking dialogue – shaping how researcher and researched take and respond to their surroundings and their own biographies 'in the making'. In the next chapter, we focus upon the relationship between walking, art and biographical research.

References

Ackroyd, P. (1991) *Dickens*. London: Minerva.

Ackroyd, P. (2000) *London: The Biography*. London: Chatto & Windus.

Ackroyd, P. (2012) *London Under*. London: Vintage.

Allred, J. (2010) *American Modernism and Depression Documentary*. Oxford: Oxford University Press.

Amato, J. A. (2004) *On Foot: A History of Walking*. London: New York University Press.

Angell, R. (1945) A critical review of the development of the personal document method in sociology, 1920–1940. In: L. Gottschalk, C. Kluckhohn, and R. Angell (ed.) *The Use of Personal Documents in History, Anthropology, and Sociology*. New York: SSRC.

Atkinson, P. (1990) *The Ethnographic Imagination*. London: Routledge.

Baker, P. J. (ed.) (1973) The life histories of W. I. Thomas and Robert E. Park, *American Journal of Sociology*, 79(2): 243–260.

Baudelaire, C-P. (2010) *The Painter of Modern Life*. London: Penguin (orig. pub. 1863).

Beaumont, M. (2015) *Nightwalking*. London: Verso.

Benjamin, W. (2002) *The Arcades Project* (Tr. H. Eiland and K. McLaughlin). Cambridge, MA: Belknap Press of Harvard University Press.

Bodenheimer, R. (2007) *Knowing Dickens*. Ithaca, NY: Cornell University Press.

Booth, C. (1968) *Charles Booth on the City*. Chicago: University of Chicago Press. (H. W. Pfautz ed.).

Booth, W. (1890) *In Darkest England and the Way Out*. London: The Salvation Army.

Brandt, B. (1938) *A Night in London*. London: Country Life.

Braude, L. (1970) 'Park and Burgess': An appreciation, *The American Journal of Sociology*, 76/3 (July): 1–10.

Brassai, G. (1933) *Paris de nuit*. Paris: Editions Arts et Métiers Graphique.

Bruyn, S. T. (1966) *The Human Perspective in Sociology*. Englewood Cliffs, NJ: Prentice-Hall.

Buchan, B. and Ellison, D. (2012) Introduction: Speaking to the eye, *Cultural Studies Review*, On Noise, 18(3): 4–12.

Bullman, J., Hegarty, N. and Hill, B. (2013) *The Secret History of Our Streets*. London: BBC.

Bulmer, J. (2012) *The North*. Liverpool: The Bluecoat Press.

Burgess, W. W. and Bogue, D. J. (1964) The delinquency research of Clifford R. Shaw and Henry D. McKay and associates. In: E. W. Burgess, and D. J. Bogue (eds.) *Contributions to Urban Sociology*. Chicago, IL: The University of Chicago Press.

Burton, G., Korda, S. and Qualmann, C. (2017) *Walkwalkwalk: An Archaeology of the Familiar and Forgotten*. Available at walkwalkwalk.org.uk (Accessed 9 January 2018).

Calder, A. and Sheridan, D. (eds.) (1984) *Speak for Yourself: A Mass-Observation Anthology, 1937–49*. London: Jonathan Cape.

Charles Dickens Museum. (2017) Restless shadow: Dickens the Campaigner, Exhibition, Dickens Museum, May–October. London (curated by J. Drew).

Clifford, J. (1981) On ethnographic surrealism, *Comparative Studies in Society and History*, 23(4): 539–564.

Collie, N. (2013) Walking in the city: Urban space, stories, and gender, *Gender Forum: An Internet Journal for Gender Studies and Women's Studies*, 42: 1–5, (online).

Coverley, M. (2012) *The Art of Wandering: The Writer as Walker*. Harpenden, UK: Oldcastle Books.

Cross, G. (1990a) Introduction. In: G. Cross (ed.) *Worktowners at Blackpool: Mass Observation and Popular Leisure in the 1930s*. London: Routledge.

Cross, G. (ed.) (1990b) *Worktowners at Blackpool: Mass Observation and Popular Leisure in the 1930s*. London: Routledge.

D'Souza, A. and McDonough, T. (eds.) (2008) *The Invisible Flâneuse? Gender, Public Space and Visual Culture in Nineteenth Century Paris*. Manchester: MUP.

Elkin, L. (2017) *Flâneuse: Women Walk the City in Paris, New York, Tokyo, Venice and London*. London: Vintage.

Entin, J. B. (2007) *Sensational Modernism*. Chapel Hill, NC: The University of North Carolina Press.

Evans, D. (2012) Introduction. In: D. Evans (ed.) *The Art of Walking: A Field Guide*. London: Black Dog Publishing.

Field, G. (2002) Nights underground in darkest London: The Blitz, 1940–41, *International Labor and Working-Class History*, 62 (Fall): 11–49.

Frank, L. (1984) *Charles Dickens and the Romantic Self*. Lincoln, NE: University of Nebraska Press.

Frank, R. (2008) *The Americans*. Göttingen: Steidl.

Gautrand, J. C. (2003) *Robert Doisneau, 1912–1994*. London: Taschen.

Gros, F. (2015) *The Philosophy of Walking*. London: Verso.

Groth, H. (2012) The soundscapes of Henry Mayhew: Urban ethnography and technologies of transcription, *Cultural Studies Review*, 18(3): 109–130.

Hall, D. (2015) *Worktown*. London: Weidenfeld & Nicolson.

Harrisson, T. (1990) *The Blitz*. Harmondsworth, UK: Penguin.

Harrisson, T. and Madge, C. (1986) *Britain by Mass Observation*. London: The Cresset Library.

Helmreich, W. B. (2013) *The New York Nobody Knows: Walking 6,000 Miles in the City.* Princeton, NJ: Princeton University Press.

Higgins, C. (2018) *Red Thread: On Mazes and Labyrinths.* London: Jonathan Cape.

Howarth, S. and McLaren, S. (2011) *Street Photography Now.* London: Thames and Hudson.

Ingold, T. and Vergunst, J. L. (2008) Introduction. In: T. Ingold, and J. L. Vergunst (eds.) *Ways of Walking: Ethnography and Practice on Foot.* London: Routledge.

Jackson, P. (1989) *Maps of Meaning.* London: Unwin Hyman.

Jeffrey, I. (2008) *How to Read a Photograph.* London: Thames and Hudson.

Jennings, H. (1985) *Pandaemonium: The Coming of the Machine as Seen by Contemporary Observers.* London: Picador.

Jennings, H. and Madge, C. (1987) *May The Twelfth: Mass Observation Day-Surveys 1937.* London: Faber and Faber.

Johnson, S. (2008) *The Ghost Map.* London: Penguin.

Jones, A. (2006) *Self/Image.* London: Routledge.

Keating, P. J. (ed.) (1976) *Into Unknown England, 1866–1913: Selections from Social Explorers.* Manchester: MUP.

Killip, C. (2016) *In Flagrante Two.* Göttingen: Steidl.

Klein, W. (2010) *Life Is Good and Good for You in New York.* New York: Errata Editions.

Konttinen, S.-L. (1988) *Byker.* Newcastle: Bloodaxe.

Madge, C. (1963) *The Origins of Scientific Sociology.* London: Tavistock.

Marcus, L. (2001) Introduction: The project of Mass Observation, *New Formations,* 44(Autumn): 5–20.

Marien, M. W. (2006) *Photography: A Cultural History,* 2nd edn. London: Laurence King.

Mayhew, H. (1851) *London Labour and the London Poor,* 4 vols. London: Griffin Bohn.

McCabe, J. (2004) Textual debaucheries and the flâneur, *New Formations,* 54(Winter): (2004/5), 154–168.

Mearns, A. (1883) *The Bitter Cry of Outcast London.* London: James Clark & Co.

Meyerowitz, J. and Westerbeck, C. (2001) *Bystander: A History of Street Photography.* New York: Little, Brown and Co.

Milburn, K. (2009) *Following the Flâneur: A Methodological and Textual Critique, Landscape, Place, Space,* 1–12. Nottingham: University of Nottingham Centre for Advanced Studies.

Miller, S. H. (2014) *Walking New York.* New York: Fordham University Press.

Mills, C. W. (1970) *The Sociological Imagination.* Harmondsworth, UK: Penguin.

Minshull, D. (ed.) (2000) *The Vintage Book of Walking: An Anthology.* New York: Vintage.

Morrison, A. (1896) *A Child of the Jago.* London: T. Nelson and Sons.

Morrison, J. and Burdekin, H. (1934) *London Night.* London: Collins.

Morton, H. V. (1926) *Nights of London.* London: Methuen.

Nicholson, G. (2011) *The Lost Art of Walking.* Chelmsford, UK: Harbour Pub.

O'Neill, M. (2016) Studying the marginalized with mixed methods. In: M. Haviid Jacobsen, and S. Walklate (eds.) *Liquid Criminology: Doing Imaginative Criminological Research.* Abingdon, UK: Routledge.

O'Neill, M. (2018) Walking, well-being and community: Racialized mothers building cultural citizenship using participatory arts and participatory action research, *Ethnic and Racial Studies,* 41(1): 73–97.

Orwell, G. (1989) *The Road to Wigan Pier.* London: Penguin [first pub. 1937 Victor Gollancz].

Orwell, G. (1937) *The Road to Wigan Pier.* London: Victor Gollancz.

Padley, G. (2017) Intelligence: Bringing art to the streets, *British Journal of Photography, March*, 7857(164): 83–85.

Park, R. E. (2005) The city. In: K. Gelder (ed.) *The Subcultures Reader*, 2nd edn. London: Routledge.

Plummer, K. (2001) *Documents of Life 2*. London: Sage.

Priestley, J. B. (1934) *English Journey*. London: Victor Gollancz.

Price, D. (2004) Surveyors and surveyed: Photography out and about. In: L. Wells (ed.) *Photography: A Critical Introduction*, 3rd edn. London: Routledge.

Price, D. and Wells, L. (2004) Thinking about photography: Debates, historically and now. In: L. Wells (ed.) *Photography: A Critical Introduction*, 3rd edn. London: Routledge.

Quennell, P. (ed.) (n.d.) *Mayhew's Characters*. London: Hamlyn. (selection from first 3 vols. H. Mayhew, 1851 *London Labour and the London Poor*).

Richardson, J. (2009) *A Life of Picasso, Vol. II: The Painter of Modern Life, 1907–1917*. London: Jonathan Cape.

Riis, J. (1890) *How the Other Half Lives*. NY: Dover (republished 1997 Harmondsworth: Penguin).

Ritchen, F. (2015) *Bending the Frame: Photojournalism, Documentary, and the Citizen*. New York: Aperture.

Roberts, B. (2006) *Micro Social Theory*. Basingstoke, UK: Macmillan.

Roberts, B. (2010) 'Ahead of its time': The legacy and relevance of W. I. Thomas and F. Znaniecki, 1918–20. In: C. Hart (ed.), *The Polish Peasant in Europe and America, The Legacy of the Chicago School of Sociology*. Poynton, UK: Midrash.

Roberts, B. (2011) Photographic portraits: Narrative and memory, [68 Paragraphs], *Forum: Qualitative Sozialforschung, Forum: Qualitative Social Research*, 12(2), Art. 6. Available at http://nbn-resolving.de/urn:nbn:de:0114-fqs110263 (Accessed 21 September 2018).

Rodger, G. (1994) *The Blitz*. London: Bloomsbury.

Russell, C. (1999) *Experimental Ethnography*. Durham, NC: Duke University Press.

Salerno, R. A. (2007) *Sociology Noir: Studies at the University of Chicago in Loneliness, Marginality and Deviance, 1915–1935*. Jefferson, NC: McFarland & Co.

Salerno, R. A. (2010). Ernest Burgess: Exploring urban marginality. In: C. Hart (ed.) *The Legacy of the Chicago School of Sociology*. Poynton, UK: Midrash.

Sandwith, F. (1935) *London by Night*. London: Chatto & Windus.

Schuetz, A. (1944) The stranger: An essay in social psychology, *American Journal of Sociology*, 49(6): 499–507.

Seaborne, M. and Sparham, A. (eds.) (2011) *London Street Photography, 1860–2010*, (Museum of London Exhibition). Stockport: Dewi Lewis Publishing.

Shaw, C. R. and McKay, H. D. (1972) *Juvenile Delinquency and Urban Areas*. Chicago, IL: The University of Chicago Press.

Sheridan, D., Street, B., and Bloome, D. (2000) *Writing Ourselves: Mass Observation and Literacy Practices*. Cresskill, NJ: Hampton Press.

Short, J. F. (ed.) (1971) *The Social Fabric of the Metropolis*. Chicago, IL: The University of Chicago Press.

Simmel, G. (1950a) The stranger. In: K. H. Wolff (ed.) *The Sociology of Georg Simmel*. New York: The Free Press.

Simmel, G. (1950b) The metropolis and mental life. In: K. H. Wolff (ed.) *The Sociology of Georg Simmel*. New York: The Free Press.

Smith, D. (1988) *The Chicago School: A Liberal Critique of Capitalism*. Basingstoke, UK: Macmillan.

Smith, G. (2003) *Dickens and the Dream of Cinema*. Manchester: Manchester University Press.

Somerville, C. (2017) *The January Man: A Year of Walking Britain*. London: Doubleday.

Sparham, A. (2018) *London Nights*. London: Hoxton Mini Press/Museum of London. [exhibition catalogue].

Spender, H. (1982) *Worktown People: Photographs from Northern England, 1937–8*. Bristol: Walling Wall Press.

Stanley, H. M. (1890) *In Darkest Africa*, 2 vols. London: Sampson et al. Pub.

Stead, W. T. (1884) *If Christ came to Chicago*. Chicago: Laird and Lee.

Stedman-Jones, G. (1976) *Outcast London*. Harmondsworth: Penguin.

Stott, W. (1973) *Documentary Expression and Thirties America*. Oxford: Oxford University Press.

Sutherland, J. (2016) *Orwell's Nose: A Pathological Biography*. London: Reaktion.

Thomas, W. I. and Znaniecki, F. (1958) *The Polish Peasant in Europe and America*, 2 vols. New York: Dover Press (First Pub 1918–20).

Thomson, J. (1880) *City of Dreadful Night*. London: Dobell.

Thrasher, F. (1927) *The Gang*. Chicago: The University of Chicago Press.

Tolson, A. (2005) Social surveillance and subjectification: The emergence of 'subculture' in the work of Henry Mayhew. In: K. Gelder (ed.) *The Subcultures Reader*, 2nd edn. London: Routledge.

Washington, B. T. (1984) *The Man Farthest Down*. London: Transaction Books (with R. E., Park) (Orig. pub. 1911).

Wasson, S. (2010) *Urban Gothic of the Second World War: Dark London*. London: Palgrave Macmillan.

Westerbeck, C. (2005) *Joel Meyerowitz*. London: Phaidon.

Wilson, E. (1995) The invisible flâneur. In: S. Watson, and K. Gibson (eds.) *Post-Modern Cities and Spaces*. Oxford: Blackwell. [also in *New Left Review*, 1/191 January–February 1992].

Wolff, J. (1985) The invisible flâneuse: Women and the literature of modernity, *Theory, Culture and Society*, 2(3): 37–46.

Wrigley, R. (2014) Introduction. In: R. Wrigley (ed.) *The Flâneur Abroad: Historical and International Perspectives*. Newcastle: Cambridge Scholars Publishing.

Yeo, E. (1984) Mayhew as social investigator. In: E. P. Thompson, and E. Yeo (eds.) *The Unknown Mayhew*. Harmondsworth, UK: Penguin.

3

WALKING, ART-MAKING, AND BIOGRAPHICAL RESEARCH

In this chapter, we extend previous discussions of the theoretical, conceptual literature linking walking, ethnography, and art by engaging with work across a multi-disciplinary terrain (sociology, urban studies, human geography, social work, arts and humanities). The intention is to articulate, consolidate, and summarise the development of practices of thinking, observing, and theorising walking in biographical research. Although walking has a long and varied history in ethnography, anthropology, urban studies, and arts practice, it is also becoming increasingly utilised in the social sciences. The emerging 'turn to walking' is part of a wider concern with lives in 'movement' in social science, as in the number of recently published works in urban sociology with a focus on the city and 'mobilities' research (Smith and Hall 2016; Roy 2016; Ferguson 2016) and arts-based biographical studies (Roberts 2015; O'Neill 2015), as well as continuing work in ethnographic and anthropological fieldwork (Turnbull 1961; Ingold 2010; Ingold and Lee 2008) and studies of urban spaces (Whyte 1943; Whyte 1988).

Here we conceive walking as a mode of experiencing and sensing the city and urban and rural spaces by: attention to the field of mobilities research (cf. Urry 2007) for its relevance to the Walking Interview as a Biographical Method (WIBM); examining walking as an embodied, sensory, and phenomenological practice in social research; and demonstrating walking as a relational, imaginative, and aesthetic practice for thinking, observing, and doing biographical research. We also outline our theoretical use of Walter Benjamin's work, as well as referring to the influence of C. Wright Mills in further developing the WIBM.

Walking, the city, and urban space: Mobilities

The 'turn to walking' in the social sciences can be associated with a wider discussion of 'mobilities' – an attention to forms of movement within contemporary societies. Bauman (and other theorists of modernity/postmodernity) discuss the way that social relations, once based upon presence with others, are more frequently 'at a distance' with multiple forms of 'imagined presence' 'and various discourses of movement': he asks us to consider how 'togetherness' is experienced through increasing mobility/mobilities in late modernity (Bauman 2001). Urry argues that the use of a 'mobilities paradigm' or 'mobilities turn' can draw attention to social relationships that are marked by 'diverse connections', often 'at a distance' and 'constituted through circulating entities' (Urry 2007: 46). Moreover, he identifies five interdependent 'mobilities' that produce social life, forming and reforming 'its contours' both distant and proximate: corporeal travel; the physical movement of objects; imaginative travel; virtual travel; and communicative travel. For Urry, the mobilities paradigm 'emphasizes the complex assemblage between these different mobilities that may make and contingently maintain social connections across varied and multiple distances' (Urry 2007: 48). He argues:

> All social life, of work, family, education and politics, presumes relationships of intermittent presence and modes of absence depending in part upon the multiple technologies of travel and communications that move objects, people, ideas, images across varying distances.
>
> *(Urry 2007: 47)*

Yet, as various histories of walking indicate (see Chapters 1 and 2), it is also significant for the 'foundation of our being human' and its development (Horvath and Szakolczai 2018: 1; see also Coverley 2012; Gros 2015). Building upon Simmel's ideas on urban life, Urry criticises the social sciences for being 'a-mobile': there has been a neglect of movement and a minimisation of the significance of its forms. Instead, the focus has been on the 'patterns' in which people interact together, at with the loss of the larger-scale understandings. Urry (2007) finds Simmel's notion of 'sociation' useful:

> Simmel distinguishes between various socio-spatial patterns of mobility ... nomadism, wandering, a royal tour of the kingdom, diasporic travel, the Court's travel, migration and adventure and leisure travel. In each case, what is distinct is its social form, the 'form of sociation ... in the case of a wandering group in contrast to a spatially fixed one' [Simmel].
>
> *(Urry 2007: 21)*

Patterns of sociation are represented in Ingold and Vergunst's sociology and anthropology of walking: in the way that social relations can be mapped out along the ground, that walking can be profoundly 'sociable' (Ingold and Vergunst 2008). Horvath and Szakolczai, in describing the experience of walking and the history of pilgrimage, also infer 'sociation', that even in solitary walking, we are never alone, but are immersed in nature, since 'walking is also source of an ongoing conversation between the body and the soul' (Horvath and Szakolczai 2018: 26). Hence, walking is a mode and process of social interaction, even with oneself. In short, the sensory, relational dimension of walking (with nature, the environment, another, or oneself) is a key theme in the literature and histories on walking.

Importantly, alongside forms of 'sociation', Simmel (1969) also explores the intense impact of city life on the senses and 'mental life' (see Chapter 2). In explaining the complexity of 'mental life' in the 'metropolis', Simmel focuses upon 'analysis of moments of co-presence' (cf. Goffman), developing a 'sociology of the senses' (Urry 2007: 24; Simmel 1969). In order to cope with the vast sensory stimuli, people may adopt a blasé attitude in order to protect themselves from being overwhelmed. Wider relationships between money, individuation, and the social, economic, and cultural life are important elements of his analysis of metropolitan life. He argues that 'the blasé attitude results first from the rapidly changing and closely contrasting stimulations of the nerves', and also by a 'blunting of discrimination' largely as a result of 'the money economy' leading to 'indiscriminate suggestability' (Simmel 1969: 51, 53).

Simmel's work is important in facilitating analyses of social mobility and mobilities (Urry 2007) and the spatial patterns of social life in the 'metropolis'. Frisby writes that for Simmel 'the sensory foundations of mental life are dominated by responses to a dynamic discontinuity of multiple fleeting perspectives', such as the speed, intensification, acceleration, shock, and impact upon the senses (Frisby 2012: 8). The impact of this includes a 'blunting of discrimination', yet at one and the same time, the metropolis also affords a kind of freedom through transcending boundaries, norms, and (for Simmel) the pettiness and prejudices of village life.

A blasé attitude is one response to metropolitan complexity; another is resistance to the sensory stimuli of urban life, as argued by de Certeau (1988), who engaged with spatial practices, specifically walking in the city, to make sense of and understand urban life. He focused especially on the way that people resist rational, disciplinary power by the paths and shortcuts they take and appropriate, creatively resisting organisational power structures (see Chapter 2). The 'act of walking is to the urban system what the speech act is to language or the statements uttered': it has an 'enunciative function' by:

> appropriation of the topographical system on the part of the pedestrian (just as the speaker appropriates and takes on language). It is a spatial acting out of the place (just as the speech act is an acoustic acting-out of language) and it implies relations among differentiated positions.
>
> *(de Certeau 1988: 97–8)*

The WIBM takes up the idea of mobilities research that social life is in movement, working with forms and practices of sociation, and that walking together opens a space for dialogue, for life stories to be told, shared, and heard. But its perspective is qualitatively different to the use of walking in 'mobilities studies' which largely focus upon its development in urban studies and is related to the use of urban space; with walking as a defined means of transport, a 'good' as well as an everyday practice, that might be disruptive of the flow of urban space (Hall and Smith 2013).

For example, Ferguson's (2016) application of the walking interview, or 'go along with' method to explore social work practice, is a useful example of the study of 'work on the move' from within the 'mobilities paradigm'. Ferguson 'shadowed' social workers over nine years, interviewing and observing them on home visits and in the car. He describes this study as constituting a 'mobile and sensory ethnography of child protection work' and argues that it is 'movement' that 'gets to the heart of what these practices are' – whether in the multiple car journeys, or 'worker's capacities to move their bodies when in the home by walking, playing with and staying close to the child' (Ferguson 2016: 193). Ferguson unpacks the 'mobile character of welfare services and what practitioners actually do and how practice is shaped by time spent on foot, in cars, travelling and moving when with service users' (Ferguson 2016: 194). He defines social work as 'a mobile practice' by outlining the sensory scale, form, and nature of this mobility. For example, the car is analysed as a space for office work to be conducted, for face-to-face practice, and as a space to process emotions, as well as a 'third space' for working directly with clients, through the 'shared experience' of a 'neutral area' (Ferguson 2016: 201).

This idea of mobile, sensory ethnography which Ferguson documents and analyses is very important in understanding connections between place, space, and human lived relations. In applying the mobilities paradigm to the practice of social work, as work 'on the move', this example demonstrates how the mobilities paradigm can inform how we can conceive 'mobile' research methods within the wider agency/structurings of current society.

However, for our purposes, walking is 'fundamental' and 'foundational' (Horvath and Szakolczai 2018: 16) to being human, to understanding 'sociality' – how we relate to others (Ingold and Vergunst 2008), the temporal and spatial dimensions to our lives (de Certeau 1988); and the sensory ways that space and place recursively impact upon our life 'stories'. The importance of walking for conducting biographical research 'situates' the individual in space, place, time – and in movement (see Chapter 4 on migration). While the mobilities paradigm helps to provide biographical research with a focus on 'movement', we also need to consider embodied, phenomenological lived lives, extending Simmel's ideas on the sociology of the senses through an engagement with sensory ethnography; using walking as a relational, imaginative, and an aesthetic practice for thinking, observing, doing, and experiencing biographical research. For example, Ferguson could have extended his research by conducting walking biographical interviews with social workers, developing the possible uses and contribution of WIBM to contemporary 'mobilities' (cf. in the work of Urry, Ferguson, and others) making use of the methodological opportunities offered by new technologies and arts to conduct research on/with individual biographies – conceived as 'moving lives'.

Walking as an embodied, sensory, and phenomenological practice in social research

In sociology, urban studies, and cultural geography, the 'turn to walking' has, on the whole, focused upon the way that space and place is formed and shaped, and the way communities and networks are constructed. Clark and Emmel (2010) have discussed the merits of undertaking walking interviews, instead of static room-based interviews, in their project on 'connected lives'. Here they seek to understand how 'individuals conceptualise their neighbourhoods', 'locate their social networks' and 'express their sense of community in relation to (local) places' (Clark and Emmel 2010: 1). They argue that walking interviews enable interviewees to have more control over the research process, and are able to take the researcher to places that are significant for the interviewee, thereby locating experiences in 'their spatial context'. In doing so, this approach facilitates the addition of extra detailed information: it elicits or prompts 'more discussion or encourage further questioning that may not occur in room-based settings'. Such practice also allows for the 'serendipitous and the unanticipated'. For instance, during one interview they 'came across' 'racist graffiti that prompted discussion about cohesion and tolerance that may not necessarily have been considered in a room-based interview' (Clark and Emmel 2010: 2).

The benefits of walking as a mobile method, as Clark and Emmel describe, is in understanding individuals' relationship to place. Walking interviews enable opportunities for 'interaction and enunciation to emerge' (de Certeau 1988: 97). As Moles demonstrated in her qualitative research in a park in Dublin, 'mobile methods' afforded her the ability to:

> watch the different cultural and social acts occurring within its boundaries, to uncover the interactions and webs that constructed the landscape of the park, and to engage with the natural and the social in different ways allowing the relationship between place and identity to emerge.
>
> *(Moles 2008: np)*

The sensory aspects of walking in the city are discussed in a deeply ethnographic way by Matos Wunderlich (2008) in relation to place. He also argues for the importance of understanding the implications of walking for urban design. Influenced by the work of Jane Rendall, he states that 'walking is a way of at once discovering and transforming the city' (Matos Wunderlich 2008: 128). Through the temporal, multi-sensory, and rhythmical nature of walking, we are able to use our sense bodies to encounter 'the features of the environment'. Moreover, this contributes to the process of generating and retaining a sense of place and belonging through the 'haptic sense' and the 'kinaesthetic' body in motion (Matos Wunderlich 2008: 125, 128). Matos Wunderlich also highlights the relationship between sensing and the emotions, the way that our attachments, the meanings associated with objects, symbolism, and imagery, are associated with and help us attach to place. She observes that when walking through places, we grow our attachment to them and we 'learn and perform socially' (Matos Wunderlich 2008: 130) (see Chapter 10 for an illustration of this process in the authors' autobiographical walks). In short, Matos Wunderlich argues that walking is a way of engaging with the world as an embodied practice, a 'mode of perceiving and living (embodying) urban places', a way of 'discovering, creating and or transforming the city' – indeed, as a critical, aesthetic, and spatial practice (Matos Wunderlich 2008; see also Ingold 2010).

This phenomenological and rhythmic quality of walking is also emphasised by Edensor (inspired by Lefebvre and de Certeau) who explores the way it intersects with temporality and space. He suggests a mobile sense of place is achieved through walking across space, and a 'mobile homeliness' can be produced as an outcome of the multiple rhythms of movement (Edensor 2010: 71; Edensor 2008). He comments upon the arts practice of Richard Long in 'Textworks', Francis Alys's 'Railings', and Jeremy Deller's 'Procession', in reflecting upon temporality and the rhythms of walking (Edensor 2010: 75). The ideas of 'pulsing space' and 'rhythmic landscape' indicate that the landscape is not an inert, fixed, bounded scene: the act of 'walking folds body, self, other humans and non-humans, time-space and place together' (Edensor 2010: 78). Both Edensor (2010) and Matos Wunderlich (2008), in exploring the 'rhythmic' nature of walking, highlight the sense of the phenomenological relationship of the body to surrounding space, formation of ideas, attachment of place and time – an emphasis that informs the WIBM approach (see Chapter 8). Massey (2005) argues against 'space' and 'place' being represented as simply the abstract (space) or the everyday/real/local (place), and instead wants the multiple trajectories of space to be recognised; space, for Massey, is plural, multiple, and unfinished. The phenomenological aspects of space and place are discussed by Tuan (1977), for whom place is a space that has been given meaning by, in, and through human experience. We can say that 'space and place are dialectically structured in human environmental experience, since our understanding of space is related to the places we inhabit, which in turn derive meaning from their spatial context' (Seamon and Sowers 2008: 44).

In summary, the attention to 'movement', as in contributions to the mobilities 'paradigm' and by other writers (above), rightly points to the fact that social science research needs to take account of 'movement' in its various forms within society. The WIBM, supported by new technologies for recording and communicating, ethnographically places individuals within the enfolding and unfolding of the relations between body, space, place, the senses, and social relations. This approach can be further explored and articulated through the analysis of walking in sensory ethnographies.

The WIBM approach (for the authors) has emerged through thinking about, observing, and doing walking-based research – and engagement with ethnographic theory and practice. Ethnography, it should be observed, is a contested idea and practice. O'Reilly provides a useful general definition:

iterative-inductive research (that evolves in design through the study), drawing on a family of methods, involving direct and sustained contact with human agents, within the context of their daily lives (and cultures), watching what happens, listening to what is said, asking questions, and producing a richly written account that respects the irreducibility of human experience, that acknowledges the role of theory as well as the researcher's own role and that views humans as part object/part subject.

(O'Reilly 2005: 3)

A key area of ethnographic practice for the development of WIBM has, again, been the attention to the sensory dimensions of social life. A powerful example of sensory ethnography that engages with walking is offered in Irving's (2010) walks with people close to death. His research is a good example of the 'push' to the senses and (following de Certeau), he states that walking is 'a practical way of worldmaking' mediated by 'different social and historical contexts' and 'bodily and environmental variables', as well as 'complex interior dialogues and imaginative lifeworlds' (Irving 2010: 24). In a photo essay, 'Dangerous substances and visual evidence: tears, blood, alcohol and pills', Irving (2010) walked with Alberto Velasco in New York in the summer of 2008, along a route the latter had walked twenty-one years earlier from his apartment to the health centre where he collected the results diagnosing HIV/AIDS, and back again to his apartment. The intention in this 'walking fieldwork' was to:

> combine image, voice and walking to uncover how a city's streets, buildings and neighbourhoods are mediated by ongoing, often highly idiosyncratic interior dialogues and emotional lifeworlds that derive from a person's current existential concerns.
>
> *(Irving 2010: 25)*

Irving argues that people's actions and behaviours are mediated by their interior dialogues, yet how can we as researchers access, observe, and experience these 'inner dialogues' without relying on what Geertz terms 'best guesses'? In Irving's research, walking is 'a performative technique' where he accompanies co-walkers 'as they narrate emergent thoughts and experiences in real time' (Irving 2010: 26).

He does not claim this method gives privileged access to the co-walker's interior lifeworlds, but rather that it enables other ways of observing, knowing, and appreciating the lived experience of another. He explains (with reference to Polanyi) that it is possible 'to dwell in another person's expressive actions, including their worlds and bodily expressions, but not dwell in the specificity of their experience' (Irving 2010: 34).

This example of a walking interview from Irving is useful to demonstrate how to get as close as possible ethnographically to the lived experience of another, to gain phenomenological 'understanding' of the lived life or aspects of a life or group through observation and sensory, performative, and mobile methods. Similarly beneficial for WIBM are Pink's (2007, 2009) studies, applying sensory ethnographic practice and digital techniques as a way of getting the feel of a place, observing and thinking through in sensory ways what it might feel like to be, walk, and live there. This approach, for Pink, brings the everyday world and the digital world together, through three important aspects: senses of place, movement, and sensoriality. Pink reflects on the centrality of movement to a 'phenomenological research method that attends to sensorial elements of human experience and place-making' (Pink 2007: 240). She describes 'walking with video' in a garden with participants David and Anne 'as they experience, tell and show their material, immaterial and social environments in personally, socially and culturally specific ways'. Walking with another enables us to 'learn empathetically', and if we use video as part of a walking/movement method, this can 'serve as a catalyst for creating ethnographic understandings of other people's experiences, and representing these experiences to a wider audience' (Pink 2007: 240).

Filming her walk with David and Anne produces a research record, for Pink, of the sensory engagement with the garden, as well as the co-walkers, and is a place-making practice. When she views the film again, she feels that she is back in that place. Pink stresses the importance of memory to the sensory experience, for example, who planted the plants and what that meant. Pink argues (following Lee and Ingold) that knowledge comes with movement, using all the senses. The work of Pink and Irving illustrates that as we walk, we observe, think through, experience, and learn/know in embodied, multi-sensory ways. Importantly, for researchers using walking as a biographical research method, concepts of place, space, and memory offer a framework for conceiving the ethnographic and biographical process and the situatedness of the ethnographer or researcher, in observing and coming to 'know' another's lived life.

Research within the field of 'mobilities' and work by visual ethnographers and anthropologists have a great deal of relevance to biographical sociology and to WIBM in particular. The methods used, and analysis of space or place and importance of sensoriality and memory, help us to see how individuals and groups give meaning to or 'shape' their surroundings and how networks are formed. The 'showing' and 'telling' of experience of the sensory, as in Pink's ethnographic tour of the garden, could be supplemented by other methods (and in other contexts) to record other sensory experiences of the participants, and not only to be mediated by the narrator or researcher. Critical here is how might the range of senses (smell, touch/feel from surroundings, sound – where the latter is not recorded) be delivered; how is a sensory ethnography, not merely a visual one, to be obtained?

Walking is a diverse practice and a lived experience, a means to an end and a means in itself. Walking as a method of doing or being in research, is not only embodied and relational, but can be *revelatory* (O'Neill and Hubbard 2010). As biographical researchers, we want to develop further the possibilities of the walking interview, by engaging with the benefits of 'storytelling' and 'art making' and specifically, the transformative possibilities of combining arts and walking in the WIBM.

Walking as a relational, imaginative, biographical method, and an aesthetic practice

The growth of interest in biographical methods can be attributed to a variety of factors: disillusionment with static approaches to data collection; a growing interest in the life course; and an increased concern with 'lived experience' and how to express it (see Roberts 2002). The 'turn' to the visual, and wider sensory and performative methods have had an important effect on biographical research – itself a long tradition of collecting and doing life story research, linked to Chicago School sociologists, oral historians, and reformers, in particular, the recording of working class lives (see Chapter 2). In developing our specifically biographical approach connected to walking, we argue that using walking methods, inspired by artists, ethnographers, and others enables or facilitates not only the sensory, phenomenological, and performative, but also the relational and imaginative – the 'emergence' in understanding of how individuals form a 'sense' of who they are and how they participate in their 'ongoing' social networks and socio-environments.

Since the 1960s–70s, artists have explored the common act of walking as a form of imaginative, artistic, or aesthetic practice in numerous contexts; often it has taken existing walking events – visiting a gallery, going on a guided city tour, a group ramble, and so on – and redefined into an 'artistic 'performance'. Walking, in fact, has become a major part of performance art – an artist/performer(s) walking (using sound, choreographed movement, etc.) through a museum, a conference, a street, countryside with elements of dance, theatre, photography (and maps, diagrams), or encounters with the audience/participants (cf. Tino Sehgal, Hamish Fulton) (Heddon et al. 2009; Myers 2006, 2010). Although performance art came into prominence in the late 1960s and 1970s, its formative ideas lie earlier, in other artistic practices by Rauschenberg and others in the 1950s and early 1960s (and even further back to early 20th century art movements, which contested traditional art, the studio, and the gallery, by ideas on 'living' and 'action': see Goldberg 2001).

Here we draw attention to the importance of walking, performance, and place in telling or constructing of our life 'stories', as well as the relational dimension of biographical work. The latter aspect of walking, both as a convivial practice, side-by-side, sharing a walk, as well as the relationship to the landscape, is a key theme of walking artist Blake Morris's work. He says '(D)espite the variety of ways artists approach walking, artistic walking works consistently explore the relationship of walking bodies to the landscape' (Morris 2017a: 1). Morris charts the development of walking art and the rise in cross-disciplinary scholarship since c. 2000, arguing that walking art is a set of 'networked, social and relational practices' (Morris 2017b: 2).

In our own biographical work, we use technology, such as digital recorders and cameras. One major technology relevant for an aesthetic practice, used extensively in walking interviews, is the camera. This use can be seen to have its artistic roots within 'street photography. Street photography is a major form of 'observation' of walkers, which developed during the 1960s–70s (especially in New York) in the work of Meyerowitz, Shore, Davidson, and others (including Ray-Jones, Steele-Perkins, Sykes, Parr, in the UK). In fact, it has a longer history in the more social documentary work of Atget, Brassai, Cartier-Bresson, Doisneau, and the later (quite different) 1950s work of Frank (2008) and Klein (2010) in the US, while Brandt, Hardy, Mayne, and others in the UK explored cultural changes, especially in working class areas (see Seaborne and Sparham 2011: 57–87). Street photography seeks to capture moments of ordinary life of people in the busy cityscape – often individuals inhabiting their own world and thoughts while (usually 'caught') in the presence of others (cf. Goffman's 'civil inattention') – recording the banal or the odd circumstance, the individual diversity, the vitality of life; even, it seems, the 'sounds' within the hard cityscape.

The street photography of Helen Levitt, artist, photographer, and film-maker is captured in a documentary short 'In the Street' that documents life in Spanish Harlem in the 1930s and 40s. Here, image making, in photography and film is 'storytelling', picturing the detail and nuances of working class lives; it is cited as influencing the development of independent films in the 1960s and 1970s (Arden 2002).

Street photography of the 'everyday' has had a resurgence in recent years in various forms, including interest in the history of the field, aided by access to and distribution by the Internet (cf. Pardo and Parr eds. 2016; Stanton 2015) and its use in fashion (cf. Bill Cunningham, in New York). A social documentary 'style' has also been maintained, as in Britain, especially after the effects of economic decline on traditional industrial communities from the early 1980s (see Konttinen 1988; Killip 2016).

The interrelations between ethnographic, biographical work and art provide potential for new, challenging practices, relations, and understandings. The 'inter-textuality' of biography/narrative/ethnography and art/photography is defined by O'Neill (2008) as 'ethno-mimesis' the combination of ethnography and art practice, where the researcher works in partnership with artists to design, conduct, analyse, and share biographical research findings using arts-based methods, such collaborations often applying participatory methods that are productive, performative, and relational.

The relational aspect of walking is important to O'Neill in her collaborations with artists, performance artists, writers, poets, photographers, and participants. Combining ethnography with arts, working in the 'hyphen', the space in between, ethno-mimesis, offers a critical theory in practice – a important theme within WIBM. For example, in relation to biographical research 'a crucial element of narrative research is the assumption that narratives are relational and reflective, being told between individuals (and groups) and involving how experiences and events are conceived—and also informative of subsequent action' (Roberts 2006:149). The interrelation between ethnography and art, as 'ethno-mimesis', provides a relational, methodological practice and a process in O'Neill's work with marginalised groups or communities (asylum seekers, sex workers, skid row residents, recipients of social work practice). This involves working together, through participatory, ethnographic biographical research, in conjunction with visual, poetic, and other artistic methods for stories to be told and heard.

The relationship of art to society is one of mediation: art is a 'feeling form' created in the relationship and tension between sensuous knowing, the playfulness and creativity of the artist and the historically given techniques and means of production (O'Neill 2008). Art is a social product, not just a reflection on its social origins, and it manifests its own specificity – it is constitutive. It can make visible experiences, hopes, ideas; it is a reflective space, and socially it brings something new into the world – it contributes to knowledge and understanding. For instance, as Nicholsen (1997) argues, photography has the power to 'pierce' us (cf. Barthes's 'punctum') and bring us in touch with intractable reality in ways that we cannot forget; it enables us to develop a broader, more compassionate, and accurate consciousness.

In arts-based research conducted with women asylum seekers and in collaboration with filmmaker Janice Haaken, it is argued that through the visual representation of the walks undertaken with women in Teesside (UK), in their photographs and a short film produced together, they were able to get in touch with the women's lives in sensory and corporeal ways (Haaken and O'Neill 2014; O'Neill 2018). This fostered understanding and critical reflection and countered exclusionary processes and practices; as well as generating greater understanding of women's resources in building and performing cultural citizenship across racialised boundaries. O'Neill argues that by using walking biographical interviews and artmaking, they were able to address issues of social justice by facilitating a 'radical democratic imaginary' (see Chapter 6).

Theorising the WIBM: Walter Benjamin – Walker, collector, storyteller

Benjamin's work is very helpful in order to theorise and explore the process of storytelling and art-making as relational, imaginative, and as a critical, aesthetic practice (see Chapter 2). Benjamin is particularly useful for understanding the processes of 'knowing' and 'observing' as we traverse the urban environment; in fact, he has been described as one of the 'great scholars of cities and the art of walking them' (Solnit 2001: 196). Walking in the city was the central focus of Benjamin's unfinished *The Paris Arcades* and its key themes of thresholds, fragments, and the 'flâneur'. He describes the flâneur as someone who goes 'botanizing on the asphalt'. He says 'strolling could hardly have assumed the importance it did without the arcades' (Benjamin 1992a: 36) that he describes as passageways, as thresholds, lined with elegant shops; a cross between a street and an 'interieur', arcades are conceived as akin to dwelling. The flâneur 'is as much at home amongst the facades of houses as a citizen in his four walls' (Benjamin 1992a: 37). Slow, meandering walks are offered by Benjamin as a protest against urban 'industriousness', and 'unwilling to forego the life of a gentleman of leisure', the flâneur(s) liked to 'have turtles set the pace for them. If they had their way progress would have been obliged to accommodate itself to this pace' (Benjamin 1992a: 54). The walking flâneur is then a somewhat different response to the acceleration and vast sensory stimuli of metropolitan life and the workings of the 'money economy' as depicted by Simmel. However, we know that Benjamin (although his work was situated within a materialist philosophy of history) was influenced by Simmel's work on the metropolis and modern life (Martinez 1984–85; Dodd and Wajcman 2016).

Benjamin has been described, on the one hand, as being 'forever on the move, a wanderer, a walker; yet on the other, a collector' (Coverley 2012: 159). He is also a storyteller and influential to artists, and informs our theoretical and conceptual framing of the WIBM, due to a number of reasons: first, he argues that storytelling plays a primary role in the household of humanity, in contrast to the role of information:

> The value of information does not survive the moment in which it was new. It lives only at that moment; it has to surrender to it completely and explain itself to it without losing any time. A story is different. It does not expend itself. It preserves and concentrates its strength and is capable of releasing it even after a long time.
>
> *(Benjamin 1992b: 89–90)*

Second, for Benjamin, a fragment of a story of a life can tell us so much more than hundred pages of information about a life. Narrative storytelling is a sensory/sensuous experience, it is the opposite of information, it can be transformative, 'auratic', 'co-ordinating soul, hand and eye' (Benjamin, 1992b: 107). Third, at the same time, he argues that the 'imaginary' is central to utopian political thinking, and in order to counter the petrification of the imagination, he stresses the need to revolutionise our image worlds (Benjamin 1992b: 89–90). There is in Benjamin's work, a call for the political and emancipatory role of the image (dialectical images) alongside the role of 'storytelling', in how we might not only understand, but also shape our social worlds (see Weigel 1996; Calderbank 2003).

Benjamin is important in the development of our WIBM, because in giving attention to 'storytelling', biographical research has a primary role in sociological understanding; it helps us to relate 'private troubles' to 'public issues' (Mills 1970) to better understand our life worlds, our social worlds (cf. Chicago Sociology); it is a sensory, sensuous experience and calls for the art of listening (see Fromm 1998; Back 2007), as well as the art of seeing (Berger 1972), and feeling, indeed, a politics of feeling (O'Neill 2008).

In biographical research, 'storytelling' creates possibilities for biographical remembering and dialogue, and enables us to see and experience the life of another. Walking with someone else to undertake a biographical interview, opens a physical, material, performative, as well as a mental, and hopefully a 'supportive opportunity' to share a life story, or aspects of one's biography. Walking through time and in space, attuned to the surroundings, environment, our co-walker(s) and 'image worlds' can offer an important means and context to share and understand a life story (and small stories), as well as the relationship between the micrology of life, and broader social structures and processes. As Benjamin discovered, walking is about seeing and experiencing the minutiae of life, as in the city, while enabling a broader understanding of society and within it, our social, temporal, spatial, and relational lives.

In summary, the WIBM has been influenced by visual ethnography, art-making, walking artists, and the critical theory of Walter Benjamin, but is also very much rooted in the influence of Mills' (1970) *The Sociological Imagination* (on linking the individual life to history, culture and structure), the developments in biographical research from the early 20th century, and particularly the work of W.I. Thomas and Znaniecki's *The Polish Peasant in Europe and America* (Thomas and Znaniecki 1958, 1996).

The history of biographical research during the late 1980s and 1990s, witnessed a 'biographical' or 'narrative turn' in sociology and the wider social sciences associated with the re-emergence of 'micro social theories' from the late 1960s onwards, and other developments (Roberts 2002; Roberts 2006: 134–153). This growth of biographical research can be seen in the formation of research centres, national associations and networks, and journals in the field (e.g., research groups within the International, European, and British sociological associations). In their overview of the history of biographical sociology, Nurse and O'Neill (2018) highlight the work of Thompson (1978; 1996), Stanley (1992, 2014), Bertaux (1981), Bertaux and Kohli (1984), Miller (2000, 2005), Roberts (2002), Plummer (1995, 2002), Fischer-Rosenthal (2005), and Schütze (1992, 2005) as amongst the foundational figures for contemporary biographical sociology, alongside influential research and guides by Chamberlayne et al. (2000), Bornat (2008), and Wengraf (2001) that spread interest in the field. Biographical research not only provides insights into how individuals understand themselves and interpret their surroundings, but also the workings of contemporary society through analysis of the relationship between the individual, history, sociation, temporal, and social structures (Mills 1970).

This first wave of contemporary biographical researchers (above) have been followed by a second, writing in the context of the rising number of 'turns' to culture, the performative, the digital and sensory research (for example, Sparkes 2015; Andrews et al. 2013; Miller 2015; Jones 2006). Both 'waves' addressed sexual and social inequalities and social issues, but the second group also work alongside artists and film-makers with an emphasis on developing new research agendas using innovative and creative methods (see O'Neill et al. 2015: chapters by Given, Haaken, Miller, Roberts, and Sparkes). For WIBM, the importance here is that including walking as part of the 'craft' of a biographical researcher extends the ways in which we are able to get in touch with 'realities' in sensory and corporeal ways that foster 'understanding' and critical reflection, as well as ways of knowing, experiencing, understanding, and imagining.

In conducting and interpreting a biographical interview, numerous approaches have been taken. For instance, one very influential procedure, the biographical narrative interview method (BNIM) has been to record the 'story' that is told, applying a non-directive active listening approach. The researcher invites the interviewee to tell the story of her life, or an aspect of her biography, for example, her working life, in her own time and in her own words without interruption (see Wengraf 2001; Fischer-Rosenthal 2005; Schütze 1992, 2005). When the narration is ended by the teller, the researcher then usually asks questions relating to the themes emerging in the narration, and then in a third and final stage, the researcher might ask more focused questions relating to the research, its patterns, structures, and themes. Analysis within biographical research is usually based on forms of grounded theory, but not always (see Schütze 2005; Frank 2010; Sparkes 2004; Riessman 2008). In fact, interpretation in biographical research can take various formats: thematic, social constructivist, narrative, ethnographical. Some biographical researchers utilise Gubrium and Holstein's approach to analysing life stories, to consider who is producing them, in what contexts, and under what circumstances they are constructed (Holstein and Gubrium 2012; Gubrium and Holstein 1998). Frank's (2010) work has also been influential – a 'dialogical narrative analysis' – and he argues that stories have several capacities and asks readers to think about how stories 'work'. In Frank's work (see also Sparkes 2004), there is a focus upon: the content of the narrative, what is said; the structural aspects, including the how of the telling; and who is telling the story and to whom it is directed, the when, why, and for what purpose? Thus, various kinds of analysis can take place in biographical research including, broadly, thematic analysis (focusing on the content of what is said and identifying common areas), structural features of the account, and cultural analysis (focusing on the how/who of telling) (see e.g., Miller 2000; Riessman 2008). In our view, the notion that the 'stories' we tell give meaning to experience must remain central to the WIBM. While there are numerous approaches to biographical interview methodology, for us a central element in biographical research is the positioning of the self in time within space and place:

The narrated and narratable self is temporally and socially located. The stories each of us tells about ourselves typically invoke a past (distant or recent), implicitly or explicitly linked to a present and perhaps to a possible future. The act of telling a story takes place within the flow of time and is situated within a sequence of social interactions between narrator and audience. Both the narration and the events recounted position the teller in a social landscape. (Jackson 2010:123)

As Miller describes: '(B)arriers of self/society and present/past/future become transparent in the biographical perspective' (Miller 2000: 158). The WIBM extends current biographical research and can draw from a plethora of recording devices (gathering information across the senses and environment), 'materials', methodologies and strategies (e.g., participatory, autobiographical, reflexive), conceptual/theoretical frameworks, purposes, and means of dissemination. Given the scope of this expansion, at the intersection of arts and biographical research, and the histories and methods that biographical research builds upon, there is now some need for a reflection on its 'progress', a review of conceptual means and frameworks, or at least a review of the expanding use of the 'mix' of eclectic techniques, and its spread across various disciplines and practices. Some critical assessment is required, keeping in mind that it is not meant to simply replace other methods as such (i.e., the traditional formal or structured interview), but to provide something innovative to capture the specificities of 'everyday life', to enhance biographical research methods by the creative inclusion and application of the WIBM.

The WIBM does have some closeness to the informal ethnographic interview – undertaken in the 'flow' of field research – as temporal, relational, and performative. But WIBM is firmly set in the present, in the 'ongoing reality' of the 'everyday scene' in orientation, i.e., how our 'stories' are formed and are ongoing within our understandings or interpretations of movement (bodily, sensual, e.g., visual, sound) through space, place, and our emergent social relations. It seeks to be in the 'active present', rather than recording an interview outside the individual's daily routine and transcribing it, and it challenges the primacy of the set interview and its 'ex post facto' transcribed 'voice in text'. By highlighting the 'relational', 'participatory', and 'performative' in research, a focus is placed upon 'communication' – how we relate to others, something we must continuously review to keep our connections with others – a theme that has been central in participant observation, feminist methodologies, and other qualitative research discussions.

The final section gives an example of a WIBM that connects and illustrates the focus of this chapter on theorising, observing, and thinking in the practice of WIBM, as well as the creative possibilities of using 'mapping' to elicit a life story.

WIBM: Walking with Donie: Theorising/observing/thinking

The following example uses the device of asking the participant to 'pre-construct' a map of a favourite or memorable walk. In the map and excerpt below, Donie Fell shares his memory of a walk to his primary school, as part of his participation in a reading group on Ethnography and Walking Methods.[1] The group were asked to draw a route of a memorable walk marking the personally significant 'landmarks' along the way.

Donie explained the map:

> I drew an L shaped map from my home to my primary school and marked the landmarks along the route. The first landmark was my friends' home, a small farm created by the Land Commission in the Thirties when the Government divided up the big estates following the Irish Rebellion.

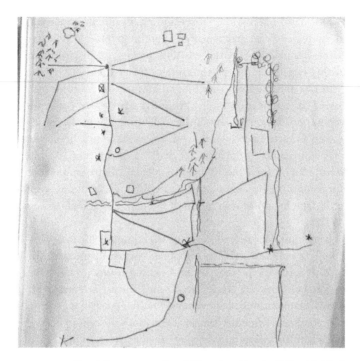

FIGURE 3.1 Donie's route to school. Drawing: Donie Fell with kind permission.

All the small farms in our locality were Land Commission farms, the bigger farms had belonged to wealthier Catholics or Protestants and predated the Land Commission farms.

The next landmark was at a crossroads where people met before moving on. If you were late and those you were meeting had moved on, they usually left a stone on a part of the wall to signify they had been and gone or two stones to say they had returned home, either way you knew where they had gone.

The following landmark was the home of a family that came to this part of the world from Wales to work as blacksmiths for the estate of the Cromwellian Jones family. They have lived in the same spot since 1655 to this day.

After that, it was down Smartscastle Hill and over the first of three streams on the route. The hill went into a hollow and rose again to a second crossroads called Penkert's Cross where we turned left for school. Down a second hill which had limestone quarries on both sides and was called the Lorry Track Hill, because a small narrow gauge track crossed from one quarry to the other and down to the river about a quarter of a mile away. We walked by Nail's lane where a mill race ran and up the final hill to the school. This hill was called Lizzie Malone's Hill after a widow who lived there.

Here, Donie is talking about the route, the meanings and memories of the landscape as though we are both present and in the present, even though he is working from memory of a time when he was a boy walking the route to school with his friends, in the past. The 'people' in Donie's narration are his friends at this time, as well as at other times, when he is older – noting the past, present, and future meaning and sense of the 'crossroads'.

> The school was called Strangsmills and was a mixed three teacher school with segregated playground. The boys played sports, the girls played chase. Schooldays were for the most part happy days, occasional blips but generally happy. The area in question was about two square miles and was filled with limestone quarries, lime kilns, mills, rivers and streams, woods and rich farmland. We swam and fished in the rivers and streams, we picked wild fruit and we gathered mushrooms in their seasons. We robbed orchards and fruit gardens.

Sharing the sense of place and space, the topographical and geographic memories and their meanings, Donie's [says his] childhood was 'for the most part happy': the connection with the landscape, the environment, the rivers, streams, kilns, and farmland are important to him. The sense of history to place is also a key theme:

> King William was reputed to have passed along the road as he made his way to Waterford city. The Dublin coach used the route and the field where they liveried the coach horses was called the Dublin Field. All the fields, like everything else, had names that made it easy to identify where to go on the roads and on the farms. In our immediate area we had the pond field, the quarry field, the woodfield, the well field, the paddock, the orchard and so on.

Donie continues giving an account of the history of roads and pathways and their connection with history and generational traditions. The 'sensorial' way Donie describes the landscape stands out; a field is not just a field, it is the pond field, the quarry field, the well field. Donie goes on to connect his knowledge of ethnographic theory with an analysis of his map and experience of the route, that reinforces the sense of history, place-making, and family, links with the land and the relational/generational aspects of his life.

> Looking at my map brought to mind Sarah Pink's conversation on 'natural lines' ['Walking with Video' 2007] and made me realise that most of our journeys were not on the roads but along the natural lines that followed well-worn tracks across the fields and through the woods. All of these were shortcuts to save time and energy. These diagonal journeys can make

your movements invisible and they followed cow paths and rights of way trodden for centuries by the people who lived in the area. The myth is that all roads started as a cow path that meandered across the fields and people used these well-worn tracks which then became pathways until finally becoming roads. Where the paths crossed developed into meeting places and trading places and people began to construct buildings and businesses along these routes. My own family have lived in the area for about two hundred years, but like other families have also married interlopers giving a local/outsider element to families, extending connections, creating invisible pathways into the next village, next townland, the next parish, the next county, into the UK and into America, Australia, and now into the EU. Pathways make the journey comfortable in the expectation of a safe arrival and of course pathways long trodden signify experience and tradition, the tried and tested handed down to the next generation to mark their own pathways.

In Donie's written account above and map, we see the routine walk to school as a way into learning about his biography, his identity, formed in relation to the land and to place, the relationships with school friends and his family history attached to the history of the land, as well as broader social and political issues – the Irish Rebellion, the Land Commission, segregation, the Church, and migration. We see here Mills's (1970) central thesis regarding the relationship between individual biography, and the links to history and social structures as very resonant in Donie's account.

Reflecting upon a routine walk, as Donie does, enables him and the reader to access rich biographical material, history, and memories that also allows access to the embodied nature of his connection and attunement to place and what this means in relation to the passing of time, social organisation and sociation (through the family, school, and church), history, and culture. Here, theorising, thinking, and observing are operationalised in the process of mapping the route, sharing the biographical memories and meanings and relating this to Pink's work. In his account of the route, we acquire a sense of the physicality and materiality, as well as the meaning of the fields in question – here Donie is observing, thinking, and theorising 'the landscape'. Such sensory experience of the landscape as an abundance of fields also emerges in Carr's (2017) account of his walk along the Irish border. Carr describes a day walking the border as 'eating up fields', and when he later remembers the border, what comes to mind are fields and 'once you've seen a hundred or so, every field starts to take on unique characteristics, minor differences seem major: a clump of hawthorn, a bath tub or 'the lie of the land' offer important differences (Carr 2017: 58).

In Donie's account we also get a sense of Benjamin's notion that a fragment of a story about a life can tell us so much more than one hundred pages of information, that stories are central to the 'household of humanity', and through the power of the imagination stories help us to both understand and shape our social worlds, give meaning to experience and place, and also contribute to the art and importance of listening. More examples of the walking interview as a biographical method will be given in the next two parts, with a focus upon experiencing and imagining in the WIBM. This first part (Chapters 1–3) concludes with an exercise to sensitise readers to doing and theorising a biographical walking interview with reference to theorising–observing–thinking.

Note

1 The reading group was conducted as part of the annual postgraduate Economy and Society Summer School at the Centre for the Study of the Moral Foundations of Economy & Society, University College Cork. The summer school was developed under the auspices of the President of Ireland's Ethics Initiative.

References

Andrews, M., Squire, C., and Tamboukou, M. (eds.) (2013) *Doing Narrative Research*, 2nd edn. London: Sage.

Arden, R. (2002) 'Useless reportage – Notes on Helen Levitt's in the street', *Afterall*, Issue 06, London/Los Angeles. Available at www.royarden.com/media/ardentexts/arden_levit.pdf (Accessed 21 September 2018).

Back, L. (2007) *The Art of Listening*. London: Bloomsbury.

Bauman, Z. (2001) *Community. Seeking Safety in an Insecure World*. Cambridge, UK: Polity Press.

Benjamin, W. (1992a) *Charles Baudelaire. A Lyric Poet in the Era of High Capitalism*. London: Verso.

Benjamin, W. (1992b) The storyteller. In: W. Benjamin (ed.) *Illumination*. (Tr. H. Zohn). London: Fontana Press.

Berger, J. (1972) *Ways of Seeing*. London: Penguin.

Bertaux, D. (ed.) (1981) *Biography and Society: The Life-History Approach in the Social Sciences*. London: Sage.

Bertaux, D. and Kohli, M. (1984) The life story approach: A continental view, *Annual Review of Sociology*, 10(1): 215–237.

Bornat, J. (2008) Biographical methods. In: P. Alasuutari, L. Bickman, and J. Brannen (eds.) *The Sage Handbook of Social Research Methods*. London: Sage.

Calderbank, M. (2003) Surreal dreamscapes: Walter Benjamin and the arcades. Papers of Surrealism, Issue 1. Available at www.surrealismcentre.ac.uk/publications/papers/journal1/acrobat_files/Calderbank.pdf (Accessed 22 September 2018).

Carr, G. (2017) *The Rule of the Land. Walking Ireland's Border*. London: Faber and Faber.

Chamberlayne, P., Bornat, J. and Wengraf, T. (eds.) (2000) *The Turn to Biographical Methods in Social Science*. London: Routledge.

Clark, A. and Emmel, N. (2010) *Using Walking Interviews*. Realities Toolkit 13. Manchester: University of Manchester, Morgan Centre. Available at http://hummedia.manchester.ac.uk/schools/soss/morgancentre/toolkits/13-toolkit-walking-interviews.pdf (Accessed 2 April 2018).

Coverley, M. (2012) *The Art of Wandering: The Writer as Walker*. Harpenden, UK: Oldcastle Books.

de Certeau, M. (1988) *The Practice of Everyday Life* (Tr. S. Rendall). Berkeley, CA: University of California Press.

Dodd, N. and Wajcman, J. (2016) Simmel and Benjamin. In: N. Dodd, and J. Wajcman (eds.) *The Sociology of Speed: Digital, Organizational, and Social Temporalities*. Oxford: Oxford University Press.

Edensor, T. (2008) Walking through ruins. In: T. Ingold, and J. Vergunst (eds.) *Ways of Walking: Ethnography and Practice on Foot*. Aldershot, UK: Ashgate.

Edensor, T. (2010) Walking in rhythms: Place, regulation, style and the flow of experience, *Visual Studies*, 25(1): 46–58.

Ferguson, H. (2016) Professional helping as negotiation in motion: Social work as work on the move, *Applied Mobilities*, 1(2): 193–206.

Fischer-Rosenthal, W. (2005) The problem with identity. In: R. Miller (ed.) *Biographical Research Methods*, Vol. 11. London: Sage.

Frank, A. W. (2010) *Letting Stories Breathe: A Socio-Narratology*. Chicago: University of Chicago Press.

Frank, R. (2008) *The Americans*. Göttingen: Steidl.

Frisby, D. (2012) Simmel's streetscape of modernity. In: G. Giannakopoulou (ed.) *David Frisby – Streetscapes of Modernity, in memoriam David Frisby*. Thessaloniki: Nisides. Available at www.gla.ac.uk/media/media_555528_en.pdf (Accessed 13 August 2018).

Fromm, E. (1998) *The Art of Listening*. London: Continuum.

Glover, N. (2005) Chapter Six 'Aesthetics, creativity, and the potential space' In: *Psychoanalytic aesthetics: The British School*, Free Associations. Available at www.psycho analysis-and-therapy.com/human_nature/glover/index.html (Accessed 29 April 2019).

Goldberg, R. (2001) *Performance Art*. London: Thames & Hudson.

Gros, F. (2015) *The Philosophy of Walking*. London: Verso.

Gubrium, J. F. and Holstein, J. A. (1998) Narrative practice and the coherence of personal stories, *The Sociological Quarterly*, 39(1): 163–187.

Haaken, J. K. and O'Neill, M. (2014) 'Moving images: Psychoanalytically informed visual methods in documenting the lives of women migrants and asylum seekers', *Journal of Health Psychology*, 19(1): 79–89.

Hall, T. & Smith, R.J. (2013) Stop and Go: A Field Study of Pedestrian Practice, Immobility and Urban Outreach Work, *Mobilities*, 8(2): 272–292.

Heddon, D., Lavery, C. and Smith, P. (2009) *Walking, Writing and Performance: Autobiographical Texts*. Bristol: Intellect Books.

Holstein, J. A. and Gubrium, J. F. (eds.) (2012) *Varieties of Narrative Analysis*. London: Sage.

Horvath, A. and Szakolczai, A. (2018) *Walking into the Void: A Historical Sociology and Political Anthropology of Walking*. London: Routledge.

Ingold, T. (2010) Ways of mind-walking: Reading, writing, painting, *Visual Studies*, 25(1): 15–23.

Ingold, T. and Vergunst, J. L. (eds.) (2008) *Ways of Walking: Ethnography and Practice on Foot*. London: Routledge.

Irving, A. (2010) Dangerous substances and visible evidence: Tears, blood, alcohol, pills, *Visual Studies*, 25(1): 24–35.

Jackson, S. (2010) Self, time and narrative: Re-thinking the contribution of G. H. Mead, *Life Writing*, 7(2): 123–136.

Jones, K. (2006) A biographic researcher in pursuit of an aesthetic: The use of arts-based (re)presentations in "performative" dissemination of life stories, *Qualitative Sociology Review*, II(1): 66–85.

Killip, C. (2016) *In Flagrante Two*. Göttingen: Steidl.

Klein, W. (2010) *Life Is Good and Good for You in New York*. New York: Errata Editions.

Konttinen, S.-L. (1988) *Byker*. Newcastle: Bloodaxe Books.

Martinez, A. T. (1984–5) Walter Benjamin a sociologist in the path of Simmel, *Humboldt Journal of Social Relations*, Fall–Winter, 12(1): 114–131.

Massey, D. (2005) *For Space*. London: Routledge.

Matos Wunderlich, F. (2008) Walking and rhythmicity: Sensing urban space, *Journal of Urban Design*, 13(1): 125–139.

Miller, R. (2005) *Biographical Research Methods*, 4 vols. London: Sage.

Miller, R. (2015) Ignore the man behind the curtain: Exploration of virtual reality. In: M. O'Neill, B. Roberts, and A. Sparkes (eds) *Advances in Biographical Research: Creative Applications*. Abingdon, UK: Routledge.

Miller, R. and Day, G. (eds.) (2012) *The Evolution of European Identities: Biographical Approaches*. London: Palgrave Macmillan.

Miller, R. L. (2000) *Researching Life Stories and Family Histories*. London: Sage.

Mills, C. W. (1970) *The Sociological Imagination*. Harmondsworth, UK: Penguin.

Moles, K. (2008) A walk in Thirdspace: Place, methods and walking, *Sociological Research Online*. Available at www.socresonline.org.uk/13/4/2.html (Accessed 22 September 2018).

Morris, B. (2017a) The walking library: Relating the landscape, *Green Letters*, 21(3): 287–299. (Accessed 3 April 2018).

Morris, B. (2017b) *Walking Networks: The Development of an Artistic Medium*. PhD thesis submitted in partial fulfilment of the requirements of the University of East London, for the degree of Doctor of Philosophy, July 2017 (personal communication with the author).

Myers, M. (2006) Along the way: Situation-responsive participation and education, *The International Journal of the Arts in Society*, 1(2): 1–6.

Myers, M. (2010) 'Walk with me, talk with me': The art of conversive wayfinding, *Visual Studies*, 26(1): 50–68.

Nicholsen, S. (1997) *Exact Imagination Late Work*. Cambridge, MA: MIT Press.

Nurse, L. and O'Neill, M. (2018) Biographical research in the UK: Profiles and perspectives. In: H. Lutz et al. (Hrsg.) *Handbuch Biographieforschung*. Wiesbaden: Springer Fachmedien.

O'Neill, M. (2008) Transnational refugees: The transformative role of art? *Forum Qualitative Sozialforschung, Forum: Qualitative Social Research*, 9(2). Available at www.qualitativeresearch.net/index.php/fqs/article/view/403. (Accessed 31 December 2017).

O'Neill, M. (2015) Participatory biographies: Walking, sensing, belonging. In: M. O'Neill, B. Roberts, and A. Sparkes (eds) *Advances in Biographical Research: Creative Applications*. Abingdon, UK: Routledge.

O'Neill, M. (2018) Walking, well-being and community: Racialized mothers building cultural citizenship using participatory arts and participatory action research, *Ethnic and Racial Studies*, 41(1): 73–97.

O'Neill, M. and Hubbard, P. (2010) Walking, sensing, belonging: Ethno-mimesis as performative praxis', *Visual Studies*, 25(1): 46–58.

O'Neill, M. and Perivolaris, J. (2015) A sense of belonging: Walking with Thaer through migration, memories and space, *Crossings: The Journal of Migration and Culture*, 5(2–3): 327–338.

O'Neill, M., Roberts, B. and Sparkes, A. (eds.) (2015) *Advances in Biographical Research: Creative Applications*. Abingdon, UK: Routledge.

O'Reilly, K. (2005) *Ethnographic Methods*. London: Routledge.

Pardo, A. and Parr, M. (eds.) (2016) *Strange and Familiar: Britain as Revealed by International Photographers*. London: Prestel.

Pink, S. (2007) Walking with video, *Visual Studies*, 22(3): 240–252.

Pink, S. (2009) *Doing Sensory Ethnography*. London: Sage.

Plummer, K. (1995) *Telling Sexual Stories: Power, Change and Social Worlds*. London: Routledge.

Plummer, K. (2001) *Document of Life 2: An Invitation to a Critical Humanism*. London: Sage.

Plummer, K. (2002) *Telling Sexual Stories: Power, Change and Social Worlds*. London: Taylor & Francis.

Riessman, C. K. (2008) *Narrative Methods for the Human Sciences*. London: Sage.

Roberts, B. (2002) *Biographical Research*. Buckingham: Open University Press.

Roberts, B. (2006) *Micro Social Theory*. Basingstoke, UK: Palgrave Macmillan.

Roberts, B. (2015) Biographical research: Past, present, future. In: M. O'Neill, B. Roberts, and A. Sparkes (eds.) *Advances in Biographical Methods*. Abingdon, UK: Routledge.

Roy, A. (2016) Learning on the move: Exploring work with vulnerable young men through the lens of movement, *Applied Mobilities*, 1(2): 207–218.

Scheff, T. (2006) Mobilization and silence: Emotional/relational dynamics. Available at www.soc.ucsb.edu/faculty/scheff/main.php?id=44.html (Accessed 25 October 2018).

Schutze, F. (1992) Pressure and Guilt: War experiences of a young German soldier and their biographical implications. Part 1 and 2, *International Sociology*, 7(2/3): 187–208, 347–367.

Schutze, F. (2005) Cognitive figures of autobiographical extempore narration. In: R. L. Miller (ed.) *Biographical Research Methods*, Vol. 2. London: Sage.

Seaborne, M. and Sparham, A. (eds.) (2011) *London street photography, 1860–2010*, (Museum of London Exhibition). Stockport, UK: Dewi Lewis Publishing.

Seamon, D. and Sowers, J. (2008) Place, and placelessness, Edward Relph. In: P. Hubbard, R. Kitchin, and G. Valentine (eds.) *Key Texts in Human Geography*. London: Sage.

Simmel, G. (1969) The Metropolis and mental life. In: R. Sennet (ed.) *Classic Essays on the Culture of Cities*. New Jersey: Prentice Hall.

Simmel, G. (1998). *Simmel on Culture*. In: D. Frisby, and M. Featherstone (eds.) London: Sage.

Smith, R. J. and Hall, T. (2016) Pedestrian circulations: Urban ethnography, the mobilities paradigm and outreach work, *Mobilities*, 11(4): 498–508.

Solnit, R. (2001) *Wanderlust: A History of Walking*. London: Verso.

Sparkes, A. (2015) When bodies need stories: Dialogical narrative analysis in action. In: M. O'Neill, B. Roberts, and A. Sparkes (eds.) *Advances in Biographical Methods*. Abingdon, UK: Routledge.

Sparkes, A. C. (2004) Bodies, narratives, selves and autobiography: The example of Lance Armstrong, *Journal of Sport and Social Issues*, 28(4): 397–428.

Stanley, L. (1992) *The Auto/Biographical: Theory and Practice of Feminist Auto/Biography*. Manchester: Manchester University Press.

Stanley, L. (2014) About the Whites Writing Whiteness project. Available at www.whiteswritingwhiteness.ed.ac.uk. (Accessed 22 September 2018).

Stanton, B. (2015) *Humans of New York: Stories*. New York: St Martins Press.

Thomas, W. I. and Znaniecki, F. (1958) *The Polish Peasant in Europe and America*, 2 vols. New York: Dover Press (First Pub 1918–20).

Thomas, W. I. and Znaniecki, F. (1996). Introduction. In: E. Zaretsky (ed) *The Polish Peasant in Europe and America. A Classic Work of Immigration History*. Urbana-Champaign, Chicago, IL: University of Illinois Press.

Thompson, P. (1978) *The Voice of the Past*. Oxford: OUP.

Thompson, P. (1996) Paul Thompson. Life story interview with Karen Worcman. Available at www.esds.ac.uk/qualidata/online/data/edwardians/biography/PaulTho mpsonLifeStoryInterview1996.doc (Accessed 14 August 2018).

Tuan, Y. (1977) *Space and Place: The Perspective of Experience*. Minneapolis, MI: University of Minnesota.

Turnbull, C. (1961) *The Forest People*. New York: Simon and Schuster.

Urry, J. (2007) *Mobilities*. Cambridge, UK: Polity.

Weigel, S. Z. (1996) *Body- and Image-Space: Re-Reading Walter Benjamin* (Tr. G. Paul, R. McNicholl, and J. Gaines). London: Routledge.

Wengraf, T. (2001) *Qualitative Research Interviewing. Biographical Narrative and Semi-Structured Methods*. London: Sage.

Whyte, W. F. (1943) *Street Corner Society*. Chicago, IL: The University of Chicago Press.

Whyte, W. H. (1988) *City: Rediscovering the Center*. Philadelphia, PA: The University of Pennsylvania Press.

EXERCISE ONE

Walking and theorising: Observing/thinking

Here the intention is to help researchers become more aware of the environment of ethnographic practice through walking, and what and how they observe (shapes, colours, movement) and to think/reflect on our walking as a daily 'experience'.

This exercise is a preparation or training for carrying out the walking interview as a biographical method (WIBM). Researchers are asked to identify a short walk, even a routine one such as to college, work, shops, visits – to reflect on what they observe and how they respond to daily occurrences, what they 'see' and how they 'take in' their surroundings in order to 'heighten' their experience and awareness - of what we 'take for granted'; what we note (familiarities, information, associations, memories); or what is 'new' each time we undertake our ordinary daily 'paths'.

As in other research, participants in WIBM must adhere to ethical, procedural and any other research guidelines of their institutions, professional bodies and local or wider legal constraints. *The conduct of the exercises must be done in accordance with relevant ethical and other professional, institutional procedures.*

The Objective of this Exercise is to 'sensitise' the participant to how we observe and think in undertaking a walk.

1. Select a walk that is very familiar to you – to work, to shops, for exercise, to a friend, to a park. Lasting no more than one hour – it may be a walk of any 'shape' – a 'linear', 'circular', 'zig-zag' path – it may be a 'drift' between two points – start and destination. You may vary the

initial route of the walk when undertaken [e.g. some 'point of interest' may have taken your eye – say why later].

2. Before the walk, note what you consider to be your 'usual' observations: thinking of previous walks on this route, what do you normally, routinely observe and think about? It maybe you take from a
number of such prior walks. You might like to draw out your route.

3. Take a means of recording – a notebook (paper or digital), sketch-
book, and/or a camera (or camera/phone). You may decide beforehand how you will record elements of your walk – but it may be you
decide at the time: but if you are leaving the decision 'open' – be
prepared.

    Alternatively, following your walk you may wish to note your
reflections in your walking diary/notebook.

- What observations did you make? 'What', 'when', 'where', 'how' –
  and 'why' for each of these.
- What were the 'surprises' (on this familiar) walk i.e. what did you
  observe that you had not (fully) noticed before?
- What do you believe was the effect of 'recording' aspects of the
  walks (i.e. how 'free', 'spontaneous' was your recording – how
  much did you seek to 'frame' what was recorded)?
- What do you believe were your 'usual' or 'main' *previous observations* on the walk – how did they differ in the Exercise?
- What were your 'usual' or 'main' *previous thoughts* on the walk –
  how did they differ in the Exercise?
- What have you *learnt* from the Exercise regarding how you usually 'observe' your surroundings?

If you drew a map of the route you took – annotate it by plotting the
observations you made (and comment on the observations in more
detail elsewhere).

4. With a 'willing' colleague – ask them to select a similar walk choice
to the one you have just completed. [It may be the colleague has
already completed the first part of this Exercise and you could discuss
it or go along on each other's' walk].

5. As you walk ask them about the observations they made and what
'sprang' to mind on their walk [or on the joint walk].

6. 'Theoretically' what do you each believe informs the observations
you have made about how we see and relate to your environment?

PART II
Experiencing

This Part documents and analyses examples from our sociological research with the Walking Interview as a Biographical Method (WIBM). In the three chapters that follow, we share examples of doing and experiencing biographical research using walking methods that facilitate a more ethnographic, phenomenological, sensory, as well as dialogic, biographical approach. We also undertake an examination of various forms of motivation for walking.

Chapter 4: Migration, memory, and place takes a walk with biographical sociologist Robert Miller, and in doing so examines the usefulness of WIBM to tell and analyse stories and experiences of migration. The chapter examines how migrant stories can be told, heard, understood, interpreted, and responded to, using walking as a method 'on the move.' Walking might also enable respondents to reflect on other 'mobilities' (cf. in identity, cross-cultural, spatial shifts, etc.). *Chapter 5: Walking as reformative and transgressive* discusses a number of forms and purposes of walking in relation to identity, as 'reformation' or 'transgression', for health, pilgrimage, activism, and/or escape. *Chapter 6: Walking in the Downtown Eastside* shares some of the walks undertaken with residents of the Downtown Eastside in Vancouver, that show how WIBM can prove to be a powerful way of communicating experience of people living out in the margins of the city and their everyday practices of citizenship and belonging, as they negotiate their environment, poverty, and social stigma.

The walks and conversations documented in this Part enable the researcher/reader to see and feel what walking methods can achieve in the telling of stories, as biographies of both people and place. WIBM research allows the reader to experience and understand how history, memory, and community/solidarity are formed in a lived, immediate, and embodied way in the lives of the research participants – it provides insight into the feelings and outlook of others.

At the end of the Part, Exercise Two invites readers to go for a walk, tune into, and take note of or document the sensory experience of walking, the sounds along the way, and the feel of the sun, breeze, rain.

4

MIGRATION, MEMORY, AND PLACE

Connecting with memory and place in urban landscapes

This chapter examines the Walking Interview as a Biographical Method (WIBM) with reference to a walk undertaken with biographical sociologist Robert Miller, that records and explores the experience in relation to his reflections on personal migration. The aim here is to show how life stories, or aspects of a life story, can be told, heard, understood, interpreted, and responded to, made possible by using the walking interview – as a 'method on the move'. The starting point of the chapter is an outline of some usage of life accounts in research on migration, in the context of major biographical approaches and analyses.

Doing biographical research

Biographical research cuts across the social and 'human' sciences (e.g., in sociology, psychology, literature, and history) with varied methodological and theoretical connections, including with ethnography, phenomenology, symbolic interactionism, ethnomethodology, and objective hermeneutics. The WIBM, drawing on ethnographic and artistic method approaches and digital technologies, facilitates the study of sensory, phenomenological, relational, and performative aspects of lived lives. Importantly, as the following WIBM with Robert Miller shows, our everyday accounts are always already 'theorised' – '*experience*' is always actively apprehended and appropriated – organised, and interpreted by our social selves. In this way, the accounts that interviewees give us are not reactive 'raw' experience, but formed in the framing and 'making sense of' the 'happening' of daily life. We 'make meaning' within 'mediated contexts' (Miller 2003), stories are part of 'symbolic interactions (Plummer 2001), and 'storytelling' is a dialogue of *imaginations* which is real in its consequences (cf. W. I. Thomas) for how people act (Frank 2012).

The WIBM extends the current ways of doing and analysing a biographical interview by a range of methods (narrative, visual, sound, etc.) and forms of interpretation and interrelates them, according to our purpose and the requirements of the research. It can encompass participatory, advocacy, performative, and artistic methodologies (see, e.g., Chapter 6). *The WIBM is the investigation of a life account, a story of a life or aspect of a life undertaken whilst walking* and can draw on a range and inter-combination of methods, modes of analysis, interpretations, and theories.

Biographical methods and migration

The use of biographical research methods to undertake sociological research on migration has its origins in particular in the Chicago School and especially in the work of Thomas and Znaniecki in *The Polish Peasant in Europe and America* (1958, 1996; Roberts 2010). There is also a long tradition of biographical research in studying the complexities involved in migration within oral history: migration stories, experiences, and trajectories. In this chapter, migration is used in its widest sense to include career, economic, lifestyle, and forced migration. Apitzsch and Siouti give a clear account of how biographical methods provide an excellent means of researching, understanding, and analysing migration experiences, yet they argue that the challenge for migration research is how to study transmigration, cross-border movements, given the 'de-coupling of geographical and social space' in current times (Apitzsch and Siouti 2007:18). Bauman (influenced by Castells) calls this landscape, or 'decoupling', the 'glocal' or 'glocalisation', the interconnection between the local and the global, which he analyses using the concepts of the 'space of flows' and the 'space of places'. The former he defines as 'imagined totalities'; for example, we can imagine a stretching of relationships across time and place (Bauman 2001:1). Bauman gives the example of supra-national business interests or nation states; however, this could be extended to thinking about more personal, supranational ties to family, people, networks. The 'space of places' might be illustrated in the coming together of people in place – he gives the example of neighbours and workmates. He argues that one of the crucial effects of glocalisation is 'a human condition suspended between two universes, each of the two subject to sharply distinct set of norms and rules' (Bauman 2001: 3). Biographical research, as we shall see, can provide 'stories of movement' as individuals cross countries and regions, re-form identities while remembering and still connecting with their origins, and reflect on personal transitions and circumstances.

In migration research the concept of 'transnationalism' is used to articulate the relationship between the local and the global in people's lives and in their migration experiences. The concept of 'transmigration' is a 'form of migration which lies at a tangent to both the region of origin and the region of settlement, and constitutes a form of existence in its own right' (Apitzsch and Siouti 2007:17). The associated term 'transnational space' is also used in migration studies to articulate the way that the experience of being both here and there is constitutive and gives rise to 'hybrid and multiple identity formations' (Apitzsch and Siouti 2007:17; see also Gilroy 1993). The experience of 'transnationalism' involves simultaneously occupying both the places of origin and destination, and is an example of glocalisation and 'the space of flows'.

Biographical research offers a productive way of better understanding the challenges of transmigration (or mobilities) and indeed glocalisation. An excellent example is *The Evolution of European Identities* project developed and led by Robert Miller (Miller and Day 2012). The Euroidentities (short title) project ran between 2008 and 2011 with seven partner teams in countries from across Europe. The project used biographical methods to study the evolution of 'European identities' and 'transgressed' the nation state perspective, once the 'natural unit of the analysis' in migration studies. The project team were looking to see the extent to which some people had a European identity that transcended that of their nation state. They found many people have a European identity that does not conflict with their national identity, or that even augments it. The complexity of identity formation is enhanced in the cases of many of the interviewees who had origins outside Europe and/or had at least one parent who originated from some other country. A key finding from the Euroidentities project was the concept of a 'European mental space', a 'collective identity', or 'orientation': 'Collective, especially national, identities are relativized by means of and in the medium of European mental space' (Schütze 1992; Schütze and Schröder-Wildhagen 2012: 256).

In understanding biographical trajectories via Bauman's terms 'the space of places' and the 'space of flows', in alliance with concepts of 'transnationalism', 'transnational space', and 'transmigration', Robert Miller is an interesting person with whom to conduct a walking interview. He was the Principal Investigator on the Euroidentities project, a leader of contemporary biographical sociology in the UK, a founder (and former chair) of the 'Biographical Perspectives' research network within the European Sociological Association, and, importantly, has experience of 'boundary crossing' due to migrating to Belfast (UK) more than forty-four years ago.

There are numerous ways of undertaking biographical research (Roberts 2002); for instance, one of the major approaches is to be found in the Euroidentities project which links identities and wider social transitions: the biographical narrative interview method (BNIM)[1] (Schütze and Schröder-Wildhagen 2012; Wengraf 2001). In whatever approach is taken, we would argue (following Apitzsch and Siouti 2007) that there is such a need to develop ways of doing biographical research that attend not only to the method of 'doing', but to the changing social contexts of exploration. The WIBM, rooted as it is in ethnographic and arts-based research, is an innovative way to research lived lives, migration and transmigration. The WIBM extends current biographical research by using and relating a range of recording devices and materials, methodologies, and strategies (e.g., ethnographic, participatory, digital, and reflexive), as well as conceptual/theoretical frameworks and means of dissemination to reveal 'moving stories' (Thomson 1999).

Migration has been an important substantive area in the development of methodological understanding and analysis in biographical research, from the Chicago School onwards. For lives 'on the move' and in glocalised worlds, there are benefits to taking a biographical approach to addressing and understanding lives over time. This is very pertinent to the growing interest in biographical methods that includes the study of the life course and lived experience; this is in part a response to the limitations of more static research approaches (i.e., the face-to-face and online interview). The biographical study of migration also fits with the desire for more creative methods to study 'lives on the move'; hence the influence of the 'turn' to visual, cultural, and performative methods in social research to capture ongoing individual social realities (Roberts 2002; Miller 2015; O'Neill et al. 2015).

Doing and experiencing biographical research differently: Walking with Robert Miller across memory, time, and place[2]

The WIBM can elicit new embodied ways of knowing, as in the experience of 'mobilities' (e.g., in daily travel routines, in migration). The following section, an account and analysis of a walk with Robert Miller, raises the theme of migration and the *experience* of walking as a form of biographical research. For a narrator (participant) and co-walker (researcher), the experience of walking, as in this case, connects them to their biographies and place in reflective and recursive ways. The phenomenological, embodied, relational, and reflective process of walking with Robert Miller elicited memories for the co-walker/researcher that also sparked a feeling of 'emplacement'.

Walking in Belfast with Robert Miller

Robert ('Bob') Miller, moved to Northern Ireland in 1972 to work initially on a research project at Queen's University in Belfast. Using an adaptation of artist Misha Myers' (2006) protocol or guidance for this WIBM, this example of a WIBM first involves imagining or visualising a walk, which is then drawn by Bob as a physical map to accompany the walk.

Robert Miller was invited to map a route he would like to share from a place he calls 'home' to a special place, a place of 'belonging', marking the landmarks along the route that are important to him. The invitation for drawing the map was sent as part of the ethics, information, and consent process. The mental 'mapping' continues along the walk and provides the opportunity for Bob to relate to the surroundings reflectively and also recursively as we move from landmark to landmark on his map.

In Bob's biographical narrative, we will find that this process of 'mapping' helped him to observe a pattern, theme, or relationship that had not been foreseen. Having drawn a map, Bob talked Maggie through the route:

I'm very close to the University in lots of ways and my own personal borders are very tightly circumscribed really.

The walk starts at his family home in Belfast, in the kitchen and garden and follows a route through the Botanic Gardens right next to his home and around the spaces and places that are important to him. The garden emerges as very important to Bob and the pleasure of living right next to the Botanic Gardens also reinforced this attachment (see Chapter 8).

Bob tells Maggie:

> The little orange crosses are where there have been incidents to do with the Troubles that I've personally known about or experienced or have been in fairly proximity and you'll see the blue is the track around the Botanic Gardens up to where we used to live and the first house we bought and then sort of down by the first place we lived which is the flat that Queen's had and then sort of around the university.

The map is detailed. It looked like an interesting mix of Bob's family and academic history as well as a biography of place, conflict, and neighbourhood, centred around the University. The 'Troubles' is a major theme of the walk. This was a period of conflict in Northern Ireland usually demarcated as between 1968 and 1998, but rooted in a much longer history, including the partition of Ireland in 1920, but going back in time to even before the

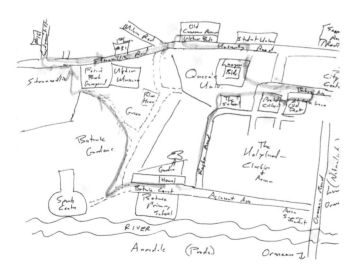

FIGURE 4.1 Robert Miller's route map. Image: with permission, Robert Miller.

16th and 17th centuries, within a context of the relationship with Britain and divisions between Unionists/Protestants (and the British Government) and Nationalists/Catholics.

Bob describes a reflection on a course he had taught for some time at Queen's University called 'Biography in Society', inspired by Daniel Bertaux's (1981) classic text:

> A couple of years ago I had some mature students in the course and it's a social change course, it's where the people do a biography of their family, family history and we were talking about the Troubles and several of the younger students said 'gosh, was it as bad as that' and myself and the other mature students were just astonished 'what do you mean'? How could you possibly not know about this?" Then it dawned on us that their parents hadn't talked to them about it, it had all happened before they were born.

Bob says that around the University (during the Troubles) was a fairly peaceful area but nevertheless 'quite a lot happened. Yet compared to the working-class areas particularly in West Belfast it just pales in comparison, but even here, as you'll see, there's quite a lot of little orange stars'.

What was emerging in the conversation with Bob, about the map were the links between his own biographical 'borders', and his relationship to the University and 'the Troubles' especially in relation to risk and belonging. At this point he had lived in the area for forty-four years and said that he tried to organise the walk chronologically, starting 'with the older stuff and work our way up to more modern'.[3]

Walking and talking with Bob around the University quarter, past the three houses he had lived in and in the Botanic Gardens, reinforced Maggie's earlier experiences of using this as a method for biographical research: again, that walking is relational, it can also be revelatory, it is firmly embodied. Taking a walk with someone in this way critically engages the thinking, sensing, feeling, and attuning body.

Home and garden

Our first stop on the walk was Bob's garden. He says that in relation to identity and borders, his walk may best be portrayed by concentric circles and the garden is the innermost circle:

> It's a communal garden … it was already a communal garden when we moved in. It's what attracted us to here … that's our communal fire pit with a couple of Christmas trees I stuck in there and lit a couple of days ago. We often have bonfires here in the summer. All this paving was laid by me because it was quite muddy and, being a good sociologist, I knew

FIGURE 4.2 Robert Miller in the communal garden. Image: Maggie O'Neill with kind
permission of Robert Miller.

if you build, if you put in a pathway, people will unconsciously walk on
the pathway because the grass would never grow because people walk back
and forth, so.

See the tree there? See the way that the branches are bent? That's caused
by the weight of my kids and their friends climbing on it when it was
smaller. So, I'm very attached to the tree in the garden.

[Indicating a bird feeder] I put this up in the autumn and take it down
in the spring because it gets in the way you know and the idea is you don't
want to encroach too much into your neighbour's space you know but they
like the birds.

Yes, yes the birds they come in. There's well that's a robin up there but
we get goldfinch and three different kinds of blue tits. And squirrels which
are lurking down there waiting for us to go away so they can come and
steal the peanuts.

And we've had a lot of fun here over the years, all our kids were
little at the same, our sons and there were some others. Oh, oh I'll show
you something just over here. We found this some years later after we'd
moved in.

Bob showed a series of bricks along the side of the house wall that had been
etched upon by 'generations' of children, starting in the 1930s and included those
of his own children and following 'generations'.

We walk past the Botanic Primary School that Bob's children had attended school. This he says is a truly mixed school (this usually refers to schools attended by children from both Catholic and Protestant families) and is 'the only school in Northern Ireland that has a qualified English as a Second Language (ESL) teacher, with twenty-two different nationalities'. Due to its location in the University Quarter, it is a favourite school for the children of postgraduates and academics and visiting scholars.

Bob shares a memory of when the kids were small and the school would have fundraising events where:

> You bought little tickets and each of the mothers brought in a specialist dish ... they were doing like their specialist stuff and it was great.
>
> I like living across from a school compared to living across from just houses.

The Botanic Gardens

The next stop or 'landmark' on Bob's map was the Botanic Gardens park a few steps away from the school and his home.

> We like the park, we've always lived around the park so even when we first came, you know it's quite an amenity, and it's more interesting than most parks because its history was, it was a Botanic Gardens and so it has a great variety of plant life in it and they have a lot of events in here which we go to.

Talking and walking through Botanic Gardens it became clear that the gardens are very close to Bob's heart and his family history: all three houses he has lived in with his family surround the park. Indeed, Bob realised in walking through the gardens that they are a central point in relation to the three houses the family had lived in and to his life in Northern Ireland. He said, looking at his map:

> And one house is there and one house is there and we're there you see so it's almost in the centre of the triangle and it's just like when we were talking there it occurred to me in fact we're clustered more around the park than we are around the university. I've always sort of thought we're near the University but in fact it's the park.

We approached the Palm House and the Tropical Ravine, the next major landmarks on Bob's map:

> It is basically a greenhouse that's designed for tropical plants from Victorian times and they're doing a major renovation because it's you know it needs it, but when we first came here because we came from Florida if we got a

bit homesick we'd go and walk slowly up and down the Tropical Ravine [laughs]. Because it was like thirty degrees centigrade and high humidity like 'Oh, this is like home' you know.

Bob added that his family used an image from the park, the view of the Palm House and the University for their Christmas card one year.

University life

This discussion of his attachment to the park 'sparked' Bob's memories of migration – to give a narrative of his journey and arrival to Belfast from Florida in 1972, forty-four years ago, and with no plans to stay. He said he was recently reflecting on his changing identity. He had not wanted to stay at his graduate university and, when an opportunity arose to go to Belfast, he took it, even though it was at the height of the 'Troubles'. He had an offer to work on a research project based in Belfast, with his plan being to complete his PhD and then apply for posts in back in the US.

> But then after I had been here a year a lectureship came up and I applied and to my astonishment I got it, I was twenty-five years old. We went back the second Christmas, to bring some data back and stuff and I went down to [town where his graduate university is located] and met two of my people who were still at the graduate school and they said 'what are you doing' and I said 'I'm a lecturer in sociology now' and one of them said 'is that sort of like a TA' [teaching assistant] and the other guy who had lived in Europe kind of went 'no, it's a bit more than a TA' [laughs] you know and yes a proper, permanent, tenure track job, as they would say in the States.

Walking past the rose garden, Bob says:

> The roses are all cut you know this is the rose garden. It's this way. There are a lot of memories all around here you see from the kids when they were young and things.
>   My eldest son fell off a tree over there, right up there and almost impaled himself on a stick. OK, yes and another time I was walking him to school and somebody went by us on a bike fast and came just like, could have hit us you know.

The University was a central focus for Bob's biography and over a significant period. Maggie said it was making her think about current academic identities: in relation to here, to the one he had 'inhabited' in the same University and same neighbourhood of around one square mile, as a lecturer at 25 years old to retirement as a professor, and its contrast to her own career trajectory. Bob continued:

> I never had a mentor, because the fellow that brought me here was a professor at 'State University'. He probably would have been a mentor but then he was off the scene. And doing the PhD, in fact the PhD was quite slow coming because the project took up a lot of time and you know being a new lecturer.

Bob says Tanaka (his almost-mentor – not his real name) gave him 'a wonderful opportunity that changed my life immensely for the better'.

Bob also joked that he probably had the most expensive PhD fellowship the ESRC had ever granted because he learnt Sociology on the project whilst also doing his PhD. He had in fact been a Chemistry major as an undergraduate who switched to Sociology at the last possible moment; and who then had to take whatever courses were available in the Sociology Department which happened by chance to include Demography and Sociology of the Family. These were core specialisms of the department at 'State University' and were instrumental in his acceptance on to their graduate programme. Then Bob met Tanaka. Here he reflects upon the major effects that chance can have on one's life:

> If I hadn't taken a course that was being given by him there I wouldn't have known him at the time. He was looking for somebody to work as a research assistant here and my life wouldn't have been the same at all, where I would have ended up God knows!

The 'Troubles' feature centrally in the walk and Bob's biographical map. Maggie asked Bob about the stress of living in a conflict zone especially through the 1970s and 1980s:

> You became used to it, the first couple, the worst, the first year and a half was always the worst then after that it gradually died back.
>
> But you've got to get numb to it in a way, I remember that first year and a half or so when you'd leave Northern Ireland it was almost it was a physical sensation of being lighter when you got out and it was a sort of paranoia of things, something that you know you just might be where a bomb goes off or someone might mistake you for somebody else or you could give somebody offence.

Bob added:

> This is where I wanted to show you, this is now a restaurant but at one time it belonged to Queen's [University] and the IRA liked to set booby-traps and there was a vacant house here which belonged to the university. They got into it and they planted a bomb that would go off when the doors opened and then they rang the RUC with a fake tip off saying there was weapons being hidden in the house. So, the police would come and search it and they would catch the police, but before the police got there a meter reader was going around and he was blown up.

FIGURE 4.3 Risky places. Image: With permission, Robert Miller.

Bob had a lucky escape in the same incident – his normal walking route to work would have taken him by the site of the bomb at the time it exploded.

An emerging theme in his walk was getting used to the Troubles, accommodating and negotiating the risk. For example, a Ph.D. student of Bob's had been born in Northern Ireland, but had gone to the States shortly after the onset of the Troubles and had come back after twenty years' absence to do her PhD:

> She was amazed about how people took the Troubles as routine and she noticed things like Catholic mothers would teach their kids Irish, but they also taught them not to speak Irish when they were in town and not to say things like not to curse using things like 'Jesus, Mary and Joseph' because that would see them as Catholic or, when you had a bomb scare, people don't run, people just put down whatever they are doing in a shop and just sort of walk briskly out. Whereas, if you had a bomb scare in Oxford Street [in London], people go nuts you know, they'd be running around panicking.

Bob described these as 'everyday adaptations':

> When my son went to Grammar School in the centre of town, the first day he came back with the parents' information sheet which was things like 'thy hair shall not be lower than the collar' and things like that, also in the event of trouble in the City we will keep the children at the school until it's safe, do not come and try to get them, we'll keep them there until it's safe. They were told for instance this was a Catholic area where Catholics

picked up black taxis to go up to West Belfast near the school and they said 'Never, ever go near there in a school uniform because you get hit you know you could get hit by a gang' and stuff like that.

We were in Canada and went into a department store [laughs] and the kids walk in, they walk up to the first person they see and they go [arms out stretched], they expect to be searched. Yes, and the guy says, what are you doing?' They said, 'Oh we're from Belfast', this is like a five-year-old kid you know and the guy goes 'oh' [laughs].

Our son would come in and he'd go 'damn you know a bloody f***ing scare you know we started up in town and there was a bomb and we had to cut back and had to go up and had to walk around' you know, like an inconvenience.

However, this also impacted upon Bob's fear for his children's safety. Bob tells that he was at an ISA (International Sociological Association) conference and shared a taxi with an academic from Israel and they talked about safety of children and bombs in conflict:

The Intifada was going on and they were having bombs in Israel and she said something like 'well you know I know whenever bombs go off I worry, but I know that the odds that my kids are caught in one are very low' and I said 'yes but until they walk through that door you're kind of thinking aren't you' and she said 'actually you're right' – because I'd done the same thing in Belfast you know. We had this like odd common connection.

Sectarian neighbourhoods and 'TINKS'

Bob described how the area where they had first lived had changed a lot over time. It had changed from being mostly families with a mix of shops to now being half student and half professionals ('Tinks' – two incomes, no kids):

But when we lived here it was quite different. It was mostly families and so the mix of shops were different. There were like two butchers, two greengrocers, stuff like that. One's Protestant and one's Catholic and so we've wandered in of course and [laughs] you know if we walked into a shop everybody would notice which shop we'd walked into, you know.

Bob says that by chance the greengrocer they settled on was Catholic.

I was in a unique position, Twy (Bob's wife) and I both, because we're American. This has always been a very pro-American place you know. It was more proAmerican in those days than now, because of the huge amounts of immigration out of Northern Ireland to the United States.

FIGURE 4.4 Shopping area. Image: With permission, Robert Miller.

Virtually everybody had relations in the States, both Protestant and Catholic, and so even quite dicey places, as soon as I opened my mouth, 'Oh, you're a Yank', you know, and so I could move across borders that it would be very unwise if you were English or Northern Irish to do. Our two sons, like my oldest son's name is Samuel and my youngest son is named Luke, Old Testament names are Protestant, New Testament names are Catholic, so when Sam was born, it's a family name you know, 'What's your baby called?' 'Samuel'. 'Oh, what a wee, that's a sweet name, Samuel's a good name'. Or 'Samuel? You named him Samuel!' You know [laughs] and then when Luke was born 'What's his?', you didn't and the person would go 'Luke? Why did you name him Luke?' and the ones who were going 'Oh, Samuel', they're going 'Oh yes, oh yes, a lovely name, a lovely' you know it was just…

Maggie says, 'you have one of each!' and Bob replies,

Yes, but that was just coincidence. Sam was named Sam because it's a family name and Luke was named Luke because Star Wars was just out [laughs] and Twy was into Star Wars.

As Bob and Maggie were walking past a convenience store, he said:

Russell's used to be a newsagents called Gardners and it was one of those places that they liked to bomb and it was bombed and they rebuilt it and they bombed and they rebuilt it. It's been bombed at least three times.

I mean there's no doubt Catholics were discriminated against, there's no doubt that they had a case, but the IRA was never particularly nice either.

I can tell the stories. A very bad taste joke I made one time, see that hotel over there, Madison's Hotel? It used to be called, I think, the Russell Court and it's a very nice place. Then it was a kind of rundown and it has the dubious distinction of having two sectarian assassinations in it within a year. One where a Protestant paramilitary was murdered and the one a year later when a Catholic paramilitary was murdered. So, it's a, it was a non-sectarian drinking place [laughs], which you know so non-sectarian sectarian assassinations or equal opportunity assassinations used to do a number, you've got me being reminiscent now.

Bob observed on Northern Ireland:

When I went to ... conferences, often there would ... be some American bore there who would be sort of saying 'Oh, America is the future and California is the future of America so if you look at California that's what the whole world's going to be like' and I go 'No, no, no, no, no, no. I'm from Northern Ireland, I'll lay you money twenty-five years from now Northern Ireland's the way to the future. We have lack of human rights, we have tight security, we have terrorism, we have people worried about getting killed you know in public, using public transport. I bet you [laughs] that we're the way of the future'. Who was right? [laughs].

Personal borders and belonging

Well, a contemporary bit of the border, this is the local shop [laughing and indicating the local SPAR] ... so, if we talk about my personal borders, oh ... see where the lights are? That's a place called Common Grounds, it's a coffee shop that's run by this church, it's kind of a community church and it's nice and it's the place where people would tend to go in the School of Social Sciences if they were going for coffee ... So, if you talk about a border that's a border at the side.

Yes, I suppose the other thing, about Botanic, you see you can easily walk into Belfast from our house and now because we're over sixty [years old] the bus fares are free here ... so, we just usually catch the bus and if the bus isn't coming we just walk.

I suppose there's little bits of me not so much in Florida anymore because my mother's now gone into a retirement home and she's moved to North Carolina in the town where I was born. So, if anything, I've got a little bit of a long awakened route back there all of a sudden; and over to London for Sam [where one of Bob's sons is living], which I know well now because we've always been going there and I'm there, you know, quite a lot.

FIGURE 4.5 Common Grounds Coffee Shop. Image: With permission, Robert Miller.

Reflecting on the housing situation and changes in the area over time Bob thought upon what the Chicago sociologists called 'zones of transition'. Much of the local area is called 'the Holy Land' due to the streets being named after sites in the Middle East. The area had traditionally had been occupied by the 'artisan working class'. However,

> I've experienced genuine social change over a medium time span first hand. [The] Holy Land, one thing about it is landlords own the property down there and they've really been very bad because it's also multiple occupancy and they fill it full of students, the kind of students [who] wreck the places but … They're starting to lose money now because the reputation is so bad that people, parents who live in the west of Northern Ireland, have heard about the Holy Land and their son says 'I want to live in the Holy Land' and they go 'over our dead body' and you know so they can't let … them to students.
>
> The middle-class is striking back, there's a street, it's kind of diagonal to where we are now and practically everyone on it are residents and they created something called 'Wild Flower Alley'. They had an alley that was behind their houses and the two streets that butt on to it and it was like, apparently, it was used for prostitution, drugs and just full of trash. They talked the council into putting gates on it so and they cleaned it up and they call it Wild Flower Alley and there are flowers in it and things.
>
> One last story – I want you to get out of the cold. The house is right there. We've been here for thirty-four years, I usually come home at lunch, I usually almost every day go into work, so you're talking about walking

FIGURE 4.6 View of the route from Robert Miller's house to his office 'I've been up
and down this street at least thirty thousand times'. Image: With permission,
Robert Miller.

up and down this street twenty times a week, thirty-four years. So, given
a couple of weeks off for holidays and things, it's about a thousand times
a year. So, I've been up and down this street at least thirty thousand times
[laughs]. And I, can I remember? I probably couldn't, can I describe the
street? Not very well, you know.

Following the walk, Maggie wrote that she had a strong sense of Bob's Belfast,
the threads and intersections that ran between home, family (in Belfast and
Florida), friendship and work, his life and identity as a biographical sociologist.
She had experienced first-hand that his work is intimately connected to the place
he was living in and the history and relationship not only to sectarianism but
the people, places, the University, and migration, a 'transcultural identity' as an
American in Belfast, and that family life is at the centre of it all. She described it
as a privilege to have accompanied Bob as he paced out these relationships and
stories along the ground. The links to Florida were imagined and embodied in
the familial relations and the Palm House and Tropical Ravine in the Botanic
Gardens, and also symbolically represented in the dense array of plants in Bob's
former office, which resembled a rainforest (and an enormous framed satellite

photograph of 'Florida from Space' behind his desk). The relationship between migration, memory, and space was central to Bob's biographical experience and his understanding of his life trajectory, which was a strong theme in the walk.

Maggie looked at the road and imagined this journey taken over so many years and the return back to family and home every lunchtime, from the University. Bob's walk led to his reflections (at the start of the walk) on his garden and the Botanic Gardens being at the 'centre of everything' when he always thought the university was. Yet, at the end of the walk it is the garden, house, and 'home' which are at the centre and starting base of his life.

Along the walk, Bob met people he was familiar with and Maggie got an even stronger sense of the conviviality to his work as a sociologist and his work and family life in Belfast – as well as the 'glocal' relations with his family in Florida.

This example and use of a map/mapping (which is only one way of doing a WIBM) gave rise to the emergence of further memories and stories along the way. In reflecting upon the walk Bob felt that the effect of assigning the task of having the interviewee draw the map beforehand introduces an 'introspective reflection' prior to beginning the actual biographical walking interview. Walking as a method is a means of 'getting close' to a biography in a phenomenological, embodied, and 'attuned' way. For Bob, the biographical and relational links between Belfast and Florida unfolded in an experiential and imaginative reflection on his life. Here we get a sense of the 'space of places' and the 'space of flows' (Bauman 2001) through Bob's account of experience of 'transmigration' and 'glocalisation'. By showing and reflecting upon how migrant stories can be told, heard, understood, interpreted, and responded to, using walking as a method 'on the move' is a means for the individual to 'retrace' their 'steps in life'.

An important point to reflect upon is not just the experience of corporeal 'being' in, and walking in place, connecting with landmarks, but the impact of the topography, as the interviewee encounters the actual places they have drawn on their map. For Bob, the experience of being there at that point in time and in those places facilitated a way of seeing a familiar place in a new way, especially when showing it to a biographical interviewer. A biographical interview will facilitate and intensify this feedback from the locality – the geography. More generally, Bob experienced that being given a non-stressful thing to do, map a walk, and share a walk, had the effect of relaxing him when discussing and relating his migration story. This is an important point, because going for a walking interview, being side-by-side with another, traversing a route, 'mediates' the experience of having attention focused upon oneself. It mediates the power relationship of a 'standard' interview and introduces a convivial, relational, dialogic dynamic to the interpretive/analytic process.

One of our arguments in this chapter is shown clearly in the walk with Bob: the *experiential* and *creative* contribution of using walking in biographical research can re-invigorate the method by 'balancing' the embodied, sensory, and mobile sense of our lives with the cognitive, reflective meaning, and memory-making in time/space/place. In the 'mattering' and 'timing' of a walk, our social lives are lived, experienced, and also imagined. The WIBM elicits a dialogic narrative and can facilitate understanding of the migratory experience by both recounter and the receiver – we can see Bob's identity 'moving' between here and there, Florida and Belfast, i.e., the importance of the Palm House as a transitional object, a place to go when they return from Florida, to maintain or sustain the 'feel' of the previous sensory experience. This would not necessarily have emerged in a life story interview undertaken in an office with the interviewer and interviewee engaged in face to face conversation with a sound recorder. Not only do we get a sense of Bob's 'trans migration' (Apitzsch and Siouti 2007), glocal experience, and 'imaginaries', the 'space of flows' and 'space of places', but we also get a view of the way that biographical narratives, as 'life stories', can be 'rich ground for the formulation of substantive theories' (Bertaux and Kohli 1984) and, as Mills (1970) advocates, personal biographies and histories are linked to broader social structures and processes.

In conclusion, the discussion of the walk with Robert Miller[4] facilitates understanding of 'theory into practice' (as above, in relation to theorisation on migratory experience). It also shows the clear benefits of the walking method in revealing the sensory, multi-modal layering of *experience* elicited in the 'moving' interview and specifically connected to the environment, memory, embodiment, and the senses. Above all, it demonstrates how wider social changes are actually also lived at the micro-level of daily individual and group experience. This chapter also 'operationalises' for the reader the framework of the WBIM by connecting theory, experience, and the sociological imagination to Exercise Two (see end of Part II) and the *Principles and Practice Guide* for undertaking a WIBM (after the *Conclusion* at the end of the book).

Notes

1 As stated in Chapter 3, the BNIM involves a non-directive, active listening approach, and the researcher invites the interviewee to tell the story of her life in her own time and in her own words without interruption. When the narration is ended by the teller, the researcher usually asks questions relating to the themes emerging in the narration, and then a third and final stage of the interview emerges when the researcher might ask focused questions relating to the research topic, patterns, structures, and themes. The interview is then transcribed and analysed. Analysis is usually based on a grounded theory, taking a bottom up approach, and can take various formats, but is usually thematic.

2 The walk was supported by a Leverhulme Trust-funded Research Fellowship (2015–16) undertaken by inviting participants to walk with Maggie O'Neill around a route of their choice on the theme of on borders, risk, and/or belonging. The walks sought to explore the participant's experiences, meanings, knowledge, and understanding of borders, risk, and belonging connected to the place/space chosen by them, in a WIBM.

3 The WIBM was undertaken in 2016.

4 The WIBM was transcribed and the transcript and soundfile were shared with Robert Miller. Maggie O'Neill undertook thematic analysis of the transcript and wrote an account of the walk in consultation with Robert Miller. See www.walkingborders.com Walk 3. This chapter was written in consultation with him.

References

Apitzsch, U. and Siouti, I. (2007) *Biographical Analysis as an Interdisciplinary Research Perspective in the Field of Migration Studies*. York: University of York. Available at www.york.ac.uk/res/researchintegration/Integrative_Research_Methods/Apitzsch%20Biographical%20Analysis%20April%202007.pdf (Accessed 22 September 2018).

Bauman, Z. (2001) *Community: Seeking Safety in an Insecure World*. Cambridge, UK: Polity.

Bertaux, D. (ed.) (1981) *Biography and Society: The Life History Approach in the Social Sciences*. Beverly Hills, CA: Sage Publications.

Bertaux, D. and Kohli, M. (1984) The life story approach: A continental view, *Annual Review of Sociology*, 10(1): 215–237.

Frank, A. (2012) Practising Dialogic Narrative Analysis. In: J. A. Holstein, and J. F. Gubrium (eds.) *Varieties of Narrative Analysis*. London: Sage.

Gilroy, P. (1993) *The Black Atlantic: Modernity and Double Consciousness*. London: Verso.

Miller, R. (2003) Biographical method. In: R. Miller and J. Brewer (eds.) *A–Z of Social Research*. London: Sage.

Miller, R. (2015) Ignore the man behind the curtain. Exploration of virtual reality. In: M. O'Neill, B. Roberts, and A. Sparkes (eds.) *Advances in Biographical Research: Creative Applications*. Abingdon, UK: Routledge.

Miller, R. and Day, G. (eds.) (2012) *The Evolution of European Identities: Biographical Approaches*. London: Palgrave Macmillan.

Mills, C. W. (1970) *The Sociological Imagination*. Oxford: Oxford University Press.

Myers, M. (2006) Along the way: Situation-responsive participation and education, *The International Journal of the Arts in Society*, 1(2): 1–6.

O'Neill, M., Roberts, B. and Sparkes, A. (eds.) (2015) *Advances in Biographical Methods: Creative Applications*. London: Routledge.

Plummer, K. (2001) *Documents of Life 2: An Invitation to a Critical Humanism*. London: Sage.

Roberts, B. (2002) *Biographical Research*. Buckingham: Open University Press.

Roberts, B. (2010) 'Ahead of its time?' The legacy and relevance of W. I. Thomas and F. Znaniecki (1918–20) The Polish Peasant in Europe and America. In: C. Hart (ed.) *The Legacy of the Chicago School*. Poynton, UK: Midrash.

Schütze, F. (1992) Pressure and guilt: War experiences of a young German soldier and their biographical implications (Part 1), *International Sociology*, 7(2): 187–208.

Schütze, F. and Schröder-Wildhagen, A. (2012) Discoverers in European mental space: The biographical experiences of participants in European civil society organisations. In: R. Miller and G. Day (eds.) *The Evolution of European Identities: Biographical Approaches*. London: Palgrave Macmillan.

Thomas, W. I. and Znaniecki, F. (1958) *The Polish Peasant in Europe and America*, 2 vols. New York: Dover Press (First pub. 1918–20).

Thomson, A. (1999) Moving stories: Oral history and migration studies, *Oral History*, 27: 24–37.

Wengraf, T. (2001) *Qualitative Research Interviewing: Biographic Narrative and Semi- Structured Method*. London: Sage Publications.

5

WALKING AS RE-FORMATIVE AND TRANSGRESSIVE

Health, pilgrimage, trespass, marching

This chapter is concerned with a number of 'forms' of walking, showing that there is a range of purposes for 'pedestrianism'. Walking can be undertaken for various broad motivations – here, as 're-formative' or 'transgressive' – and lead to differing modes of 'experience' and 'expression'. A number of examples are discussed: walking for health and pilgrimage, or as trespass and marching. The chapter then considers 'walking' as a form of social escape and in relation to identity formation – how we re-imagine or reconstruct a sense of who we are, and could be.

History of walking

As we have discussed earlier in this book, there has been considerable interest in recent years, as witnessed by the popularity of a number of books and in journalism, on the history and philosophy of walking (see Amato 2004; Baxter 2016; Bryant et al. 2016a; Gros 2015; Hazan 2018; Horvath and Szakolczai 2018; Nicholson 2011; Smith 2015; Solnit 2014). Minshull (2000), for example, gives a diverse, comprehensive edited anthology of 'historical' excerpts from a numerous literary works (cf. Wordsworth), philosophy, the Bible, and other sources, providing an informative catalogue of quotations. 'Walking' as a subject permeates our cultural traditions, as well as our own personal history and recollection, as in various kinds of walks we have undertaken – for leisure, with family and friends, commuting, shopping and so on. Some of the recent texts on walking display common themes: walking in streets, deserts, or wilderness, and literary or philosophical musings. The themes considered in this chapter are: health, pilgrimages, activism, and escape. 'Walking' can be defined as an individual's movement, usually on two legs (with some arm and body shift), but it also may be aided or only made possible by various mechanical, human, or other assistance (e.g., a wheeled chair) and commonly undertaken at a regular 'walking pace' (i.e., not a jog or run). A 'walk' can vary greatly in time from a few minutes to hours, sometimes interrupted by some pause to rest, to talk, to reflect, to check on the way, to view.

Motivation

The act of walking is closely connected with biography; for instance, our early walking as recorded, say in a photograph with parents, or we will have memories of walking to school (or to the school bus), holiday rambles, or organised hikes on trips and camps. Walking can be intertwined with a particular identity; for instance, it may also have been keenly connected to our political activism as a student protestor, issue activist, or political party member – while no longer perhaps 'active', we may have saved old badges (pins) and photographs which act as personal reminders of former campaigning walks.

One way of considering the various 'modes' or types of walking is according to 'motivation' (cf. Gerth and Mills 1954; Mills 1940), purpose or objective. Motivation is dependent on context – the reason for doing a particular action as informing or arising from a situation. It is, therefore, connected with 'timing' – as the spur to action, or during action, or in retrospect ('rationalisation') (cf. Matza 1964, on 'neutralisation') – so 'allowing' actions to take place, but can also be seen as emerging, to be ex post facto, or different from an initial reason.

Walking 'itself' has risen in 'popularity', with issues (especially pollution) surrounding car journeys now leading to search for alternatives. It may be a 'returning' activity as people decide: 'It's quicker on foot', or by declaring: 'Once it was the only way', so it could be becoming fashionable, as perhaps a show of 'individualism' and 'independence'. Its popularity may also tie in with the recent 'search' for 'slowness' and 'mindfulness' – life as better 'lived' or appreciated by a slower pace, allowing for contemplation and awareness, living more fully 'in the moment'.

There may be a personal motivation for walking, in terms of feeling a need 'to make a difference', some specific form of change, hence a focused purpose around a social or political issue; again, an activism that has a personal and social import. It may be for a 'cause', such as to join a war (e.g., international republican volunteers travelling to the Spanish Civil War) or against one; or walking for reform, such as to draw attention to the living conditions of one group to another; or due to habit. It can also be 'to be with nature'; to see the sights, to gain physical and mental change; as a key part of a job (as street cleaner, walking athlete, in policing and security); or as a 'necessity' – as a refugee, for asylum (see Minshull 2000).

Some walks, it appears, may be done for 'altruistic' reasons: for instance, to support charitable causes, perhaps for ensuring 'reciprocity', in return for help one has received. Walking can also be or become 'aimless' – to be open to experience, a 'drift' (Debord), finding one's own route, or a 'flâneurism' within the streets or the arcades of the city (Benjamin 2002: 416–55) (see Chapter 2), 'half-consciously' appreciating the signs of the past and the distractions of the present. Walking can be for discovery: for instance, the metal detectorist seeks to uncover an historical artefact lying beneath the earth being trod, the bird watcher to record a particular kind of bird. A walk may start with, be sustained by, or become a focus for memories of someone who acts as an absent companion, 'a ghost'; it may be a walk to 'search' for an understanding of a person and their generation, or a relationship; or re-enact a personal or previous well-known journey (Somerville 2017; Stewart 2017).

Motives may not be well-formulated by a person, and there may be a mix of reasons to walk, some probably changing in importance 'along the way', from pre-planning to redefined in reminiscence, with some reasons even 'added' or 'subtracted' during the walk. A simple before and/or after analytical model of motivation, or one based only on 'clear' reasons, is rather restrictive – instead, motives should be conceived as 'in process', with shifting emphases, neither wholly 'rational' nor 'emotional', and subject to rehearsal and renewal according to reflection within action. On a wider cultural level, the forms and motivation of walking may vary historically (e.g., due to changes in cityscapes, transportation, commuting distances).

Respondents taking part in walking interview biographical research may have a range of motivations for agreeing to participate and in choosing the particular walk. Their reasons may be influenced by a wish to re-visit a previous routine walk, or create a new experience, if only in the imagination. For instance, a migrant may wish to be interviewed along a certain road, past a particular statue, building, or line of trees, because in earlier walks on this route these features have 'reminded' them, say, of parts of their home neighbourhood in a different country (see O'Neill and Perivolaris 2015). A key interview element will be a wish to 'tell their story': of their participation in an event, a biographical theme (family, career), or even of their life span. Walking for a purpose – such as for charity fund-raising, for health benefits, in protest to defend or widen political and social rights, as 'forced' or escape (e.g., for asylum, refuge), or as a 'getaway' for new experiences – may be defining for a whole life (and brought by or induce a 'conversion' or 'turning point'): a subject's walking interview can reveal ('re-create') this life experience as if in 'miniature'.

It is difficult (if not impossible) to produce a clear taxonomy of walks, with types easily definable and placed in some neat pattern according to clear, 'steady' motivations (e.g., personal and social purposes), or length, landscape, history, and so on. Here, we will outline two broad motivational forms – re-formative and transgressive – in which personal and social expressions of walking can be examined as connected, and later including walking as escape, which draws particular attention to identity formation.

Re-formation – Health and pilgrimage

'Re-formative' as a walking motivational form lays stress on both personal physical and/or mental 'renewal', as well as having broader societal connections – as part, perhaps, of wider social trends, opportunities, or policy proposals.

Thus, individual motivations and activities are linked to wider social institutions through attempts to re-organise one's personal life which may well fit with forming or taking social objectives. Implicit here are questions of self or identity – and how individual action is replicated across social strata and related to institutions (e.g., in social policy, resource allocation, religious practices).

Health

Walking is increasingly associated with 'good health', with media news items frequently stating research findings on the positive effects of exercise on the body, through its contribution to strengthening muscles, the work of the heart and respiratory system, and for a sense of wellbeing due to the release of beneficial chemicals. In addition, walking may be medically recommended for recuperation from an injury or an operation, or broadly advised for the elderly who are beginning to be restricted in movement by physical diseases. Exercise can be easily measured by everyone, in terms of steps per day and heart rate recorded by tracking/monitoring technologies on wristbands, smartwatches, or other devices. 'Walking for health' groups, particularly for the elderly, have proliferated, as doctors have advised activities for physical and mental improvement where appropriate.

How someone walks may indicate ill-health and aging. *The Times* (UK) reported recently on research that recommended office workers should walk for an hour a day to mitigate the possible effects on health of sitting for long periods, even the chances of dying early; a few minutes regular walking in the office, to work, or during the lunch break, brought measurable effects in research, with 'moderate' activities, including domestic chores such as gardening or cleaning and playing with children, also being beneficial (Smyth 2016: 20). 'Walking meetings' outdoors have also been recommended (Lay 2017), while the good effects of dog-walking have also been included in similar advice. In counselling programmes, the idea of walking with individuals as 'moving therapy' has also been advocated, and more broadly as an aid to positive approach to life and work (and their balance). Particularly in the last twenty years or more, there has been a proliferation of organised charity walks (for cancer research, local hospices, or health education, etc.) sometimes inspired by a specific person's illness or a tragic event. Individuals and groups may often walk over long distances to raise funds for 'good causes' (in the UK, this is commonly from Land's End to John O'Groats, or on national walking trails). 'Walking with someone' can also mean 'to befriend' – to take a walk with a person in his or her ill-health, pain, bereavement, recovery from injury etc., to give mutual support, to be in solidarity.

Broadly, walking has increasingly been recognised as a 'health giving' activity in various ways: producing individual wellbeing, happiness, contentment, pleasure, positive outlook, or invigoration, (see Gros 2015:139–45). Walking, in addition to improving health, according to Amato, 'allows the feet to lead the mind and heart; it gives us back our body and senses … an altered state of mind for prayer, reflection, or simply talking to oneself' (Amato 2004: 276). Recently, Raven-Ellison has engaged in 'mapping' his 'moods' when walking across Britain's parks and cities by using sensors to monitor degrees of stress, interest, excitement – giving a geolocational mapping of emotions (Sillito 2017).

Walking can be for educational (often health associated) reasons – the pleasures (and pains) of walking may be coupled with sightseeing, perhaps with an individual guide and commonly with a guide book detailing historic sites, locales, or marvellous landscapes. Walks are outlined and organised by city councils, tourist boards, parks, museums, commercial organisations, or enthusiasts. Walking has grown to become a major 'business', for instance, some tourist companies specialise in walking holidays. There is an 'industry' of clothes, boots, sticks, hats – and books of walks and maps, internet sites, newspaper or magazine features, etc. on routes in cities and regions – to see buildings, sites from novels, places associated with the famous (politicians, artists, sports people, musicians etc.) often marked with commemorative plaques, historical events (e.g., battlefields), well-known vistas (e.g., in national parks), and so on.

Today, travel writing is a major literary genre (including accounts of walking: cf. Eric Newby, and more recently, Nicholas Crane (2008); Rory Stewart (2017); Bee Rowlatt (2016), and very many others), although it does have a long history to the 17th century and earlier (e.g., Defoe); 18th century descriptions of landscapes and walks (cf. the walking of Wordsworth, de Quincey); Johnson and Boswell's London ramblings and Scottish journey; and accounts of colonial officials, missionaries, traders, 'explorers and travellers', artists, botanists, anthropologists, etc., particularly during the 19th century to the mid-20th century (cf. H.M. Stanley; Gertrude Bell; Freya Stark; Alfred Russel Wallace). There are also the traditions of popular travel writing/journalism (cf. H. V. Morton in 1930s Britain and abroad), and well-known novelists' accounts (cf. Evelyn Waugh's travel writing, R. L. Stevenson's walk in central France which has been retraced by later hikers, Hilaire Belloc's pilgrimage to Rome, and Graham Greene's *Journey without Maps*, and so on: see Amato 2004: 101–7, 205–7; Dodd 1982); Crane 2008).

Apart from the much-discussed benefits of walking for physical and mental health, it may also help in stimulating thought and imagination (as Thoreau and many others have observed). Perhaps the act of walking – like music – fills part of the mind, while the rest is then released to focus on other tasks: writers and scientists have used walking deliberately to stimulate ideas and solutions to problems.

The link between outdoor exercise and general health was prominent in the 'mass' walking and fitness 'movement' of the 1930s (in the UK and elsewhere). Walking activity was able to expand with increasing leisure time and people becoming more able to take holidays away from home.

> One of the positive features of life in the inter-war period was the growing
> availability of holidays for people of all classes. Partly this was due to the
> spread of paid holidays, for in the early twenties only about one and a half

million people [in the UK] had paid holidays, whereas by 1939 the figure was over eleven million. British holiday resorts reached a peak of popularity in the thirties

(Stevenson 1977: 41; see Cross 1990)

Stevenson argues that 'the other great passion of the inter-war period', that encapsulated a 'get away from it all' spirit, was hiking and rambling which became almost 'a national mania' in the UK:

> The Youth Hostel Association founded in 1930, opened its first hostel in Winchester and had over 400 by the end of the thirties, offering cheap overnight accommodation. Over a million 'nights' were booked in the hostels by 1939, and the movement had over 100,000 members … epitomizing the faith which many people had in fresh air and healthy, physical exertion as a positive force for betterment in an often-depressing economic climate. Other organizations, such as the Ramblers' Association, sprang up to cater for the new enthusiasm for the outdoors.
>
> *(Stevenson 1977: 42–3; Amato 2004: 205, 215–7)*

In addition to the mass hikes of the Ramblers Association (formed nationally in the early 1930s), there was the growth of 'inexpensive escapism' of nudism, sunbathing, cycling clubs (e.g. Clarion), and 'keep fit' organisations, including the 'Women's League for Health and Beauty, which had 166,000 members by 1939' and 'did much to popularize the new cult' (Stevenson 1977: 42–3; Amato 2004: 205; see Graves and Hodge 1994). There were also 'codes' and 'guidance' on the 'correct' way of walking (manners, dress, posture, gait) by groups, reformers, and professions (Amato 2004: 217). Of course, many individuals, such as Laurie Lee and Patrick Leigh Fermor, were venturing on foot much further than a local hike in the 1920s–30s, and even guides on the practicalities of how to take part in the 'art' of long-distance 'tramping' appeared (Lee 1971; Fermor 2014; Graham 1927).

The 'respondents' in a walking interview may not have had the freedom previously to walk with comparatively little restriction (in time and place) for health and leisure. Their movement may have been circumscribed by personal resources, laws and authorities, family commitments, or physical and mental difficulties; their current walk may well be affected by experiences of their previous necessity to walk from danger and oppression, or merely by memories of their routine walks (in home street, shopping area, etc.) undertaken in their past life in their country of origin.

Pilgrimage

'Religious' walks can have a number of forms across major faiths – including outdoor processions to mark central figures (e.g., Christian Saints' Days) or within religious services (in wedding rituals, funerals). A pilgrimage may be undertaken for a number of religious reasons – to affirm faith, give penance, seek a cure or express gratitude for return to health, to discover a new path in life, as a duty, to visit a significant holy site – famously in Christianity, pilgrimages are undertaken to Rome, Santiago de Compostela, Lourdes, or (in the UK) to Canterbury, Bury St Edmunds, and Winchester. Historically, the walking pilgrim's appearance gained a degree of a symbolism (e.g., a staff, a pouch) (Amato 2004: 51–5). There are religious notions associated with pilgrimage, such as 'conversion', 'seeing the light' (an 'epiphany') on a journey (e.g., St. Paul), or the idea of 'walking with God'. The act of walking within religions can be said to have a 'spirituality' – as a lone contemplative exercise, say, of renewal or on 'life' (on fate, chance, direction, fulfilment, will, and choice, etc.), or (again) as a sharing experience with someone – their pain, thoughts, as a 'friendly companion', helping them on their way as someone to 'lean on'. The term 'pilgrimage' has also become used in more secular ways as a personal journey – perhaps returning to one's origins, experiencing a 'turning point', a 'fork in the road' in life. It can mean an adventure, a tour, or an odyssey to a special place, to give your respects (to a national monument, family grave, historic battlefield), to pay homage, display a 'devotion' to an activity. In both religious and non-religious meanings, 'pilgrimage' can also be used to denote metaphorically life as a whole – a 'progress' (cf. Bunyan) through life's challenges towards its (final) resolution, or even a devotion to helping someone else on 'life's journey'.

For Gros, a 'pilgrimage' is an important cultural activity, rather than a lone or desultory wandering, he says it has rules, aims and end point (Gros 2015: 107). Interestingly he adds that there is a utopian 'presence' or mythic elements and 'regeneration' at the base of pilgrimage (Gros 2015: 121). While the medieval Christian pilgrim followed penitence and devotion, contemporary millenarian movements were anticipating imminent salvation and a new order (with later echoes, some have argued, in 20th century secular political ideologies: see Cohn 2004). In a religious pilgrimage, we are usually retracing our own, or a given path, across a landscape and town in the 'steps' of many others often centuries ago – following previous accounts and set rituals. Solnit says the distinctive 'repetition' and 'imitation' of the pilgrimage creates something 'deep' – a 'spatial' and 'spiritual theatre'; in moving through the 'same space', we have the 'same thoughts', 'becoming the same person' (Solnit 2014: 68). Horvath and Szakolczai's (2018) book on walking discusses four pilgrimages they have completed and their experience is that walking is a 'liminal in-between condition, implying a contact with the void' and aims 'to regain what was lost' (Horvath and Szakolczai 2018: 173). Walking, for them 'secures a balance literally in-between extended time and unlimited space' and part of the process is to 'get an apprehension of reality' beyond utilitarianism, use value and 'freed from exchangeability' and 'to become real again' (Horvath and Szakolczai 2018: 181).

The pilgrimage is closely associated with storytelling – a pilgrimage story may vary in forms of genre, in narrative incidents and personal commentary, and in number of tellers (cf. Chaucer's *The Canterbury Tales*). We can follow the route taken by the pilgrim's account and its happenings, how the particular teller formed their own account of the well-trodden path, within the group narratives of previous tellers – as it unfolded (Solnit 2014: 71–2). In a sense, the pilgrimage as described in prose, poetry, pictures, is not simply a journey, or a metaphor for life: it is a life itself in 'miniature' – which leads to the thought of the correspondence between walking interview research and the pilgrimage, in sharing life's narration in time and through space.

Transgression – Trespass and marching

The idea of walking as 'transgressive' immediately brings to mind popular phrases such as a 'walk on the wild side' or, simply, to cross a 'boundary', to 'trespass' by breaking a restriction to entering property, or a moral code. It also may be associated with a symbolic walk (for civil or social rights) which may be legal or illegal – perhaps a commemoration of an earlier such walk, or as metaphor for a life struggle, such as a 'freedom walk'. A transgressive walk can also be in a sense, a 'micro politics', such as crossing in the road in the wrong place or when the 'green figure' on the crossing post does not show (which could bring a fine), as a minor statement of non-conformism, as not obeying the official behaviour of the street as laid out by authorities. In this way, a walk may be a 'mini rebellion', a small everyday resistance by taking your own direction and making your own 'walking narrative', perhaps sometimes a symbol of a broader personal detachment from dominant social mores and rules. For Field, artists can show how the anonymity of the urban space can be made to give a new approach to 'being' in daily life by walking as a new experience or perspective of surroundings: as a freedom to change the city into a playground or maze, by marking its surfaces, or politically and collectively through theatre as parade, or protest (Field 2009). There are overlaps, here, between art and transgression – 'the art of protest' – in 'kit' or accoutrements and rituals: protest marches can have banners, badges, pins, slogans, masks (of politicians, heroes etc.), T-shirts, particular songs, band tunes, and chants on heroes, villains, and causes. These walks have a choreography, are time-judged and 'street planned' according to traditional routes and anniversaries etc., perhaps providing a street theatre, a processional pattern, or defiant carnivalesque atmosphere (see Comino-James 2017). 'Marches' and 'processions' may also be employed by artists choreographing their own events or engaged in existing ones to support protests, celebrations, commemoration etc. with 'performers' who may be local people (Evans 2012: 63–91). Of course, there are also official restrictions on the right to march and of protest (when, where, how) and forms that are denied in law or in practice.

To walk can be an 'exercise' in rights and democracy, a collective effort, a unifying statement that 'we are here', as an established 'fact', occupying public spaces and avenues – inverting, resisting, attempting to overturn dominant stereotypes and assumptions, seeking to have a presence recognised by others and to create different modes of life and identities to those given through domination and marginalisation (see Chapters 6, 7). We should not overlook, however, that a march may be against what many or most see as undemocratic cause, or in support of some 'unprogressive' change: as against equality for certain groups and for the 'rights' of another, against what is regarded (by some at least) as immoral or irreligious, in favour of existing hierarchies, vested interests, or for the return of a former 'regime', or to commemorate a 'reactionary' past. Thus, 'transgressive' walks – protest marches and processions – can take in many forms in symbolism and action, and for many disparate 'causes': in a sense, each example is different, existing in a certain context and time with its particular 'membership', organisation, 'collective culture' and effect, and degree of 'transgression'. A walk may be a 'symbolic stance', a 'moving vigil', an act of social solidarity, as against a colonial power, a march allied to armed insurgency, a mass disruption with religious fervour, to extend or protect civil/political rights (voting, antidiscrimination), a call to curb activities of certain groups, against wars and armaments, to demand or safeguard jobs, against impending legislation, for animal rights, to defend existing traditions, etc., commemoration of a victory, a past religious event, a trespass, an industrial walkout, a walk to call for liberation.

To transgress is to be 'against' what we see as the 'given routine' – the socially accepted mores, dominant institutional values, or cultural identity, or to the political 'status quo': it can be a 'stepping aside or outside' – rather than a 'frontal' physical, verbal, or other assault, a subversion which can appear superficially conformist (even 'over-conforming'), a quiet non-acceptance, a peaceful process, in a written or other form of opposition, or merely a 'revolution' within the mind. So, the means of actual 'non-acceptance' are varied, the tactics and strategies can be complex and creative, from confrontation to a daily micro-resistance – as found against totalitarian regimes and foreign occupations: a 'guerrilla warfare' traversing through petty non-compliance in 'ordinary' everyday life to an outright physical challenge.

Trespass

The 'mania' for healthy walking in the 1930s (and other outdoor pursuits) had more 'political' correlates during the period. Marches (cf. May Day) and parades (from the 19th century) in protest, to make rights and allegiances visible within the 'nation' (Amato 2004: 209), were not merely made on the street, but also in the countryside. When large numbers of walkers, often working class and unemployed, left northern UK cities for the hills at weekends, there were great areas of open countryside not accessible to them for 'rambling'. Many walkers saw their activity as set against the historical injustice of wealthy landowners who should not have the sole right to use the land for their hunting or other pursuits. In 1932, several hundred walkers from Manchester and elsewhere (e.g., Sheffield) engaged in a mass trespass on Kinder Scout, an area of high, open moor in the Peak District. Their objective was to gain the right of access for walkers to areas of countryside denied to the public (Beer and Lennon 2019). The police, local press, and landowners were made aware of the protest walk, and so the walkers were met on the moor. The walkers' leader, Benny Rothman, and several others were arrested for trespass, and some were jailed for several months. The severity of the punishment gave impetus to further protest and campaigns to 'open up' the countryside. Eventually (post-World War II), national parks were established: The Peak National Park came into being in 1951, and was followed by nine others. The long distance (over 260 miles) Pennine Way (suggested in 1935) was completed in 1965, and other national trails established, such as the South West Coast path (630 miles) created in 1978 (see Armitage 2012; Armitage 2015).

There is debate on the degree of effectiveness of the 'direct action' on Kinder Scout in 1932; there had been ramblers and cycling clubs from the early years of the century, and previous attempts during the 19th century to enact the right to roam and protect public pathways (Hey 2011; Taylor 1997). The right to open country and common land was established by the Countryside and Rights of Way Act 2000 and implemented in 2005 in England with the public access across mapped spaces on moorland, mountain, and lower areas amounting to nearly 900,000 hectares. In Scotland, similar attempts were made in the 19th century and early 20th century to extend the right of access. During the interwar period, as in England, a range of working class climbing and other clubs were formed to pursue countryside activities; access to land was introduced with the Land Reform (Scotland) Act 2003.

The extension of 'right to roam' can be set within the centuries-long history of restrictions on social movement and growth in property legislation. Where a person can walk in accessing rural and urban spaces (today and historically) has been covered by a mesh of regulation (customary practice, local byelaws, and civil and criminal law). Such regulations are intimately related to the formation of social and civic life, including demotic rights and participation. For example, historically, vagrancy legislation in the UK and elsewhere was concerned with the control of populations 'tramping' around the country – as part of the regulation of unrest, controlling labour market supply and wages, and curbing dissent, crime, and disruption of trade – and possible conflict (cf. 'roaming gangs'), particularly at times of economic disruption and political instability (Amato 2004: 68–9; Marx 1976: 873–913). In the 19th century, workers' autobiographies indicate that 'tramping' (including migration abroad) for work – geographical and occupational mobility – was much more common than has often been assumed (Burnett 1977: 16). Regulation of those in, or seeking, work, and the vagrant, criminal, and destitute, took 'evolving' historical, legal, and institutional forms. The Vagrancy Act 1824, for instance, was concerned, in part, with regulation of the street to keep 'suspected persons' away from areas of trade and warehousing, and prevent prostitution and display of 'obscene' pictures. It came at a time of mass migration from Ireland and Scotland and large numbers of unemployed ex-military. The Act was immediately before the Metropolitan Police Act 1829, which placed the 'overseeing' of the street in London onto a 'modern professional' basis, and the new 'work-housing' of the destitute by the Poor Law 1834.

The access to land has been something of a persistent 'low level class war' stemming back for hundreds of years as wider land use was restricted by, for instance, the Norman Conquest which brought the dispossession of land by carving out tracts for hunting. The curtailment of common rights to wood, grazing, etc., and access to local paths can be seen in the long-running implementation of 'Enclosure Acts' and the Scottish Highland Clearances of the late 18th to early 19th century, leading to movement to the towns and mass emigration. The access and use of space are dependent on centuries of contestation, played out daily at a local level:

> in a class society, based on the needs of capital and the protection of private property, the poor and propertyless are *always* in some sense on 'the wrong side of the law', whether actually they transgress it or not ... We can see this clearly ... in the eighteenth century ... in the long, deep and protracted struggle, in progress throughout the century, between customary rights and traditions, and the encroaching bourgeois notions of property and law. The crimes of the forest were only one episode in the longer story of the 'remaking' of English life and society in its bourgeois form – a process which often depended rather more on the selective use of terror and force than on more 'civilising' influences.
>
> *(Hall et al. 2013: 190–1; see Thompson 1977)*

In fact, the Waltham Black Act of 1723 brought in fifty new capital offences covering tree damage, poaching, and other activity; by the end of the century, there were around two hundred such penalties (Potter 2015: Ch. 20).

It can be argued that 'walking' is imbued with a demotic impulse, as sharing or access to land is a challenge to exclusive property ownership, just as in a wider sense, those groups whose lives do not recognise the hard lines marking national sovereignty, may make physical demarcations more porous (Solnit 2014: 162).

However, by the mid-19th century, groups were being formed to protect footpaths and open spaces and challenge landowners. 'Walking' in the 19th century must also be placed in a contrasting cultural context of widening of social access to urban parks, botanical rambling and study, the influence of religious, commercial, and other ideas on the need for public recreation: 'walking' became an expression of both conservative and radicals' notions of 'Englishness' in identifying with the countryside (see Bryant et al. 2016b: 24; Taylor 1997). Today, issues surrounding the public access or openness to land – in the countryside, but also increasingly in the city – remain very important: for example, the surveillance and control of public spaces; the privatisation of publicly owned land (e.g., playing fields) and buildings (and renting 'back' for profit); limitations on access to spaces (e.g., due to payment); control of 'loitering', drinking in public, protest, and other activities; and use of private security firms (employed by individuals, corporations and public institutions) in overseeing shopping malls, urban spaces, private office and housing developments, etc., raise vital questions of democratic rights, social equality, and citizenship. The campaigns for access to the countryside in the 1930s in the Peak District and earlier 19th century struggles for access remain relevant; for instance, the concern today about the privatisation of public spaces involves its impact on civic and political interaction, as (it is argued) the 'participatory citizen' is being 'replaced' by the individualised consumer. Here, there are concerns for the defence of the rights to peaceful protest, issues of official surveillance and restriction, upholding legal rights such as to take photographs in public, issues on public dress, and so on. There is the further concern to resist forms of social 'segregation' – the official or other public assumptions that certain groups of people should not be walking in particular places or at certain times, and thereby defining who are 'allowed' on the streets. Women have marched to assert that they should be free to walk the streets when they wish without violence, fear, and hindrance or discouragement (cf. 'Reclaim [or Take back] the Night' walk campaigns, and see also Gay Pride marches, early 1970s onwards).

Concern for the countryside, including the loss of wildlife and open land, and threats due to the effects of pollution, commercial, and public exploitation, and climate change has led to renewed activism (e.g., on access, habitat protection, road development) during the last 30 years. Many groups, including artists, have taken up issues involving the countryside, for instance, photographer and activist Fay Godwin (some years ago) produced powerful images of the 'forbidden' landscape supported by works by well-known poets (Godwin 1990).

Marching

Alongside the hiking and rambling of the 1930s, there was another form of mass walking by working class people – local and national 'hunger marches' by the unemployed. These marches were protests to make visible the plight of unemployed industrial workers – in 'depressed' or 'distressed' areas – to government and the wider population, to give the 'social reportage' and official reports on the social conditions of neglected areas walking 'flesh and blood' (Stevenson 1977: 58; see Cole and Cole 1937; Orwell 1989). Hunger marches and protests by the unemployed and trade unions had a deeper origin; for instance, in South Wales, a tradition of communal action can perhaps be traced to the early 19th century 'Scotch Cattle' raiding parties of coalminers, rural 'Rebecca' rioters against road tolls, and Chartist demonstrations, including the march of the 'Newport Rising' (1839) (which led to around twenty marchers being shot dead and three leaders transported) and, of course, to emerging trade union struggles, through to the Great Pilgrimage (1913) for women's suffrage (Robinson 2018) and the General Strike (1926) (Francis 1984: 61–2; Francis and Smith 1980; Jones 1986; Beer and Lennon 2019). We should also note here the wider contemporary political international context of 'marching' in the 1930s: 'bread queues', hunger protests, workers' rights demonstrations, and anti-colonial struggles abroad (cf. Gandhi's significant march of civil disobedience in India, 1930).

Hunger marches (and demonstrations) in Britain by the unemployed took place from the early 1920s, and could be said to have had 'strong military overtones' in organisation to maintain discipline (Francis 1984: 62; Kingsford 1982: 182). During the early 1930s, the National Unemployed Workers' Movement was formed under the leadership of Wal Hannington to campaign for Public Assistance Committees to raise their rates for unemployed workers suffering greatly at the height of the Depression (Hannington 1937; Hannington 1940; see also Cohen 1937). The marches were met with hostility from the TUC and the Labour Party. The Hunger Marches gave a break from the daily boredom and desperation of unemployment, a feeling of togetherness, an intent to show the wider public the plight of the unemployed and their communities, and for many also an outlet for a belief in radical societal change. Local protests during the 1930s were opposed by the authorities, who declared fears of a 'red rabble' and outbreak of violence (Branson and Heinemann 1973: 36–7). A notable National Hunger March and petition was organised in 1932, with large groups of unemployed from across the country converging on London, gaining material and emotional support from towns as they went. Despite the authorities' hostility to the march, a very large crowd welcomed them in Hyde Park in London. Even so, violence erupted, with mounted police charges, and the leaders of the NUWM were arrested (Branson and Heinemann 1973: 39).

While the economy recovered in the early 1930s, long-term unemployment persisted in areas of basic industries, such as in coal valleys in South Wales, and campaigns continued for higher levels of relief (see Evans 1999). A further national march was planned for 1934. However, this time while there was opposition from the authorities, the action of the police at the end of the march was rather different (Kingsford 1982: 167–99). Earlier, to monitor the policing of the march, a Council for Civil Liberties (now *Liberty*) had been formed by lawyers and others. Shortly after its end, the Government restored benefits to former levels, although payment issues remained and demonstration marches continued, as in South Wales where a large march to a public assistance office in 1935 resulted in the jailing of unemployed men after the 'Blaina Riot' (Branson and Heinemann 1973: 40–5; Evans 1999; Francis 1984: 70–2; Hannington 1940: 120–47; Kingsford 1982: 197).

The most well-known march against unemployment – the Jarrow March – took place in 1936 when about 200 men along with local MP Ellen Wilkinson (author of *The Town that was Murdered*, 1939) walked to London from North-East England following the closure of the shipyard in Jarrow. The march did not appear to have a great deal of effect at first, but began to take on 'iconic' status within the Labour movement; for instance, in 1986 on its fiftieth anniversary (and again at a time of high unemployment), the march was re-enacted. It continues to serve as a direct inspiration for a range of current campaigns, including marches on the future of NHS and other social issues, and walking its route is a source of observation on parallels with contemporary Britain (Maconie 2017). What, unfortunately, has received insufficient attention has been the role (although often restricted) of women on the hunger marches, women's suffrage marches, the number of marches by organised blind workers who pioneered this kind of protest, and also marches by war veterans during the inter-war period (see Reiss 2005; Reiss 2007; Reiss and Perry 2011).

A well-known workers' march in the UK, part of the Durham Miners' Gala (UK), which is over 130 years old, has former miners and trade unionists walking with their bands and banners. They assemble in a large crowd and are addressed by local and national leaders (including leading national Labour politicians). The gala is a celebration of labour rights and trade unionism, as well as a memorial to the mining industry – a display of community and social solidarity. O'Neill (in collaboration with artists) has documented these gatherings and the reasons that people give for taking part – in terms of tradition, the solidarity and experience of past industrial and communal struggle of mining, family history, and the fight for social justice.[1]

A protest has its individual experience within that of the wider group, and may also be a singular entity, one person walking to make their point – towards a police line at a demonstration, or in defiance against an armoured vehicle suppressing street activities, with possible dire consequences for the protestor. In addition, we can say we can have 'transgressive imaginations', or commit 'transgressions' merely in the mind when walking, and do not act upon them, or at least do not translate them into full realisation in action.

Escape and identity formation

Walking may act as a form of 'escape' and could be described as occurring when the prime focus is an 'exercise' in *identity formation* – it can have both 're-formative' and 'transgressive' aspects. As Cohen and Taylor (1971) argue, we attempt to find various avenues of 'escape' in daily life when we are feeling dissatisfied with our 'routines' and 'scripts'. Thus, to enable 'fantasies' and escape from 'boredom', we briefly leave 'paramount reality', although society keenly regulates these 'free areas, escape routes and identity sites'. In 'activity enclaves', such as hobbies, sex, and sports, people find 'self-expression and identity work', or internal 'new landscapes' of adventures and holidays, or in 'mindscapes' of drugs or therapies (Cohen and Taylor 1971: 94–5; 97). However, some 'extreme escapers' attempt to go 'over the wall', spreading out in time and space their spare time activities that become central to their life (Cohen and Taylor 1971: 175). So, for instance, the next 'holiday' becomes a dominant preoccupation, 'summer clothes' are worn through the winter, the holiday tan is artificially 'topped up', a more extended trip is planned and dreamed about, or holiday home bought, etc. all to 'prolong' the holiday 'feel', 'look', and 'values' of leisure, 'holidaying' becomes a 'life-style'. The 'mundane escape' of the passing fantasy, the weekend hobby or rented cottage, the two-week holiday, may take a more central defining aspect – extended in time and/or space, in a process of 'becoming' 'who we really are'.

Walking can also involve our various selves, secret selves, 'enclaves' in which we regard our 'inner self' (selves) as a separate arena of self-expression. The formation of the self and walking can be intimately connected – the activity may confirm the self (as physically and mentally 'alive'), as an expression of the self (an 'extension' of self); provide an escape for the self (from the rigours of the mundane); can be a search for the self (a period of inner reflection); or for a new or renewed self (an attempt to 'find' the self); or walking back to our selves. It may also become a 'drift' or aimlessness, a shifting and loss of 'centredness'. Walking may also be an 'adventure' (cf. Simmel 1998; Lyman and Scott 1984) – not merely to walk through the unfamiliar city area, countryside, wild place, or to see new sights, but also an inner movement outwards, to 'de-familiarise' what has previously been experienced, to look afresh at, or to actively place the personal past in a new wider socio-cultural interpretation.

In this way, we can say, a religious pilgrimage to a shrine and secular journey to a particular site, or protest activism may be psychically extended, and become a central activity for identity and self, more a life-long *quest* (cf. Horvath and Szakolczai 2018). Some forms of walking may also be considered at least in part, to be expressions of *wider* social attempts to give life meaning, via group allegiances, as responses to societal shifts in social solidarity, migration, and 'mobilities', etc. (see Chapter 2); here, immediate motivations having deeper socio-cultural 'springs to action'. For Klapp, writing in the late 1960s, fashions, fads, cults, recreation, and celebrity and hero worship were part of 'collective search for identity' through new symbols (Klapp 1969: vii). He argued that 'mass society' eroded individuals of meaning, while 'social mobility' destabilises relationships. People, he argued (writing prior to the advent of social media) with 'hundreds of friends' find they do not really know them and 'reference points' or 'identifying rituals' are insufficient: it is unclear when someone is being 'true' and 'sincere' or merely 'posing' (Klapp 1969: 29–35). As Park earlier described (in 1925), in the city, the 'more intimate' long-lasting associations of the 'smaller community' are replaced; people live together, but do not know each other, thus relations are 'fortuitous and casual': an 'individual's status is determined' by 'conventional signs – by fashion and "front"– and the art of life is largely reduced to skating on thin surfaces and a scrupulous study of style and manners' (Park 2005: 31; cf. Goffman 1971: 32–40, 109–40). Whether 'walking' is such a 'collective search for identity' in these terms can be debated, but as in the 1930s, there is a broad 'social movement' associated with walking which encompasses health, fitness, exploration, and the appreciation of the countryside and 'discovery' of wilder places, and which also involves differing (often high) levels and kinds of motivation, and processes self and identity formation.

Walking can also be regarded as 'performance' – a routine in the sense that we 'perform' each day (and we 'prepare', by deciding on clothes to wear, etc., and 'rehearsing' what we are about to do) – an 'everyday promenade'. We are broadly aware of expected social courtesies or etiquette in conversation, social conventions relating to situations, and social obligations. We are aware of body imagery, movement, and our own 'projections' on how others and situations are to be perceived. The glamour and styles of magazine fashion pages reveal what is 'on trend' (or not), the 'health and fitness' magazines give examples of body imagery regimes, the 'make up' and body perfume industry, tanning and nail salons, clothing advertisements and fashion blogs, and the 'health, fitness and diet industry' with their advertisements and recommendations all provide 'constructions' of what image (according to gender, age, etc.) to project and 'how to be' – to look better, feel better, as someone who 'cares' for themselves and for what others assess. Of course, some walks are 'full-scale' 'performances' in the sense that they are particular forms undertaken in a certain manner – as in the 'rituals', for example, of the fashion 'catwalk', a politician taking the election stage, or in the choreography, costumes, effigies or sacred figures, chants or songs of religious or other processions.

There is a degree to which we all wish to 'project' autobiographical statements about ourselves (an 'identity construction') by the way we dress and walk – our 'bearing', how we 'act', 'present' ourselves to others (and our self) – and, in return, 'read' the demeanour and gestures of others as in walking (by no means entirely accurately) (see Goffman 1972; Roberts 2006: 73–5; Roberts 2008). At times, we are more self-consciously aware of the 'performative' nature of walking – as walking 'down the aisle' at a wedding, as a pall bearer at a funeral, receiving a scroll on a degree ceremony stage, etc. which we rehearse in our minds, logistically and emotionally, beforehand and have a 'template' having witnessed others in the role. In the performance of walking, there is a process between how we are shaping both our 'inner' sense of self, and how we 'present' ourselves. 'Walking' as a pursuit can become a central 'performance', not simply an associative wearing of walking clothes and shoes (boots) as a 'practical' everyday 'fashion', but as part of a 'dominant' identity: in terms of specialist clothes, 'kit', skills, and planning, for the coast-to-coast tramping, immersion in wilderness trails or exploration, long-distance charity challenges, etc. These activities may be fuelled by a 'need' to be 'doing' something different, making a 'contribution', 'seeking freedom' or a new life: the 'performance' of the walker becomes part of a self-reorganisation, to being an outdoors exercise enthusiast, one who appreciates scenery, an explorer of the 'wild', a 'Walker'.

Walking may be implicated in identity formation in a number of ways. This may vary from walking as a pastime (like a hobby or other leisure time activity), but becoming (as above) more important than work (or other major status), and even may replace it, as walking may become the main focus in retirement, or turn into an occupation itself (e.g., an interest in hiking may lead to a holiday guide business). Forms of walking may become 'central' to identity in self-definition as a hiker, activist, or traveller in defining oneself to others. Walking can also be identity-forming by 'pulling together' symbols and signals – routine meanings given to place are important: a park, a shop, the street, can be symbolic markers giving feelings of 'home' or 'belonging', walking out in the countryside or trek may become part of such attachment. Walking provides the opportunity to 'make sense' of our surroundings and our position within it; we can be said to have layers or a succession of created boundaries of the immediate, routine settings and relationships which give nearest attachments of the street, through to the locality, the town or city, region and nation. These immediate, local, regional, national and other 'identities' overlap and interpenetrate in a series of boundaries that shift according to time, setting, and usage. Walking in a location stirs memories of the place as visited on previous occasions, or similar places, and the feelings and events experienced. We may even revisit and re-walk a location to 're-live' what went before, and to assess those memories and associated emotions, and judge what has changed in the social environment – and in 'who we are' (see Chapter 10). For the study of biographical narrative-making, here there is a concern for how identity formation takes place – how we construct 'coherent', but adaptive personal accounts within the circumstances of multiple social mobilities across time and place.

Walking can be part of the daily 'identifying rituals' through which we can place and form 'ourselves' – our routines, such as visiting local cafés, shopping, appointments at health practices, friends we meet, etc., within the shifts in the social composition, and technological and environmental changes that are (and we recognise) taking place. The repeated, longer acts of walking may reflect or become a central, deep, facet of identity, for example, Dickens's compulsion to walk may have been a physical release to prevent (for him) the peril of spiritual stasis on the one hand, while on the other, to calm the disturbances of excess of thought by immersion in activity – in the long walk from London to home, or in the night-time exploration of the city itself (see Frank 1984). In short, in Dickens, to walk was to 'be', to exist, but also to attempt to 'control' the demands of the psyche, to 'know' through 'walking his autobiography', his personal 'route'.

Our 'mental mapping' of daily life is a constituent of routine narrative and identity formation; it provides for degrees of social 'anchorage'. However, such identity formation is not unproblematic; routine walking observation is a more complex phenomenon than it appears: in what we notice and select, we rarely examine how we 'look', 'view', 'gaze', and how we more broadly 'sense', apprehend, and interpret. Indeed, we do not reflect much on the experiences of our less common walking, for which we may have planned in detail, such as a paid holiday 'sightseeing'. In fact, we can say that 'sightseeing' overlaps with other forms of social vision (and sensual–emotional experience); 'sights' are socially constructed (socially planned) for various effects, can have or be meant to have resonances from previous periods, stimulating types of 'desirability' for what they are or contain, project 'power' or accessibility, and so on. Even so, while the 'objects' of 'sightseeing' are a large degree often 'constructed' (e.g., we are given expectations of holiday 'sights' from our knowledge of them through the media) and 'consumed', it has the possibilities for the creation of meanings not intended, for subversion, and recasting – and resistance. Travel and sightseeing can be both affirming of expectations and for creating new attachments and identities (see MacCannell 2013; Urry and Larsen 2011).

'To walk' can be an expression of 'being alive' to a wider range of sensual, physical, and emotional experiences in movement; for some it is a transition from a 'stagnation', as active – it brings new sights and sounds, which require interpretation and integration, bringing possibilities for the renewal of identity, and for the self in performance and narrative.

Re-formation, transgression, and escape and identity formation

In summary, there are then many 'forms' of walking which could be described. Here, the concentration has been on 're-formation' and 'transgressive imaginations': indicating those that seek a 'renewal' physically and mentally; the act of walking as a symbol, a statement, to challenge social mores, legal prescriptions, the existing order, by individual or group activism; or attempts by individuals to 're-create' themselves by a 'step 'outside' the set boundaries of the routine world to achieve a 'new freedom' and 'escape'. Walking can be undertaken and experienced for a number of motivations and range in forms that can include health, pilgrimage, and forms of protest.

Repetition of a walk (or one similar) requires us going over 'old ground', memories of 'incidental moments', the inconsequential and the important, the happy times and the disappointments. The Walking Interview as a Biographical Method (WIBM) is participatory, but a walk could be solitary, perhaps even recorded by the respondent and interviewed by the researcher later with the recording, or both could repeat the walk. For the WIBM, a research walk may be a 're-tracing' of steps with an individual: a person's health regime, a pilgrim's journey, a campaigner's protest, or a person's self-realising, 'liberating' wander. Walking, in fact, is involved in routine identity formation and may become a central facet of how an individual portrays the self and how they wish to be regarded.

Note

1 See Maggie O'Neill's blog of walking biographical interviews found at: at www.walkingborders.com (accessed 22 September 2018).

References

Amato, J. A. (2004) *On Foot: A History of Walking*. New York: New York University Press.
Armitage, S. (2012) *Walking Home*. London: Faber & Faber.
Armitage, S. (2015) *Walking Away*. London: Faber & Faber.
Baxter, S. (2016) *A History of the World in 500 Walks*. San Diego, CA: Thunder Bay.

Beer, H. and Lennon, R. (2019) People's landscapes, *National Trust Magazine*, Spring, pp. 28–29.

Benjamin, W. (2002) *The Arcades Project* (Tr. H. Eiland and K. McLaughlin). Cambridge, MA: Belknap Press of Harvard University Press.

Branson, N. and Heinemann, M. (1973) *Britain in the Nineteen Thirties*. Frogmore, St. Albans: Panther.

Bryant, C., Burns, A., and Readman, P. (2016a) Introduction: Modern walks. In: C. Bryant, A. Burns, and P. Readman (eds.) *Walking Histories, 1800–1914*. Basingstoke, UK: Palgrave Macmillan.

Bryant, C., Burns, A. and Readman, P. (eds.) (2016b) *Walking Histories, 1800–1914*. Basingstoke, UK: Palgrave Macmillan.

Burnett, J. (1977) *Useful Toil*. Harmondsworth, UK: Penguin.

Cohen, P. (1937) *Unemployment Insurance and Assistance in Britain*. London: George G. Harrap.

Cohen, S. and Taylor, L. (1971) *Escape Attempts*. Harmondsworth, UK: Penguin.

Cohn, N. (2004) *The Pursuit of the Millennium*. London: Pimlico.

Cole, G. D. H. and Cole, M. I. (1937) *The Condition of Britain*. London: Victor Gollancz.

Comino-James, J. (2017) *Shout It Loud, Shout It Clear*. Stockport, UK: Dewi Publishing.

Crane, N. (2008) *Great British Journeys*. London: Weidenfeld & Nicolson.

Cross, G. (ed.) (1990) *Worktowners at Blackpool: Mass-Observation and Popular Leisure in the 1930s*. London: Routledge.

Dodd, P. (1982) *The Art of Travel: Essays on Travel Writing*. London: Frank Cass.

Evans, D. (ed.) (2012) *The Art of Walking: A Field Guide*. London: Black Dog Publishing.

Evans, N. (1999) 'South Wales has been roused as never before': Marching against the means test, 1934-36. In: D. W. Howell, and K. O. Morgan (eds.) *Crime, Protest and Police in Modern British Society*. Cardiff: University of Wales Press.

Fermor, P. L. (2014) *The Broken Road*. London: John Murray.

Field, A. (2009) Promenade shows must step up and put the joy back into walking, *The Guardian*, 26 March 2009 (Theatre: Theatre blog), https://www.guardian.com.stage /theatre.blog/2009/mar/26/promenade-shows-walking (Accesssed 30 May 2019).

Francis, H. (1984) *Miners against Fascism*. London: Lawrence and Wishart.

Francis, H. and Smith, D. (1980) *The Fed: A History of the South Wales Miners in the Twentieth Century*. London: Lawrence and Wishart.

Frank, L. (1984) *Charles Dickens and the Romantic Self*. Lincoln, NE: University of Nebraska Press.

Gerth, H. and Mills, C. W. (1954) *Character and Social Structure*. London: Routledge and Kegan Paul.

Godwin, F. (1990) *Our Forbidden Land*. London: Jonathan Cape.

Goffman, E. (1971) *The Presentation of Self in Everyday Life*. Harmondsworth, UK: Penguin.

Goffman, E. (1972) *Interaction Ritual*. Harmondsworth, UK: Penguin.

Graham, S. (1927) *The Gentle Art of Tramping*. London: Robert Holden.

Graves, R. and Hodge, A. (1994) *The Long Weekend, 1918–1939*. London: W. W. Norton and Co.

Gros, F. (2015) *The Philosophy of Walking*. London: Verso.

Hall, S., Critcher, C., Jefferson, T., Clarke, J. and Roberts, B. (2013) *Policing the Crisis*, 2nd edn. Basingstoke, UK: Palgrave Macmillan.

Hannington, W. (1937) *The Problem of the Distressed Areas*. London: Victor Gollancz.

Hannington, W. (1940) *Ten Lean Years*. London: Victor Gollancz.

Hazan, E. (2018) *A Walk through Paris*. London: Verso.

Hey, D. (2011) Kinder Scout and the legend of the mass trespass, *Agricultural History Review*, 59(II): 199–216.

Horvath, A. and Szakolczai, A. (2018) *Walking into the Void: A Historical Sociology and Political Anthropology of Walking*. London: Routledge.

Jones, D. J. V. (1986) *The Last Rising: The Newport Insurrection of 1839*. Oxford: Clarendon Press.

Kingsford, P. (1982) *The Hunger Marchers in Britain, 1920–1940*. London: Lawrence and Wishart.

Klapp, O. E. (1969) *The Collective Search for Identity*. New York: Holt, Rinehart and Winston.

Lay, K. (2017) Walk the walk for better meetings, say health chiefs, *The Times*, 12 September 2017, p.3.

Lee, L. (1971) *As I Walked Out One Midsummer Morning*. London: Penguin.

Lyman, S. and Scott, M. (1984) Adventures. In: J. Douglas (ed.) *The Sociology of Deviance*. Boston, MA: Allyn and Bacon.

MacCannell, D. (2013) *The Tourist: A New Theory of the Leisure Class*, rev. edn. Berkeley, CA: University of California Press.

Maconie, S. (2017) *Long Road from Jarrow: A Journey through Britain Then and Now*. London: Ebury.

Marx, K. (1976) *Capital*, Vol. 1. Harmondsworth, UK: Penguin.

Matza, D. (1964) *Delinquency and Drift*. New York: Wiley.

Mills, C. W. (1940) Situated actions and vocabularies of motive, *American Sociological Review*, 5(6): 904–913.

Minshull, D. (ed.) (2000) *The Vintage Book of Walking: An Anthology*. New York: Vintage.

Nicholson, G. (2011) *The Lost Art of Walking*. Chelmsford, UK: Harbour Pub.

O'Neill, M. and Perivolaris, J. (2015) A sense of belonging: Walking with Thaer through migration, memories and space, *Crossings: Journal of Migration and Culture*, 5(2): 327–338.

Orwell, G. (1989) *The Road to Wigan Pier*. London: Penguin [first pub. 1937 Victor Gollancz].

Park, R. E. (2005) The city. In: K. Gelder (ed.) *The Subcultures Reader*, 2nd edn. London: Routledge.

Potter, H. (2015) *Law, Liberty and the Constitution*. Woodbridge, UK: Boydell Press.

Reiss, M. (2005) Forgotten pioneers of the national protest march: The National League of the the Blind's marches to London 1920–36, *Labour History Review*, 70(2): 133–165.

Reiss, M. (ed.) (2007) *The Street as a Stage: Protest Marches and Public Rallies Since the Nineteenth Century*. Oxford: OUP.

Reiss, M. and Perry, M. (eds.) (2011) *Unemployment and Protest: New Perspectives on Two Centuries of Contention*. Oxford: OUP.

Roberts, B. (2006) *Micro Social Theory*. Basingstoke, UK: Palgrave Macmillan.

Roberts, B. (2008) Performative social science: A consideration of skills, purpose and context [122 Paragraphs], *Forum: Qualitative Sozialforschung/Forum: Qualitative Social Research*, 9(2): Art. 58. Available at http://nbn-resolving.de/urn:de:0114-fqs0802588 (Accessed 19 April 2018).

Robinson, J. (2018) *Hearts and Minds*. London: Doubleday.

Rowlatt, B. (2016) *In Search of Mary: The Mother of All Journeys*. Richmond, UK: Alma Books.

Sillito, D. (2017) Mood swings: The man mapping Britain's emotions, *BBC NEWS*. Available at https://www.bbc.co.uk/news/uk-38788928 (Accessed 1 May 2019).

Simmel, G. (1998) The adventure. In: D. P. Frisby, and M. Featherstone (eds.) *Simmel on Culture*. London: Sage.

Smith, P. (2015) *Walking's New Movement*. Axminster, UK: Triarchy Press.

Smyth, C. (2016) Office workers told to walk an hour a day, *The Times*, 28 July 2016, p.20.

Solnit, R. (2014) *Wanderlust: A History of Walking*. London: Granta.

Somerville, C. (2017) *The January Man: A Year of Walking Britain*. London: Doubleday.

Stevenson, J. (1977) *Social Conditions in Britain between the Wars*. Harmondsworth, UK: Penguin.

Stewart, R. (2017) *The Marches: A Borderline Journey between England and Scotland*. London: Vintage.

Taylor, H. (1997) *A Claim on the Countryside: A History of the British Outdoor Movement*. Edinburgh: Edinburgh University Press.

Thompson, E. P. (1977) *Whigs and Hunters*. Harmondsworth, UK: Penguin.

Urry, J. and Larsen, J. (2011) *The Tourist Gaze 3.0*. London: Sage.

Wilkinson, E. (1939) *The Town that was Murdered*. London: Victor Gollanc.

6

WALKING IN THE DOWNTOWN EASTSIDE

Experiencing the WIBM as participatory, visual, and ethnographic

This chapter takes as starting point biographical walking interviews undertaken with residents of the Downtown Eastside (DTES), a 'skid row' neighbourhood in Vancouver, Canada as part of O'Neill and Stenning's (2013) participatory action/arts research.[1] Whilst the intention, at the time, was to conduct walking interviews as part of gathering residents' living experience of community, politics, and resistance, in hindsight, this work takes on new meaning and resonance for this book in developing the Walking Interview as a Biographical Method (WIBM) as a means of sharing the *experience and application of* creative, sensory, and participatory biographical methods, and what the WIBM can contribute to community-based research.

O'Neill and Stenning (2013) found walking-based interviews to be transgressive (crossing social, physical, and emotional or psychic borders), a powerful way of communicating about lived experiences across cultural divides, and as an 'embodied resistance' to the social stigma experienced by the residents/co-walkers. During the biographical walking interviews, participants told O'Neill their stories about arriving and living in the DTES, their everyday routes and 'mobilities' (i.e., within DTES as residents, workers, as activists, artists, and in negotiating and living with poverty), the myriad of ways that they feel a sense of belonging to and interrelate with their environment. Being poor and contending with the dynamics of power, stigma, and humiliation associated with poverty within the DTES or 'skid row' emerged strongly in their narratives and walks. Residents spoke about the importance of resistance and resilience and their struggle for recognition, living in the 'depressed margins' of the city of Vancouver. Their narratives strongly resisted the 'fascination' and voyeurism 'that brings people to the DTES to look at the poor people' (O'Neill and Stenning 2013: 220).

Context: Borders – Physical, material, and relational

Using the example of O'Neill and Stenning's (2013) research, walking methods will be shown as particularly relevant, helpful, and potentially ground-breaking way of doing participatory action research with marginalised people, a method that is respectful, supports dignifying representations, and in doing so, challenges myths and stereotypes associated with being poor. The DTES is consistently described in the mainstream media as a problem community and 'Canada's poorest postal code'. It is a clearly demarcated and bounded area, specifically around eight city blocks situated between Gastown and Chinatown. As the research found, the borders of the DTES are also subjective, in that they are internalised by some of the residents who participated in the project. For one of the participants in particular, the border marking the DTES was almost impenetrable, as the stigma she experienced coming from beyond the borders of her 'community' was almost too much to bear. She stayed physically and mentally within the 'frame of reference' of her 'imagined community'; that was also a 'demos', a collective spirit of belonging and participation in 'community' forged in part in relation to the exclusionary communities beyond the DTES.

The available socio-demographic data at the time of the research (2010–11) in the DTES included a gender breakdown of the population as being 62 per cent male and 38 per cent female, with more than 50 per cent over 45 years of age, a low percentage of children and youth, and a high percentage living in single room occupancy dwellings in hostels. There was a ratio of around 50:50 Canadian-born and immigrants, and more than 10 per cent of the city's Aboriginal population lived in the DTES. Unemployment rates were high, with a large proportion living on social assistance/disability (Downtown Eastside Community Monitoring Report 2006; Pederson and Swanson 2009). The DTES has a number of homeless shelters and key organisations supporting those in need in the area, through food security projects such as the 'roving' kitchen, food drops, and soup kitchens, often organised by faith-based organisations. The key social issues reported in O'Neill and Stenning's (2013) research by the participants were poverty, stigma, mental health issues, drugs and addiction issues, crimes of poverty, sexual violence, and the impact of gentrification at the time of the 2010 Olympic Games.

The history of the DTES, in recent years, is also bound up very much with the history of violence against sex workers, particularly the crimes of Robert Pickton, and the missing and murdered women, the majority of whom are First Nation. An Annual Womens' Memorial March to honour these women has taken place every year since 1991 in response to the murder of a Coast Salish woman on Powell Street in Vancouver. Indigenous women disproportionately continue to be missing and go missing, or are murdered (see also Chapter 7).

Tourist websites warn people to take care when travelling through the DTES. O'Neill and Stenning (2013) were cautioned not to have cameras on display, as some residents react strongly to 'poverty tourism'. Yet their experience of walking around and getting to know the geography of the area, when setting up and conducting the research, was positive. People spoke to them on the street, and were interested to know why they were there and keen also to talk about the area and the issues they experienced. O'Neill and Stenning engaged in an ethnographic process of 'feeling their way' and mapped out the streets and support agencies, contacting some first by email and telephone (United We Can and PACE) and calling in to others (*Megaphone* and Enterprising Women Making Art) to share what they hoped to do and invite involvement. Stenning had worked at Simon Fraser University, knew the area and had documented the DTES in photographs in an earlier visual ethnography (O'Neill and Stenning 2013). As the principal investigator, O'Neill was based there for much of 2010–2011 and felt that the relationships she made helped to create a sense of connection to the place, individuals, and the groups she worked with. The overall aim of the research was to produce a critical recovery of the history of the DTES in collaboration with the people who live there, to tell a different story, from the inside, using participatory action research, and visual, ethnographic, and biographical methods.[2] For the development of WIBM, here the emphasis is on the ethnographic, participatory approach when applying the method in community based-research.

Walking biographies of people and place

O'Neill and Stenning (2013) wanted to get beneath the prevalent stereotypes associated with the DTES by conducting walking biographical interviews, but also to see, feel, learn, and understand more about the area from the perspectives of the people who live there. In documenting the lived experiences of those who lived in the DTES, they (O'Neill and Stenning) also realised that they were documenting a shifting 'biography of the place'.

Walks, as a way of conducting biographical research, were undertaken with community members as 'co-researchers' (who were residents in DTES) and some carried out walking based interviews with each other. 'Community co-researchers' are both the project co-ordinators/workers and residents helped by each organisation – United We Can (binners and bottle collectors), PACE (former and current sex workers), *Megaphone* (street newspaper vendors), Enterprising Women Making Art (EWMA) affiliated to Atira women's housing (women artisans, some who were living in housing supported by Atira), and AHA Media (a group of citizen journalists and social media consultants) – and formed the research team.

The project produced a collaborative research report, an exhibition of photographic and digital stories, as well as a 'dialogue day' hosted by Langara College at Simon Fraser University's DTES campus. The dialogue day offered an open invitation for residents, staff, and students to attend the event, learn about the research findings, and take part in 'dialogue groups' led by the core research team of community co-researchers. The research was documented through photographs and sound files. A video made by AHA Media and an exhibition, curated by the core group of the community co-researchers, was launched in DTES at the close of the dialogue day.

Participatory action research practice and process

The collaboration between the research partners was agreed as being based upon the principles of participatory action research: inclusion; active involvement; valuing all voices; and action-oriented interventions. The aim was to produce useful knowledge (to be shared locally, nationally and internationally) that represented the sense of 'community/communities' and 'belonging' experienced by the residents of the DTES. Partnerships and collaboration were at the heart of the research.

The projects and agencies contacted were all supportive of the participatory nature of the research being proposed and moreover that it would be shaped and, indeed, designed by the research team of project managers, residents, and university researchers. The project managers in turn, opened up opportunities for workers, volunteers, and clients who were also residents, to meet with us to discuss taking forward the research. A research team began to develop. Residents or members from each organisation volunteered to work with us as community co-researchers. Eighteen people volunteered and took part in the research; of these, a base group of six formed the core research team, finalising the research brief and design, developing the analysis in one-to-one and group discussions, and curating the exhibition and organising the dialogue day. All were committed to and in agreement with the participatory nature of the research and liked the idea of walking as a method alongside visual methods, i.e., photography. The participatory and inclusive ethos of the research combining biographical and arts-based research was crucial to the active involvement of the participants and agencies, as well as the potential impact and application of the research to informing policy and practice.

Arts-based methods – Mapping, walking, sensing, and visualising

It was agreed by organisational and individual participants that walking methods would enable a more corporeal, sensory connection to the area and the everyday lives of the participants, and also facilitate understanding about its history. Community co-researchers, those taking part in the walking research, were invited to create a map of their daily routes in the DTES, and these routes would then be walked with Maggie or a member of the core research team. Photographs would be taken by the community co-researcher and conversations recorded. The ethical implications of the research were discussed with all of the participants and informed consent forms and participant information forms were created in consultation with the core research team, following the principles of participatory action research.[3]

The second phase of the research involved arranging and carrying out the biographical walking interviews using the route maps of their everyday lives that people had drawn. Interviews were carried out on the move based upon the questions around 'What is it like to live in the DTES?' The walk followed the important landmarks people had mapped, the points and places that were important and familiar to them. Images of landmarks and places were captured on a disposable camera and conversations were recorded on a flip video and/or a sound recorder. These recordings were shared with the narrator/participant – and were the basis of the analysis for the report, subsequently published in *Megaphone* (a street community newspaper.)

The filmic recordings of the walk (if taken) using the flip video were not made fully public, but rather were used in the process of analysis, alongside the photographs with each participant. AHA Media worked with *Megaphone* to document and film one of the 18 walks with a core member of the research team. A digital story was produced in filmic form by AHA Media that was shared as both part of the exhibition and the dialogue day. Two participants chose to walk their map alone, take photographs, and discuss them with Maggie O'Neill afterwards. Two community researchers from *Megaphone* and PACE conducted one each. Maggie conducted the remaining walking interviews.

The third phase of the research involved interpreting the key 'themes' in conversation with each participant, based upon their photographs and sound recordings; and then also with the core research group. The thematic interpretation and further analysis of the themes identified continued during the process of curating the images for exhibition. The exhibition took place at the Interurban art gallery in the DTES, organised by the core research team.

The DTES research demonstrates that the WIBM can be used as part of a wider set of practices (as in collaboration with community agencies and participatory action research) involving participants. The outcomes of the walks, photographs, sound files, film clips/video can be disseminated in a number of ways (photographic exhibitions, reports, and via community newspapers etc.). The participatory research approach facilitated raising issues of marginalisation, communal stereotyping, poverty and resistance to wider audiences. The walking interview using multi-media methods enabled a sensory depth and richness of marginal experiences to be documented, and then when reviewed within the analysis, providing a fuller portrait of individual lives and community.

Walking with another as a research method can be a powerful route to understanding our lives and experiences. Most of the co-walkers (participants/narrators) were able-bodied, some were on disability allowance, and one used a wheelchair. The walks were led by the 'community co-researchers' in that they were in 'situational authority' (Myers 2007), so they led the researcher around their route/ walk. This more person- or community-centred approach to conducting research supported the participatory aims of the project. It also creates a space for listening and dialogue, for life histories (and also biographies of place) to be heard, experienced, and shared within the context of community-based research.

The core research team (all resident in DTES) found that doing a walking interview enabled them to reflect upon, express, and feel what 'community' means in a lived, immediate, and embodied way through recounting their biographies in situ. It was also apparent that people's stories are lived out in place *and* memory. Walking, it was found, is creative and productive, embodied, relational, can also be revelatory and opens a 'space' for dialogue when walking with another. The WIBM showed that in walking we engage with participants in multisensory ways and can elicit phenomenological and biographical understanding. Moreover, as we move from scene to scene and place to place, our consciousness moves too, and memories can be sparked by the landscape, the sense-scape we encounter, eliciting emotions, talk, meaning, listening, and understanding, as the two examples shared below illustrate. Walking together involves 'sociation' (Simmel 1969), it brings us in touch with 'our being human' (Horvath and Szakolczai 2018), and situates the walkers, their bodies, and their biographies in space, place, and time. Walking in the DTES, for O'Neill, was also a way of discovering the area, and enabled a sense and attachment to place to be both produced and retained, alongside immersion in and participatory analysis (in the collaboration with the community co-researchers) of the social issues, and understanding the politics of community, belonging, and social justice.

Step-by-step, community, resistance, and recognition

The notion of 'community' was a strong emerging 'theme' in the interview analysis by the core research team. The residents and local community organisations of the DTES have a long and deeply embedded history of community activism and resistance to gentrification and regeneration, as well as a desire to raise awareness and challenge political issues such as stigma, poverty, drug use, and homelessness. O'Neill and Stenning (2013) state that they learnt what 'community' means, looks, and feels like for residents, in contrast to the depiction of DTES as a 'no go' area, or a place where 'down and outs' live. The biographical 'stories' given by walkers (residents and agency workers) via the maps, photographs, and digital recordings gave the sense of 'community' as lived experience. The following section demonstrates this process and practice and the usefulness of the WIBM within communal, participatory research through two examples. First, a woman who, when made unemployed following an accident at work, says she was initially denied benefits and did not have the means to support her life other than in the DTES (this was a common story); and second, a young man who ended up living in the DTES due to drug addiction. Both describe their lives 'spiralling downwards'.[4]

Walking with Amanda

Amanda (not her real name) met Maggie at the Woodward's Building, a former department store and famous location in the DTES. The first 'landmark' on her walk was the building where she was first accommodated after living in a homeless shelter:

> I live … smack dab in the middle of the poorest postal code in Canada. Prior to that I had a good job, I had a workplace accident, was denied benefits and lost my income.

Maggie asks what it is like living in the DTES:

> From the outside eye it looks dysfunctional and yet like any dysfunctional family we make it work. What I am really interested is the arts community. The arts community is very vibrant, it is hustling and bustling and we have events all the time, arts related, and we get reviews in the local posts and we are very happy with that. I have been featured a couple of posts and that is fun.
>
> But there is a strong sense of community here. I find that a lot, especially on the street, a lot of people that spend time on the street, they tend to police each other.

Walking a block further we come to another housing association, described as safe, affordable housing for women:

> I have a small unit. It's for single women, women only and it helps with security and safety. Everyone has to present ID and it is partly in response to the Pickton murders. He was choosing women at random, sex trade workers and vulnerable women in the DTES taking them off and he became a serial murderer … so here if they do not see us for twenty four hours, they search for us. That is different for me, I have always lived independently, always owned and had my own home, first time in my life. This is part of my spiralling downwards from a loss of my income. So, I find myself living here and I am working really hard because of what I want. I want to get myself a nice studio. I am grateful to have a home but I want to not feel crowded. Now I have beads and cloth everywhere.

She went on to talk about her current work and her passion:

> My work is good, it surprises me really. I am very proud of my work. I work with recycled products in my work, antique shops and thrift stores they don't have to be made again, they are already there. Recycling and found objects and things that have been cast away.

We approach a community garden behind a fence and Amanda stops to show it to Maggie. It is a social enterprise where she volunteers and looking at the produce growing, especially the treasured strawberries, led to her comparing the vegetables in Vancouver with the traditional vegetables from Ontario where she had lived previously, and what life was like there:

> I come down here to weed and help out with the flowers and being from back East our traditional meal consists of root vegetables as winters are cold in Ontario so things that could last through the winter are treasured like corn, three sisters soup. On the West Coast the food is salmon and fish

products and rice, it is really interesting the areas have different mainstay in their meals. Well, here we are growing strawberries, highly treasured by my First Nation people, they are to my people what salmon are to Coast Salish. They would be dried, put in bread and baking.

I come from the land of the forest we had long houses, we would have frozen to death in tepees, but most foreigners are knowledge seekers, that is my target market tourists who are knowledge seekers. Especially people who want to know about the culture and the local indigenous people to this area, how they live, their culture and belief systems.

Walking towards the next landmark on Amanda's route, we move beyond the two block boundary of the core DTES. She spoke about her biography in the context of the history, politics, and governance of First Nations people in Canada:

It is really interesting to see how life has changed for First Nations people. We carry a card that says this is who we are, where we are born and what nation we belong to. The benefits of that card are dental care, medical care; however, that has not always been respected. It is really interesting as well from an outside perspective how First Nations women have been discriminated. For example, I was born and raised on a reserve and I married out, so I lost my status as a First Nations woman. I was legally not an Indian any more. We are governed by the Indian Act. So I lost my status. I proudly tell people I have been an Indian for 20 years now. When men married a non-native she became an Indian. There is more equality now, so your status remains regardless of who you marry.

Amanda has been involved in First Nations politics for some years and reflected on the impact of the residential schools:

In 1894 an amendment to the Indian Act stated that all children should to go to school, but boarding or residential school. Children had to be taken to go to these schools and if they did not go they could be arrested. Five year olds and parents were arrested and thrown in jail. Children were taken away. I am a product of the system. I didn't go but mother and father did. She was away for twelve years and he was away for fifteen years so they became institutionalised. The purpose was to take the Indian from the child, they were 'civilising us'. That is Lizzie and her gang and her forbearers … I am not a monarchist. I recognise that it is difficult or impossible to have parenting skills … I could not understand at the time but I sure do now. We never had opportunity to have a discussion with them when they were alive to talk about what that must have been like, so you almost have to learn models of parenting over again.

We arrive at a white building; it is the First Nations Employment and Enterprise Centre. She says:

> Its mandate is to assist First Nations people off reserve and help train for jobs, help them into different types of training and to get jobs. It is an employment agency as well. They also do a lot of training in the construction business. They helped me to put together my business plan. I come here for specific business advice. It is a place of welcome, everyone feels at home. We have access to these wonderful computer banks, print off resumes; I printed off my business plan here to proof read it and have it critiqued.

Inside, there are beautiful examples of Coast Salish weaving and craft that Amanda drew attention to, noting the importance of the patterns and richness of the cloth and the wood. Amanda was warmly welcomed and introduced Maggie to the staff there. Amanda tells Maggie how she was sponsored to undertake an advanced management course at the local University through her engagement with the Centre and that having raised three children as a single parent, she had realised that 'education is the key to having a good life' and that two of her children are university educated.

We walked back into the DTES, Amanda wanted to show the only fresh produce store in the heart of the DTES, reinforcing the importance of the community gardens where fresh vegetables are grown in gardens based in old parking lots and community spaces:

> This is one of our local food markets, prices are great, some of the good stuff is on the other side, we can take pictures of them.

Speaking more about her children:

> I just turned 18 when I had my first child. That's the way it was back in my area. Because of that my kids are grown and so I can travel like I do now. It is far too beautiful to leave here.

On arriving back at the Woodward's Building where the walk had started, Maggie thanked Amanda for sharing her walk and her story, that it was a privilege to share her walk and had gained a deeper and better understanding of life in the DTES.

The walking interview with Amanda gave Maggie an insight into First Nations politics and history as well as the sexual and social inequalities experienced by Indigenous people. It showed Amanda's resistance and resilience in the course of her life to date, challenging stigma and discrimination. The 'landmarks' along the way that were important to her life in the DTES were:

Woodward's (a former department store now providing some social housing, owner-occupied apartments and a food store); the housing agency; community garden; and the First Nations Employment and Enterprise Centre. These landmarks and places formed a jumping off point for sparking memories and sharing more detail about her biography. The community garden led to her talk about favourite foods and recipes from the place where she grew up, a different and colder part of Canada. The visit to the enterprise centre led to her showing her pride in her children, the importance of education, and her struggles as a single parent. In contrast to the dominant media representations and other heavily stigmatised representations of the DTES and the people who live there, the walking interview with Amanda both resisted and challenged prevailing 'tropes' – in a sense serving to de-stigmatise them and representing her own life in the DTES with dignity.

The walking interviews, including Amanda's, revealed a different 'picture and story' of dignified lives, with attachment to others and place, through listening to and 'attuning' to their biographies as captured in their narratives and photographs. This WIBM approach should, therefore, not be mistaken for research that operates a 'tourist gaze'. Through 'immersion' connection and involvement by the embodied and sensing researcher, operating in 'the space of places' and 'the space of flows' (Bauman 2001; see Chapter 4) the WIBM (drawing on ethnographic, participatory, and biographical research), can challenge dominant conceptions of inequalities and the imposition of social stigma, as the walk with Steve illustrates.

Walking with Steve

The walk undertaken with Steve (not his real name) is an example of one variety of WIBM, in that he walked alone and then 're-lived' the walk in conversation with Maggie. He talked about the route map he had drawn before his walk and then later discussed the photographs he had taken. Later still, he wrote the following narrative relating to his walk and the photographs of landmarks he had taken, and then emailed it to Maggie.

First, he refers to:

> pictures of my 'happy place' – for after work I bike down to the liquor store and buy a six-pack of cider for the night. After that I go to a spot where I usually run into old binners [collect bottles and cans from bins for recycling] and that one bin used to be my favourite bin when I binned, before I started working again. There used to be graffiti there that made it more welcoming, at least for me it did, but the City removes it for some reason.

The time after work he described as 'calm' where 'you get to meet all the local people; and talking about community, there is a tight knit group of binners'

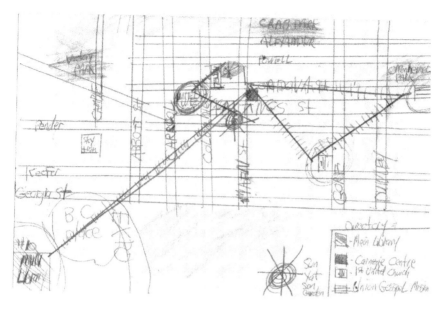

FIGURE 6.1 Map of Steve's walk. Image: Printed with kind permission.

that support each other. Food support and shelter are important landmarks on his map:

> They serve two solid meals a day every day of the week and plus shelter the homeless every night also. Now of course they can't feed everyone or shelter everyone so how it works is like this. For the meals, you line up for two servings for lunch and two servings for supper. During the wait in line we get to meet new people or see the same face every time and get familiar and comfortable with each other.

The image above was taken in the foodline at a shelter:

> For the shelter, you also have to line up and its first come first serve. But for all the shelters, the community works together and if we are not social able, which some people are not, then the community will ask you to leave. For example, if you steal or fight/hurt fellow people then one day as a group you will be asked to leave and the local shelters will ban you from the premises. As you stay longer at these locations you get to know the locals plus the workers/volunteers and eventually start a dialogue with each other and become friends, and your group of friends will grow after a while.

FIGURE 6.2 Food line. Image: Printed with kind permission UWC.

Steve went on to describe what he called 'bad places' associated with the Winter Olympics:

> Now don't get me wrong, the 2010 Winter Olympics had a lot of benefits to it. There was a lot of employment and lots of bottles available for binners. But also, the poor had to sacrifice stuff like housing. I lost my 'hotel' due to making available space for tourists, but at the end my 'hotel' was never used but all the tenants were still evicted.

Steve was not the only participant who said they had been evicted from their hostel whilst they were renovated for tourist rooms during the Olympics. Housing is, and was, a major issue, as is, similarly, being cautioned or prosecuted for begging or 'pan handling'. He says:

> Just before the 2010 Winter Olympics, we had the city pass the 'Civic Act' which is totally against the poor of the DTES. The Act prevents from people to panhandle, they call it 'aggressive street soliciting'. I was put into jail for the night just for panhandling in front of a bank. I don't bother anyone or even ask for change I just open and close the door and hold my hat out with a smile on my face. But this Act prevents anyone panhandling plus it also stops people from setting up camp at any area in the city.

Steve had made a life in the DTES and said that the work he was given as a binner really helped him to progress with his life at a time when he could not have managed to work fulltime because of addiction. He shared a strong sense of belonging to the community of binners and to the DTES; despite being poor, he stated 'we are all still human'. He also expressed a desire to stay 'under the radar':

> It is difficult for me to show how our community at the DTES is because of our life. I for one do not like my picture ever taken and like most of us down here are reasons of family/friends looking for us, police warrants, not wanting employers to connect us to DTES. Now these reasons seem hard-core but most of us down here are downtrodden and poor and are drug addicts. But we are still humans and as humans we still develop a community, we are social beings. There are so many different communities going on in the DTES. There are the soup kitchens, the shelters, the help groups, community centres and even independent groups help with a hearing ear or food or clothes or even just standing on the street with a smile helps.

He expressed profoundly both through his photographs and his narrative the importance of individual lives and experiences as testaments against social stigma, prejudice, and discrimination; and the importance of the 'community' in DTES to his own survival:

> Now for me I ended up down here after losing to a drug addiction and finally in jail for trafficking drugs. I was depressed and moved into a single room occupancy (SRO). I lost my finance, friends, and income, then too embarrassed to talk to family and close friends, I became an alien and just lived off the food and shelter. Some can say without the structure of the DTES I could have easily died, but because of the way things work down here I survived my depression and then eventually found a job. They are a non-profit organisation that recycle bottles. They employ the down and out people that was me and give them a stepping stone to get back into the community and back into life. Even though it is only minimum wage, I could work four hour shifts. I was not able to hold down a job before 'cuz of the eight hours/five days, too depressing plus pay checks, could either start 'cuz of no money or ended up blowing all my check at once. At least here I was able to just work four hours and three or four days a week with cash pay at the end of the day. Give me a start to get my life back on track and out of my depression 'cuz of giving me direction to my life.

Steve, again, stresses the importance of 'community' for personal life:

> The community down here works where the longer you live here, the more people you recognise and vice versa recognise you that eventually you/we become comfortable with each other and start a dialogue and then the rest is human nature, we are all social beings.

Steve's photographs and everyday route map helped him to tell his story of living in the DTES; in the written narrative, there is a strong sense of 'the right to have rights' as a member of the DTES and the way that community develops, as well the support and recognition he found there. For, as he says, in resistance to the social stigma experienced, 'we are all social beings'. Having Steve as a community co-researcher talk Maggie through the walk helped to elicit biographical material and connection to place, which was enhanced by the discussion of his photographs. The sensory, material, and phenomenological aspects of walking with another can be present, albeit through the description and attention to photographs, and through the activity of telling or recounting other lived experiences and memories. We also begin to appreciate the 'micrology', the 'small stories' Steve tells, how broader social and cultural processes and structures impact and are lived, within daily life.

In summary, stories such as Amanda's and Steve's also demonstrate that memories continue in the present – are retrieved, reshaped, and operate, as they interplay with current individual and group socio-cultural experience and memory. As Kuhn states:

> It is impossible to overstate the significance of *narrative* in cultural memory – in the sense not just of the (continuously negotiated) contents of shared/collective memorystories, but also of the activity of recounting or telling memory-stories, in both private and public contexts – in other words, of *performances of memory*.
>
> *(Kuhn 2010: 293)*

The *performances of memory* and the walking and visual (photographic and filmic) methods allowed a broader 'communal' story to emerge, in the 'intertextuality of individual and collective biographies and photography': the participants' 'struggle for recognition' against depictions of the people and the area as 'other', 'different', and 'abject' (O'Neill and Stenning 2013: 216). Moreover, that participatory methodologies promote 'recognition, participation and inclusion in the production of knowledge and public policy' and are instrumental in helping to create opportunities for these issues to be raised and for dialogue to take place' towards social justice (O'Neill and Stenning 2013: 219).

Walking towards a sense of community and mattering

What became clear across the walks, during the day of dialogue and the launch of the exhibition is that 'stigmatization operates as a form of governance which legitimizes the reproduction and entrenchment of inequalities and injustices' (Tyler 2013: 212), which was challenged by the participatory, biographical, and visual research on many levels. Maggie says that her warm memory of and connection to the DTES and Vancouver is indelibly connected to these walks that introduced her to the community, the people, as well as the dominant landmarks on their walks, and the beauty of the surrounding environment – CRAB Park, the mountains, and the sea. The sensory, relational, and embodied aspects of conducting walking interviews were experienced in the connections and attachments to both people and the place, through the senses and emotions, the objects, imagery, and symbolism encountered along the way (see also Matos Wunderlich 2008).

The WIBM with Amanda and Steve illustrate that first, biographical research conducted when walking can be productive and support dignifying self-representation for the co-walker (participants) via the subject–subject embodied relationship that develops between the researcher and co-walker in the rhythm of walking (Amanda in this case) as we attune to each other, the environment and see, feel, and think on the move. Second, that active listening is vital to biographical and participatory research and this also supports a relational dialogue that minimises power relations (of researcher/participant) and promotes understanding. Third, that this in turn can promote social justice, especially when the biographical walking research can be shared more widely, in this case through the day of dialogue, the exhibition, and the report in *Megaphone*.

These two examples of WIBM also show how the relational/community construction aspects of an area or neighbourhood can be experienced and understood. The maps that the eighteen participants created, the photographs, film, the walks, and conversations along the way, and the writing the community members and researchers sent to Maggie during and after the project powerfully represent aspects both of their own biographies, as well as what 'community' looks like, feels, and means as people living and working in DTES.

The walks, images, and stories of Amanda and Steve enable us to see and feel the participants' sense of 'community' as relating to 'mattering' (to be of importance, to count) and connecting with others (see Schultheiss et al. 2011). Their stories showed the importance of relationships and friendships as 'mattering', as well as basic material needs being met, are all important for community building, well-being, and sustainability. The politics of the area, history, and place are also central in Amanda and Steve's accounts, and in accounts of others in the research, through comments on and attachments to buildings, places, and objects. For example, during many of the walks, Maggie was shown with great pride a local painted greygreen fence. Here artwork by community members was attached to the fence. The fact that it remained untouched by graffiti or vandalism during the entire research project and beyond was very important to her co-walkers. It symbolised a different message about the DTES, an example of the creativity as well as dignity they associated with their DTES.

The eighteen walks and their representation in the exhibition helped to build a picture of how the co-walkers (participants) relate to their socio-cultural and built environment, and construct and sustain community. WIBM can help to deliver how individuals see, hear, touch, give meaning to their environment and personal relations, that in turn creates a 'sense of community' as a set of social and material relationships.

One community co-researcher said: 'I feel very intimate in this community and connected, people are accepted, here are people from all works of life here'. Following a walk with a woman living in the heart of the DTES in social housing, she sent an email to Maggie as a follow-up to their conversation around her photographs and their walk:

> there is another thing that contributes to the strong sense of community amongst us is that, whether this is a result of being poor, or whatever other dynamic is in operation here; (I say poor because that is my rationale) – so one of the reasons for the strong sense of community, for me, is that people who live in DTES (not counting gated communities such as co-ops), the people who are out and about, there are not too many pretences; there is honesty and integrity to emotions, behaviour. There is a directness of approach and communication. a 'tell it as it is', and also the language, the sentence structure, is succinct, brief, quick, to the point ... sharp, lively, it's heavily based on street, rez (reservation), ghetto lingo and I love it.

The WIBM can show the *relational* aspects of 'belonging' and 'community' as evidenced in the walking interviews by Steve, Amanda, and others. Community co-researchers described strongly bonded relationships based upon feelings of belonging and shared issues and experiences. 'Mattering' was also represented in people's stories of the long history of local activism and resistance. *Megaphone's* archive of published stories by residents and articles on key issues for the DTES is evidence of the cultural memory of the community's activism. The memorial to the missing women in CRAB Park was a landmark on the maps of most participants – a material expression of community intervention and memory/memorial.

The two walking interviews discussed above (and others undertaken in the DTES) were a precursor to our development of the WIBM. They illustrate how a walking interview as a biographical method can not only capture something of the lived, sensory experience of residents, using walking alongside participatory and visual methods, but reveal the relational connections and communal conceptions that develop in an area of deprivation. The findings from the research highlight: poverty and the organisation of social difference in DTES; the experiences of First Nations people; the strength of the 'community', constituted by many groups and 'communities'; the creativity and creative energy on display; the resilience of community members in the face of poverty, social problems, and extreme social stigma and 'othering', as shown in the multiplicity of stories and biographies of people living there. The WIBM, through the sensory aspects of walking in the DTES, uncovered what it means to live in a poor neighbourhood and to be 'poor' in a 'feeling' and relational way. The experience of waiting in the food lines 'a two hour wait for a five minute meal', budgeting, where to access cheap or free clothing and the stress involved in always having very little

FIGURE 6.3 The Women's Memorial, CRAB Park. Photo: Printed with kind permission PACE.

money, especially the week before welfare payments are made, were shared in along the walks. Alongside the material and embodied experiences of poverty, there emerged a strong sense of belonging to the DTES community and communities in the interviews. Co-researchers talked about how it feels to live there, the spirit of mutual support and solidarity, the social struggle and activism that exists and has developed over time, particularly in the face of gentrification, regeneration, and racism.

The walks with Amanda and Steve showed the mobile, ethnographic, and participatory aspects of walking research. These examples contribute to the development of the WIBM by using creative and multi-sensory methods that can be seen to capture 'complex, sensory and embodied lives' and that 'working in the space between art and storytelling … can bring something new into the world and offer a change-causing gesture … a space for dialogue and reflection' (O'Neill and Stenning 2013: 240). This chapter has developed O'Neill and Stenning's (2013) findings by highlighting possible ways of doing WIBM for community studies, underpinned by an ethnographic and participatory approach for sharing better understanding of the lives of marginalised residents, their individual and collective biographies, towards social justice and human dignity and against stigma and 'othering'. The WIMB as a way of engaging with lived lives as an embodied practice and a means of understanding through the use of all the senses is, we argue, a critical, ethical as well as a mobile practice.

Finally, the participatory and policy-oriented possibilities of the WIBM are evident in this chapter. Five organisations and groups of people came together to conduct participatory, biographical walking research in the DTES, led by a research team made up of academics and local residents, workers, and organisations. The interviews showed not merely how poverty and stigma impact on an individual and community, but how, in fact, research can show, in its dissemination, the vitality, resistance, and communal solidarities of people. The wider research had a diverse range of outcomes to meet a variety of 'audiences': for example, the report, a dialogue day, an exhibition, and recommendations to authorities on policy, regarding food poverty, citizenship, planning. Thus, WIBM (in this case working with a range of social agencies) can record the voices – the feelings, forming of meanings or 'ways of seeing' the lived environment, the communal outlook, the impact of dominant cultural views – of local people.

In summary, the participatory biographical research discussed in this chapter contributes to the WIBM by highlighting the political and emancipatory role of the image and sensory walking biographies in how we can understand and also shape our social worlds. The experience and application of WIBM can lead to embodied calls for dignifying representations that challenge and resist stigma and othering, and contribute much to community-based research for social justice.

Notes

1 This chapter was developed in consultation with Prof. Philip Stenning and draws upon and extends research undertaken by O'Neill (principal investigator) and Stenning (co-investigator) funded by the British Academy in 2010–2011 in the DTES, Vancouver (see O'Neill and Stenning 2013). Documentation by AHA Media, one of the community partners, is available here: https://ahamedia.ca/2011/06/09 /community-arts-dialogue-community-politics-and-resistance-in-vancouvers-do wntown-eastside-part-1/

and here: https://ahamedia.ca/2011/06/30/aha-media-filmed-at-community-arts -dialogue-community-politics-and-resistance-in-vancouver's-downtown-eastside- --part-2-on-june-18-2011/, and Durham University Medical Humanities Blog is here: https://medicalhumanities.wordpress.com/?s=community+politics+and+resi stance (Accessed 15 August 2018).

2 The Vancouver Police Department supplied the disposable cameras that we gave to community members for the WIBM and they also supported the production of the Sister Watch poster. The research team were grateful for this support.

3 Ethical approval for the research was given by Durham University (UK). The ethical process must be very thorough in participatory research and is usually developed in collaboration with the research participants. It can, however, be difficult for university ethics review boards to both understand the participatory process and grant ethical approval before the research tools and methods have been designed and agreed. For more discussion and guidance see: (a) toolkits and guides at the Centre for Social Justice and Community Action at the University of Durham: www.dur.ac.uk/social justice/ethics_consultation/ and (b) a toolkit for using walking and theatrebased methods funded by the Economic and Social Research Council and the National Centre for Research Methods. The toolkit emerged from the 'Participatory Arts and Social Action Research' project that originated out of the need for the UK social science community to gain a better understanding of how participatory action approaches can engage

marginalised groups in research that co-produces knowledge. http://eprints.ncrm. ac.uk/4120/1/2.%20Toolkit%20PASAR%20Final%2030%20Jan%2018.pdf (accessed 1 April 2018) and a training video is available here: www.ncrm.ac.uk/resources/online/ participatory_research_methods/ (Accessed 1 April 2018).

4 Both participants gave consent for their maps, words, and images to be shared in the project report and subsequent publications.

References

Bauman, Z. (2001) *Community. Seeking Safety in an Insecure World*. Cambridge, UK: Polity.

Downtown Eastside Community Monitoring Report. 10th edn. (2006). Available at https ://sunnvancouver.files.wordpress.com/2011/05/2006dtesplanning.pdf. (Accessed 23 September 2018).

Horvath, A. and Szakolczai, A. (2018) *Walking into the Void: A Historical Sociology and Political Anthropology of Walking*. London: Routledge.

Kuhn, A. (2010) Memory texts and memory work: Performances of memory in and with visual media, *Memory Studies*, 3(4): 298–313.

Matos Wunderlich, F. (2008) Walking and rhythmicity: Sensing urban space, *Journal of Urban Design*, 13(1): 125–139.

O'Neill, M. and Stenning, P. (2013) Walking biographies and innovations in visual and participatory methods: Community, politics and resistance in Downtown Eastside Vancouver. In: C. Heinz, and G. Hornung (eds.) *The Medialization of Auto/Biographies: Different Forms and Their Communicative Contexts*. Hamburg: UVK.

Pederson, W. and Swanson, J. (2009) Our place our world: Mapping downtown eastside community assets and challenges. Carnegie community action project. https://su nnvancouver.files.wordpress.com/2011/02/ccapmappingweb2.pdf. (Accessed 23rd September 2018).

Schultheiss, D. E., Watts, J., Sterland, L. and O'Neill, M. (2011) Career, migration and the life CV: A relational cultural analysis, *Journal of Vocational Behavior, Special Issue on Migration: Vocational Perspectives on a Complex and Diverse Transition*, 78(3): 334–341.

Simmel, G. (1969) The metropolis and mental life. In: R. Sennett (ed.) *Classic Essays on the Culture of Cities*. New Jersey: Prentice-Hall.

Tyler, I. (2013) *Revolting Subjects*. London: Zed Books.

EXERCISE TWO

Walking, sensing, experiencing[1]

Building on Exercise 1, the aim is to help readers become aware of walking as a sensory experience – not simply visual – but to be conscious of experiencing and feeling (the breeze, sun, sounds, etc.).

Think of a place that is familiar to you: the garden, the park, or the campus. Visualise that place, think of where you might walk. Think of yourself walking there. Plan a walk in the location, or simply go and walk there!

When you arrive, spend a few minutes slowing down your breathing. Stand and 'tune in' to the place you are in. Close your eyes, listen with care and attention, open your eyes, and then walk, slowly becoming aware of your surroundings, the birdsong, the feel of the breeze, various noises, etc.

You could record your walk on an audio recorder and/or take photographs to 'remind' you of 'sensing' experiences.

Now think of a place that is more unfamiliar to you and follow the instructions above.

The duration of the two walks is up to you!

Enjoy tuning into the sounds and sensations and textures along the way. Listen to your recordings on your return.

How did you feel in those places?

- Were there any similarities or differences between the locations?
- What thoughts come into mind about how you experienced the locations?
- What is the most enduring memory of your walks?

- What did you learn about yourself: for example, how you usually walk and sense your surroundings?
- Note down your experiences and reflections in a 'walking diary'.

[Note: The conduct of the exercise must be done in accordance with relevant ethical and other professional, institutional procedures, and legal requirements]

Note

1 For inspiration, you might like to look at walks with Chris Watson (award-winning sound recordist/sound artist) on www.walkingborders.com.

PART III

Imagination

This final Part engages with sociologists, activists, and artists in the UK and Vancouver, Canada to better understand how we 'imagine' the practice of walking in biographical research and the *use* of imagination. We have argued in this book that using the Walking Interview as a Biographical Method (WIBM) as influenced by arts-based and ethnographic, performative, phenomenological methods, enabled us: to get in touch with our 'realities' that demand critical reflection; to experience and value the importance of innovative ways of consulting, connecting, and 'understanding' lived lives; and to reflect on and utilise arts-based walking methods as embodied, relational, sensory, and multi-modal.

Here we emphasise the role of the 'imaginary', the part played by the imagination in biographical research and how this may facilitate a 'radical democratic imaginary'. By this, we mean the opening of a 'democratic space' for critical reflection on a 'life story', or a particular aspect of a biography that involves walking, moving through places and time. Walking methods also open an arena for reflection on how we imagine our lives, as well as how the researcher uses 'imagination' in the process of producing a reflective opportunity for biographical research to take place. At the end of Part III, we include a third Exercise to facilitate the experience and application of the imagination in biographical research. A fourth 'model' WIBM Exercise and a Principles and Practice guide is provided after the Conclusion.

Chapter 7: Walking, sex work, and community: Towards a radical democratic and imaginative space for addressing sexual and social inequalities includes four walks with a common theme of sex work in London, Liverpool, a northern UK city, and Vancouver, as an imaginative method for doing biographical research that connects the sociological imagination and the lives as told, to broader social structures and processes. *Chapter 8: The phenomenology of walking in a garden* engages our imagination through the experience of gardens, and suggests that concepts such as 'maze', labyrinth', and 'panorama' are methodological metaphors for how we may 'investigate, collect and communicate' walking interviews as biographical research. *Chapter 9: Walking artists: Critical dialogues and imaginaries* shares a series of walks with 'walking artists' to explore the relationship between walking, autobiography, and place. Excerpts from two walks with walking artists are presented, followed by a discussion of the possibilities or 'ways forward' for biographical research inspired by walking artists. Here we explore walking as imaginative, relational, and biographical. In *Chapter 10: Autobiographical encounters in time and space*, the authors re imagine and report autobiographical walks in the places they were raised – Scrooby (in Nottinghamshire, UK) and Consett (in County Durham, UK) to examine each other's 'roots and routes'. These very personal walks raise awareness of the role of remembrance, memory, lived experience, and the sensory, multi-modal aspects of walking in place and in our imaginaries.

7

WALKING, SEX WORK, AND COMMUNITY

Towards a radical democratic and imaginative space for addressing sexual and social inequalities

As a methodology for conducting biographical research, this book suggests that 'walking' brings particular advantages for understanding 'lived lives', especially when combined with ethnographic, visual, and participatory forms of practice. Walking methods can help articulate the material, phenomenological, embodied, and imagined, yet transitory, sense of lived lives by giving priority to walking and thinking (Weigel 1996). Here, as Weigel, referring to Walter Benjamin, says, 'the images of our perceptions and ideas, and the metaphors with which we are surrounded, are seen by Benjamin as 'body-and image-space' (Weigel 1996: x). Benjamin thinks in images. Another way of articulating this is expressed by Solnit, for whom walking includes 'that crucial element of engagement of the body and the mind with the world, of knowing the world through the body and the body through the world' (Solnit 2014: 29). Walking involves moving in time and space, but it also means becoming 'attuned' to our environment – knowing the world through the body, but also through the employment of images. Capturing the sense of walking as an 'imaginative' sensory and visual activity is key to the Walking Interview as a Biographical Method (WIBM). There is also a connection to how individuals 'feel' their emotional state. For example, Solnit (2014) refers to the way in which walking modulates alienation.

In this chapter, we draw upon four walks to show connections between creativity and the sociological imagination in understanding biographical lives within broader social structures and processes. In doing so, we also reflect upon walking as an imaginative, sensory, and visual method and how walking can offer a 'radical democratic space' for identifying and addressing sexual and social inequalities. The walks referenced in this chapter were undertaken with two academics, a health worker, a former CEO of a sex work support organisation, and a hostel resident. The walks were undertaken in four urban areas, in the places where sex is bought and sold – in London, Liverpool, a northern city in the UK, and Vancouver.[1]

Walking is an everyday practice in the lives of sex workers, especially street sex workers, in the practice of outreach and support workers, and in the experience and practice of the researchers working with sex workers and related organisations and communities. Walking, as we shall see, is also a way of remembering sex workers who are dead or still missing, and to advocate for an end to violence, harm, and criminalisation of sex workers. On 17th December across the globe, sex workers and sex worker rights activists march to raise awareness of violence against sex workers. On this day, people march to 'end violence against sex workers'. On 14th February for the last twenty-six years in Vancouver, Canada, the missing women's memorial march takes place to honour the missing and dead women, especially from Indigenous First Nations communities, some of whom were sex workers. Walking, on these days of remembrance, is for protest and advocacy, as well as in memory (see Chapter 6). In the walks explored in this chapter, we learn not only about the biographies of the co-walkers, but the entanglement of their working and personal biographies, situated in place, space, time, memory, and history – the history of sex work, sexualities, and of supporting sex workers' rights.

A sociological imagination

Stories and storytelling having multiple capacities, can balance multiple perspectives, and display differing accounts, and they have the capacity to arouse the imagination: 'they make the unseen not only visible but compelling' and indeed, if a story 'does not arouse the imagination, it will not be much of a story' (Frank 2012: 41–2). The role of the imagination in walking is foregrounded in the walks in this chapter, as an opportunity for giving personal accounts, generating dialogue and understanding of lived lives, as well as sexual and social inequalities. Imagination is deeply implicated in the process of walking as described by various writers, artists, musicians, and commentators, and walking aids the process of creativity. For example, Solnit's approach to walking calls attention to imagination in the way that walking connects body and the earth; it can give unpredictable encounters, whilst all the time re-shaping our experience of the world, 'the way each act reflects and reinvents the culture in which it takes place' (Solnit 2001: 276). In this sense, walking is generative, it helps to make culture and citizenship (O'Neill 2017a), and we need to walk to have a 'living democratic city' (Careri 2017: 13).

The process of walking as an imaginative tool for the biographical sociologist to undertake, document, illustrate, and analyse life stories is inextricably connected with the concept of the 'sociological imagination':

> The sociological imagination enables us to grasp history and biography and the relations between the two within society. That is its task and its promise. To recognise this task and this promise is the mark of the classic social analyst.
>
> *(Mills 2000: 6)*

Indeed, Mills claims that those who are 'imaginatively aware of the promise of their work have consistently asked three sorts of questions' and these are to do with (i) the structure of society, continuity, and change, (ii) the situatedness in human history, and (iii) the imaginative ability to move from micro to macro analysis, to see the general in the particular, or as Adorno aptly put it, 'the splinter in your eye is the best magnifying glass' (Adorno 1978: 50).

Moreover, Mills identifies the distinction between 'the personal troubles of milieu' and the 'public issues of the social structure' as a defining feature of sociology, and importantly, that the sociological imagination is a 'most needed quality of mind'. The promise and challenge of sociology is to 'make clear the elements of contemporary uneasiness and indifference' (Mills 2000: 8).

It is our experience that the biographical researcher focuses upon the story of a life, the way that lives are told in relation to the social contexts of telling, the psycho-social matterings (to be of importance, to count), and that the internal and external dialogues that emerge in the telling are important for biographical sociology and wider sociological analysis. For example, biographical sociological research can help people make sense of what has happened and is happening in their lives, cultures, communities, and broader society. It 'sensitizes social scientists to the heuristic possibilities of biographical research in gaining important insights into the workings of contemporary societies and the relationship between biographical and collective social processes' (Riemann 2003: np). These themes are interrogated in the following walks and examples of WIBM.

Walking with Nick Mai in Soho

Nick Mai, an academic film-maker on migration and sex work, was invited to take Maggie on a walk that was meaningful to him connected to the theme of borders, risk, and belonging. He was asked to draw the route and talk her through it before setting off.

> Yes, so today we are going to walk around Soho, around its borders and inside Soho and we will explore some of the ways in which I am related to the place, some of the features of the place and, unfortunately, some of the ways in which it has changed, because Soho has become a very, very different place.

At the start of the walk with Nick, he says there are a lot of *Amarcord* memories in the walk he has planned. He explains that this refers to Fellini's movie *Amarcord* and means 'I remember'; in it, the director reminisces about his adolescence and a past long gone.

They look at the map together and he says:

> So here is my map. The peepshows, the big construction site, the Soho Estate place and the place I used to live. Old Compton Street as a safe space

where people were holding hands at the beginning and not at the end
... Yes, I think I showed you everything. And the borders. You see how
bounded it is? These big streets act like borders.

In taking the walk with Nick, it became clear that it was only a partial mapping
of Nick's biography, and especially his early years in London, his attachment to
Soho, and his academic and filmic work on migration and sex work. He spoke
about the layers of migration embedded in Soho, and importantly, the shifting
landscape of the area and the capitalist regeneration 'juggernaut' that is changing its face and spirit with 'everything being branded and sold'. This layering
also maps what Nick calls the 'moral gentrification', the convergence of moral
conservatism and gentrification, alongside his arrival, connection, and sense of
belonging to the area.

Nick arrived in London as a fifteen-year-old on a language school visit:

> That was the first time and that's when I discovered *Time Out*, the fabulous
> gay and lesbian section ... which used to be extensive, you know. I came
> from a small town in Italy which wasn't very intensely homophobic, but it
> still was a very small place in quite a conservative country. Suddenly I have
> seven pages of events including gay canoeing or tennis playing. Not only
> clubbing, but a life, there was a life to be had here.
>
> So, that stuck in my head for a long time. As we were passing by, with a
> typical kind of rucksack that was popular amongst Italian kids, people were
> shouting 'gay night, gay night Monday night' so it stuck in my head for a
> few years. So, on that famous evening of 1989 we went in, me and a friend
> of mine, on yet another language course [laughs]. You know by then we
> were quite fluent, but never mind.

Nick tells Maggie that he arrived in the Thatcher years, the Berlin Wall was still
up and he said the UK was a very different country:

> There were lots of migrants in the disco, and it was very interesting to
> see how for many of us, London in those years was like an articulation of
> ourselves that we couldn't express at home. Because of the pop music that
> emerged, the gay pop music specifically like Marc Almond or Boy George
> ... Those people used to be in Soho and so it became a place where we
> could imagine to be.

Furthermore, he explains his growing sense of identity to his migration and
sense of belonging to Soho now:

> I refer to what I told you before about myself and my relationship to
> London in the 1980s and 90s, to explain that when you feel that existen-
> tially you have a possibility of being who you are somewhere else, then risk

becomes an opportunity. Risk is experienced as a limit to something you want to be and so you just take it. In the case of my migration the risk was HIV and all of that, but we just needed to come here, to become who we thought we were then.

Walking along Charing Cross Road, the border of Soho, towards the Cross-Rail site, was a constant sea of boarding and construction. Nick pointed out the 'vintage' gentrification and the 'clink' of 'money, money, money' represented on the advertising boards:

> This black wall that you see over here is what we are talking about. Today we are going to see a very gentrified Soho, or a Soho that is being gentrified. All of this is now going to be rebranded into a string of higher end restaurants and chains. This is what's going on in Soho, restaurants which did not belong to chains before, are now being bought and transformed into chains. The whole neighbourhood is being boarded up and restructured, the whole thing is quite an intense and violent intervention.

Nick described the Soho in construction that they were walking through as the backdrop to the gentrification and commodification of sexualities, referring to the ways in which sex workers and sex clubs were presented as adding character to the branding of Soho by people refashioning and consuming the area, instead of being considered as people who live and work there. 'Everybody's now become useful for this kind of venture. I think it is the society we are living in. Everything is being branded and sold'.

> So, you see, it's going to be shops, shops, shops. Luxury flats, luxury flats, the whole bloody city's being converted into luxury flats. Luxury flats, luxury for who? Who can afford it? Consuming everything. Consuming Soho. Bloody everything. And then, oh look, you can also do a sound history of Soho. But the tragic thing is that Soho is being killed by the same people, or the same kind of dynamics that are memorialising it!

The landmarks along the way were the places, buildings, clubs, and bars that were part of Nick's biography; his life in place, time, and memory. His narrative was interrupted and diverted by the smells of the Italian deli, the sounds of construction workers, and the vehicles that made him jump out of their path.

Passing an Italian deli, Nick says:

> I forgot this one was here. Can you smell this?

Maggie says:

> Oh, it's gorgeous.

Nick says:

> Come and have a smell, the smell of Parmesan and all this mix, it reminds
> me of when I was a kid. My Granny used to have a shop like that. I was not
> allowed in but I always found a way.

This memory led to a conversation about Nick's childhood, his relationship with
his Granny, and the importance of this memory and family.

The walk with Nick illustrates that walking is a very creative way of doing
biographical research and arts-based methodologies, including walking biographies, might generate greater knowledge and understanding of social issues,
communities, as well as a single life in its social, historical, and cultural contexts.
The walking interview with Nick in Soho reveals an individual in dialogue in
relating their biography, remembering their childhood through passing smells,
and articulating how they interrelate with the visual culture and materiality of
place, in this case offering a critical reading of the changes in Soho and the role
of global capitalism.

This brief excerpt is 'evidence' of the historical, political, and structural relations
that are involved in the interlinkages between the personal and the public, not only
to explain the general in the particular, but also that the WIBM facilitates the ability
to creatively and critically interpret the social and cultural relations marked out along
the walk through Nick's eyes, senses and biography. The role and importance of
the relationship between 'body-and-imagespace' is also highlighted in this excerpt.
Walking through Soho, passing the visual signs and symbols he draws our attention
to, are a central part of 'tuning' into his account of his biography and belonging to
the place. The visual and sensory gentrification of Soho is experienced as 'shocking',
marketising the history of Soho as 'vintage' for easy consumption. Creative and critical interpretation in the WIBM can be further unpacked by discussing the relationship between creativity, biography, and the imagination.

Creativity, biography, and imagination

'Creativity' depends upon imagination. As Winnicott (1982) stated, creative
perception is fostered by a negotiation of the gap between self and other, and
creativity is linked to play and playfulness (Glover 2005: 2). Critical theorists
Theodor Adorno and Walter Benjamin discuss creativity and the imagination
with reference to the concept of 'mimesis'; this is not to be understood as imitation, but rather as playfulness. Play and imagination being intimately connected, one cannot have one without the other. O'Neill (2008) argues that in
the 'mimetic moment' of cognition, we can develop a critical perspective that
includes 'empathy' as sensuous knowing. It is through this imaginative process
that we can connect or attune to another in the process of walking with another
as a biographical research method. In the walk with Nick, Maggie connected/
attuned to his experience and critique of the 'moral gentrification' of Soho,

empathising with his account of his migration journey to be the person 'he wanted to be'. Soho was also the place where he (and others) could 'become who we thought we were then'.

'Creativity' has gained in emphasis in qualitative research practice, especially as social science has reached out to the arts for inspiration and new techniques (see Kara 2015; Mannay 2010). However, when examining methodological innovations in research, Wiles et al. (2011: 2) discovered that although there was limited scope for actual innovations in their mapping of qualitative research, there was a rise in researchers engaging with creative ways of *doing* research, and the biggest growth was in those using arts-based methods. Part of the 'reaching out' to artistic practices has been the opportunity to collaborate with artists and this has raised the possibilities for dialogue and sharing through what O'Neill terms 'ethno-mimesis' (O'Neill 1999). The WIBM provides a particularly innovative and creative example of such collaboration across the arts and social sciences (see also Chapter 9).

Walking with another not only opens the opportunity to walk side-by-side, thus 'modulating' power relations, but also places the narrator in 'situational authority' (Myers 2007) by disrupting the traditional interviewer/interviewee hierarchical relation[s]. Walking with another also opens a 'potential space' for dialogue, attunement, and sharing, and as a biographical method influenced by the arts, creates the opportunity for reflection in the mimetic moment of cognition. One outcome is that the 'potential space' created in the act of *walking with* might bring something new into the world, that can include contestation, imagination, and critical discourse; indeed, a 'radical democratic imaginary' (O'Neill 2008).

This notion of the walking interview as 'modulating power' relations, placing the narrator/co-walker in 'situational authority', and opening a space for dialogue that connects 'personal troubles to public issues', seeing the general in the particular and vice versa (and providing an example of the importance of the visual and sensory aspects of walking), is illustrated below by a walk undertaken in a northern city (UK) with Faye (not her real name), a woman living in a direct access hostel.[2]

A walking workshop was undertaken by Maggie O'Neill in collaboration with Open Clasp, a feminist theatre company, as part of its residency in the direct access hostel. The hostel provides emergency accommodation for women who are homeless. The residency introduced the women to interactive theatre techniques, included a trip to the theatre. Working in participatory ways with the women, the characters and themes for Open Clasp's next play 'Sugar' were developed with them, from the 'ground up'. The walking workshop (Walkshop) aimed to support this process.

Walking with Faye and Open Clasp

Maggie introduced the concept of a walking interview and, supported by hostel support workers and two Open Clasp staff members, including Creative Director Catrina Mchugh, asked the group to imagine a favourite walk or a walk they take every day and draw it onto paper (see O'Neill and McHugh 2017). Although several women mapped their everyday routes and special places as part of the Walkshop and then talked to us about the walk and what it meant to them, only one woman wanted to walk us through her map. In walking us from the direct access hostel to a park in the city centre (her favourite place), Faye told her story which is also, in part, a biography of homelessness in the city.

The conversation along the walk with Faye was recorded into a digital sound recorder and she took photographs of the landmarks along the way that were important to her, and that she wanted to share. Faye led the way, through the places where she worked to the city centre, where we experienced the visual presence, reality, and materiality of homelessness. Faye asked how can it be possible, in 2017, for so many people to be homeless living in the centre of a major city?

Faye's walk took place largely in the borders and margins of the inner city, the liminal spaces, alleyways, and underpasses, where sex is bought and sold, until the final stop in the centre of the city, the park, where we enjoyed what Faye called a 'posh coffee'. During the walk, Faye shared aspects of her biography, including the tree she passes every day, a special landmark, asking permission to walk over its legs/roots; the sex work outreach organisation that supports her; and the place where drugs are bought and sold. Faye spoke of a childhood marked by loss, and that her first sexual encounter with a 'client' was to be able to buy batteries for her Walkman. O'Neill and McHugh write that through Faye's walk, they were attuned to her story, her experiences, and reflections on border spaces and places both real and imagined in a sensory way, and connected to her bravery and resilience and search for belonging as feeling/being in place and at home, albeit 'on the move' (O'Neill and McHugh 2017: 219).

The walk facilitated connection or attunement to Faye's lived experience, her lived life, in embodied ways, as well as its sensory and affective dimensions. On returning to the hostel Faye shared the walk with the group of other residents. First, she wrote a sentence on the back of each photograph to explain why she had taken it (Maggie had processed the photographs near the park). Then she curated the photographs, placing them around the map. She talked us all through the walk and each photograph. Faye ended her account of the walk by thinking forward to a future possible self.

> If I could do anything, I'd like to be a support worker you know and like work with young people and try to sort of make sense of it with them. But you know, I just sometimes think that I don't know who to reach out to get a life, I want to establish myself as a person because I'm just like, I feel I'm just floating between situations at the minute and I don't know what's going to happen to me, it's scary. I just want to be productive, I don't want to just exist.
>
> (O'Neill and McHugh 2017: 220)

FIGURE 7.1 Sharing a walk. Image: Maggie O'Neill, printed with kind permission Open Clasp.

Faye imagines a hoped-for future as a support worker, but the material and psycho-social relational reality of her life weigh heavily, so that she does not only not know who to reach out to, but feels lost and not in control, she is 'existing', rather than being 'productive' in her terms. In writing about the walk with Faye and thinking through the relational sense of Faye's walk and the potential change-causing gesture of documenting the walk as a photoessay, O'Neill and McHugh write that the photo essay 'is a biographical as well as a social document of the history in which it is produced'. Moreover, it calls us to reflect upon, challenge, and transform the sexual and social inequalities in evidence here, towards social justice for women (O'Neill and McHugh 2017: 213).

The walk with Faye and the Walkshop contributed to the scripting of a play 'Sugar' that will raise awareness about women's lives and reach a range of publics and audiences. The play offers an example of a 'radical democratic imaginary', as it will open and keep open a critical space for reflection and understanding about women's experiences of homelessness, the impact of austerity and poverty, as well as violence and abuse. A radical democratic imaginary is defined as the opening and keeping open of a 'space' to reflect upon repressed elements of the imaginary (see Cornell 1995). A radical democratic imaginary is also the 'space' for the creation of the arts and literature. For example, in the use of forum and play back theatre, pioneered by Brazilian Augusto Boal as part of what he termed 'Theatre of the Oppressed' (Boal 2000) – an 'interactive theatre' for empowerment and action, inspiring social change and grass roots activism – is similar to what Open Clasp aim to achieve in their work. Open Clasp are committed to research that produces knowledge and theatre for social change, working with women (the 'oppressed' – the stereotypical subjects of research), in partnership and collaboration. Creativity and the imagination are relational and constitutive; they bring something new that helps to regenerate research, especially biographical research through the WIBM, by facilitating 'voice' and seeking change.

The processes and practices involved in biographical research, as well as arts-based methods such as theatre, film and photography, are inherently creative and relational, as expressed in the walk with Faye and the walk with Nick discussed above. The WIBM can also be a useful and important contribution to the relational practice of hostel key workers and social workers, to assist them in getting to know the individual stories behind the 'client', and may be useful in supporting earlier interventions (see Roy et al. 2015: 167; Ferguson 2016; Schütze 2008).

While there are benefits in 'combining' or, rather, interrelating arts practices and biographical research, there are also challenges which need to be considered. Roberts (2007) asks readers to take cognisance of the importance of critique, reflexivity, and acknowledgement of arts practice for biographical researchers in the use of performative research – how it can be conducted and in how researchers might be trained (Roberts 2007: para.121). Further, the importance of ethical issues on how we conduct research remain, but might occur differently, in adopting or adapting arts-based methods. In thinking through the challenges of WIBM, we also need to keep in mind the complexity of walking as a means of connecting with lives as told – in terms of imagination, memory, meaning, and space, how can this complexity be both imagined, theorised, and represented?

Biography, memory, and meaning

As the section on the walks with Nick and Faye illustrate, the biographical 'stories' we create, hold, and tell, can heal, empower, challenge, and transform our relationship to the past and the future. They are also important psycho-socially, as narratives of 'self-making' which can take various forms (Smith and Sparkes 2002; Sparkes and Smith 2003; Sparkes and Smith 2005; Phoenix and Sparkes 2007). The process of memory and meaning-making is, then, important to how we produce or construct a biography of 'self'. For in constructing a biography, we are shaping, and re-shaping a sense of self – attempting to achieve coherence in our relation to others and our social worlds. In the walk with Nick, he reflects upon his migration journey as intricately connected with his 'coming out' and finding who he wanted to be and become. In Faye's walk, we get a sense of her everyday routines, her connection to place, and the impact of place on her identity as a woman, a sex worker, and someone who experiences homelessness. In both walking interviews, recollection and memories are central to the sharing of experience, moving backwards and forwards in time to construct and reconstruct 'self' and biography.

In documenting the process of recollection in relation to memory, most experiences, according to Winter and Sivan (1999), leave 'long term memory traces', recorded in our 'episodic memory' system – the system which encodes 'what happened'. 'Autobiographical memory appears to be the most enduring kind of memory … combat experience is particularly dense because it is personal and dramatic. Harrowing moments are denser still' (Winter and Sivan 1999: 12). 'Memory work' involves an active staging of memory; a questioning attitude to the past and its reconstruction through memory, and questioning the transparency of what is remembered. Khun (2007) takes what is remembered as material for interpretation. Here there is a performative aspect to remembering, as Kuhn (2007) argues, through which the traces of the past that remain in the present are the raw material of (new) stories about the past. We can, therefore, understand memory as a 'medium' and not simply an instrument for exploring the past. Benjamin spent considerable time exploring memory and remembering, especially in relation to place, and discussed different 'memory models' (Laanemets n.d.: 71). Benjamin stated that 'epic' and 'rhapsodic memory':

> must yield an image of the person who remembers, in the same way a good archaeological report not only informs us about the strata from which its findings originate, but also gives an account of the strata which first had to be broken through.
>
> *(Benjamin 2005: 576)*

Memory work for Benjamin (in his early writing) thus involves 'archaeology', digging into the past, turning over the soil, again and again; inspecting the soil and strata (see Chapter 10). He also associates memory and remembering with 'topographical' work, mapping, and experiencing with his corporeal body, exemplified in his view of the Paris Arcades as a storage for collective memory. This connects the epic with rhapsodic (voluntary and involuntary) memory i.e., the repetitive, careful examination of one's history with the embodied revelatory aspect of remembering in place (see Chapter 10). Influenced by Proust and Freud, Benjamin describes the importance of voluntary and involuntary memory (Jones 2006: 154–6). The former may be enlisted in digging through the past; but it is the latter that can help to articulate the shock or surprise – the revelatory possibilities, connected to walking, the way that a place or landmark or object might reveal, in an involuntary way, a memory previously forgotten or hidden and that enables us to grasp the phenomenological aspects of walking. For example, when Faye stops to thank the tree for allowing her to walk over its 'legs', and when she tells us, as we approach a road leading under a bridge, a dimly lit, dark liminal space, of her first sexual exchange with a 'client', we experience the walking biographical interview as revelatory as well as relational, involving voluntary and involuntary memory, linked to place. There are, as Roberts (2002) discusses, various forms of memory that are important to biographical research and analysis.

Walking with Rosie Campbell and Shelly Stoops in Liverpool

The relationship between voluntary and involuntary memory – and relations between memory, biography, and meaning – is further exemplified in a walk led by Rosie Campbell (an academic) and Shelly Stoops (a health worker) who are both supporters for sex workers' rights and researchers in Liverpool. Rosie and Shelly outline a walk through Liverpool, the areas where street sex work takes place, and at the same time delineate their own history as researchers, outreach staff, and activists challenging stigma and violence against sex workers, whilst supporting the women working both on and off street in Liverpool, for the past twenty years. The walk and conversations evolved around their shared practice, addressing violence, coercion, and control, as well as their shared commitment to promoting rights and social justice for sex workers.

The walk with Rosie and Shelly started in a small café over a cup of tea. They were asked to draw a map of the walk they would take Maggie on. We discussed the ethics of the research and they completed the consent forms (that had been sent in advance of the meeting), and they agreed for the conversation along the way to be recorded and transcribed, and that they or Maggie would take photographs of the landmarks along the way. The transcript would be shared with them and the interview would be written up with their collaboration for the Walking Borders Blog. Both were familiar with Maggie's participatory methods and way of working to conduct biographical research. They shared their map and the route and in doing so they talked about why they wanted to do this walk: the regeneration of the area; residents' action against sex workers and displacement of sex work; their shared history in responding to sex work in Liverpool via research and activism; the development of the Merseyside hate crime approach to addressing violence against sex workers; and Rosie's recent PhD on this topic. They had previously documented the differing responses of residents, with some campaigning against sex work taking place in the area, with some residents supporting sex workers, especially in relation to safety – a key theme of their ongoing work. A central theme of the walk was violence against sex workers.

In the process of walking with Rosie and Shelly the places along the route evoked many memories for them. Indeed, the route was chosen because of memories of their past outreach work and activism; it illustrated their profound commitment to relating what they learnt about women's lives, in support of a common humanity and justice for sex workers. The walk also reflects other memories, revealing how deeply connected they are to the city, its history, politics, and culture.

Rosie: I've moved away from the city just in the last two years after nearly twenty-nine years here, I cry every time I come into the city, you know my heart lies in Liverpool.

Shelly replied 'I cry every time you leave'. Further into the walk, Rosie states, out of the blue: 'Oh, I feel at home here, we've talked about that, but I feel at home, not just in the city but in this area and on the beat'.

Both Rosie and Shelly's biographies are an important part of the narrative that emerged along the walk. Rosie's own biography as a student and then an academic and an outreach worker represents a lifetime of work supporting sex workers. Shelly was working as a helpline coordinator of a domestic abuse project and met two sex workers and then, as a consequence, changed the direction of her work towards supporting sex workers. The two met for the first time at a local project in the late 1990s. The walk elicited memories of some of the murders and rapes of sex workers in the area, of their long history of working together and the inspirational, resilient women they had met; the difficult times and the humour they had shared.

Their work was instrumental in the development of the Merseyside approach to addressing crimes against sex workers as hate crime. They describe being on 'outreach' together, and were once talking about hate crime when they suddenly came across a stencilled graffiti – an image of Peter Sutcliffe (a serial killer) and the words 'Warning: Peter Sutcliffe operates in this area'. This led to them having discussions about the issues experienced by sex workers and the work of the Merseyside Police Hate Crime Unit and it was agreed that sex workers should fit into its remit. The incorporation of sex workers, as a group vulnerable to hate crime, was a landmark decision by a police authority, and an important outcome of Shelly and Rosie's shared commitment to addressing crimes of violence associated with the stigma and 'othering' of sex workers.

There were some very poignant moments when the places we walked, the trees, buildings, walls, and fences evoked memories of their being together on outreach, and the women they worked with and supported. Walking in an area that had been transformed with new buildings, Shelly pointed out that it had previously been an area of grass and trees, where the women used to do 'business'. Rosie added:

> I just think of the hundreds of people we've spoken to, just to catch up with their lives. I remember a lady who was beauty therapy trained telling me the best nail varnish tips, just here, I'm just remembering this amazing conversation with her.

Their working biographies reflect a commitment to social action and the promotion of social justice for sex workers, that connected their memories of working together, the pioneering work they had conducted in the city, to stories of sexual inequalities, violence, and coercion. Their memories emerged in both voluntary and involuntary ways during the walk. At the end of the walk, one of them said:

> For us both the walk has been highly meaningful, being together (which we don't get to be as often now) reflecting on places, people and times shared, on struggles, trauma and achievements. It has been highly poignant, sharing such intense memories of people and places we cherish.

This walk focused specifically on the sites of sex work and what emerged were the losses, the murders, and violence against women selling sex on the street. But the theme of gentrification was also central, especially in relation to displacement and pricing of ordinary people out of the city centre and housing market; also, the former locations of sex work in the 1980s are now gentrified areas. The theme of social justice, for women in particular, resonates through the walk, as do the interrelated aspects of biography, memory, and meaning. Maggie gained a strong visual mental map of the Liverpool she had been shown by Rosie and Shelly, the shifting sites of where sex was bought and sold; the history of sex work connected to the docks, the seamen, and the colonial past; the sites where outreach took place; and the memorial sites where women were raped and/or lost their lives. In this sense, the walk told a partial, moving biography of Liverpool, through their biographical memories of working and connecting with women sex workers, issues of justice, and resonances of place.

Walking with Kerry Porth in Vancouver: Biography and cartography

The accounts of life that individuals give are not uniform, coherent, or unchanging, they are subject to memory, re-interpretation, and circumstance. As Bourdieu (1996) argues, the linear chronological biographical narrative is an 'illusion', that tellers constantly lose threads, that the narrative is partially motivated by a concern to give meaning, to create relationships between past present and future, to give meaning to identity. By this, he means we construct identities through the 'stories' we tell to give meaning to our lives. Our accounts may also be seen to serve numerous purposes; as Riessman (2008) says, we use narratives in different ways, 'to remember, argue, justify, persuade, engage, entertain, and even mislead an audience' (Riessman 2008: 183).

As we have seen in the walk with Rosie and Shelly, biographical research can be involved in the production of social justice through knowledge production, that reveals 'social actors' own way of knowing the field, through generating 'understanding' (Fowler 1996: 12). Bourdieu's use of the concept 'understanding' is relevant here (Bourdieu 1996). In biographical research, our 'understanding' involves attempting to situate oneself in the place the interviewee occupies, in the social space in order to understand them and:

> to give oneself a general and genetic comprehension of who the person is, based on the (theoretical or practical) command of the social conditions of existence and the social mechanisms which exert their effects on the whole ensemble of the category to which the person belongs.

> (Bourdieu 1996: 22–3).

Walking is an appropriate way to get to know 'the field' – in Bourdieu's sense of 'understanding'. For example, in February 2016, Maggie returned to Vancouver (see Chapter 6) to walk with Kerry Porth at the 26th Annual Missing Women's Memorial March. The march is a pilgrimage, a remembrance, and a performance of advocacy and activism. Family members, friends, and citizens walk through the Downtown Eastside, stopping at the landmarks where women had died or were last seen, and burn sweetgrass and leave a rose in remembrance.

Kerry, at the time of the interview, was chair of Pivot Legal Society, a legal advocacy group that addresses legislation and policies that undermine human rights, and a former CEO of PACE, a Sex Worker support project offering services to Sex Workers in the Downtown Eastside. Pivot is also committed to the de-criminalisation of sex work, arguing that criminalisation leads to stigma, discrimination, and violence. Meeting up on the morning of the march in a coffee shop, Kerry explained the map of the walk she had been asked by Maggie to draw.

Kerry says:

> The Memorial March starts at the Carnegie Centre at the intersection of Main and Hastings. We go down Main Street, we end up coming down to the bottom of Main Street which is here, and so there's a very bad drawing of an overpass but the mountains are in the background and there's an

FIGURE 7.2 Kerry sharing her map. Image: Maggie O'Neill, printed with kind permission Kerry Porth.

overpass and then over here is CRAB Park and this is where the Memorial Stone is. So, the inscription says 'The Heart Has Its Own Memory' and this is where people go to have memorials for the murdered women, it's a large rock with an inscription in it.

   People leave tobacco and flowers and they light candles and I've attended a number of memorials there. At the close of the walk there is a candle ceremony there and they light candles and then they move on to the Japanese Language Hall and they have a feast there, I've never been to that part of it.

Kerry says that the memorial stone is in honour of all people who have died, been murdered or have gone missing in/from the DTES, but has come, over time, to be associated with the Pickton case (see Chapter 6). She goes on to say:

   CRAB Park is kind of a cool thing. CRAB stands for Create a Real Accessible Beach because there was no place for people to get to the beach down here and so it was a social justice thing and so it's just weird because you have the craziness of the Downtown Eastside and you just go over this little bridge and there's this big, peaceful park with a beach and yeah. So, I've gone there you know on my own when you need to think and it's a nice place to go. So yeah those are my two favourite places.

Kerry points to her map:

   Yes, so we're just going to be a block up that way and that's Main and Hastings, our most famous intersection and then we walk down Main Street to Alexander. This takes us through Gastown and that's always kind of an interesting part of the march because you've got very wealthy tourists there.

   We stop at various places along the way where women were last seen and they'll lay a rose for them … the march sometimes spreads out over a couple of blocks but they always have the elders at the front so at least people don't get left behind that way because you walk at their pace.

The sense of community and support gained from organisations like PACE and Pivot are crucial to marginalised residents of the DTES (see Chapter 6). Kerry stated that Pickton was charged with twenty-six murders and convicted of six, that Vancouver has the 'second highest urban Aboriginal population in Canada, the highest is in Winnipeg', and that 'the women's memorial march continues to honour the lives of missing and murdered women and all women's lives lost in the Downtown Eastside'.

   Increasing deaths of many vulnerable women from the DTES still leaves family, friends, loved ones, and community members with an overwhelming sense of grief and loss. Indigenous women disproportionately continue to go missing or be murdered with minimal to no action to address these tragedies or the systemic nature of gendered violence, poverty, racism, or colonialism.

Whilst waiting in a circle for the walk to start, having been handed pink hearts with the missing and dead women's names written on them, Kerry states that 'the hearts are new this year and the banner in front of us, the panels were either sewn by women at the Women's Centre or by family members and so they're representing each of the serial killer victims'. She goes on to talk about the extent of gentrification and displacement of people from the DTES.

> Young hipster professionals think it's edgy to live down here, but the people who call this place home and who have been here for so long feel that they're being displaced and this community has such a long history of displacement for its Indigenous people. There was a black community that was erased from down here, the Japanese community was erased.

A former colleague joined us and responded to Kerry's point by saying that this current wave of people moving into the DTES is yet 'another generation of appropriation of land, space, community and it's sickening and it needs to stop'.

The conversations along the walk focused on the evolution of the March over the years, the way that sex workers/sex work had been erased from recent narratives about the walk (that focused upon Indigenous people's experiences) and the importance of campaigning for the rights of sex workers and to end violence against them. The conversations were punctured by periods of silence as roses were laid and sweetgrass burnt by the elders leading the walk.

The 'sensory' dimensions (environmental and relational) of the walk were in high relief; it also rained hard throughout and the silence, contemplation, and memorialisation at each stopping point produced a powerful sense of solidarity and commemoration. Maggie asked Kerry about the purpose of the burning of sweetgrass:

> it is burnt as an offering and a rose is left at the site of where a woman was found or last seen. And that's what people use to smudge with so that's a spiritual cleansing. So, what you do is you cleanse your eyes so that you can see clearly, you cleanse your ears so that you can hear clearly, you cleanse your mouth so that you speak kindly, then I think you pull it over your head, you know over your body, down your arms, down your legs so that you're strong, and then the last is your heart.

Walking with Kerry had covered the evolution and politics of the March, but also the relationship to the bigger picture of violence against sex workers and violence against Indigenous women. The March itself is a memorial and memorialisation, a reminder and a symbol of protest and resistance. The start and close of the walk is marked by a healing circle, the rituals (sweetgrass and laying of roses); the colours and banners, traditional blankets and clothing, the drumming and women's warrior song all add to the rhythm of the walk, the walking, stopping, remembering, all are a reminder of our social connectedness around the issues of social justice for marginalised community members in the DTES.

Importantly, the March is also an example of a radical democratic imaginary; over a now twenty-six-year history, it has opened and continues to keep open a space to honour and remember the missing and dead women, to claim that Indigenous women and girls' lives matter, and to challenge the sexual and social inequalities that underpin the continuing need for this claim. The walk is an example of the importance of remembering, not simply memorialising the missing and murdered women. Kerry told us about Tina Fontaine, as an example of this deeply troubling issue of violence against Indigenous women and girls. Tina was 15 when she was found dead. A report published by the Royal Canadian Mounted Police (RCMP 2014) put the total of missing and murdered Aboriginal women at 1,181. Indigenous women account for 16 per cent of female homicides and 11.3 per cent of missing women, yet they make up only 4.3 per cent of the Canadian population.

The walk with Kerry is also an assertion of the right to the city and to space, transgressing the borders and boundaries of stigma, race, and sexual and social inequalities and gentrification. The walk is 'a history in the present' and a reminder of the marginalisation of the people associated with the DTES. This marginalisation is an outcome of race, class, and colonial history, the stigma and violence attached to marginalised peoples. It is therefore vitally important to keep these issues on the agenda, connecting private troubles to public issues, drawing attention to memory (both voluntary and involuntary in walking) and biographies. The importance of place, activism, rights, and outreach support surrounding sexual identities and sex working, have been key themes in the four walks in this chapter.

Reflecting on the importance of bodies and place, Dee Heddon (2008: 100) (see Chapter 9) comments that a 'deep mapping' – we might call this cartography – can occur through autobiographical work in place and that narratives can 'adhere to sites' (Pearson and Shanks 1997: 51). This is very apparent in all four walks. Imagining, remembering, and drawing a map is an embodied experience, that calls upon memory and enables us to locate or situate ourselves in relation to place and space. Mapping is described by O'Rourke as the ways in which 'walking meets mapping through wayfaring and wayfinding' (O'Rourke 2016: xx). The Missing Women's Memorial March in Vancouver's DTES is probably the most salient example here of the way that narratives 'adhere to sites' in the route of the walk, the long history of the walk, and the way that it opens a forum for repressed elements of history (the oppression and disposability of Indigenous women and sex workers) to be kept alive and on the political agenda.

Importantly, the four walks in this chapter, given as examples of the WIBM, illustrate the usefulness of using maps and cartography, of the 'deep mapping' that can occur, when starting a walking interview with a route map, and for the map to form the initial stage setting the frame and scene for the research/biography to unfold. Walking through Soho, a northern city in the UK, Liverpool, and Vancouver, led by the co-walker[s] participants, shows the various dimensions of WIBM, the importance of the landscape or environment, the relational work that takes place, the emergence of involuntary and voluntary memory, and the visual/sensory relationship to space and place, whilst walking.

Biographical imagination, walking, and memory

The relationship between biography, memory, place, and embodied learning through walking is evidenced in the excerpts from the walks detailed in this chapter. The discussion of the walks has facilitated a shared sense of the visual, material, phenomenological, embodied, and imagined, yet transitory, sense of lived lives, as well as giving priority to the imaginative aspect of walking and thinking as 'body and image space' (Weigel 1996).

The four examples of the WIBM have illustrated the importance of reflecting on walking as embodied in place and in time, operating relationally and recursively. In Vancouver, the enactment and representation of the 'mattering' of the missing women's memorial walk, over long-term history through the eyes and experience of Kerry, enables us to reflect upon and critique society (its sexual, social, and racial inequalities) through biography and history as a crucial aspect of the sociological imagination. This also includes reflecting upon space, place, time, memory, and injustice, during the walk.

The walking interviews in this chapter indicate the significance of place and attachments to objects and landmarks that seem to invoke not only a sense of belonging to place, but as in the excerpt from Nick Mai's walk, also that the meanings people give to place can tell us something of their identities and sense of belonging, as being 'in place', 'between', or 'out of place'. These findings will be addressed further in the autobiographical walks discussed in Chapter 10.

Our use of the 'biographical imagination' here is both the imagination we use in constructing our identities/self as well as imagination of the researcher in understanding the lives of others through biographical research: the WIBM. The WIBM can produce narratives that generate social knowledge to inform and raise awareness, as well as counter the sanitised, demonised, or hidden aspects of the lived cultures of marginalised, as 'othered' by wider society. In doing so, the WIBM can produce knowledge as a form of social justice. Informed by analysis of memory, this 'micrology' can illuminate broader structures, practices, and processes enabling 'understanding' and possible action/interventions.

In the next chapter we explore the 'phenomenology of walking' in a garden, connecting the imagination and imaginary to emotion and memory invoked by 'gardens': the ways that our memories, emotions, and senses of, and in, gardens, connect to our biographies, lived lives, and wider socio-cultural traditions.

Notes

1 O'Neill's Leverhulme Research Fellowship was undertaken between 2015–2016 and sought to explore walking as a method for conducting research on borders, risk, and belonging; conduct walking research with participants/co-walkers (artists, academics, researchers, and residents in the UK and across the globe) to access their experience and reflections on border places and spaces; advance innovations in biographical and visual/ performative methods; and reflect on the impact of the collaborative research findings and walks. Available at https://walkingborders.com (Accessed 1 January 2018).
2 A direct access hostel is a hostel that provides emergency temporary accommodation at the door.

References

Adorno, T.W. (1978) *Minima Moralia*. London: Verso.

Benjamin, W. (1992) *Illuminations*. London: Fontana Press.

Benjamin,W. (2005) *Walter Benjamin: Selected Writings*, Vol. 2, Pt 2 (1931–1934). M. Jennings, H. Eiland, and G. Smith (eds.) Cambridge, MA: Belknap Press of Harvard University Press.

Boal, A. (2000) *Theatre of the Oppressed*. London: Routledge.

Bourdieu, P. (1996) Understanding, *Theory, Culture and Society*, 13(2): 17–37.

Careri, F. (2017) *Walkscapes: Walking as an Aesthetic Practice*. Ames, IA: Culcidae Press.

Cornell, D. (1995) *The Imaginary Domain*. London: Routledge.

Ferguson, H. (2016) Professional helping as negotiation in motion: Social work as work on the move, *Applied Mobilities*, 1(2): 193–206.

Fowler, B. (1996) An introduction to Pierre Bourdieu's 'Understanding', *Theory, Culture and Society*, 13(2): 1–16.

Frank, A. (2012) Practising Dialogic Narrative Analysis. In: J. A. Holstein, and J. F. Gubrium (eds.) *Varieties of Narrative Analysis*. London: Sage.

Glover, N. (2005) Chapter Six: Aesthetics, creativity, and the potential space. *Psychoanalytic Aesthetics: The British School*, Free Associations. Available at www.psychoanalysis-and-therapy.com/human_nature/glover/index.html (Accessed 23 September 2018).

Heddon, D. (2008) *Autobiography and Performance*. London: Palgrave Macmillan.

Kara, H. (2015) *Creative Research Methods in the Social Sciences: A Practical Guide*. Bristol: Policy Press.

Kuhn, A. (2007) Photography and cultural memory: A methodological exploration, *Visual Studies*, 22(3): 283–292.

Laanemets, M. (n.d.) Places that remember. Available at www.eki.ee/km/place/pdf/K P1_09laanemets.pdf (Accessed 1 January 2018).

Mannay, D. (2010) Making the familiar strange: Can visual research methods render the familiar setting more perceptible? *Qualitative Research*, 10(1): 91–111.

Mills, C. W. (1970) *The Sociological Imagination*. Harmondsworth, UK: Penguin.

O'Neill, M. (1999) *Adorno, Culture and Feminism*. London: Routledge.

O'Neill, M. (2018) Walking, well-being and community: Racialized mothers building cultural citizenship using participatory arts and participatory action research, *Ethnic and Racial Studies*, 41(1): 73–97.

O'Neill, M. and McHugh, C. (2017) Walking with Faye from a direct access hostel to her special place in the city: Walking, body and image space. A visual essay, *Journal of Social Work Practice*, 31(2): 207–223.

O'Rourke, K. (2016) *Walking and Mapping: Artists as Cartographers*. Cambridge, MA: MIT Press.

O'Neill, M. (2008) Transnational refugees: The transformative role of art? [53 paragraphs], *Forum Qualitative Sozialforschung/Forum: Qualitative Social Research*, 9(2): Art. 59.

Pearson, M. and Shanks, M. (1997) Performing a visit: Archaeologies of the contemporary past, *Performance Research*, 2(2): 41–53.

Phoenix, C. and Sparkes, A. (2007) *The Narrative Construction of Self in an Ageing, Athletic Body, Narrative and Memory.* Huddersfield, UK: University of Huddersfield, 73–80.

RCMP. (2014) Missing and murdered Aboriginal women: A national operational overview. Available at www.rcmp-grc.gc.ca/en/missing-and-murdered-aboriginal-women-national-operational-overview (Accessed 23 September 2018).

Riessman, C. K. (2008) *Narrative Methods for the Human Sciences.* London: Sage.

Riemann, G. (2003) A joint project against the backdrop of a research tradition: An introduction to "Doing Biographical Research" [36 paragraphs], *Forum Qualitative Sozialforschung/Forum: Qualitative Social Research*, 4(3): Art. 18. Available at http://nbn-resolving.de/urn:nbn:de:0114-fqs0303185. (Accessed 14 August 2018).

Roberts, B. (2002) *Biographical Research.* Buckingham: Open University Press.

Roberts, B. (2006) *Micro Social Theory.* Basingstoke, UK: Palgrave Macmillan.

Roberts, B. (2015) Biographical research: Past, present, future. In: M. O'Neill, B. Roberts, and A. Sparkes (eds.) *Advances in Biographical Methods.* Abingdon, UK: Routledge.

Roy, A. N., Hughes, J., Froggett, L., and Christensen, J. (2015) Using mobile methods to explore the lives of marginalised young men in Manchester. In: L. Hardwick, R. Smith and A. Worsley, *Innovations in Social Work Research: Using Methods Creatively.* London & Philadelphia: Jessica Kingsley Publishers, 155–172.

Schütze, F. (2008) Biography analysis on the empirical base of autobiographical narratives: How to analyse autobiographical narrative interviews – Part I, *Biographical Counselling in Rehabilitative Vocational Training – Further Education Curriculum Module, B.2.1.* Available at www.zsm.ovgu.de/zsm_media/Das+Zentrum/Forschungspr ojekte/INVITE/B2_1-p-140.pdf (Accessed 25 October 2018).

Smith, B. and Sparkes, A. C. (2002) Men, sport, spinal cord injury and the construction of coherence: Narrative practice in action, *Qualitative Research*, 2(2): 143–171.

Solnit, R. (2001) *Wanderlust: A History of Walking.* London: Verso.

Solnit, R. (2014) *Wanderlust: A History of Walking.* London: Granta.

Sparkes, A. C. and Smith, B. (2003) Men, sport, spinal cord injury and narrative time, *Qualitative Research*, 3(3): 295–320.

Sparkes, A. C. and Smith, B. (2005) When narratives matter: Men, sport, and spinal cord injury, *Medical Humanities*, 31(2): 81–88.

Weigel, S. (1996) *Body- and Image-Space: Re-Reading Walter Benjamin.* London: Routledge.

Wiles, R., Crow, G., and Pain, H. (2011) Innovation in qualitative research methods: A narrative review, *Qualitative Research*, 11(5): 587–604.

Winnicott, D. W. (1982) *Playing and Reality.* London: Routledge.

Winter, J., & Sivan, E. (1999). Setting the framework. In J. Winter & E. Sivan (Eds.), *War and Remembrance in the Twentieth Century* (Studies in the Social and Cultural History of Modern Warfare, pp. 6–39). Cambridge: Cambridge University Press.

Worsley, A. (ed.) *Innovations in Social Work Research.* London: Jessica Kingsley Publishers.

8

THE PHENOMENOLOGY OF WALKING IN A GARDEN

Introduction

When we use the word 'garden' in conversation, we are drawing on strong images and preconceptions, which are informed by rich histories and traditions; behind our everyday notion, there are layers of meaning both personal and passed on by wider culture. At first thought, a garden may 'merely' mean to us a pleasant scene of plants, trees, paths and corners, ponds, and vistas. We may immediately have images of our own garden, or another we pass or frequent, possibly a 'public' garden, which may be part of a larger park that has been 'decorated' in areas with some formal plant displays and sculpture. But associated with many of these thoughts on gardens is something deeper, emotions and memories shaping our experience of walking within their confines: particular 'gardens' are set in our personal, biographical time, while our conceptions also draw on wider cultural traditions.

The 'garden' is a place redolent with history, faith, fable, and legend: The Hanging Gardens of Babylon, the Garden of Eden, Vauxhall Gardens, the Tuileries, Tivoli Gardens, Alhambra's Generalife, Seville's Alcázar, Kabul's Babur, Kew Gardens, gardens 'real' and 'imagined' (or both), conjure up images and wonder, as sites for pleasure and diversion, of 'paradise' or 'arcadia' ('lost' and to be 'found'). Here, we could trace the history of gardens and how earlier 'classical' Chinese, Islamic, or other forms had a wide influence on Western and wider design, and also broader developments in the shaping of landscape (see *SHGDL* 1998–). Included here would be an examination of the changes in design, say in country British gardens as they 'extended' from the enclosed gardens of castles, to formal gardens of the large country house, 'evolving' into the wider landscaping (tree planting, artificial lakes and hills, etc.) of 18th century designers, and then to the creation of even more 'natural' vistas. There is the influence of medieval cloisters and herb gardens, gardens of ancient Roman villas and the Italian Renaissance (and first botanical gardens), the changing scenes and buildings of the Chinese garden, the varied composition of Japanese gardens (e.g., rock gardens), and the differing Persian and Islamic (e.g., courtyard) styles, and the English cottage garden. Relevant also is the lasting influence of literature and art, such as the Romantic movement (cf. Wordsworth, Hazlitt, Constable) with its effect on our 'sense' of the natural environment in terms of the 'appreciation' or 'feeling' of beauty, the pastoral idyll, the picturesque and the powerful grandeur of the 'sublime' (Craven 2016; cf. Wordsworth's *A Guide through the District of the Lakes*, 1810, Selincourt 1977).

Important in any 'review' of garden history is the way in which 'gardens' became cemented in our consciousness as places of recreation and retreat, while recognising that how we see 'historical gardens' today may not be quite how their originators and first users felt about them (see Felus 2016). Gardens (flowers and trees) have long and complex layers of cultural and religious meanings (see Graves 1961; Frazer 1987; Lewis-Stempel 2015: 163–4, 188).

Gardens and parks (both public and private) have historically taken various (and often mixed) forms: as pleasure gardens (Downing 2009); memorial gardens (with commemorative statues or plaques etc.); zoological gardens; botanical gardens (Eden Project, Kew Gardens, Chelsea Physic garden, and Edinburgh Botanic Gardens) (Rutherford 2015); residential and allotment gardens (Willes 2015); and urban garden squares (cf. those in Bloomsbury designed by Repton); and wildlife gardens. The location of gardens can be in a courtyard and cloister, under glass (greenhouses), walled, on a roof, in built-up urban spaces, in shopping malls, office concourses, on former viaducts, at sides of pavements, or in very hostile natural environments (e.g., in a desert or beside the sea: cf. film-maker Derek Jarman's garden on the beach at Dungeness, South England; see Jarman and Sooley 1995). A consideration of how we conceive gardens today draws in a wider debate surrounding the 'heritage industry', regarding the (ideological) construction and presentation of the 'past' (with issues of conservation, preservation, commercialism, nostalgia, identity formation, national decline, etc.) as presented to visitors to the English country house and garden, and other 'historical sites', by charitable and national bodies and wider culture (in literature, media, art, and so on) (cf. Hewison 1987; Wright 2009). We can say that the individual (and communities) constructs versions of the 'past' (as gone, continuing, to return), its meanings and importance from an interplay of personal and social 'resources' (narratives, images, interactions) – both are involved in a complex cultural process of 'history-making'. While the 'heritage industry' may relay certain values and imagery, its version of 'tradition' is by no means 'uni-dimensional', or merely received and uncontested (see Samuel 1996; Roberts 2004).

Often gardens will have permanent buildings and sheds (e.g., for storage of implements, greenhouses for plants, etc.), or hobby or 'garden' rooms and offices. They may have sculptures, pergolas, barbecues, ponds, bird-feeders and baths, fountains, ornaments, planters, benches, sofas and chairs, tables, and seasonally occasional awnings or umbrellas. Gardens are now placed increasingly on roofs of houses, and large residential and commercial buildings, for aesthetic or eco- logical and environmental reasons: to 'green the city', to conserve energy and plants, and to provide more 'natural' living (cf. an older, famous roof garden is above a store in Kensington, London: Byers 2017; Yudin 2017).

The garden may have many 'functions': as a place of rest, a solitary arena for reflection, or for religious contemplation set apart from worldly distraction, or, broadly, as an extension of an interior – a 'room outside' (cf. Brookes 1969). It may also be for assignations (as in historical romantic fiction 'courting rituals'), for couples that may not want to be easily observed. Of course, it is a setting to observe the beauty of nature – flowers, plants, and trees, and butterflies, birds, and insects – and, perhaps, to 'lose oneself', at least for some moments, in the surroundings. Commonly, the garden or park is also an arena for families and friends to enjoy company, to eat, drink, and play – have 'fun and games' – and sunbathe or even sleep (on the grass, in a hammock, on a lounger, etc.). As the seasons change, activities will rise and fall accordingly. Gardens may be places for both informal (e.g., cooking a barbecue meal for family and friends) and formal (e.g., a wedding reception) garden parties (cf. the Queen's Garden Parties, UK).

Despite the variety of gardens – in size, ownership, access, content, variety of function, and so on – it would seem there is often a common theme in how they are perceived – as a place of and for 'recreation': as plants undergo revival, so we can have renewal in mind, body, and spirit. This has an appeal that is found in the 18th–19th century ideas of the 'natural state' and subsequent 'back to nature' ideas, a former state with the 'natural' as a source of harmony and wellbeing, lost by growing urban and industrial complexity and associated physical, mental, and social ills (cf. as itemised by the new 19th century focus on the gathering of 'moral statistics'). At night, the garden can take on a different character, bestow- ing an apprehension and anxiety, perhaps from an 'ancient fear of the forest': such as the perception of trees in threatening semi-human shapes (cf. L. M. Boston, *The Children of Green Knowe*, 1955) – the flitting outlines and sounds of creatures, as shrubbery and trees take more sinister form to startle the unwary. The dark wood or forest has hidden dangers, and perhaps with evil or mysterious fairytale, mythical, fantastical, or folkloric inhabitants (cf. the 'foliaged' Green Man: see Anderson 1990), while open, sparse parkland in the gloom of dusk has an eeri- ness, loneliness, and mystery (cf. Antonioni's film *Blow Up*), just as do the ill-lit, deserted night bars, streets, and corners (cf. Hopper's paintings) in the urban environment. The single silhouetted walking (male) figure, a distinct theme in the history of photography, symbolises both these timeless spaces and an alien- ated mood (Dyer 2007: 146–56). So, while a place of pleasure – amusement, enjoyment, and recreation, even desire (for the 'infinite') – the garden can also be a place of anxiety, uncertainty, and dread.

To walk in a garden is to meet an unfolding sensual experience, and also 're-live' some of our preconceptions residing in previous similar perambulations (see the walk with Miller in Chapter 4). These current and past understandings, sensations, and feelings will inform, to some extent, how someone will relate to a companion in conversation, as in a walking interview. It may well be that a 'respondent' directly draws parallels to a garden or park in a former home or town – a vivid reminder and comparison with experiences of 'another life', before migration for work, or asylum due to persecution, or other migration.

Garden and the city

The notion of a 'garden' can be situated within a broader 'cultural' construct of the 'country and the city' (at least in the UK) (see Williams 1973; Williams 1976). It is allied to conceptions of the 'rural' – or 'rurality' – with a range of social and national meanings. One of the strong features of 'Englishness' is the peaceful vision of the village green, rose-covered cottages, trees in rolling landscape, and perceived social harmony (albeit based on status hierarchy and social inequalities). In World War II, such portrayals of the village and landscape were part of the propaganda for what was being fought to preserve, as the necessary 'timeless' milieu for a certain set of 'national values'.

While such ideas of 'rural', 'countryside', and even 'garden' had an element of 'timelessness' (although, the 'rural' landscapes of Britain have been changed by human intervention over thousands of years, cf. Hoskins 1955; Crane 2016), there is also within this notion of the 'rural' the setting for social renewal and 're-moralisation'. In 19th century Britain, the idea of transferring ('replanting') the criminal or poor of the cities to institutions in rural areas was common, as in General Booth's map outlining a schema for moral and practical education in 'farm colonies', before sending them overseas to serve the Empire (Booth 1890). The fate of children sent abroad until as late as the 1950s from charity orphanages in the UK, often to work under harsh conditions, has become a prominent issue in recent years in Australia, and latterly, the UK.

The 'decline of the city' and the 'flight' to the suburb or countryside became an increasing social and political (ideological) concern during the 1960s. Famously, Jacobs (1961) detailed the pressing issues of city neighbourhoods and gave a critique of 1950s urban environmental ideas and housing policy. She celebrated the liveliness of the neighbourhood (e.g., Greenwich Village), the 'human scale' needed for social conviviality, and varied uses (social interaction, recreation) of urban spaces (the street and green areas) – features which urban planning should safeguard. Later, radical urban geographers during the 1970s began to focus on the processes of city, and the construction of space and social networks, as a site for production and consumption, power distribution and economic inequalities, and social segregation (cf. Harvey 1973; Castells 1977).

The issues of 'structures of secondariness' – in employment, housing, policing, racism, and other dimensions – in the formation of inner city areas, and a repressive shift in the nature of State action but also local community culture and resistance, also became subject to deeper analysis (see Hall et al. 2013: 339–62). In the scrutiny of these internal and external dimensions, the 'street' became an ethnographic focus of study as the context to understand cultural diversity and everyday encounters, proximities and divergences, and contestation – how the 'local' is shaped by 'evolving' customs and historical and present interplay of space and group, within the contexts and effects of global and other changes (see Hall 2012). Activities as mundane as 'walking' can be linked to ordinary movement in urban spaces, to social institutions, and to interconnections with social inequalities and power, including questions such as access and resources (see Shortell and Brown 2014).

The idea of the 'rural' was 'built in' to the growth of 'suburbia' in the UK from the 1930s–1950s, and concerns regarding city living – houses were to be given a garden at the front and rear, often having decorative wooden 'beams' on the outside, windows with small stained glass panes of rural or 'natural' motifs (a sun or plant), and sited on roads given names with rural associations ('drives' and 'avenues' often being compounded with addition of names of a tree, flower, or a Romantic poet). It seems there was an attempt to somehow (re)connect through symbol, style, and design an expanding suburbia (spreading across the fields) with a 'romantic tradition' and 'renewal' regarding nature – traceable from Wordsworth's poetry, to Humboldt's explorations, to the movements for preservation and conservation (e.g., U.S. natural parks fought for by campaigner John Muir and others in the Sierra Nevada) which was not simply an appreciation of vista, but a spiritual conception of 'oneness' with and of nature (Amato 2004: 208; see Wulf 2015). A notion of the rural was firmly embedded in 1930s suburban growth at time of the 'opening' of the countryside to the car and the campaigns for walking access to the hills and moors (see Chapter 5). The 'country vs. city dualism' is still a very strong, if shifting, but usually 'simplifying', distinction in England, a long cultural response to the social disruptions and uncertainties brought by industrialism and urbanism (see Williams 1973; Williams 1976; Jennings 1985).

There were various interventionist responses in the 19th century (in the UK and elsewhere) to the slums and terrible conditions of city life for workers and poor (e.g., in housing, sanitation, parks), including placing 'reformative' institutions for offenders (and orphanages) in the countryside and 'model industrial villages' (New Lanark, Saltaire, etc.) to 'improve' the workforce and their circumstances (Yallop 2016; Booth 1890). There was also, in the 1930s, the effects of the Depression (and Government's slowness to act) which motivated voluntary, charitable, and religious groups (e.g., Quakers) to go to into the 'distressed' areas (of heavy industry) in South Wales and elsewhere to set up self-help employment, environmental, and health improvement schemes, including communal gardens and allotments (cf. Jennings 1934). Fifty years later, another rise in unemployment in the 1980s brought a series of Government initiatives (as a response to criticism) including 'Garden Festivals' (e.g., Ebbw Vale, Wales 1992) – to beautify, reclaim derelict industrial sites, and 'breathe new life' into affected areas as a spur to new housing and private investment. A little earlier there had been various 'community development' and other projects in the late

1960s and early 1970s (e.g., Six Towns Project, UK). Today, the idea of 'greening the city' is common, but it is not a new idea and can be found in earlier ideas of the 19th–20th century of parks being the 'lungs' of the city, and extracting pollutants, as in the trees of London streets. There was also the important early 20th century development in the UK of the 'garden city' and 'garden suburbs/estates' for cities in the countryside, as promoted by Ebenezer Howard in *Garden Cities of To-morrow* 1902 (e.g., Letchworth 1903; Welwyn Garden City 1920), as both 'humanising' and 'naturalising' the built environment by bringing benefits of the rural to the urban through social planning (Willes 2015: 289–317).

Rather different, was the inter-war (although having earlier 19th century origins) 'plotlander' or smallholding movement (in the UK and various countries), where working class families (and others, such as artists) lived in shanties and chalets in self-organised communities (Willes 2015: 303–6; Hardy and Ward 1984). We must also remember that there was the opening up and provision of municipal city parks in the 19th century (cf. Roundhay Park, Leeds, UK 1872 – on the site of an 11th century Norman hunting estate) and, of course, the later establishment of the National Parks (in the UK and elsewhere) and their recent extension, and officially planned 'green belts' established around cities. Recently (January 2017), the UK Government has announced the building of fourteen 'garden villages' and three 'garden towns'. One recent campaign proposal has been mooted to establish Greater London as a huge urban national park to enhance health, biodiversity, and the environment (Raven-Ellison 2014).

A movement to 'green the city' – with city farms, tree planting, conservation areas, verge planting, and a renewed interest in allotments – has gathered pace in recent years, but can be fitted into a much longer 'movement', including the construction of 'urban parks' (cf. Willes 2015: 341–73; Otterbourg and Roberts 2016). However, the declining level of official funding of existing urban public parks (and so, commercial pressures) is an increasing concern (in the UK) (see Communities and Local Government Committee 2017; Moore 2017; see also Comedia 1995; Elborough 2016).

Nature writing and walking

The burgeoning of 'popular' literature about walking – overlapping with a renewal of 'nature writing' – is connected to an attempt to relate the experience of being within 'nature', while at the same time being philosophically informed and reflecting ecological and social concerns. These writings commonly also have a strong autobiographical account, relating to how we are 'formed' within landscape – the countryside's multiple sensations, frequently containing writing reflecting a mixture of literary (often 'Romantic'), historical, and poetical sources. There is often some 'spiritual' approach to the outdoors – an intention to create a 'heightened' awareness of the varied surroundings with the detail of sounds, smells, climate, time of day or night, etc. in giving a 'depth of feeling' of a 'unique' space or landscape (field, river, marsh, moor), its fauna and flora, and its 'borderlines' (cf. Attlee 2012; Cowen 2015; Deakin 2008; Dee 2013; Donaldson 2017; Farley and Roberts 2012; Harrison 2016; Pavord 2016; Jamie 2005, 2012; Macfarlane 2008, 2013, 2015; Thomson 2013; Warwick 2017; Wohlleben 2017). In these works, there is usually an allusion to the private, hidden, traces, tracks, clues, and so on, under the immediate 'surface' appearance of terrain (cf. Gooley 2015), perhaps emphasising that in uncovering the appreciation of both the detail of nature and its wider landscape, there is also some inner personal revelation or quest. Interestingly, there has also been a growing notion of the 'wild', as indicated in titles of books, TV programmes, and leisure activities etc. associated with swimming, food, holidays, and even in leaving some garden and field areas relatively untended. In the genre of 'countryside literature', the act of walking seems to be informed by the imperative of getting closer to, within, at 'one' with nature, and thereby enabling 'release' and 'freedom', and fulfilment. These various arenas provide conceptions, expectations, or a 'frame of thinking' that helps shape how we perceive walking in a garden (or park), in so doing influencing our narratives of the experience and how we relate to 'nature'

The garden path and bench

The 'garden' figures in our everyday language – within differing speech contexts, it has implicit meanings and associated action. The idea of the 'garden path', for example, enters routinely into everyday speech and 'sayings': to 'lead someone up' (or 'down') the garden (path)' is to mislead, deceive, seduce, or start in one place, but take someone unwitting (who may have been distracted by the equivalent of the beauty of surroundings) somewhere else. The scents and mysteries of the garden have been long associated with metaphors of sexual activity, and transportation to different states of ecstasy or dreaming – along a sensual path.

A garden walk is a movement through scene to scene – unlike seeing a painting, which is only one given vista. However, walking around a gallery at a particular exhibition, from painting to painting of flowers, vistas, etc., and from room to room, may have strong similarities with a stroll through a garden, if as the paintings 'demand' your belief in the 'now' of the room is suspended, and each painting scene is perceptually (and otherwise emotionally and sensually) 'entered'. We begin to revisualise the two-dimensional picture, in depth, and 'broaden' its height and width – appreciating and 'living', moving within the picture and its perspective. Today, augmented and immersive reality, 3D, and 360 degree photography are now allowing the surface, the screen, the canvas to be 'entered', more 'fully', and to enhance, enable, extend our imagination, and our participation in the scene, 'almost in reality'; for instance, to walk down the garden path.

On a garden walk, we may take time to pause, and sit. An ubiquitous fixture in the garden and park is the 'bench' (in wood, sometimes aided by metal): it waits patiently, fixed in all weathers and seasons and reflecting their moods, and in day and night, for its next sitter, as a static 'spectator' on human life, and observer of nature (see Dyer 2007: 131). The park bench can be a site for an assignation, exchange of secrets, or a 'pick-up'; a 'sofa in the living room of the outdoors'. The park bench is often donated in commemoration to a departed loved one (with a dedicated plate) becoming a site to lay annual flowers for a former sitter – it comes to represent illness, old age and death (as, it has been be said, the armchair did in Picasso's work, as well as a protection for the sitter: see Richardson 2009). In recent years, artists have utilised the bench as a 'resting' place in parks or city streets for reclining statutes often of famous deceased persons (which the living can sit alongside) or 'characters'. The park bench has been used as a 'sound installation' by artist Christian Boltanski with the words (from letters) of soldiers on the way to World War I, possibly not to return, recorded and played to the sitter (*The Whispers*, Folkestone Triennial 2008). The park bench gives minor respite from a walk, a point of reflection, an opportunity to read, to gaze at others, or look closely at flowers or insects, or to lazily scan the scene. In a walking conversation or research interview, the act of bench-sitting may mark a corner, a pause, perhaps allowing a 'turn in the narrative', to expand on something just raised, take a break for a new topic, or provide increased physical (face to face) 'attention' to the other. The park bench has its own 'narrative' as a life cycle, beginning with its installation (its 'feet' often secured with bolts and concrete) and ending with broken slats, decay, removal, and then destruction.

Garden, walking, and sentencing

Lancelot 'Capability' Brown, the famous 18th century landscape designer, amongst others (cf. earlier Charles Bridgeman), transformed the grounds of numerous British country estates into 'naturalistic vistas' of utility and pleasure (see Brown and Williamson 2016). He once described the approach of his work in terms of sentences – to place a 'comma' or 'full stop' is to mark where there was a 'turn' or 'interruption' in a view or to start a new 'subject'. Thus, to walk one of his landscapes is to traverse a sentence. Taking this further, we could allude to sentence elements – nouns, verbs, adverbs, adjectives – as the subject 'content' of the garden: the flowers, trees, grass and the form, qualities and movements they make. (Here, it is interesting to note the long debate by scholars on correspondences between trees and shrubs' names and letters in Celtic alphabets, Graves 1961). Perhaps we should include some (recent) additions to parts of 'sentences': emojis, a single ideogram or ideograph that represents a concept, idea or phrase in single pictorial form (face, hands) which have proliferated due to the mobile phone (although older), and the emoticon, a text based form using punctuation, letters, or numbers, that grew with 'typing' for the display of emotion – as (new) elements, images to be employed in 'recording' particular vistas, feelings, thoughts (BBC/R4 2017). The term 'sentence' can be used to delineate a whole or part of a life – for instance, from criminal trials, as in a 'sentence' as a 'term' or years or life (or death) – so denoting something set out for us with restricted (or no) choice (and so allied with 'fate') regarding our future.

Prisoners literally walk much of their sentence, around the prison yard (i.e., 'walk the line') and its ('punctuated') corners or by pacing the cell. A walk as a 'sentence' could be seen as condensed life – punctuation being its 'key points'. A life can be conceived as (or as if) a book (in paragraphs, chapters) in 'understanding' our current experience: a book can be (as if) a life (autobiography, biography) written in retrospect, or still to be completed – or, in reading, by 'turning a page', coming eventually to the last page, the final line, The End. A biographer may follow 'in the footsteps' – the past journeys and life – taken by subjects, and recorded in their 'footprints', reflecting meanwhile on their own writing 'sidetracks' and life (Holmes 1985; Holmes 2000). However, a belief found in many cultures is that to damage a footprint is to harm the walker who made it (see Frazer 1987).

A text based analogy of walking as writing has its limitations. James Agee famously experimented with writing, in the late 1930s and early 1940s in his book *Let Us Now Praise Famous Men* (Agee and Evans 2006), in an agonising attempt to put the complexity of ethnographic experience into words, recognising that a sentence is like the 'winding' direction of a walk; in particular, he showed an innovative use of punctuation, especially the colon to depict what cannot be expressed in text (Agee and Evans 2006: 98; see Stott 1973: 310–11; Rabinowitz 2010). Again, a sentence can also be read – and 'reading' (like writing) may also be compared with walking. For Solnit, books and walks (as 'reading') can 'resemble' each other – re-walking a landscape makes it a stable text in memory and thought (Solnit 2014: 77). Perhaps a closer connection is between the daily walk and the diary – the 'routine' of the format coupled with the recorded uniqueness of each entry. Thoreau 'thought with his feet' – walking observations shaped the structure of his books (Amato 2004: 143). It follows, maybe, that speaking (to oneself or in conversation) and its 'verbal punctuation' in both in analogy and practice is associated with writing and reading: speaking can be 'walking' just as walking can be 'speaking'. There is also the interrelation between walking and counting: we may count our steps – as in 'pacing out' a distance or to keep a tally of the distance or circuits taken (cf. Darwin's kicking of a stone to mark each of his 'sand walk' rounds at Downe House, while Dickens 'counted pages as well as miles' (Bodenheimer 2007: 179) – as we 'calculate', give an 'account' of our lives'. Walking itself can be (likened to) following a song or musical piece – the percussion of the feet, the rhythm of the body's movement, our inner or outer voice following a melody, perhaps becoming 'lost in rhythm – in motion' as if a dream (in the 'suspension', the 'zone') – and a means of describing immersion in the undulating landscape (cf. Bruce Chatwin, *Songlines*, 1987). The garden itself may be chosen as a particular place to 'walk and write' (perhaps in the mind), or more likely, sit and write (cf. George Bernard Shaw's revolving garden writing hut, following the daily sun's round).

The walking interview can involve one or more of these 'expressive' elements – writing, reading, speaking, counting, singing/listening, and associated emotions and senses – as we 'punctuate' and record and recall our lives and those of others. A walk is for 'exercise' – and is also an 'exercise' in these expressive elements. In relating our biography (in walking) we compose and 'edit' – reveal, secrete, fantasise, celebrate, and account.

Garden – Geometries and secrets

Gardens are constructed to be 'appreciated' at 'walking pace', to stimulate and satisfy sensual pleasures and meet the need for 'recreation'. At their most sensual, they raise the individual to a certain state of consciousness, as if 'walking on air' – a lightness of movement and being, a reverie of spirit: a feeling that oscillates between transcending surroundings and its cares, another realm where the 'scene' is vivid, abstracted – an ecstasy through a feeling of happiness, as if from good news, a feeling of heightened sensitivity to the joy of living, of 'being alive', a 'oneness with nature', but it also may have a deeper, forbidden, darker side. While the garden, at its most intense in 'sensualness' is an idyll of peace and rest, (again) it can be a foreboding place or a temporary, uncertain refuge in the face of fear and threat.

A garden can have secret doors, tunnels, arches, and openings. The forming of secret or secluded parts have a long history in the construction of gardens (cf. Persian gardens). Gardens in the Georgian era could be designed to enable pleasures and 'sins' to be indulged in through opportunities for secretion in byways, foliage, and follies (see Felus 2016). 'Secrecy' stimulates the workings of the mind and imagination: in the mind's eye, creating a parallel or new world, one timeless/or 'out' of time. The garden, at least for some, is a place where other worlds or dimensions can exist, perhaps walking through a mysterious door in an old wall can give a fleeting promise of new vistas and life; not surprisingly children's books have featured such devices of escape, fantasy, and enchantment, towards overcoming personal situational difficulties, with themes of transformation and growth (cf. F.H. Burnett, *The Secret Garden*, 2012). In half-light, the secret door or entrance gains in mystery. Perhaps, surprisingly, Stone Age cave art has relevance here: in the cave, the effect of the dark tunnel, lit only with flickering lights that lead the way, catching the eye, brings imaginative, almost psychedelic effects, as wall-painted animals appear to move as if on a cinema screen, with such perception perhaps aided (it has been argued) by a drug-induced midworld state of half-sleep/semi-consciousness (see Lewis-Williams 2004). The garden is a place for 'secreting', 'hiding', and 'camouflage', especially 'under the 'cloak' of night. But we should not see these elements as unusual 'deception'; they are what we do routinely in life, part of how we live and represent ourselves, as integral to how we form our life accounts by constructing, (again) by 'editing' or 'sentencing' our written and spoken accounts before delivery (see Leach 2006; Simmel 1906).

The 'secret' or 'locked' garden has a parallel in the 'maze' or 'labyrinth' also often found in the garden – which has some correspondence with the ziggurat, a building whose levels become progressively smaller as it rises, so it has a three-dimensional, rather than a walled or diagrammatic pattern. As remarked earlier (in

Chapter 2), many 19th century 'explorers' described entering parts of the city as if they were dark tropical forests. Writers spoke of their experiences of the city, especially the slums, with trepidation that the 'way out' may not be found, the streets as 'labyrinths' – an intertwining or matting, a bewilderment of sights, sounds (noise), smells, and secrets, peopled by 'alien' beings. 'Labyrinth' and 'maze' are often used interchangeably, but the garden (and other sited) maze is intended to baffle due to offering alternative routes, whereas the labyrinth has only one set path, to the centre; the former appears to give free will (and the destination may not be achieved), the latter a fixed route to 'salvation' (Solnit 2014: 71; Elkin 2017: 134; see Higgins 2018; Ingold 2013a; Ingold 2013b; O'Rourke 2013).

The maze and the labyrinth, therefore, confront us in different ways, in terms of how we are presented with and make choices, what they allow and demand, each 'corner' bringing anticipation and possible unexpected interactions with other people and sites. In life, there are mazes and labyrinths and we seek their centre, their meaning; they may represent life itself – in both we take 'turns', but are likely to continue to follow and search for, but not achieve, the simple narrative (answer) we desire. As Solnit observes, the labyrinth and maze give 'stories': ones that we bodily tread with our feet, with our eyes not being able to see the complete path, just as when we read or listen to a story (or when we write one) (Solnit 2014: 71–2). We can also say that in life we 'filter' consciously and unconsciously the myriad informational, sensual 'stimuli' we encounter in the urban/rural scape: we avoid, dismiss, 'hide and seek', bear with, experiment, etc. elements in the paths we choose or must take (Hall 2017: 4). Of course, our knowledge concerning the 'scenes' we encounter is incomplete, even if we are returning.

Interestingly, there has been a revival of the garden mazes and designs from the 1960s and 1970s (and older 18th–19th century or ancient ones restored, cf. Saffron Walden, UK), not only in country house grounds and parks (n.b. the extensive work of Adrian Fisher, see Higgins 2018: 88–91), but in children's playgrounds and other outdoor sites, and art gallery installations, perhaps due to increasing recognition of their entertaining fascination and the educative value in puzzle-solving, their meditative and therapeutic use, and the emerging search for 'alternative experience'; in addition there has been possibly associated rise of 'land art' (Solnit 2014: 71). Mazes and labyrinths have a very old history and have commonly been associated with religious experience (cf. Christian pilgrimage and penitence or 'route to heaven', old 'pagan' or 'folkoric' festivals, such as the 'maze dance', or the walk in and out as representing death and rebirth), and classical myth e.g., the ancient labyrinth of Crete: Higgins 2018). They differ from the intricate interweaving paths of ancient 'Celtic knots' (as on standing stones, book illumination, jewellery, etc.) that have no beginning or end (unlike single or double open spirals), whose various symbolic meanings, perhaps, include 'life as circular'.

Walking in the wider garden or landscape itself can also be like going through a maze or labyrinth – if there is a complex of interlocking pathways that seem to have similar features. Meanwhile, in the city, its streets (again as commentators have long noted) may seem to take such patterns. However, the garden and the city share another motif. The garden often has 'moving' 'panoramas' – the 'walking vistas' of openness, colour, and light (Smith 2003: 76–90), and the city also has its panoramic views. Further, the perceptions of the garden and city also have something else in common – 'adaptation': this concept is from evolutionary thought as found in plant ecological study, with its ideas on habitats, symbiosis, 'zones', and the natural history of organisms. The notion of adaptation influenced sociological understanding in Chicago Sociology on the diversity of urban cultural milieu and the formation of concentric circles defining city districts, in particular the 'adjustments' in social group relations, and the individual 'life history' (see Roberts 2006: 18–19; Smith 1988: 136–7; see Chapter 2). The garden and the city (following Chicago Sociology) can each be considered as not merely 'natural' but as 'living' social organisms, as adaptive to their environments, and also as related to our experiences and 'adjustment in the "biographical"' – to walk in a garden or wider urban/rural scape is to 'trace' their 'life history' and our own biography (Ackroyd 2000; Smith 1988: 123).

For Schuetz, the 'stranger' – the migrant – does not have the given cultural 'scheme of reference', the 'thinking as usual' supported by a 'degree of knowledge' for 'standardised situations' in 'tested recipes' in joining a culture, but instead faces a 'state of transition' where the 'shelter and protection' offered appears as a 'labyrinth' in which there is a loss of 'sense' of 'bearings' (Schuetz 1944: 499, 507). Schuetz argues that not only may the 'crisis' of the immigrant take 'milder forms' (e.g., joining a closed club, attending college from a rural background, enlisting for the army, acceptance to a spouse's family, etc.), but that the experience of 'strangeness' and 'familiarity' are part of our general interpretation of the (labyrinthine) social world. Occasionally, we may find our 'cognitive themes' of understanding 'reality' have 'slipped away', our usual 'scripts' have shifted or do not seem relevant – as an unknown experience or one that now seems different (e.g., where geometrical forms and relations between elements of a scene may now seem very peculiar and disturbing) or the current situation becomes 'enveloped' by associations with a former time and place (Cohen and Taylor 1978: 155–6). 'New situations', including the more disorientating, where 'contours' of 'relevant knowledge' are disrupted, are met with a process of inquiry, application of facts and meaning, and (if successful) an adjustment in our 'stock of experiences' and personal biography (Schuetz 1944: 500, 507). A walk in a garden or city can, therefore, be conceived as a series of 'adjustments' (or adaptations) in our experiences – to individual psycho-social interactions with the 'stimuli' or conditions experienced in the surrounding 'socio-cultural environment' (cf. Park, Thomas, Wirth on 'mental life' in the city: see Smith 1988).

Forms of mazes were used in ancient fortifications to confuse and trap attackers. Now with computer visual technologies, such graphics as mazes and labyrinths can be in formulated in 3D and are used as part of screen action games. With digital technologies, to take a walk (or cycle or run) can be done 'as if' in the scene, as 'game-like'. Further, we are now on the edge of 'transmitting' other sensual and physical responses by apps and add-ons to hand held digital devices. To walk as/as if to speak, write, read, count (and vice versa) becomes a virtual experience which may include a range of source materials, from an 'actual walk' and additional elements (film, text, voice, graphics, etc.) assembled in various 'mash ups': collaged/montaged, layered, interlinked, in multidimensional ways, and provided with 'augmented' elements or a 'virtual world'. Thus, an actual walk can be retraced in the real world, or on a single screen, in headset 'glasses', or in a room with computer screen/projection, and re-constructed and revisited in multiple ways. In applying this technology for WIBM study, the 'virtual walk' can be related to 'layers' of other materials within aspects of research, including interpretation, analysis, and theorisation.

Historically, the idea of the maze or labyrinth has featured prominently in literature and art, but has also inspired contemporary artists such as Ilya Kabakov, Yayoi Kusama, Richard Long, and Mark Wallinger (Higgins 2018: 87, 147–9). The layout of an artistic exhibition can seem to be like a maze or labyrinth – on occasion, these forms are deliberately used by artists (or curators), for instance, to give a disconcerting walking experience or provide a 'narrative device' for showing a life/lives and 'works'. As metaphors for life, the maze and labyrinth provide not merely 'straight' linear routes, but combinations of decisions and directional 'paths'. Narrative models of identity formation can be show that we may take not only linear, but circular, cyclical, spiral, static, fragmentary forms in relation to 'temporal orders' of individual, natural, and cultural processes; in addition, life narratives are also formed in 'temporally parallel and overlapping gestalts of possible lives' (Brockmeier 2002: 462; see Brockmeier 2000). Perhaps what provides the attraction of a 'real' maze or labyrinth on the ground is not only its puzzle to be solved, but also something deeper – the metaphor it gives for the structures within our mind as we grapple with the mysteries of life?

We need to 'reconfigure' research – to recognise fully, particularly in the new age of digital, layering of data (text, image, sound), augmented reality and so on, that research practice is more than simply linear (it is also circular, etc.) or even two-dimensional, but it is multi-directional, 'moving' in content, time, and space, and simultaneously, exploring the 'possible' (in 'fantasy') directions of inquiry. The garden's paths, and its labyrinths or mazes, here, become a metaphor for the complexity of the social world, and how it is experienced, navigated, understood, and represented, in both its 'realities' and 'possibilities'. It can also be a guiding metaphor for the WIBM as engaged in a methodological 'layering' and interconnecting of materials and analysis.

Garden, identity, and space

The 'garden' in its domestic, public, and other guises is a site that is bounded, segregated, and stratified socially in a number of ways, for example, in terms of gender, age, income, etc. Bhatti et al. (2009) examine the experience of the domestic garden 'as an intimate place in everyday life' by investigating the 'prosaic pleasures' and 'enchanting encounters' that are shown in its 'multi-sensorial engagements and emotional attachments'. They describe a number of 'modalities' in the 'everyday' – the tasks involved in the 'cultivation' of the garden; the 'sensuous and embodied experiences' involved using the idea of 'haptic perception'; the 'caring' for the garden and others; and the 'emotional attachments' and memories of 'body/space' (as from childhood) by drawing upon 'garden narratives' (Bhatti et al. 2009). Using a particular story, Bhatti (2014) elsewhere, describes 'gendered leisure' – its 'complex emotions, resistances and ambiguities' – so while a garden can be a 'domestic chore', it can also be a 'creative activity', and possible avenue for 'self-expression' and 'alternative discourses' that can inform a remaking of self. In this view, following Foucault's (1998) notion of 'heterotopia', the garden is 'a contradictory space', giving the self possibilities. In a further article, Bhatti (with Church) argues 'gendered meanings' of the garden, an arena where gendered relations are acted, are very important in how the how the 'home' is socially formed (Bhatti and Church 2000).

At a wider level, Parry et al. (2005) investigated how traditional 'gender roles and relations' were in operation in the use of a community garden, according to the 'division of work', 'initiative' and 'leadership'. They found a complexity of resistance and reproduction, but that 'many women' were 'empowered' enabling them to look for new responsibilities and opportunities outside the sphere of the garden (Parry et al. 2005). Here, an historical perspective can further demonstrate women's complex connection to 'the garden'; for example, Bending writes of 'green retreats' or the seclusion of 18th century upper class women on country estates. Letters and diaries show how such women shaped an identity in a complex relation to their surroundings and the diverse 'culture of the garden' (Bending 2013). Historically, the activities of a country house park or garden were often organised according to time of day – in Georgian times, the morning for walks and conversation, recreation or sports in the afternoon and, perhaps, entertainment such as fireworks during the evening or night (see Felus 2016). Finally, Bhatti and Church (2004) in a survey of garden owners examined 'meanings of gardens and personal experiences of nature', arguing that the garden does not merely foster sensual relationships with nature, but gives significant opportunities for both privacy and sociability. These activities can be considered as negotiations or practices in a response to the complexities of modern social and environmental circumstances (Bhatti and Church 2004: 37). The (domestic) garden, we must remember, apart from being a site of 'informal mores' regarding access, division of labour, etc. is also subject to official or other rules – which can include the line of boundaries, height of fences and hedges, rules on usage and development, tree protection, and which may be a site of dispute (e.g., with the landlord, neighbours, authorities).

Gardens can be an 'expression' of the self (e.g. as in gardening activity), but also metaphorically it can stand for its blurring and camouflage, and (as in a labyrinth or maze) to represent that life is not simply a linear path, but has its turns, mysteries, and surprises. The experience of walking within a garden can be intimately connected to a conception of self. By 'merging' into the 'vegetation' of life's surroundings, attention is drawn to issues of the nature of the self, its production, expression, and representation. The act of walking within a garden may induce a sense of being able to 'fade' against the background of varied patterns, colours, or shapes of flowers, plants, and shrubs or to be a dark silhouette, especially, set against the stark, bare garden shapes in the murk of winter. The garden is also 'on the move', a daily and seasonal movement in flickering shapes, colours, and light. A 'blurring' or 'camouflaging' of self into the garden background undermines the assumption of a unitary (static) self. Instead, the self is conceived as shifting, mobile, as unstable or multiple. This process of fading or merging can also have its opposite, the 'emergence' from the 'organic' as an attempt at a more definable, stable selfhood. Some of these dimensions of blurring and 'camouflage' of the individual self have been explored by artists, such as photographer Francesca Woodman, in her self-images in woodland and a derelict room, with Gothic, Surrealist, and other influences. Woodman paid particular attention to the body in how the 'figure' is emerging – or dissolving into background of trees or wallpaper, is present-absent, depicting identity but giving it an unstable status (see Townsend 2006: 42; Tellgren 2015; Leach 2006; Pedicini 2012).

Garden, the body, and art

There are some close interrelations between the 'garden' and the 'body' – the former often used metaphorically to represent the latter. In the nursery rhyme 'Round and round the garden', the hand of a child becomes the garden – where a circular motion is made by someone's finger on a child's hand with the addition to the title 'like a teddy bear', and then the finger is moved saying 'one step', 'two steps' to the elbow, and 'tickle under there [the arm]'. The rhyme may have originally included a 'hare' rather than 'bear', raising the possibility of the rhyme's origin in the mythical or symbolic properties of the hare in various religions and legends, or the correspondence between learning to count and catching hares. The garden is also associated seemingly paradoxically with the body in both play and in rest – each implicated in personal 'recreation'. In a sense, walking merges both of these facets together, being both exercise and an activity for 'mindful' 'renewal'. The walk in a 'garden' and in the fields has been very long associated with romance and liaisons (as in novels and poetry); for instance, some flowers are symbols of passion, love, or fidelity, and they give settings for sexual encounters (for pleasure, knowledge, downfall and guilt, eroticism and technique), as the foundational biblical story of The Garden of Eden and *The Perfumed Garden* 'guide' demonstrate. The 'garden' featured in the 'sexual liberation' and 'flower power' of the 1960s as a metaphor for a peaceful, natural state in the 'moment' of youthful eclectic 'hippy culture' (in songs, poster art, drugs, clothes, meditation, communalism, in counter-culture and protest, etc.), with all its contradictions and ambiguities (cf. 'pastoral', utopian, mystical, political oppositionalism, 'permissivism', individualism, etc.: see Clarke et al. 1976: 57–71). 'Hippy culture' became symbolically characterised in the luscious sensuality of hair, the flower as representing peace and love, a notion of 'returning to the garden', and 'journeys' (pilgrimages) i.e., to San Francisco and Woodstock, as almost mythical places (paradisiacal gardens) for harmony. Associated here (perhaps) is the individual 'mind as a garden' to be tended – where we cultivate our own myths, organising our feelings, a setting we can visualise (as recommended in some therapies) to feel calm, and to cordon off ('repressive') daily cares.

The garden can also be a place for the 'exotic'. Professional plant collectors, botanical scientists, and others (cf. Royal Navy ship personnel) sent back specimens from around the world (including in Wardian glass cases) to adorn the 19th century country house gardens and herbariums, or to be studied and classified by naturalists and recorded by artists (e.g., Wallace 2017: 328). Historically, the garden itself has been a site for artistic expression – in its very structural design, construction, and use of technologies: its paths, benches, arches, artificial lakes and fountains, terraces, follies, statues, mosaics, ornaments, etc. as well in the patterning and arrangement of flowers, plants, trees, and topiary, etc. to provide changing 'vistas'. Numerous styles of garden design have historically resulted in the 'extreme': some being very patterned and formalised, others aimed towards a more 'wild' or 'natural' effect, reflecting differing modes of appreciation or sensibility. The garden and its particular contents have been central subjects of domestic and professional painting and drawing for hundreds of years (e.g., flower illustration), such depiction often taking older mythical or religious themes, and have been very common subjects for photography, featured in TV documentaries and dramas (especially 'costume dramas'), and also in films. Interestingly, the oldest existing piece of film (by Le Prince) is of figures at leisure in a 'suburban garden scene' (in Leeds, UK, 1888).

Some artists have often been concerned with the 'transition' and relation between inner and outer vistas, between the room and garden, in their work (i.e., views through open windows). Matisse's studio(s), for instance, could be regarded as both scenes for painting and a work of art – and, in part, 'garden-like' (e.g., with flowers in vases, potted plants, floral decoration on fittings, in elements in hanging canvasses, and a connected indoor aviary, etc.), diluting the difference between the room (with its objects he painted), his works, and the garden. Thus he 'extended' his perceived working environment in space and time, colour and movement, just as his pictures 'reached out' beyond their frames. He travelled to the South of France, Spain, North Africa, and the South Seas being influenced by the vibrancy of textile design, the form of collected objects, and experience of striking vistas of light and colours; he sought to bring the 'arcadia' of his travels and his garden into the 'confines' of the studio, while simultaneously moving the studio outwards 'through' the window (see Buchberg et al. 2014; McBreen and Burnham 2017; Spurling 2009). Finally, sculpture (and mosaics) has been a particular feature of gardens for hundreds of years (cf. Classical sculpture and 18th century gardens). In recent years, there seems to be a revival of garden sculpture and rise of 'sculpture parks', with modern sculpture and landscape works exhibited in country house parks. In Northern England, there is the major Yorkshire Sculpture Park (opened in 1977) which includes galleries and walks passing sculptures and 'land art'.

Whereas much of the domestic garden or park garden can be considered as 'artful', this also implies 'artificial' in the sense that they are constructed. Indicated here is not particularly that there is 'artificial grass or flowers', but that there is a large industry behind the fantasy and reverie (sometimes revelry) of the pensive, de-stressing site of the garden. The 'garden' does not merely produce its plants, but is a site for the application and consumption of products from across the globe. Commercial garden centres supplying gardeners sell not only a fantastical array of flora, but a huge range of mechanical devices and machines, tools, posts and fencing, sheds, bricks and paving, chemicals, gazebos and lights, chairs and tables, birdbaths and feeders, plastic gnomes, 'stone' animals and birds, seeds and pots, greenhouses, barbecues, awnings, swings, bouncy castles, trampolines, and paddling pools. This industry extends to radio and TV garden programmes, magazines, books, country house visits and other tourism, shows and competitions, tree experts, gardeners, designers, nurseries, importers, and growers. The 'garden industry' is not simply a major feature of the modern economy; culturally it is involved in shaping what we perceive – what we want and how we enjoy – 'the garden' and how we use it, including the experience of our walks within it.

Artists have recently interrogated traditional ideas on the 'landscape' (e.g., from Romanticism) and 'garden' and sought to bring a new conceptualisation which includes ecological concerns with pollution, energy issues, and our body and identity in relation to nature, and how we interpret our environment – with notions, for example, such as the 'viral landscape' of sculptor/installation artist Helen Chadwick (Sladen 2004), the 'metabolic landscape' of photographer Gina Glover (Glover et al. 2014), and Andy Goldsworthy's site-specific sculpture, installations, or land art using snow, mud, twigs, leaves, and stones. Rugg (2010) gives a critical contextual assessment of the 'garden' in outlining a number of temporary and 'interventionist', 'site-specific' art projects (e.g., a US campus garden, the underside of a motorway in Melbourne) that raise considerations of food production, consumption, and urbanisation – as well as relating the spatial to questions of selfhood, identity, displacement, and loss. Thus, she argues, rather than consider the garden as an 'Arcadian space' or a 'refuge', the garden can be used to reflect on conflict, control, and appropriation, and the global environmental crisis. This view highlights the important contemporary campaigns to conserve and protect the landscape, as part of the long movement that has seen (in the UK) the granting of 'national park' status (see Chapter 5), areas to be safeguarded as 'green belt' land, and a wide range of (ongoing) protest against forms of development.

Garden, auto/biography, and time

There are a number of ways people relate their lives – commonly in a chronology from childhood, through family, educational, and work experiences along the way, with some evaluation of their life and its events. Within this chronology, certain events may well be described as pivotal by the individual in terms of the subsequent 'course' of their life, e.g., a migration, a death of someone close, an illness or injury. However, lives can be told in other ways, not simply chronologically: its 'telling' may take one or more themes through which the life can be understood by the teller and listener. 'A told life' may particularly focus on educational and work career, health, 'love life', or places lived: for example, Forster describes her life according to the houses she has resided in (Forster 2014). 'Gardens' may also feature strongly in a life-telling, and may be a 'prism' through which someone focuses on, or 'makes sense' of, experiences – a family garden fondly and nostalgically remembered, a later needed refuge from exterior conflicts, a treasured place of personal renewal, a site for a memorial, a current garden that raises powerful memories of a previous one (see Miller in Chapter 4). Wider landscapes may also serve as 'frames' for memory (of a holiday, a former home area, etc.), perhaps coming into mind when a later garden or broader vista is encountered (see Schama 1995). A memory may be 'triggered' merely by a particular smell of a flower or tree, or an incident such as once a sharing a bench with someone may provide a frame for a recurring memory of a time past and now 're-experienced' (see Chapter 10).

'Time' 'enters' the garden 'biographically' along a number of registers. Time is recorded in growth, maturity, and decline (and renewal) of plants and trees. The idea of a 'life cycle' of plants and insects has been transposed to the study of human life as stages of development or personal 'growth'. A public garden may well be subject to formally displayed open and closing times dependent on seasonal light – the 'opening day' regulated by gate operation. The length and direction of shadows – as on a sundial – indicates the time of day. Like a sundial, an individual casts a shadow, but when walking it seemingly alters its trajectory – at one moment, the individual 'catching up' with the shadow, at another, leaving it behind, or if at the side, as a parallel companion. At differing points, a walking interviewer may walk in the actual shadow of the other person. As if their 'shadow', the researcher in a walking interview walks 'in time' ('in step') with the interviewee, sharing 'biographical time', and within the various 'timings' of the elements of the scene (e.g., day/night, the seasons). Of course, the 'shadow' (like the photograph) can have religious, folk, or literary/visual cultural significance associated with the soul, self, disguise, or death (cf. a 'shadow of oneself', 'shadow of death') or in 'prefiguring' ('foreshadowing') the future (see Frazer 1987). Also, to cast a shadow over someone can be as protector or healer, while 'shadowing' can be a work practice to show a task to someone learning a role, but can also mean to trail unseen (as in policing, security surveillance) or to stalk.

The passing of time due to the changing of the seasons may be observed (in the garden or meadow, cf. Lewis-Stempel 2015) with the emergence of particular flowers (snowdrop, crocus, daffodil) in sequence, and the varying height and position of the sun between the solstices. Plants may be arranged by gardeners as a large clock face – a clock which itself 'fades' as the flower heads die. The seasons carry a complex of meanings: the Spring can be associated with rain, water, renewal, earth, growth, greening, and warming, and childhood; the Summer, with blue sky, heat, sensual 'fullness', a transcendental or uplifting feeling, and early adulthood; Autumn with turning and falling leaves, browns and orange, and middle age; Winter with white and dark, frost or snow, cold, downwards, the solid ground, old age and dying. A walk according to time of day or season (depending on the overall clime) can bring differing perceptions of colour and form according to light and shadow, so varying associations and feelings may arise – the garden is a 'natural clock' recording and implicating not only time, but also experience and memory (cf. the work of interactive, video/computer installation artist David Rokeby). A daily walk is often 'circular', like the move-ment of hands on a clock: footsteps may be seen as seconds, walking a length of path as minutes; a footstep is like a memory as experienced in space. In walking research, the interviewer is a companion for the journey, taking the same geo-metrical route.

The garden is a site both of growth and flowering, but also 'degeneration' – the aging, death, and decomposition of its inhabitants (a 'life history'), and of clearing of the 'pruned and the dead', forming compost heaps and bonfires – organic matter and dust; a place of failed efforts by fauna to survive predators and flora to compete with others (for air, space, light, and nutrients). Degeneration and combustion can metaphorically correspond to the poles of character that Dickens identified in *Bleak House*, how some individuals, due to obsessive con-cerns either 'de-generated' or 'burnt up' (spontaneously) due to personal obses-sion – dying due to a stasis or repetition (Frank 1984). But, of course, a garden can re-awaken, be reborn from its hibernation, a plant may survive the rigours of winter or neglect. Birds, flowers, and insects reappear according to season. Here, is a comparable view of the self as having to renew its narratives to avoid obsession, stasis, and a premature end (Frank 1984). The self, like the garden after winter, can be renewed from its 'stasis' (n.b. Oscar Wilde, *The Selfish Giant*, 1882). In this narrative conception, to have a 'viable' self is to 'narrate' – to give accounts, to tell our story – to be able to move perspectively and reflectively in time backwards and forwards. In using the 'walk' as a key to an interview method (as 'on the move'), a possible temptation is to conceive a narrative as linear, and hence the danger of retreating, perhaps implicitly, to only a chrono-logical, unidirectional conception of narrativising, whereas, commonly, we also construct narrative accounts that (perhaps despite our intention) disrupt chronol-ogy and the singular story (Roberts 2004). We also have various 'small stories' in daily interaction (Bamberg 2006) and larger narratives of our lives (say, accord-ing to work, family, education) and metaphors (cf. 'my life has been a journey') that we variously draw on. The garden seems particularly associated with child-hood and old age in biography – in rather simple terms, at one end, a time when wider social interaction is not yet achievable and a safe, supervised area to play is needed, at the other, when restrictions of mental and physical health arise (or simply greater 'home' life, nonwork time is available) a place for rest, meeting, contemplation, and pleasure.

A garden or park can be a lonely place, one of melancholy – fostered by the damp air, misty swirl, and wet grass and puddled path. It may be that we go to the garden because we hope for that mood, or another in different weather (although a sunny day may itself engender loneliness, if we are alone in a lively park). A garden can be a place of reflection on life and relationships, and for memories, commemoration, and memorialisation – in this it has overlaps with the cemetery (cf. 'a garden of rest') (see Chapters 4, 10).

The garden and the Walking Interview as a Biographical Method

Qualitative research involves personal communication, between researcher and participant, as in any relationship – 'meeting and greeting'; the 'monitoring' of a situation and relationships; a sensitivity to others, their feelings, outlook, and responses; and, for the researcher to be self-reflective, as well having a wider under-standing of social institutions, groups, and social change. The Walking Interview as a Biographical Method (WIBM) involves an 'encounter' with the 'subject' (with some prior description of the research, consent, and other relevant ethical issues addressed). Trust and rapport have to be established and maintained. It involves an awareness of time – the given situation, time passing, and how the past and future flow; in short, the current situation as an experienced 'moment' (cf. Husserl) which requires attention and concentration, but is 'ongoing' (Dyer 2007), an extension of moments past and future – moments as in 'process'. The method also necessitates a consideration of 'structuring' – how within the processes of the 'micro' setting, there are dimensions of 'structure' – processes (or action) are not divorced from the structuring of situations, they interpenetrate – thus, class, gender, ethnicity are 'lived' out in an 'interaction order' and not simply 'structural' macro formations (cf. Goffman 1972; see Roberts 2006: 70–1). The 'garden' is a particular location for a walking interview, one amongst many such arenas, in which the researcher may be engaged with a respondent, sharing the experience. Walking in a garden, as in other cases, can bring a whole gamut of personal resonances stimulated by the 'scene': of other occasions remembered bringing reflection on the passing of one's life, memories of family history and its members and relationships, as well as cur-rent general mood and circumstances. WIBM commonly takes place in locations, such as the garden, that have particular connections and evocations for participants that they re-share and experience afresh with the researcher (see Miller, Chapter 4 and Heddon, Chapter 9 of this book).

The WIBM carried out within or through a garden or park (or other settings) will take place via differing forms of interaction and different environmen-tal aspects of the setting/scene. Goffman's insights on interpersonal behaviour and the 'production of the social self' are very relevant to an understanding of

WIBM, and the 'interaction order' in which it takes place. He describes 'face-to-face or mediated contact' as part of a 'world of encounters'; individuals act out a 'pattern of verbal and non-verbal acts' in which there is an evaluation of 'impressions' given to and by others (Goffman 1972: 5; Roberts 2006: 74). Goffman is very suggestive here, in employing several key metaphors to describe social life – drama, ritual, and game – and in his ideas on self-formation. Alongside his useful account of the 'interaction order', he examines the 'production of the social self' in interaction with others (see Roberts 2006: 64; Branaman 1997). The procedure of WIBM itself can be described, following Goffman, as an 'occasion' constituted through 'social organisation'– a 'normatively stabilized structure' based on the 'co-mingling of persons' but which is a shifting 'social gathering' as people enter and leave the interaction (Roberts 2006: 74; Goffman 1972: 1–2).

There is something 'ritualistic' about walking in a public garden – we monitor our actions (cf. the route being taken and its features, our gait and gestures, impression to others, etc.) and perhaps notice that something may have changed in surroundings, while also paying 'attention' to how we are feeling (cf. cold, hot) as our thoughts 'wander' away from the situation to other concerns, 'apprehensions', hopes, plans, joys, and memories. Goffman's ideas on ritual as 'routinised' and 'expressive' are relevant for garden or park walking (Roberts 2006: 73; see Cuff et al. 1990: 161–2). As Collins argues (commenting on Goffman), 'ritualistic behaviour has a number of levels in face-to-face presence, i.e. the mutual awareness of two people, the sharing and intensification of an emotional mood, and the interactions involved as shaping future feelings, thought and behaviour' (Roberts 2006: 72; see Collins 1994: 72). 'Civil attention' to a companion will also go alongside 'civil inattention' to others – awareness of the person walking a dog, the couple chatting on a bench. Even conversation has a ritual and sharing of mood – 'a symbolic world' or 'a little social system' with its own rules and boundaries' (Roberts 2006: 72).

Walking is also 'performative'. The idea of 'performance', linked to a notion of life as (if) 'drama' (as in Goffman), has gained a great deal of currency in social science in the past fifteen or more years – as an area of study, as a means of collecting information, and as a mode of dissemination, especially in participatory forms of enactment/re-enactment (Roberts 2008; Goffman 1971). Of use here, for WIBM, is the notion that to walk is to in some way perform to others, a 'personal front' of 'appearance' and 'manner' (Goffman 1971: 34–5), and even to one's self (i.e., as we monitor, review, and internally 'comment' on our 'accomplishment' of a walk). For example, in the historical rise of the public garden, it appears that the 'stroll' could become very much a conscious 'stylish saunter taken mainly to be seen', an expression of upper-class status, fashion, and manners: a promenade (with cane and parasol) (Gros 2015: 169, 171, 210; Amato 2004: 71–100). Interestingly, how we think can be related to how we walk: in considering a task, some changes in arm movement may be observed – with perhaps some gender difference – without the walker even being aware (Whipple 2017).

Walking in a garden

The garden walk can be an 'immersive' experience through a number of differing registers in terms of types and degree of 'enclosure': the immediate intensity of sensual encounters; the effects of the colours, forms, and sounds (conversations, birds); weather of the seasons; the light of time of day, etc. A scene is given meaning, not merely as a 'setting' of memory but can also *be a memory* – memorised as visualised. The 'verbal' can also be visualised: that is why doing other visual tasks at the same time perhaps becomes more difficult – our brain is partially distracted. While a painting or photograph of the 'scene' is not changing and multi-sensual, unlike the view of the walker which is 'on the move', new technologies are allowing for a garden walk to be re-experienced or experienced for the first time – on (headset) screens 'artificially' in 3D. The 'reality' of a garden walk can also be 'augmented' by additional sensual elements, images, audio, information (e.g., on the history of the area), and other 'data', etc. These developments can include the range of senses, not only sight and sound, but smell and touch, and 'appreciated' according to the capabilities of researcher and 'researched'. Attempts by artists to 'extend' the studio (a room), its 'scenery', in time, movement, and space, is enhanced by these new technologies. The possibilities arise of new 'psychedelic' and 'synaesthesic' methodologies – with new awareness of the differing possible appreciative ways of listening/hearing; speaking and conversing; smelling and touching; and observing and spatial living, for example, our memory of an event (e.g. a garden walk) is likely to be richer and longer-lasting the more the various senses have been involved and were interconnected. The garden walk can be 'recorded' across the various sensual/practical dimensions and as related to walking as reading, writing, drawing, talking, counting. It can be 'replayed' as a virtual walk within a studio (via multi screens or headsets). The WIBM should be conceived as having to 'traverse', interpret, and analyse these sensual, relational, and spatial dimensions.

A garden walk can seem to transcend time and space – as a 'timeless movement' within a scene of contemplation, reflection, and reverie, and as a 're-creation' – a phenomenological journey. The garden may well be a site for memories held by the interviewee of a past walk within it, or stir memories (by the scent of a flower, a particular path or fountain) of another garden or broader life in different town or city – and the life journey in time and space taken to the present existing site. A walk in a garden is a phenomenological sensual experience and a physical activity, but one also set within memory experience – with invocations and resonances that draw us towards, or that we search out through, our senses and our emotions, and define previous and continuing life. A garden walk is also a joint, relational experience – a 'conversation' not merely with oneself, but also a 'dialogue' with oneself and the environment. To walk with another brings additional dimensions – a mutual awareness, sharing and 'passing' within the shifting scenes of the garden. The WIBM employs both dialogue and narration – a 'feeling' of the occasion, its emotional dimensions and shifts; a 'telling' of experience; a sensual–cognitive 'reading' of the surroundings; and a 'writing' (in text, sound, images, etc.) about the walked path – by 'composition'. It involves a 'counting' – a mapping of steps or circuits of path, but also an 'accounting' or evaluation through the time duration of the walk, and in later discussion. Finally, could the 'labyrinth', 'maze', and 'panorama' be not only features and representative of a garden, but also metaphors for how we investigate, collect, and communicate WIBM research, especially now in using digital materials – how we explore the 'certainties' and 'choices', 'mysteries' and 'pleasures' in our own lives and those of others?

References

Ackroyd, P. (2000) *London: The Biography*. London: Chatto & Windus.

Agee, J. and Evans, W. (2006) *Let Us Now Praise Famous Men*. London: Penguin (Orig. pub. Houghton Mifflin, 1941).

Amato, J. A. (2004) *On Foot: A History of Walking*. New York: New York University Press.

Anderson, W. (1990). *Green Man*. London: HarperCollins.

Attlee, J. (2012) *Nocturne: A Journey in Search of Moonlight*. London: Penguin.

Bamberg, M. (2006) Stories: Big or small – Why do we care? *Narrative Inquiry*, 16(1): 139–147.

BBC/R4 (Radio 4). (2017) Emoji: The future on of language. *Word of Mouth*. Programme, 21 February 2017.

Bending, S. (2013) *Green Retreats: Women, Gardens and Eighteenth Century Culture*. Cambridge, UK: Cambridge University Press.

Bhatti, M. (2014) Garden stories: Auto/biography, gender and gardening, *Sociological Research Online*, 19(3): 1–8. Available at http://socresonline.org.uk/19/3/12.html (Accessed 25 April 2018).

Bhatti, M. and Church, A. (2000) 'I never promised you a rose garden': Gender, leisure and home-making. *Leisure Studies*, 19(3): 183–197.

Bhatti, M. and Church, A. (2004) Home, the culture of nature and meanings of gardens in late modernity, *Housing Studies*, 19(1): 37–51.

Bhatti, M., Church, A., Claremont, A. and Stenner, P. (2009) 'I love being in the garden': Enchanting encounters in everyday life, *Social and Cultural Geography*, 10(1): 61–76.

Bodenheimer, R. (2007) *Knowing Dickens*. Ithaca, NY: Cornell University Press.

Booth, W. (1890) *In Darkest England and the Way Out*. London: The Salvation Army.

Boston, L.M.(1955) *The Children of Green Knowe*. San Diego: Harcourt Brace.

Branaman, A. (1997) Goffman's social theory. In: C. Lemert, and A. Branaman (eds.) *The Goffman Reader*. Oxford: Blackwell.

Brockmeier, J. (2000) Autobiographical time, *Narrative Inquiry*, 10(1): 51–73.

Brockmeier, J. (2002) Possible lives, *Narrative Inquiry*, 12(2): 455–466.

Brookes, J. (1969) *Room Outside*. London: Thames & Hudson.

Brown, D. and Williamson, T. (2016) *Lancelot Brown and the Capability Men*. London: Reaktion Books.

Buchberg, K., Cullinan, N., Hauptman, J. and Serota, N. (eds.) (2014) *Matisse: The Cut Outs*. London: Tate Publishing.

Burnett, F. H. (2012) *The Secret Garden*. London: Vintage.

Byers, D. (2017) Canary Wharf gets green spaces — 55 storeys up, *The Times*, Friday, 10 March 2017.

Castells, M. (1977) *The Urban Question*. London: Edward Arnold.

Chatwin, B. (1981) *Songlines*. London: Jonathan Cape.

Clarke, J., Hall, S., Jefferson, T. and Roberts, B. (1976) Subcultures, cultures and class. In: S. Hall, and T. Jefferson (eds.) *Resistance through Rituals*. London: Hutchinson.

Cohen, S. and Taylor, L. (1978) *Escape Attempts*. Harmondsworth, UK: Penguin.

Collins, R. (1994) Erving Goffman on ritual and solidarity in social life. In: Polity: *Polity Reader in Social Theory*. Cambridge, UK: Polity.

Comedia. (1995) *Park Life: Urban Parks and Social Renewal* (in association with Demos). Stroud, Gloucestershire: Comedia/London: Demos (L. Greenhaigh and K. Worpole).

Communities and Local Government Committee. (2017) *Public Parks*, Seventh Report, HC 45, 11 February 2017. London: House of Commons.

Cowen, R. (2015) *Common Ground*. London: Hutchinson.

Crane, N. (2016) *The Making of the British Landscape*. London: Weidenfeld & Nicolson.

Craven, T. (2016). The romantic thread in British Art: A point of view. In: T. Craven, D. Matthews, and A. Ball (eds.) *The Romantic Thread in British Art*. Southampton, UK: Southampton City Art Gallery.

Cuff, E. C., Sharrock, W. W., and Francis, D. W. (1990) *Perspectives in Sociology*, 3rd edn. London: Unwin Hyman.

Deakin, R. (2008) *Wildwood: A Journey through Trees*. Harmondsworth, UK: Penguin.

Dee, T. (2013) *Four Fields*. London: Jonathan Cape.

Donaldson, C. (2017) *On the Marshes*. Dorchester, UK: Little Toller Books.

Downing, S. J. (2009) *The English Pleasure Gardens, 1660–1860*. London: Bloomsbury.

Dyer, G. (2007) *The Ongoing Moment*. London: Abacus.

Elborough, T. (2016) *A Walk in the Park: The Life and Times of a People's Institution*. London: Jonathan Cape.

Elkin, L. (2017) *Flâneuse: Women Walk the City in Paris, New York, Tokyo, Venice and London*. London: Vintage.

Farley, P. and Roberts, M. S. (2012) *Edgelands*. London: Vintage.

Felus, K. (2016) *The Secret Life of the Georgian Garden*. London: I. B. Tauris.

Forster, M. (2014) *My Life in Houses*. London: Chatto & Windus.

Foucault, M. (1998) Of other spaces. In: N. Mirzoeff (ed.) *The Visual Culture Reader*. London: Routledge.

Frank, L. (1984) *Charles Dickens and the Romantic Self*. Lincoln, NE: University of Nebraska Press.

Frazer, J. G. (1987) *The Golden Bough*. Basingstoke, UK: Macmillan.

Glover, G., Rayner, G. and Rayner, J. (2014) *The Metabolic Landscape*. London: Black Dog Publishing.

Goffman, E. (1971) *The Presentation of Self in Everyday Life*. Harmondsworth, UK: Penguin.

Goffman, E. (1972) *Interaction Ritual*. Harmondsworth, UK: Penguin.

Gooley, T. (2015) *The Walker's Guide to Outdoor Clues and Signs*. London: Sceptre.

Graves, R. (1961) *The White Goddess*. London: Faber & Faber.

Gros, F. (2015) *A Philosophy of Walking*. London: Verso.

Hall, S. (2012) *City, Street and Citizen*. Abingdon, UK: Routledge.

Hall, S., Critcher, C., Jefferson, T., Clarke, J., and Roberts, B. (2013) *Policing the Crisis: Mugging, the State, and Law and Order*, 2nd edn. Basingstoke, UK: Palgrave Macmillan (orig. pub. 1978).

Hall, T. (2017) *Footwork*. London: Pluto.

Hardy, D. and Ward, C. (1984) *Arcadia for All*. London: Mansell Publishing.

Harrison, M. (2016) *Rain: Four Walks in English Weather*. London: Faber & Faber.

Harvey, D. (1973) *Social Justice and the City*. Baltimore, MD: The Johns Hopkins Press.

Hewison, R. (1987). *The Heritage Industry*. London: Methuen.

Higgins, C. (2018) *Red Thread: On Mazes and Labyrinths*. London: Jonathan Cape.

Holmes, R. (1985) *Footsteps: Adventures of a Romantic Biographer*. London: HarperCollins.

Holmes, R. (2000) *Sidetracks: Explorations of a Romantic Biographer*. London: HarperCollins.

Hoskins, W. G. (1955) *The Making of the English Landscape*. London: Hodder and Stoughton.

Howard, E. (1902) *Cities of Tomorrow*. London: S. Sonnenschein & Co.

Ingold, T. (2013a) The maze and the labyrinth: Reflections of a fellow-traveller. In: C. Watts (ed.) *Relational Archaeologies: Humans, Animals, Things*. Abingdon, UK: Routledge.

Ingold, T. (2013b) The maze and the labyrinth: Walking and the education of attention. In: C. Morrison-Bell, M. Collier, M. and A. Robinson (eds.) *Walk on: From Richard Long to Janet Cardiff*. Sunderland (UK): University of Sunderland Learning Development Services.

Jacobs, J. (1961) *The Death and Life of Great American Cities*. New York: Random House.

Jamie, K. (2005) *Findings*. London: Sort of Books.

Jamie, K. (2012) *Sightlines*. London: Sort of Books.

Jarman, D. and Sooley, H. (1995) *Derek Jarman's Garden*. London: Thames and Hudson.

Jennings, H. (1934) *Brynmawr: A Study of a Distressed Area*. London: Allenson & Co.

Jennings, H. (1985) *Pandaemonium: The Coming of the Machine as Seen by Contemporary Observers*. London: Picador.

Leach, N. (2006) *Camouflage*. London: The MIT Press.

Lewis-Stempel, J. (2015) *Meadowland*. London: Black Swan.

Lewis-Williams, J. (2004) *The Mind in the Cave*. London: Thames and Hudson.

Macfarlane, R. (2008) *The Wild Places*. London: Granta.

Macfarlane, R. (2013) *The Old Ways: A Journey on Foot*. London: Penguin.

Macfarlane, R. (2015) *Landmarks*. London: Penguin.

McBreen, A. and Burnham, H. (eds.) (2017) *Matisse in the Studio*. London: RA Publications/Boston: MFA Publications.

Moore, R. (2017) The end of parklife as we know it? *Observer* (9 July 2017): pp. 6, 7, 9.

O'Rourke, K. (2013) *Walking and Mapping: Artists as Cartographers*. Cambridge, MA: MIT Press.

Otterbourg, K. and Roberts, S. (2016) Urban Parks: Bringing nature closer to home, *National Geographic*, April 2016.

Parry, D. C., Glover, T. D., and Shinew, K. J. (2005) 'Mary, Mary quite contrary, how does your garden grow?': Examining gender roles and relations in community gardens, *Leisure Studies*, 24(2): 177–192.

Pavord, A. (2016) *Landskipping: Painters, Ploughmen and Places*. London: Bloomsbury.

Pedicini, I. (2012) *Francesca Woodman*. Roma: Contrasto.

Rabinowitz, P. (2010) 'Two Prickes': The colon as practice. In: C. Blinder (ed.) *New Critical Essays on James Agee and Walker Evans*. Basingstoke, UK: Palgrave Macmillan.

Raven-Ellison, D. (2014) Why Greater London should be made into an urban national park, *The Guardian*, Tuesday, 27 May 2014, Available at: https://www.theguardian.com/local-government.../greater-london-national-park-city (Accessed 1 May 2019).

Richardson, J. (2009) *A Life of Picasso, Vol II: The Painter of Modern Life, 1907–1917*. London: Jonathan Cape.

Roberts, B. (2004) Biography, time and local history-making, *Rethinking History*, 8(1): 89–102.

Roberts, B. (2006) *Micro Social Theory*. Basingstoke, UK: Palgrave Macmillan.

Roberts, B. (2008) Performative social science: A consideration of skills, purpose and context [122 Paragraphs], *Forum: Qualitative Sozialforschung/Forum: Qualitative Social Research*, 9(2): Art. 58, May. Available at http://nbn-resolving.de/urn:nbn:de:0114-fqs0802588 (Accessed 23 September 2018).

Rugg, J. (2010) *Exploring Site-Specific Art: Issues of Space and Internationalism*. London: I.B. Tauris.

Rutherford, S. (2015) *Botanic Gardens*. London: Bloomsbury.

Samuel, R. (1996) *Theatres of Memory*, Vol. 1. London: Verso.

Schama, S. (1995) *Landscape and Memory*. New York: HarperCollins.

Schuetz, A. (1944) The stranger: An essay in social psychology, *American Journal of Sociology*, 49(6): 499–507.

Selincourt, E. de (1977) *Wordsworth's Guide to the Lakes*. Oxford: Oxford University Press.

SHGDL (1998–) *Studies in the History of Gardens & Designed Landscapes*. Taylor & Francis.

Shortell, T. and Brown, E. (eds.) (2014) *Walking in the European City*. Abingdon, UK: Routledge.

Simmel, G. (1906) The sociology of secrecy and secret societies, *American Journal of Sociology*, 11(4): 441–498.

Sladen, M. (ed.) (2004) *Helen Chadwick*. Ostfildern-Ruit: Hatje Cantz Verlag.

Smith, D. (1988) *The Chicago School: A Liberal Critique of Capitalism*. Basingstoke, UK: Macmillan.

Smith, G. (2003) *Dickens and the Dream of the Cinema*. Manchester: MUP.

Solnit, R. (2014) *Wanderlust: A History of Walking*. London: Granta.

Spurling, H. (2009) *Matisse: The Life*. London: Penguin.

Stott, W. (1973) *Documentary Expression and Thirties America*. Oxford: Oxford University Press.

Tellgren, A. (ed.) (2015) *Francesca Woodman: On Being an Angel*. London: Koenig Books.

Thomson, H. (2013) *The Green Road into the Trees*. London: Windmill Books.

Townsend, C. (2006) *Francesca Woodman*. London: Phaedon.

Wallace, A. R. (2017) *The Malay Archipelago*. London: Penguin (orig. pub. 1869).

Warwick, H. (2017) *Linescapes*. London: Vintage.

Whipple, T. (2017) Women juggle better (at least for a while), *The Times*, 25 January 2017.

Wilde, Oscar (1982) *The Selfish Giant*. Harmondsworth: Puffin.

Willes, M. (2015) *The Gardens of the British Working Class*. London: Yale University Press.

Williams, R. (1973) *The Country and the City*. Oxford: Oxford University Press.

Williams, R. (1976) *Keywords*. London: Fontana.

Wohlleben, P. (2017) *The Hidden Life of Trees*. London: William Collins.

Wright, P. (2009) *On Living in an Old Country*. Oxford: OUP.

Wulf, A. (2015) *The Invention of Nature*. London: John Murray.

Yallop, J. (2016) *Dreamstreets: A Journey through Britain's Village Utopias*. London: Vintage.

Yudin, A. (2017) *Garden City: Supergreen Buildings, Urban Skyscapes and New Planted Space*. London: Thames & Hudson.

9

WALKING ARTISTS

Critical dialogues and imaginaries

In this chapter, we engage with the work of artists who use walking in their arts practice and explore the imaginative, relational, and biographical aspects of walking. We have argued that walking with another focuses attention on the sensory, kinaesthetic, mobile dimensions of lived experience and the ways that differences are materialised, embodied, and experienced. In the first section, we connect with the work of walking artists and the 'walking museum', we examine their objectives, outlook, and methodology, including how they are recording, representing, and 'creating' art through walking. Excerpts from two walks with walking artists, as examples of the Walking Interview as a Biographical Method (WIBM), are shared in the second section. In the final section, we discuss the possibilities or 'ways forward' for biographical research, inspired by walking artists. This chapter further extends our discussion of themes highlighted in the book – theorising, experiencing, and imagining walking as a biographical method – and signals the importance of memory, place and cartography (taken up again in Chapter 10) to the WIBM, specifically in the examples of the two walks with women walking artists.

The WIBM brings a new approach to biographical research – asking how do we relate corporeally, sensually, kinaesthetically and biographically to our 'present', our immediate environment, our 'pasts' and the places and spaces that are familiar and unfamiliar? These dimensions can be analysed using a variety of interpretive theories and schemas – narrative approaches; phenomenology; textual and image analysis and their relations. In this chapter, we draw upon artistic and arts-based approaches to help us think more carefully, culturally, imaginatively and critically about walking as a biographical method for doing research.

The WIBM can 'tap into' a multitude of dimensions of individuals' experiences – their lifeworld and their interpretation – and so enable biographical work, 'learning' and understanding to take place. In the process and practice of WIBM, we go beyond the limitations of the traditional informal interview (i.e., through a more 'holistic' attention to place and its interpretation) by relating diverse elements of experience and practice into something new – a more situated, 'moving' account of individual life.

The walking practice of two artists, Clare Qualmann and Dee Heddon, is introduced and discussed in this chapter through sharing a walk with each of them. Their work brings to the foreground that we should not assume a homogenous, singular, or exclusive conception of what it is 'to walk' (Heddon 2008). To this end, we later include *Principles and Practice: A Framework* (following the *Conclusion*) to aid biographical researchers, as well as reflect in the chapter on the need for technical help when 'walking' in conducting the WIBM to address the variability of the senses and spaces where we walk. In any research, individuals, including both researchers and researched, have differing capabilities (see Young and Temple 2014; Heddon 2015; Butler and Taylor 2009). For example, what it means to walk and how, under what conditions and circumstances and with what ambulatory techniques and tools, such as motorised support. Qualmann's perambulator walks and night walks draw attention to the environment and the gendering of space, and Heddon's walks with Sue Porter in a project called 'Walking Interconnections' direct attention to walking with disabled people, not only to aid better city and sustainable planning, but to understand what it means to walk, and the resilience and fortitude necessary if you are walking using a wheelchair. As Taylor puts it in conversation with Judith Butler:

> I always tell people I'm going for walks – I use that word even though I can't physically walk. I mean, to me, I think the experience of going for a walk is probably very similar to anybody else's: it's a clearing of the mind, its enjoying whatever I'm walking past. And my body is involved even though I'm physically not walking. I have my own ways in which I engage my body, my balancing. But yeah, I use the term walking. And most of the disabled people I know use that term also.
>
> *(Butler and Taylor 2009: 186)*

Walking as art practice

As illustrated in previous chapters, 'thinking and feeling' can be 'embodied' in walking. Walking is implicated in being social, and as 'social beings', we are walkers. We can understand our sociality – and subjectivity – more deeply if we study our walking 'routines': indeed, 'thinking and feeling are ways of walking' (Ingold and Vergunst 2008:1–2). In this section, we explore the work of artists, for whom, one could argue, walking is represented in their art as ways of 'thinking and feeling'. We look at their practices, their methods, and how they record, represent, and create walking as art practice.

> Since the early 1950s, when Guy Debord and his friends wandered through Paris on day-long drifts, and the late 1960s, when Richard Long trampled

a patch of grass in a field and snapped a photo of the result (A Line Made by Walking), contemporary artists have returned time and time again to the walking motif, discovering that, no matter how many times it has been done, it is never done.

(O'Rourke 2013: xvii)

The connection between walking and art is of course much older than this, as prehistoric cave paintings, landscape paintings, and indeed early photography show (see Horvath and Szakolczai 2018; and Chapter 1).

As walking artists Dee Heddon and Cathy Turner make clear, the histories of walking are largely histories of men who walk (Heddon 2008; Heddon and Turner 2012). Richard Long and Hamish Fulton are credited with being the earliest of the contemporary British walking artists, creating new forms of landscape art. Hamish Fulton describes himself as a 'walking artist' and the entire history of his work from the late 1960s has walking at its centre. He says that he began to make short walks, and then to make photographic works about the experience of walking; he declares that if he does not walk, he cannot make art. Fulton says that walking is not itself an art material, but rather uses what is already there and he likes to include some narrative or words: 'Every walk I make is recorded in words (I do not offer the relief of wordless art) … Walking … allows us the opportunity to be influenced by nature and gain an attitude of respect for all life-forms not just human life' (Fulton 2010: 8–14). Fulton (2010) has outlined the importance of walking as: a political force; a commitment and experience; as producing art and life. Some of these elements of walking as art practice are explored in the next section.

Walking as a practice, method, experience, and a political force in society

For both Long and Fulton, documenting, recording, and sharing walking as art is central to their practice, whether it is a singular or a collective walk, a sensory, immersive experience or is done in the two-dimensional form of writing and image-making. For Fulton, especially, one gets the sense of a life made by the experience of walking (rather than objects) – which he records through images, sounds and texts.[1]

'Walking' has been widely taken up by artists; for instance, the Museum of Walking, the Walking Artists Network, WalkingLab, and The Walking Library for Women Walking are all examples of walking as art, for research, as method, experience, and practice. *The Museum of Walking* is led by Andrew Stuck and develops walking events, 'walk shops' that are artist-led, with a central focus on 'walking creatively' using walking as art. Stuck also has a web platform devoted to 'Talking Walking', that is now in its tenth year, with over seventy-five podcasts of his interviews with artists and walkers about how and why walking 'inspires their work and shapes our world'.[2] Stuck's consultancy, 'Rethinking Cities', connects walking to research on the built environment, education, health, and transport sectors. The Walking Artists Network (funded by the AHRC[3]) was developed by Clare Qualmann in collaboration with other walking artists. The network is for those who define themselves as walking artists, and anyone who is interested in walking as a mode of art practice. Clare Qualmann and Amy Sharrocks (with advisory input from Dee Heddon) curated two Walking Women events in 2016 in London and Edinburgh in partnership with a range of artists, universities, and other bodies.[4]

WalkingLab[5] is an international research-creation project that seeks to create collaborative networks and partnerships with those interested in walking, walking methodologies, and public pedagogy. The aim is to explore the entanglement of human and non-human environments and ecology across the following key themes: 'land and geos, affect, transmaterial and movement' drawing upon 'new materialisms, critical race theories, and queer theories' (Springgay and Truman 2018). Co-directors Springgay and Truman undertook a residency in Iceland and led what they called a series of 'itinerant reading salons' and 'stone walks' through the landscape, exploring place, energy, and participation.

The Walking Library is an art project led by Misha Myers[6] and Dee Heddon (Heddon and Myers 2014, 2017) and explores the relation between walking and books; it was also conceived in response to the domination of men in the history of walking. They say:

> The idea for The Walking Library was prompted initially by our encounter with repeated references to books carried on long walks during the nineteenth century; for example, in 1818 John Keats walked across the Lake District and to Scotland with Dante's *Divine Comedy* and John Muir, on his thousand mile walk to the Gulf in 1867, carried Robert Burns' poetry, John Milton's *Paradise Lost*, William Wood's *Botany* and a small *New Testament*. We became interested in the relationship between mobility, place and books, how the experience of reading is changed by the journey and the places where a book is read and vice versa.
>
> *(Heddon and Myers 2017: 32)*

Although women walking artists feature seldom in the texts devoted to the history and/or philosophies of walking (see Gros 2015), there is a rich history of walking arts practice by women artists, with a clear focus upon the body, movement, embodiment, the materiality of lived lives, and challenging sexual and social inequalities. For example, in the 1970s, Adrian Piper made a series of works called *Catalysis* that explored in embodied, thinking, and feeling ways the experiences of dislocation and alienation, which has been described as a 'socially charged critique of homelessness' (O'Rourke 2013: 15–16). In Brixton, UK, the scene of race riots and increased police surveillance (e.g., stop and search) and institutional racism, Mona Hatoum performed 'Roadworks' in 1985. Walking barefoot, Hatoum dragged military style boots, 'the boots that the police and skin heads used to wear' (Hatoum 2016: np) tied by the shoelaces to her ankles along the footpaths, along her route. Her slow, deliberate walk was filmed and the result is powerful and compelling. Speaking about this work, Hatoum says that politically, her lived experience has influenced her work; she is interested in the phenomenology of space and works with 'feelings of displacement, disorientation, estrangement'. In 'Roadworks', 'you have the symbol of vulnerability, this woman being followed by the boots of the state and racist thugs'. Her intention is to make the familiar strange, inspire critical awareness, 'and make you question things that you normally take for granted' (Hatoum 2016: np).

The theme of embodiment was also the focus of Janet Cardiff 's *Her Long Black Hair* (2004), an audio walking tour of Central Park (NY). Walkers were given a set of photographs, a cd player, and a map and invited to walk the route devised by Cardiff. During the walk, they listen to music, the narrator, and sound samples from Central Park. Hatoum and Cardiff's walks (like those of Qualmann and Heddon) open an imaginative space to both disrupt viewers' embodied, everyday lived experience of space and place, challenge their normative experiences, and invite viewers and participants to experience and think differently about them. An important point to remember, for the biographical researcher, is that space is never a fixed surface, but an 'ongoing product of interconnections' and made meaningful depending on who occupies it and for what purpose (see Heddon 2008: 100; Massey 1994). In an interview, Doreen Massey (2013: np) discusses the importance of dynamising space and the 'intimate connections' between stories, space, and time. She reflects upon a point made by Raymond Williams, that when travelling across a landscape, by train, it may seem like a flat surface/space, but in fact you are travelling through a million stories, that space and time is intimately connected via stories, and at any point, one could stop and connect with the stories contained in the houses and buildings, the places along the route.

How we come to know a place is often by walking, by developing a mental or cognitive map of place and in time – walking is 'place-making'. In a recent walk with Maggie and Bea Rose (an artist), Fahira Hasedzic (a former refugee from Bosnia in the mid-1990s) recounted how when she first arrived in the city, she left her flat and could not find it again. After dark, everything looked so different. A university building has a special place in her memory of arriving and place-making, as this was the landmark she looked to to find her way home in the dark in those early days (see O'Neill et al. 2018). Fahira created an imagined, embodied mental map, that served to counter the initial alienation and facilitated a sense of home and being in place, that she was able to regain through seeing the landmark of the university, building in her memory a cognitive/mental map of the area.

In the work of the artists discussed above and in this next section, walking can be defined as an engaged experience, a practice, an imaginative method, and central to this is an understanding of walking as place-making, through the walking body, the experiencing body, and the thinking body.

Walking as place-making and embodied learning

Walking is an act of place-making and how we interpret our surroundings and our position within it. Artist Claire Blundell Jones describes walking practice as a resistant transitory 'place-making' gesture. She says:

> I have been escorting tumbleweeds with a leaf blower through towns and cities since 2006 … In strolling, one becomes aware of suburban details and social space … Sauntering feels transformative; like a constant state of becoming, allowing for play and daydreaming. In the current arena where vehicles dominate, meandering is becoming increasingly unfamiliar, regarded as aimless and wasting time it is perceived as a lower social status activity … Mere ambulation through the unknown could be interpreted as 'going off the path' in life, which is connoted through the word 'tramping'.
>
> *(Jones 2010: 87)*

Artists whose practice involves attention to walking as 'place-making' also include Lottie Child (2010), Tim Brennan (2010), and Tamara Ashley and Simone Kenyon (2010). Child describes 'street training', which includes taking hold of, making, and re-making public space through 'climbing, testing, penetrating, playing with, nurturing, building and/or p★★★ing on boundaries; physical, mental and social in the perpetual making of public space' (Child 2010: 85). Brennan's 'performative' walks, he calls 'manoeuvres'; at places along the route, he also invites contributions from participants:

> This has been established through my manipulation of the guided-walk form that I distinguish from other categories of 'performance art' or 'live art' and which are described as 'manoeuvres'. As a mode of 'discursive performance' each 'manoeuvre' has involved my recitation of quotations to targeted groups of participant walkers at various intervals along a route. I have designed each route and selected and sequenced quotations prior to each performance.
>
> *(Brennan 2010: 80)*

Tamara Ashley and Simone Kenyon (2010) undertook the 270-mile walk 'The Pennine Way: The Legs That Make Us' and walking the backbone of England, they invited other artists to join them at certain stages and make artwork in response to their walk. They say '(D)uring the project we collected words, thoughts, photographs, film, drawings, sound recordings, injuries and kinaesthetic memories' (Ashley and Kenyon 2010: 83).

In the work of these artists, the process and practice of walking is about placemaking, 'dynamising space' (using Massey's term), and unearthing, sharing, and/or making stories in the walking or performance, sharing their experience and inviting or challenging the co-walker or audience/viewer to see things differently, against the grain. For example, Brennan's 'Luddite Manoeuvre' (2010) is a creative, kinaesthetic, and memorable way to learn about the history and politics of the Luddites in Loughborough, bringing to the surface the memories of place that also works as a political force in mapping and walking this hidden history.[7]

Clare Qualmann, Gail Burton, and Serena Korda created work together as walkwalkwalk between 2004 and 2010. Their work is an example of walking as placemaking, but is also very much about embodied learning. Clare describes walkwalkwalk in a WIBM with Maggie[8] as:

> a walking project that explored our routine walks. From its outset, that was the goal, to re-explore the places that we are familiar with, or that fell on our routine pathways. But as the project developed, we realised it had this kind of side-effect of tracking some changes that were happening in the city, and at that time, there were some significant shifts going on as the East London Line extension was coming right through.

The group led night walks, walking in spaces and places that they might not feel comfortable during the day, setting up a brazier and making food/soup in those places, inhabiting them in a different way. Together, the women artists took hold of and changed their experience of the spaces and places. In a walk with Maggie (see the following section), Qualmann says that walking at night (see Chapter 2) changed the way they felt about space; that at first they felt anxious about 'unpromising looking dark alleyways, yet when we did some fly-posting – using stories that we'd written from encounters along the walk and putting them back onto the route, it changed the way we felt'. The night walks shifted how they felt about the places, their behaviour in those places, and the process of sharing this with others was experienced as empowering.

Dee Heddon has a long history of using walking as part of her performance practice, and together with Misha Myers and Cathy Turner ensures walking women artists are acknowledged and have an audience (Heddon and Myers 2014; Heddon and Turner 2010). Heddon and Turner (2010) ask what are the limitations placed on women's walking and what are the implications for the gendering of space? They interviewed a number of women artists whilst going for a walk with them and captured the many ways that space is gendered and embodied.[9] They examined the cultural value attached to scale of walking, the contrast between the epic monumental walk versus the small-scale walk in a domestic space: for example, Cathy Turner (a member of Wright and Sites), discusses her 'attempts to drift (using Debord's method of the 'derivé') with a baby in a domestic space, as simultaneously the other [male] members were filmed drifting through cities', and the importance of problematising these binaries that highlight the gendering of space. They also reflect upon walking as a communal, rather than a solitary pursuit, and the differences between the 'improvisatory and embodied experience' of walking, leading to sharing and understanding with others (Heddon and Turner 2010: 15).

The walking arts practice of the aforementioned artists and Heddon and Turner's interviews with women walking artists, enable us to see, experience, and understand walking as imaginative, relational, embodied, as well as a biographical and an aesthetic practice. Collaborating across arts and social science (ethno-mimesis) through a methodological, performative approach that involves working in partnership with artists in the space between art and ethnography is one important way of doing biographical research (O'Neill 2008). O'Neill argues that through 'walking biographies' and the visual representations of the walks, we are able to get in touch with our 'storied lives' in sensory and corporeal ways, that foster understanding and critical reflection (O'Neill 2015: 73). Working in the 'hyphen', the space in-between (ethno-mimesis), offers an opportunity for critical theory to be inserted in practice. This critical engagement with walking as a means of doing biographical research can be furthered by reflecting upon Benjamin's work to explore the interconnection between storytelling and art-making.

Storytelling and art-making

Walter Benjamin, walker, collector, storyteller has been described as one of the 'great scholars of cities and the art of walking them' (Solnit 2001: 196; see Chapter 3). In *The Storyteller*, Benjamin tells us that storytelling plays a primary role in the household of humanity, in contrast to the role of information. For Benjamin, a fragment of a story of a life, can tell us so much more than a hundred pages of information about a life. For Benjamin 'narrative storytelling' is a sensory/sensuous experience; it is the opposite of information, it can be transformative, auratic, 'coordinating soul, hand and eye' (Benjamin, 1992: 107). At the same time, he argues that the 'imaginary' is central to utopian political thinking and to counter the petrification of the imagination, he stresses the need to revolutionise our image worlds and the political and emancipatory role of the image (dialectical images) (Benjamin 1992: 89–90).

The role of the 'image' is an important feature of Benjamin's work. Weigel (1996) and Calderbank (2003) explore Benjamin's notion of dialectical images; the 'politically emancipatory significance of the image for the way that we develop the capacity to actively intervene in and shape the world around us'

(Calderbank 2003: 6). For the artists discussed in this chapter, walking is an imaginative experience involving visual, image-making, embodied, and performative ways of intervening in the social world. Walking is an experience, not an object, and involves the use of creativity, the body, and the imagination. The WIBM connects the imagination, biography, the body, and the relational act of storytelling.

In the two excerpts of walks in this next section, conducted with artists Clare Qualmann and Dee Heddon, the relationship between sharing biographical material and the relational and embodied experience of walking with another is captured in the images and the narratives of both walker and interviewer; between walking, seeing, and imagining, between body and image and space, between walking and storytelling. The interviews are also about gendering space and challenging this through critical interventions of walking as art practice.

A walk with Clare Qualmann: Walking as imaginative, embodied, relational, and biographical

Walking artist Clare Qualmann met Maggie outside Exit 3 Aldgate East Tube Station, London after accepting her invitation to do a WIBM on the theme of borders, risk, and belonging. Clare had both mapped and planned a walk from Aldgate East to Stratford Olympic Village, following mainly the route of her walkwalkwalk project's night walks. Clare says:

> So we're starting near Aldgate East tube and we're going to walk around to Old Castle Street where the building that used to be the Women's Library which is part of London Metropolitan University is, and then we're going to wiggle our way through around Brick Lane, up past the old Shoreditch Station and then through Bethnal Green and then when we get to the end of what was the walkwalkwalk route, we're going to carry on east and we're going to, so I've kind of sellotaped another map on to this map. So, we're going to walk across or around the edge of Victoria Park and then on. And the reason I want to do that is because that will take us to the London 2012 Olympic zone which is another important site of borders and boundaries and edges and a highly contested space.

The walk was to take us through many borderlands, liminal and in-between spaces, for example, a 'nomadic garden' developed by local people in an area between two communication lines – tube and rail – literally the in-between spaces, the edges, in a site left over by planners. Approaching the nomadic

FIGURE 9.1 Nomadic Gardens. Image: Maggie O'Neill with permission Clare Qualmann.

garden, we wondered about the stories associated with this place, the deep narratives, layered over time, embedded in the land and place.

Clare says:

> Yes, it's so lovely. So, this space was a wood yard and a scrap yard with a gate at the other end, a closed off space, and then for ages it was just empty and fenced off; and then I assume there was permission process but now it's fantastic, it's become this. This wonderful little chunk of allotments and community activity.
>
> 'In-between' spaces were a theme in Clare's walk made real in the sensory experience of walking by the canal and train lines.

Clare says:

> This, where the road goes over and somehow it makes the light reflect in the canal underneath the road in a beautiful way, and I love the sound under these bridges too, but this feels like an edge to me this feels like a kind of boundary.

FIGURE 9.2 Community space between the tube and railways lines. Image: Maggie O'Neill with permission of Clare Qualmann.

FIGURE 9.3 Canalside. Image: Maggie O'Neill with permission of Clare Qualmann.

FIGURE 9.4 Decorated railway arch. Image: Maggie O'Neill with permission of Clare Qualmann.

Later, Clare continues:

> So, this railway arch I want to tell you more about, it was important for our walk because, well, none of this was here, in fact very little activity was here ... So we made use of the space, we would use it as a place to pause on our night walks and inspired by the street drinkers we'd set up a brazier and have a fire and cook soup and popcorn.
>
> So, there would be a meal on the night walks and then because nobody ever challenged us, we got more and more confident [laughs] with doing things in the space. So, we did one walk where we set up a generator and screened a film and it felt like wow, how extraordinary to find this space of possibility right in the city and all you have to do is come here and do it.

Qualmann's imaginative use of walking arts practice and use of the disused railway arch in the night walks highlight the importance of women taking hold of public space and making it theirs, particularly given that they would not ordinarily visit this space alone, or at night time, for safety reasons.

We also experienced the sensory and imaginative aspect of walking at one point during the walk by the canal. It was a beautiful spot with the sound of water and the reflection of the surrounding environment on the water. Walking under the canal bridge, we were aware of moving in and out of different spaces and across thresholds: from the noisier canalside, with boats and cyclists going by, to the quiet spaces, under canal bridges, a shift in atmosphere with our voices echoing and resounding in the space between concrete and water. Later we talked about the contrast with noisier street spaces, a shopping centre, housing, and the more controlled, designed spaces shaped by capital, such as the Olympic Village and park and the Westfield Centre.

FIGURE 9.5 A borderspace. Image: Maggie O'Neill with permission of Clare Qualmann.

The walk was a relational experience, walking together, side-by-side, with Clare leading the walk. It is in this relational sense that we come to understand walking as 'social being' (Ingold and Vergunst 2008). In the process of walking, a space for dialogue and sharing is facilitated. Our social understanding emerges in and through relationships, and this relational dimension of walking is a central aspect of the Walking Interview as a Biographical Method. Identities, biographies, and relationalities are lived out in the process of walking together. The relational and convivial aspect of walking is implicit in walking side-by-side and is a strong theme in Qualmann's walking arts practice.

The concept of 'ethno-mimesis' is relevant to the imaginative and relational aspect of the WIBM with Clare. It expresses the practice and process of working at the boundaries of sociological research (ethnography, biography, narrative) and the arts: the playful, imaginative nature of artistic activity (O'Neill 2008; O'Neill et al. 2002). Ethno-mimesis facilitates a 'potential space' (Winnicott 1982), a dialogic and reflective space, what Winnicott (1982) called the 'in-between' space between objective reality and creative perception. In walking together, our imaginations were sparked in negotiating the space between self and other and environment.

The relational, imaginative dimension of the walk with Clare was a collaborative process of getting to know Clare's work and biography through the walk and the experience or immersion in the spaces and places Clare shared with Maggie. Walking with another can also be revelatory; at one point along a walk, a wheelchair user passed us as we were standing looking at a building that Clare described as a 'spectacular cash and carry'.

FIGURE 9.6 'Spectacular cash-and-carry'. Image: Maggie O'Neill with permission of Clare Qualmann.

We were immediately cognisant of the depth of the kerb, the nearby roadworks, and how she would negotiate the paths. Clare then talked about a project that Dee Heddon and Sue Porter undertook about walking with wheelchair users called 'Walking Interconnections' noting the 'resilience and acceptance by people when there's no dropped kerb' and 'how disabled people's embodied knowledge can contribute to the sustainability debate'.

In summary, the WIBM with Clare had covered a lot of ground, both under our feet and in relation to the themes that emerged. The relational, embodied sensory and imaginative process of conducting a WIBM was evidenced. The walk was a biography of place too, given the social and environmental changes over time, and Clare's references to these. The gendered nature of walking was a key theme, and especially what it means to walk with children, prams, and pushchairs. Clare talked about the inception of walk-walkwalk, their night walks, as well as her perambulator walks in Scotland

and her 'spinning stories' and 'jam walks'. Threaded through our conversation, these walks linked with the landmarks, places, and spaces along the route. Clare shared fragments of her biography, not only as an artist, but as an academic, researcher, mother, teacher, and manager, and how walking as an arts practice started. She talked about organising her work and art practice around children, the need for being organised, as well as negotiating city spaces with children in prams, the roads, transport systems and routes. The perambulator walks emerge as a resistance to the gendered nature of the environment and the constant need for embodied, negotiation of space with children in prams and/or pushchairs.

This walk (like the walk with Nick Mai, Chapter 7) also highlighted the shifts and changes taking place along the route; gentrification, regeneration, redevelopment, and their impact. Clare reflected upon 'things that are gone', such as Bethnal Green Town Hall, now a 'posh' hotel, the demolished buildings along our walk, including a mission church, and buildings where there had been a change of use – a former laundrette and the women's library.

The following walk with Dee Heddon both reinforced and developed further some of these themes, especially the political and relational aspect of walking.

A walk with Dee Heddon in Kelvingrove Park, Glasgow

Maggie invited Dee to walk with her; she was keen to learn more about her biography as a walking artist. They met at Dee's office and after a cup of tea, headed out to Kelvingrove Park in Glasgow. It was a breezy day and the park was quiet with solo walkers, couples, and at one point a group of young men chatting by a monument.

At the start of the walk, Maggie raised the important question of 'why walking' is part of Dee's art practice. Dee explained that she had written a book on 'autobiography and performance' in 2007, examining how theatre practitioners use autobiographical narratives in making their work, looking 'at what we call "site specific performance" so performances made for and in response to sites, we might call it "site responsive" now actually'. Dee says that she 'kept coming across performances where walking was a major part of the practice, as part of an autobiographical practice, but they were all by men [laughs] and I thought well, that's just a bit unacceptable'.

In collaboration with Cathy Turner, Dee wanted to explore the question of women artists using walking. They put out a call to women artists and conducted ten walking interviews. She calls this method 'peripatetic interviewing'.

> We invited them to take us on a walk of their choice to talk about their walking work ... It was a really lovely way to do the research and then we published two essays about walking women, and the purpose of that really was to bring to visibility the practice that had been so marginalised, if not

just completely ignored, but also to think through that what might it mean to be a woman walking – does it mean anything different without that being an essentialising gesture?

Dee says that that was the beginning of 'why walking', and that her work is ongoing. She goes on to talk about the relational and biographical connection walking has for her and her practice.

> I turned forty, seven years ago and it wasn't a research project, it wasn't intended to be a research project, it was intended as a birthday present to myself, because I'd been thinking a lot about walking and doing, you know, walking interviews and writing about walking. I decided to throw a walking party.
>
> I sent out forty invitations to forty different people, friends, family, folk I didn't know, folk I knew well or folk I'd only sort of acquaintances that I wanted to get to know better and I invited them to take me on a walk of their choice and I spent five years gathering up those walks.
>
> I wrote a thousand words about each walk and blogged it and took three pictures, well, illustrated it with three pictures, I took hundreds of pictures, but I chose three pictures to illustrate each walk and I absolutely loved it as a project. So, that was my first walking art project but it was absolutely intended just as a birthday present.

Although it took five years to complete the book, the purpose was about spending time with people, as 'that's what walking allows'. It facilitated Dee to think 'What is it to be a walking friend or walking side-by-side and everyone said, I mean everyone categorically said, "I had to think really hard about the gift of the walk that I was going to give you"'. One of the walks was an autobiographical walk with her Dad – he took her back to his childhood home. 'We could still stand out and look at the house outside and we hadn't ever done that, so you know so that was interesting to me, it sort of revealed things I hadn't really thought about'. Another friend had intended to take her on a walk that she did weekly with her father 'but he passed away before we managed to do the walk with him, so we did the walk anyway as a sort of memorial walk to him, so what the walk meant changed in that intervening period for her'. The youngest walker Dee walked with was a three year old 'who wanted to take me to the Kelvingrove Art Gallery because that was her favourite place in Glasgow, that's brilliant isn't it?' Dee says that the interviews with women artists politicised walking for her.

Walking as political and relational

The walks Dee undertook:

> brought into sharper focus that whilst there might be lots of nice pleasurable cultural things, there's also a politics attached to the practice of

walking and in the world of art and aesthetics, as in so many other spheres, the women artists are absolutely marginalised in that discourse.

More than this, in contrast to that idea of the walk as a way to escape your everyday, I don't know, burdens, let's call them that, expectations, burdens, cultures, whatever the women artists that we were walking with really used walking as a way to root themselves into those everyday relationships ... I think we talked earlier about relationality, but they were using walking absolutely as a relational material, so it's that side-by-side again. I think that what attaches itself to walking is that relational capacity, walking 'with', not walking 'away', and I don't think we'd say that there are not men who don't use walking as a relational practice, but we were just struck by the recurrence of it in the work of the women that we walked with, but also that it's not written about anywhere, and what we hear always is the striding out, the conquering of the landscape, the heroic figure on their own or with a donkey, rather than the convivial talking and sociability that's afforded by walking and the sharing that's afforded by walking.

In her own practice, Dee has worked for some years now across autobiography, walking, and theatre/performance. What emerges from her work, from the perspective of biographical sociology is an imaginative, creative, interdisciplinary process of art making as method, practice, and performance. Heddon's work connects walking and performance and focuses upon the relational, repetitive, evocative, and revelatory aspects of walking side by side.

At one point in the walk we reached what appeared to be a very high and steep set of stone steps, and we both remarked on how difficult it would be for those with limited mobility to get down the steps. Dee spoke about her work with Sue Porter, Walking Interconnections, at this point – a project that is also a good example of the relationship between method, practice, politics, and performance. Dee says:

Sue herself was a wheelchair user and very much an environmental activist, and as she became increasingly disabled, she began to find that activist community practically inaccessible to her ... So she might want to go to an activist meeting and it would be in a town hall where there was no accessible toilet or the toilet was you know hundreds of metres away ... and it is a problem. So, she wanted to use walking to impress upon other people that in their everyday lives people with disabilities are always problem-solving, having to find deep inner resilience, accepting challenges that can't be overcome, but accepting them in a way that allows them to get up again the next day, rather than giving in to defeat.

In the project, 'an environmental activist went on a walk with a self-identified disabled person' and the conversations were recorded and transcribed by Dee, who then made a thirty minute play from twenty-five hours of recording. The play, called *Going for A Walk* aimed 'to make more publicly accessible the everyday experience of disabled people'.

> So, I learned so much, I was like, gosh, the amount of planning and forethought and mitigation strategies always weighing up risks and benefits on every walk. So the play does say things like, 'Oh well we can't go down here now there's steps' but it would also say things like, or it would capture moments that would be like, 'gosh look at the sun or listen to the trees', so it was in a way an attempt to remind folk that, for most folk walking is a pleasure of some sort, but the type of walking that you do is differential, always differential depending on the time of day, whose body, what body and what type of space.

Walking back towards the entrance to the park, Dee reflects upon the autobiographical element in her walking arts practice, she says:

> I do not want to assume any easy or transparent relationship between a lived life and its portrayal. All autobiographical productions involve processes of selection, scripting, editing, revising. Autobiographical performances strategically work with life experiences, but rather than rendering them selfevident, the important task is to discern the subtext.

In the walk with Dee, the key emerging themes are the connection between self and place, home, performing the self, and the relational, connective, and gendered aspects of walking. Dee comments 'where Carl Lavery can walk fifteen miles alone in Mourning Walk, I know that if he were me he would be continuously looking over his shoulder and scanning the horizon ahead, rather than contemplating his father' (Heddon 2008: 113) The walk also raised the political aspects of walking and the learning gained in Dee's 'peripatetic interviews' with women walking artists, and the interventionist potential of walking by sharing the walks/performances involved in Walking Interconnections with Sue Porter.

This layering of biography, time, space, embodiment, and memory are reflected upon by Heddon (2008) in her discussion (elsewhere) of Crab Walk by artist Phil Smith in Teignmouth, Devon. Smith goes home to Devon and recovers the sites that had childhood significance in a performance called 'Crab Walk'. Smith performed to small intimate audiences in a beach hut and tells a story of walking to the places he visited as a child with his grandparents, following a 'map' of childhood holidays with his 'Nan' and 'Pop'. Dee says, 'this walk was about finding that precious feeling again. When this seaside was that magical playground' (Heddon 2008: 106). In describing biographical performance and the re-imagining of the walks with his grandparents, Heddon reminds us that stories are 'spatial trajectories' that can also 'traverse and organise places' (Heddon 2008: 106). Smith's performance helps us to understand how space is 'dynamised' through the layered and complex story of his early memories, his childhood told in place.

Walking as art practice and the WIBM

Qualmann and Heddon's walking arts practices are instrumental in drawing attention to the imaginative, embodied, relational, biographical, and playful aspect of walking, documented in the 'gifting' of walking and the autobiographical examples of walking they shared with Maggie.

Engaging with the work of walking artists, and the walking interviews with Clare Qualmann and Dee Heddon, has helped to explore and articulate the processes involved and the relational work undertaken by walking artists, and especially the creativity, reflexivity, and imagination involved in walking as process, method, and practice. The walks with Qualmann and Heddon highlight the way that walking facilitates biographical, relational, embodied understanding, and engaging with the arts-based practices of walking artists can help us to better reflect upon lives appreciated in context, and importantly, with critical awareness. Walking as art, for both artists, can also be political.

We have reflected, in this chapter, on the transformative role and possibilities of art and storytelling (via Benjamin) as biographical work, with the aim of enhancing knowledge and understanding across an interdisciplinary terrain – the arts and social sciences – by theorising, experiencing, and imagining walking as method. Inspired by walking artists, we have highlighted the sometimes neglected sensory and embodied experiences of conducting biographical research, and importantly, how this can help us to map ways forward, with critical attention given to the WIBM as imaginative, relational, embodied, sensory, and as a political practice. The importance of memory, place, and cartography to the WIBM is highlighted in the walk with Qualmann and we take this up specifically in the next chapter. In Chapter 10: Auto/biographical encounters in time and space – Roots and routes, we discuss the themes of autobiography, place, and history, as well as cartography, to further explore and explain the WIBM. The following chapter provides auto/biographical accounts by the authors of walks each has imagined and taken in the places where we grew up, Scrooby in Nottinghamshire and Consett in the North-East of England.

Notes

1 For more information see Fulton's website at: http://www.hamish-fulton.com (Accessed 13 August 2018).
2 See for example interviews with Heddon and O'Neill at www.TalkingWalking.net: Available at http://www.talkingwalking.net/?s=heddon and http://www.talkingwalking.net/maggie-oneill-talking-walking/ (Accessed 11 August 2018).
3 The AHRC is a research council called the Arts and Humanities Research Council, which funds academic research (via research competitions).
4 Somerset House, the Live Art Development Agency, the Walking Artists Network, the University of East London, Deveron Arts, Forest Fringe, and Geography Workshop.
5 WalkingLab is co-directed by Stephanie Springgay and Sarah E. Truman (www.walkinglab.org). Initial funding came from the Social Sciences and Humanities Research Council, Canada titled 'Performing Lines: Innovations in walking and sensory methodologies'.

6 Maggie's inclusion of walking in her arts-based research practice was inspired by meeting Misha Myers and hearing her keynote speech at a conference.

7 For example, two crime, justice, and punishment walks in Durham and York were similarly created to enable students to engage with history, theories, and concepts of criminology in embodied and imaginative ways. The walks are a pedagogical tool that facilitate the process of walking in place as both 'dynamising space' and history in the present, uncovering the hidden history of place and landmarks. See http://www.yorkcrimewalk.co.uk and http://ghostsofourfuture.com/the-crime-walk/ (Accessed 12 August 2018).

8 See Walking with Clare Qualmann at: https://www.walkingborders.com/?p=559 (Accessed 23 September 2018).

9 Including walks with: Elspeth Owen, Clare Qualmann, and Gail Burton; Misha Myers; Tamara Ashley; Simone Kenyon; Asna Laura Lopez de la Torre; Emma Bush; Sorrel Muggridge; and Rachel Gomme.

References

Ashley, T. and Kenyon, S. (2010) The Pennine way: The legs that made us (a return journey). in S. Pink, P. Hubbard, M., O'Neill and A. Radley, (eds.) Walking Ethnography and Arts Practice (Special Issue), *Visual Studies*, 25(1): 83–84.

Benjamin, W. (1992) *Illuminations*. London: Fontana Press.

Brennan, T. (2010) The manoeuvre, in S. Pink, P. Hubbard, M. O'Neill, and A. Radley (eds.) Walking Ethnography and Arts Practice (Special Issue), *Visual Studies*, 25(1): 80–81.

Butler, J. and Taylor, S. (2009) Interdependence. In: A. Taylor (ed.) *Examined Life*. New York & London: The New Press.

Calderbank, M. (2003) Surreal dreamscapes: Walter Benjamin and the Arcades. Papers of Surrealism, 1. Available at: www.research.manchester.ac.uk/portal/files/63517385/surrealism_issue_1.pdf (Accessed 23 September 2018).

Cardiff, J. (2004) Her long black hair (audio walk). Available at www.cardiffmiller.com/artworks/walks/longhair.html. (Accessed 23 September 2018).

Child, L. (2010) Street training in Loughborough: On climbing, testing, penetrating, playing with, nurturing, building and/or pissing on boundaries-physical, mental and social-in the perpetual making of public space, in S. Pink, P. Hubbard, M. O'Neill, and A. Radley (eds.). Walking Ethnography and Arts Practice (Special Issue), *Visual Studies*, 25(1): 85–86.

Fulton, H. (2010), Walk, in S. Pink, P. Hubbard, M. O'Neill and A. Radley (eds.) Walking Ethnography and Arts Practice (Special Issue), *Visual Studies*, 25(1): 8–14.

Gros, F. (2015) *A Philosophy of Walking*. London: Verso.

Hatoum, M. (2016) Interview with Mona Hatoum. http://the-talks.com/interview/mona-hatoum/. (Accessed 23 September 2018).

Heddon, D. (2012) Turning 40: 40 turns. Walking & friendship, *Performance Research*, 17(2): 67–75.

Heddon, D. (2015) Going for a walk: A verbatim play, *Studies in Theatre and Performance*, 35(3): 177–188.

Heddon, D. and Myers, M. (2014) Stories from the walking library, *Cultural Geographies*, 21(4): 639–655.

Heddon, D. and Myers, M. (2017) The walking library. Mobilizing books, places, readers and reading, *Performance Research*, 22(1): 32–48.

Heddon, D. and Turner, C. (2010) Walking women: Interviews with artists on the move, *Performance Research*, 15(4): 14–22.

Heddon, D. and Turner, C. (2012) Walking women: Shifting the tales and scales of mobility, *Contemporary Theatre Review*, 22(2): 224–236.

Heddon, D. E. (2008) *Autobiography and Performance*. Basingstoke, UK: Palgrave Macmillan.

Hind, C. and Qualmann, C. (2015) *Ways to Wander*. Axminster, UK: Triarchy Press.

Horvath, A. and Szakolczai, A. (2018) *Walking into the Void: A Historical Sociology and Political Anthropology of Walking*. Abingdon: Routledge.

Ingold, T. and Vergunst, J. (eds.) (2008) *Ways of Walking: Ethnography and Practice on Foot*. Aldershot, UK: Ashgate.

Jones, C. B. (2010) Walking, the Western and the tumbleweed, in S. Pink, P. Hubbard, M. O'Neill, and A. Radley, (eds.) Walking Ethnography and Arts Practice (Special Issue), *Visual Studies*, 25(1): 87–88.

Long, R. (1967) A line made by walking. Available at www.tate.org.uk/art/artworks/long-a-line-made-by-walking-ar00142 (Accessed 23 September 2018).

Massey, D. (1994) *Space, Place and Gender*. Cambridge, UK: Polity Press.

Massey, D. (2013) *Doreen Massey on Space, in Social Science, Bites, Podcasts*. Available at www.socialsciencespace.com/2013/02/podcastdoreen-massey-on-space/ (Accessed 23 September 2018).

Myers, M. (2010) 'Walk with me, talk with me: The art of conversive wayfinding', *Visual Studies*, 25(1): 59–68.

O'Neill, M. in association with Giddens, S., Breatnach, P., Bagley, C., Bourne, D., and Judge, T. (2002) Renewed methodologies for social research: Ethno-mimesis as performative praxis, *The Sociological Review*, 50(1): 69–88.

O'Neill, M. (2008) Transnational refugees: The transformative role of art? [53 paragraphs], *Forum: Qualitative Sozialforschung, Forum: Qualitative Social Research*, 9(2): Art. 59.

O'Neill, M. (2015) Participatory biographies: Walking, sensing, belonging. In: M. O'Neill, B. Roberts, and A. Sparkes (eds.) *Advances in Biographical Research: Creative Applications*. Abingdon, UK: Routledge.

O'Neill, M., Giaquinto, B. and Hasedzic, F. (2018) Migration, memory and place: Walking as a convivial methodology in participatory research. A visual essay. In: M. L. Berg, and M. Nowicka (eds.) *Convivial Tools for Research and Practice*. London: UCL Press.

O'Neill, M. in association with Giddens, S. Breatnach, P. Bagley, C. Bourne, D., and Judge, T. (2002) Renewed methodologies for social research: Ethno-mimesis as performative praxis, *Sociological Review*, 50(1): 69–88.

O'Rourke, K. (2013) *Walking and Mapping: Artists as Cartographers*. Cambridge, MA: MIT Press.

Shortell, T. and Brown, E. (2014) *Walking in the European City: Quotidian Mobility and Urban Ethnography*. Farnham, UK: Ashgate.

Solnit, R. (2001) *Wanderlust*. London: Viking.

Springgay, S. and Truman, S. (2018) *Walking Methodologies in a More-than-human World. WalkingLAB*. New York: Routledge.

Weigel, S. Z. (1996) *Body- and Image-Space: Re-Reading Walter Benjamin*. London: Routledge.

Winnicott, D. W. (1982) *Playing and Reality*. London: Routledge.

Young, A. and Temple, B. (2014) *Approaches to Social Research: The Case of Deaf Studies*. Oxford: Oxford University Press.

10

AUTO/BIOGRAPHICAL ENCOUNTERS IN TIME AND SPACE

Roots and routes

In this chapter the authors return to some biographically formative spaces and experiences, to examine our 'roots' and 'routes' – our starting points or the 'path(s)' taken as a biographical research method. In mapping, walking, and reflecting on walks taken long ago in our hometowns, our present circumstances are in 'dialogue' with, and 'responding' to, previous attachments (e.g., to 'home', 'family', 'place', 'location'). In the memories of 'then' and the experience of the 'now', as we walk, we reflect upon what is remembered, what in the moments of the present shapes the past – what are the continuities or disjunctions in meaning, feeling, and memory? Is the past 'past', or is it still here, in how we 'are', our sense of belonging, self, and identity? How do our 'root(s)' and the 'routes' form and shape the most important aspects of who we are?

Walking and autobiography

The Walking Interview as a Biographical Method (WIBM) requires a 'reflective' approach, not merely on the 'research role' being undertaken, including the relationship with the participant, but also on the wider personal life and its bearing on the research process. One element of this consideration of the researcher's 'position' is the memories of walks that 'come to mind' – perhaps even 'involuntarily', or by more direct recollection. In writing this book, researching on topics to be covered, various previous walks 'in life' (including as part of earlier research) became 'apparent', sometimes from many years ago.

The process of researching and writing this book enabled Maggie to have the time to reflect on walking as part of her ethnographic, creative practice, and the participatory research she has conducted for almost three decades, as well as more personally and autobiographically. In this chapter, she reflects upon walks in Consett, taken with her Mam and Dad as a child, and on her return to Consett for a university art project in 1981, a year after the Thatcher government had presided over the closure of Consett Iron Company.

As an adolescent, Maggie's art teacher would organise youth hostelling and walking trips that had a profound impact upon her, reinforcing her love of walking and nature that had been established when living in Consett and walking in the surrounding countryside. Later, at university, protest walks included 'Anti-Nazi League' and 'reclaim the night' walks, and as an academic at Durham University, she undertook walks with artists during the annual miners' gala over a three-year period, walking with Margareta Kern, John Perivolaris, and Alan O'Cain, interviewing the banner holders walking through the streets of Durham. At both Durham and York Universities, she led walks on the development of crime, justice, and punishment to facilitate more embodied and convivial teaching and learning practices to introduce students to theories and concepts in criminology. Walking is also central to her sense of wellbeing, and given the opportunity, she will walk as a means of de-stressing, to elicit creative reflection, and as a weekly 'constitutional'. In the section below, she traces walks undertaken in Consett as a child growing up and reflects upon them.

For Brian, walks and walking are also very much part of his personal history and current life. He particularly remembers numerous protest marches in the 1960s as a student, and later, as a political activist, many local and national marches and campaigns in the 1970s–80s – against racism, in support of the NHS, trade union struggles, and protest marches against unemployment (under the Thatcher government) (e.g., the National Miners' Strike 1984–5). At the same time, there were also the various leisure pursuits (e.g., holiday coastal walks) and later walking holidays in parts of the UK and Europe (Italy, Croatia, Turkey, especially in recent years). One very personal memory is as an adult rambling with his late father along the banks of a canal accessed from the garden gate of his parents' bungalow that looked out across the water and fields. In the section below, he describes a regular walk he took through a local cemetery (near where he now lives), how it raises memories of his childhood village and its cemetery next to his family house, and a return to the village some years ago.

Walking in Consett – Maggie O'Neill

At the centre of the map (below) is the first house I remember us living in, Number 8 Foster Street. My parents paid £100 for the house in 1960 and they sold it to move into a council house in Moorside when I was seven. I realised, on drawing the map, that this house retains centre stage in my memory and imagination of Consett. I have drawn the walking routes taken with my Mam and later on my own, to my Nanna's, Grandma's, and Aunty Kay's: three important women and figures in my life history. The landmarks on the map are Consett Iron Company, the places we used as playgrounds, the overgrown slag-heaps, railway sidings, and the countryside, and the library, park, swimming baths, cinema, shops, St Patrick's school, and St Patrick's Church.

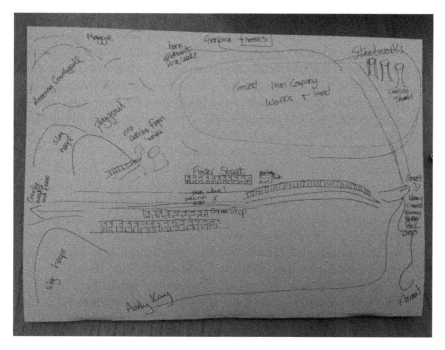

FIGURE 10.1 Maggie's map of her childhood walks in Consett. Image: Maggie O'Neill.

Shopping, conviviality, and the park

My earliest memory of walking is with my Mam (we called her Mammy, but I soon stopped that when we moved to the Midlands as one of my school friends laughed at this; in the Midlands, Mammy became Mum), holding onto the pram as we walked from our house, a two-up, two-down terraced house. It was on the same road as the Railway Inn pub. The town was dominated by the Consett Iron Company's steelworks. Mam had to be watchful on washing day, as red iron oxide dust she described as 'iron ore' would cover the washing out on the line, as the 'works' belched out red dust that I can smell right now in my nostrils, whilst re-imagining the days when a red layer would cover everything. It evokes a feeling of comfort and belonging.

I loved going out shopping with her. We would walk across the road, onto the railway bridge, over the bridge into the town centre, to the market and to certain shops, the church, the library, the park. It took a long time to get wherever we were going, as she would greet and stop and chat with women en route. Shopping was a convivial experience. I remember her quick purposeful step, and keeping up with her was a challenge.

The library was a favourite place. Aunty Theresa taught me to read at four years old and I lived in books, they were to be my sense of home and belonging after the move to the Midlands; an escape and imaginary domain where I learnt about life and language beyond my immediate horizons, the village, school, miner's welfare, and church; and my feelings of alienation in the place that was now home. Going swimming with Mam and her sisters and my cousins, and to the park came a close second to the library. Looking back, I realise that I learnt a lot about my Mam in the process, that she was warm and positive and engaging. She is the eldest of eleven and shopping often included a walk to my Nanna's house where Mam would have a cup of tea and my uncle Jim, her youngest sibling, would humour us children and make us laugh. Her Granddad was sometimes there, sitting on a hard-backed chair with a glass of water in front of him, a quiet man. The water often remained untouched, with bubbles eventually appearing. He had raised his own sisters and brothers to save them from going into the workhouse when their mother died in Ireland. Newly married, he and his wife Ellen raised one son, my Grandad, Thomas and his young siblings, Kate, Pat and John. Nanna's house was rarely quiet, the fire seemed always to be on with tea in the pot on the table by the window. Nanna rarely seemed to sit still; occasionally she would let us play with her hair, dressing it up, she had white fine hair. More usually she was in the small kitchen, cooking.

Mam's sisters, who were also living in Consett, were her companions, especially Patsy and Kay, and Theresa the youngest sister would often babysit. We also visited Kay, a much longer walk or bus ride to Leadgate, who was great fun; she would chase us around the furniture and talk to us as equals rather than as 'children'. I in turn later 'babysat' for her four boys, my cousins. My sister and I moved in to Kay's house when Mam went into hospital to have our two brothers. I can still remember very clearly the feeling of loss and comfort of being with Kay during those times. My sister and I had both been born in our Nanna's house, as was the norm then – the girls returning to their Mam's to have their babies.

We also walked to my Grandma's house at The Grove, to visit, and sometimes for tea or Sunday dinner if my Dad was on a late shift at the steelworks. The walk to Grandma's was longer and we would sometimes take a bus. Her house had a coal fire and range, an outside toilet with newspaper cut up neatly on a string (as toilet paper), and a garden full of vegetables and rhubarb. In our house, we had an inside bathroom, that my Dad had fitted with a friend; and white toilet paper. My Dad told us stories of bathing in the tin bath in front of the fire/range.

Mam told us of the day when two young men came to Grandma's door asking for their 'da' and she answered that they had the wrong house. They hadn't, they were the children of a previous marriage that my Grandma, until that moment, was unaware of. Across the narrow road from Grandma's was a horse that we would feed through the fence with crusts of bread, oblivious to the nettle stings, and then Grandma or Mam would rub our legs with large dock leaves. It was a two-bedroom house with an outside toilet and she brought up five children there with my Granddad, who died in his mid-fifties. He was a union organiser, like my Dad.

Dad was union secretary for the steelworker's union, when working at the steelworks in Consett and then was branch secretary for the Warwickshire miners' union whilst in Coventry. He played a huge part in the national miners' strikes of 1972, 1974, and especially the 1984–5 strike.

In these early days, walking was convivial and a large part of it was relational and familial too. We also walked, I now realise, because it would have been difficult to get a pram and four young children onto the bus on her own; and to save money. I also have early memories of my Dad taking my sister and I to the park, probably to give Mam a break. He worked shifts at the steelworks and when he took us shopping, he was much more extravagant than my Mam, and of course we loved this, the buying of food and treats that Mam would be more careful about, or not even consider; and the pleasure we gained knowing that he was transgressing the shopping budget norms and the treats in store for us.

Walking was also about play and playing. We were encouraged to 'go out to play' and would often return for our tea, playing at friends' houses sometimes involved eating there too, although this was rare. My strongest memory of walking and playing was with my best friend, a girl who lived at the end of the street, also called Margaret. We would walk for miles, along country roads leading out of Consett, playing in the old railway sidings and on the slag-heaps that were grown over with wild flowers, weeds, and grasses, long jumping the puddles, and testing our agility by walking along the railways lines as trapeze artists. Once a lady stopped us along the main road, offered us a drink, it was very hot, and advised us to turn back into the town. We did not follow her advice. I also remember being forced out 'to play' with my sister, despite our protestations that it was too cold. We huddled by the back door and then in the shed (used to be an outside toilet) at the end of the back yard, where we were soon joined by an older girl who lived a few doors down. She would take us swimming sometimes and to the cinema, we soon forgot about the cold.

Our family migrated to the Midlands in 1969, my Dad took a job as a fitter with the Coal Board. My Mam and four children travelled by train and were collected in a Coal Board minibus in Coventry along with other families and were dropped off at our respective Coal Board houses, on what seemed like an enormous estate, populated not by trees and grasses, but by pylons, an army of them seemed to march through the estate at intervals. The journey was eventful; my youngest brother was not yet twelve months old. It was a long journey. Other families were on the train, there was a small migratory group headed to the coalfields of the Midlands. I never settled in Coventry, it was so alien, my accent was mocked, there were endless rows of Coal Board housing, grey, pebble-dashed, and in this grey flat landscape loomed the row of electric pylons, instead of trees, grass, and hills. It was also a long walk to the bus stop and I was told never to take short cuts, keep to the main roads and would often run the last stretch after dark to our house (in a cul de sac) as a teenager returning home from seeing friends in Coventry, news of recent rapes or muggings at the forefront of my imagination. I am sure looking back it was much safer than I imagined.

I had to take two buses to get to my school, Cardinal Newman Comprehensive, and to meet with my friends who were mostly living in Coventry or Holbrooks, the catchment area for the school. Despite passing the 11-plus, I was allowed to go to the comprehensive, the cost of school uniforms and other items prohibitive and, I imagine, my socialist parents wanted a comprehensive education for their eldest child and daughter. My siblings followed me. Bus money was often spent on sweets during the summer and I would walk home, this was much easier when we lived on the village in Keresley.

We moved from the Newdigate estate a few years later to another Coal Board house, a smaller, more established community, Keresley village, and lived in what my Dad called a 'Dutch' house. I would spend ages at the telephone box in the village queuing to talk to my friends and sometimes Aunty Kay.

During the miners' strikes of 1972 and 1974, we lived on food handouts and whatever Mam could afford from the picket duty pay Dad would bring home. Burning candles and playing card games and telling stories when the lights went out.

Soon we were on the move again, moving to a larger house back to the Newdigate estate. Four bedrooms instead of three. We were there for a couple of years and then back to Kerelsey village, to a three-bedroomed house and within a year I moved out myself, moving to Nottingham to work for social services as an administrative assistant in 1977, and in September 1978, I was a student at Nottingham Polytechnic on the CNAA B.Ed. degree programme specialising in Sociology and Creative Arts Education.

My favourite tutors (all male staff in those days and mostly women students) were the artist Ken Longcake, education scholar Pete Shuttleworth, and critical sociologist Conrad Lodziak. Con's influence was significant, he introduced us to the Frankfurt School, to a history of critical theory and encouraged me to think I could do a master's degree (M.Phil) to take forward my passion for the transformative possibilities of art and arts-based research, drawing upon Benjamin and Adorno. Pete's radical politics, commitment to the power of education, and great integrity were important, and Ken's wonderful artworks, aesthetic practice, ordinariness, lack of ego, and support were instrumental in the development of my scholarship.

Thinking about these three teachers now, I realise that biographically they pointed to the path I would take, marked by education, art, and critical theory. In 1999, my first book was an edited collection of feminist papers on the work of Adorno and the transformative role of art and critical theory.

Protest and memorial walking

As a student in 1980, I walked with my Dad at the annual miners' march in Berryhill in Mansfield alongside Tony Benn and Arthur Scargill flanked by the National Union of Mineworkers banners; these were formative years politically. I would also walk in the anti-Nazi and reclaim the night marches, with friends and fellow students.

A member of the Labour Party since my student days, with a lapse during the Blair years, this walk with my Dad, union leaders, and miners, as well as with fellow student activists, was emotive and deeply expressive of solidarity, addressing social and sexual inequalities to be further explored and expressed through class politics, being a labour union representative at university, and the disciplines of sociology, critical theory, women's studies, cultural studies, and criminology. Later still, these themes would be expressed by undertaking biographical, as well as participatory action and participatory arts research. My sense of belonging to the North-East, to the social and political history and culture is palpable. I have such great fondness and connection to the post-industrial landscape of Teesside, expressing something of the images I remember of Consett Iron Company, 'the works' (now erased). Whilst working in Durham, I undertook four years of documenting the annual miners' gala, walking with banner-holders and interviewing them about the meaning of the march and 'big meeting'. The landscape around Consett and Weardale is incredibly beautiful.

I returned to Consett to undertake an arts project for my undergraduate degree in 1981, walking from Consett to 'the works' and on to the newspaper office and my Grandad's house (on my Mam's side). A three-bedroomed house where he and Annie my Nanna, who died in her mid-sixties, raised eleven children.

It was freezing cold; 'the works' had been closed by the Thatcher administration in 1980. I took a series of photographs and then created a series of etchings of our old house and street; and a painting of 'the works' – closed, bereft, and monumental in the snow. The artist Ken Longcake, our tutor, was patient and supportive of my attempts at oils and acrylics and the image below was certainly inspired by him. He encouraged me to be bolder, not only with the palette, but with the forms and lines and energy of the work. I can remember him talking me through the perspective here; it isn't quite the way I intended.

FIGURE 10.2 Consett Iron Company. View from 'The Grove'. Acrylic painting: Maggie
O'Neill.

Grandad, who was still working as a lollipop man (a person who helps children
cross the main road in front of the school – holding a long pole with a circular
symbol on top to identify him or her) for the local Catholic primary school (the
school I had attended) welcomed me and made me hot tea. It would be the last
time I saw him, as he died a few months later of a heart attack, on the school premises, after work – aged 83. This image reminds me of that visit with him. He was a
quiet, gentle, humorous man, who was kindness personified.

There were dark times ahead for Consett following the closure of the steelworks. Thousands of people, mostly men, lost their jobs: the estimates are
between three and four thousand were made unemployed; some never worked
again. The ski chalets and dry ski slope that sprang up in an enterprising fashion
on the site of the old works, gave way to various small enterprises, including
disposable nappies.

The photographer Julian Germain captured the closure and aftermath in
'Steel Works' (1990), combining photographs by Tommy Harris, a local press
photographer, with Germain's own, producing a social history; indeed, one
could argue, a biography of Consett through images. The book is described as
a postmodern visual history writing. Tommy Harris's (freelance photographer
and steelworker) images are wonderful, scenes of family and community life,
juxtaposed with Germain's. What Germain loved about Tommy Harris's images
were the details that he had cropped from the image before publishing in the

local newspaper. The details cropped from the images tell a richer more detailed story of community life.

Aunty Kay's husband, my Uncle Eddie never had a permanent job again, but a 'portfolio' of temporary jobs and travelled as far as Lincoln to get work. Many young people of my cousins' generation have two and three jobs or a series of temporary contracts working in factories and farms and two of my cousins are also retained firemen alongside their 'day' jobs. The ski chalets and dry ski slope gave way to the production of Phileas Fogg's tortilla chips in 1993, and this in turn also closed in 2014 with the loss of 103 jobs (Lynch 2014).

It was reported in 1995 that the population of the town from 1981 had fallen from around thirty thousand to twenty-four thousand, with only six per cent of school leavers finding jobs by that date. By 1998, it was commented that the fear of joblessness and the lasting economic effects of the 1930s, and the continuing decline of the basic industries of coal and steel had brought a generational cycle of experience of unemployment (see McElvoy 1998). At the last census in 2011, the population of Consett was 27,394, and nearly four decades after the closure of 'the works', Office of National Statistics data shows that unemployment is still a major issue. Consett is described as a 'dormitory town' where people take advantage of low-cost housing, but work elsewhere.

Walking in a nearby cemetery (2016–17) – Brian Roberts

Two years ago, I moved home after twenty years living in northern England some 200 miles, to a city in the south, initially into a rented flat while looking for a house to buy. The flat was part of a number of low-rise blocks, most of them making a square surrounding a formally patterned garden with fountains, raised brick beds for bushes and plants, and benches. Most days, I would walk through the square and often take photographs of the ripples and bubbles made by the fountains in the water and passing on across a narrow road into a small cemetery on the slope of a hill whose grounds were being left 'wild' to encourage traditional fauna and flora of the area. Across the bottom corner of the cemetery, a flat wide tarmac path ran which was quite busy with residents and students taking a short-cut to make their way to and from town. I would diverge from the path, go up one side of the slope of the cemetery on a stony track that narrowed to a grassy imprint, and then back down to the tarmac path in a rough circle. At points, I would look at the graves as they caught my eye – their headstones and names, dates and dedications, statues and crosses. On the top of the slope, I would sit for a while on one of two benches in the shade of a tree and look down on the path crossing below with its pedestrians flowing by to and from college, the shops, and home, and beyond to view the houses in the lower valley and a hill that sits on the opposite side. Sometimes I would wander haphazardly around the graves reading the dedications (where legible) and the details of lives.

This week (in September 2017), I returned to the hillside cemetery after a year – again after walking through the formal grounds of the square. I had driven past in the car recently and vowed to walk there again, retracing the steps of my previous visits. As on other occasions, my thoughts turned to the youth of many of the pedestrians passing through the cemetery and that of the incumbents many of them killed in World War I – young lives a hundred years apart – on both the poignancy and tragedy of lives cut short and the brevity of life itself. This time, I was also again reflecting on my own life, and relatives no longer present. I realised while sitting on the bench, especially on this visit, that many of the memories of my childhood village were connected to walking and to seeing, playing in, and passing through, its cemetery.

Cemeteries, time, memory

The experience of my walking in the local cemetery on the more recent and previous occasions made me think of the passing of time, and of stasis and move-ment – the 'quick and the dead', the passing pedestrians across the bottom of the cemetery while I sat on the bench under the tree, the dead lying around beneath the stones while the long grass, trees, and bushes moved in the breeze. On sitting on the bench again and re-viewing the graves of the young World War I soldiers, I thought particularly of my grandfather, a coalminer during both World Wars and pictures of my uncle, a miner who died aged thirty-four in World War II in 1942, and the fact that they were both buried in the cemetery next to our house in the village when I was a child. The walk in the 'current' cemetery 'took me back' to their graves, and my early life in the village where our family lived until I was eight years old. It was as if each of the two cemeteries had become a lens – giving a moment or series of moments through which we see backwards and forwards in time (Brockmeier 2001; Roberts 2011).

These walks in the cemetery brought one clear memory of my grandfather to mind, the time (when I was around four to five years old) when he challenged me to a race around the corner of my grandparents' cottage to the outside toilet (about twenty yards away) and back to the front door. As my grandfather walked slowly with the aid of a walking stick (he had been disabled in mine work), I thought the challenge was easy. Off I set, not glancing back, got to the toilet, and headed back to the cottage door – without seeing my grandfather! I believed I had won the race since my grandfather was still there at the door. However, he declared he had won the race, explaining that he had been so fast that he had been there and back unseen. Although, a little annoyed at the 'trick', it pos-sibly began to make me think about movement, speed, and time. A couple of years later (around seven years old) I began to wonder that if I ran fast enough around a corner could I see people motionless. This notion was then reinforced at school when a radio programme often played music each week for us to dance to – and when the music stopped, we were instructed to be still like a tree: of course, some of us on purpose kept moving a little later than others who were now standing still. Around this time, I set out to dream in colour and float to the ceiling when I slept (Roberts 2011).

On my recent visits to the local cemetery, seeing pedestrians walking across its lower corner while so many other inhabitants had 'stopped' (were in graves), again made me consider how some remain 'walking' after others, and how the pedestrians had started their 'life journey' long after others of the 'same age'. My cemetery walks and resting on the bench beneath the tree brought to mind the cemetery over our garden wall in the village churchyard, which I would see from our garden, perhaps in sitting on the bench under a mulberry tree, when I was a child. They brought the thought that the world we live in is 'inhabited' by our predecessors and successors – those who walked here before, along these paths and roads, and other spaces, whose footsteps we now tread in, just as others (some of our contemporaries and successors) will move through these same spaces 'in time' when we have 'stopped'. The garden or park bench, I reflected later (in writing this book), is not only associated with respite and contemplation but, as a 'place of rest', can also act as a symbol of infirmity, aging, and death (and a site for memorialisation) (see Chapter 8).

My developing understanding of time as witnessed by my 'grandfather's trick' and the school music and dance programme (and, interestingly, both have been retained clearly in my memory), was perhaps bolstered by a nascent 'historical consciousness'. This awareness was probably due to living in a 17th century house in which we had to keep a 'museum room' open to visitors (as part of a rental agreement) and in a village with an important history (see below), in addition to being mainly surrounded by a cemetery containing the dead of the long past and where more 'contemporary' deceased of the village were also buried.

A return to the village (2010)

The 'reminiscences' of the 'cemetery of my childhood' and associations with my grandfather brought into mind while sitting on the cemetery bench in my recent walks also reminded me of another – physical – 'return' to my village. About seven years ago, I made a special trip to the village to see what had changed (and what I remembered). It had been about twenty-five years since my last visit made with my mother and father.

On my return visit, I went from one end to the other slowly by car, stopping now and again, getting out and walking about to see sights I remembered – from Gibbet Hill Lane and Mill Lane (in the north, nearer the local town), along where I played in bushes with friends, crossing the river where we swam, along the common land where gypsies annually camped, and we fished in a stream, passed the mill and mill cottages, and up to where our house – the Old Vicarage – stands and the churchyard and then down to the village hall (where the main London–Edinburgh rail line is a little way down the lane), on to the end of the village where it meets the old Great North Road at the former public house, and then finally to my old school (now a private residence). I made sure I walked around the cemetery to visit my uncle's grave, but now found it being encroached by a large bush and the writing on the headstone shaling away. I was disconcerted by not being able to find the grave of my grandfather.

In this recent 'pilgrimage' visit to my origins, what was I 'looking for'? I wanted to gauge how I felt about the village and my history – influences on my life – and how I perceived continuities and discontinuities: was the past 'gone' or was it still with me? I wished to see if my feelings were still the same: I had seen the past as 'past' with little connection between my village childhood and now – but was there to be a renewed connection with my childhood and adolescence, perhaps a greater sense of emotional recognition than on previous occasions years before? Interestingly, the visit brought a shift in my feelings to the village and our house, a renewed 'recognition' – I now felt more continuity, or return, a reconnection: it was no longer 'the past' (as 'gone'), but had formed significantly who I am now – I began to 'recognise' that key basic elements of 'learning development' (in perceptions, senses, skills) had been laid down. Further, it seemed as though some aspects of this learning had lain dormant or only partially realised in adulthood, and was now coming through again towards the latter part of my life. An 'enthusiasm' begun then had 'powered' my interest in accumulating knowledge and understanding, but some parts of my development had remained relatively unfulfilled (i.e., the poetic, visual, sensual, artistic). I began to write more about my early life and development. In short, I used to see the village as 'gone' – a time and place distanced – but began to see continuities as if I was 'returning' to it, and wondered on the relation: 'the boy the man, man the boy' (see Roberts 2011).

The village provided my boundaries, and how I developed – appreciation of sounds and colours, and understanding of time, skills in reading and writing – in imagination and a wider consciousness of place (Roberts 2011; see also Roberts 1999). Looking back on my early life in the village, there are at least two processes of time involved – how I was developing in consciousness as a boy (including an understanding of 'time') and later, especially after the 'return' visit to the village, how my biographical perceptions have shifted – in the 'historical consciousness' of my life (Roberts 2011).

Walking as a child in the village in the 1950s

My memories of my childhood in the village are often associated with walking. I remember having the 'freedom' of the village, being able to walk and run around the lanes and farms with friends exploring, climbing, building 'dens', playing various 'adventure' games and 'hide and seek' from when I was quite a young child. As children (my siblings or friends), we would walk around the fields when harvesting was taking place. I would also see my mother working picking potatoes or some other crop. We would walk into the countryside, such as on the other side of the railway, along the path through marshy ground to cross the river bridge into the woods with its mass of bluebells and blackberries. Occasionally, I would go alone into the woods to climb trees, once falling ('luckily') into a soft bed of nettles. I walked (in 'pit boots') daily a few hundred yards to school on the edge of the village with my older brother and sister. After school, a usual walk was from home going downhill to my grandparents in Mill Cottage to watch children's programmes on their 'coin in slot' television.

I walked each week (or when younger, I would be in a large baby 'pram') with my mother to the nearby town (about a mile and half), to the cooperative store to shop and occasionally to go to the doctors, and, less often, our family went to the 'pictures'. I broke my right leg when I was five. I was jumping from a tree with a friend, I landed and rolled a little, but much to my surprise, I could not get back to my feet. My Dad was called and he carried me home on his back. Excitingly, I went by ambulance to hospital in the city ten miles away. My leg was in plaster for six weeks and I was not able to stand at first. I was transported around (much to my embarrassment) in the baby 'pram' until I could walk again. My older brother and sister and I could walk through our garden gate into the churchyard, past the graves to the path to the church porch. We were members of the choir, and after dressing in the vestry, processed down the nave in our surplices with the vicar leading each Sunday to the sound of the organ, between the congregation rows, to the choir stalls, and back at the end of the service.

I was very much aware of the life of the village – the local farmers herding cows going past our house to the farm milking sheds, the occasional 'tramp' going past the village and visiting door-to-door salesmen, or gypsies who camped each year in the village also selling wares door to door. I was also curious about the disabled man in the village in his hand-pedalled wheelchair.

A developing childhood in Scrooby

Until I was eight years old, the village – Scrooby – formed the 'parameters' of my world, where my sensual understandings developed, notions of time arose, and I began to read, write, and explore the countryside (Roberts 2011). Interestingly, the Rupert Bear books were a favourite reading. Rupert lived in the village of Nutwood – in a cottage in a fictional, idyllic English village. Did I have some identification with his wanderings into the countryside with his 'pals', just as I played around the village and surrounding fields; was there some correlation then in my mind between life in the two villages?

Much of the history of the village I did not know, but I was very aware of the Pilgrim Fathers and their voyage to America (see below). In fact, we had many American and other visitors to view our house, who walked around the garden and were shown into our 'antique room' to see old plates, furniture, cauldron, fireplace etc. Many took photographs of the house, garden, and of my sister, brother and I, and later posted copies to us.

The garden surrounded the house on three sides, and had a large lawn with the mulberry tree (and its companion bench), vegetable area (including rhubarb, gooseberry bushes), and a wall on the church cemetery side The house, garden, and the village formed the boundaries of my world – a microcosm in which my senses and intellectual abilities, social understandings, and social attachments developed. It was a 'maze' of streets, paths, cemetery, farmyards, and field tracks to experience and explore, where my interest in reading and study, in 'finding out' (especially in history and geography) was set 'in motion'.

Scrooby is a small ancient village (population c.300), in north Nottinghamshire, England, UK. Our family's rented a 17th century house, the Old Vicarage, next to the church – it was nearly surrounded by the churchyard, and we had our small ironwork gate and path to the church. The graveyard was higher than our garden, and the tops of the gravestones could be seen over the wall – my uncle's grave was close to the wall, and later (as an eleven-year-old), I attended my grandfather's burial there (a year or so after we had left the village).

In 2020, the village of Scrooby may well become (at least a little) better known. It has a central place in the history of the Pilgrim Fathers – 'puritan' religious 'separatists' (from the Anglican church) who sailed to America from Plymouth in 1620 to avoid persecution, and the 400th anniversary of their voyage and settlement is to be celebrated in the village and elsewhere (see Bunker 2011; Philbrick 2007). Scrooby and its surrounding villages provided the key membership of the Pilgrim Fathers, including William Brewster, an early leader who was from the village and William Bradford (leader of the colony and writer of its early history) was from nearby. The village school I attended was named after the Pilgrim Fathers' ship, the Mayflower; the trans-Atlantic sailing of a replica – Mayflower II – made international headlines in 1957 (when I was seven years old) and was celebrated in the village. Some years ago, on a visit to America, I went to see Mayflower II. Locally, this history has again received more attention in the last few years with postings on village and county websites, and the involvement of local museums. In former times, it had an archbishop's palace where Henry VIII and Cardinal Wolsey had briefly stayed. It is also mentioned in the Domesday Book and was featured later when common land enclosure legislation was enacted in the late 18th century.

The village lies on the Great North Road (prior to the later bypassing by the A1 and then the M1) which used to be the main route between London and Edinburgh, and so was a 'posting' stop for horse carriages. An 18th century turnpike improvement of the road to 'bypass' the village was built; the tollgate was the site of a murder, and the origin of the name of Gibbet Hill Lane was due to a subsequent hanging and exhibition of the body. The main London to Edinburgh railway line (from the 1840s) running by on the edge of the village carries trains at high speed, and the village had its own station until the 1930s. The most prominent resident when I lived in the village in the early 1950s was Group Captain Insall, VC who restored and lived in the former mill; he was friendly with my (Welsh) grandparents who were near neighbours in a row of tiny 'mill cottages'. My grandfather had retired from being a coalminer at the pit in the next village. I learnt many years later that Group Captain Insall was a pioneer of aerial photography, in particular known for his photographs of the Neolithic 'woodhenge', a mile and a half from Stonehenge, in 1926, which led it to be designated a 'henge' (rather than a 'barrow'). Last year I visited both 'henges'. In 1958, our family moved to a nearby town, Retford ten miles away, famed as a Victorian 'rotten borough' (as mentioned in *Middlemarch*, Eliot 1871–2) and a stop off for Bryson on his well-read travels (Bryson 2015). I travelled to our new home in the back of the removal van with my father; I could see the road 'moving' away, and with it the village through a gap under the vehicle's rear doors and my previous life.

Auto/biography: Roots and routes

The walks above alert us to the power of memory and how we 'recover' past events. Walking can bring back memories of previous locations – sometimes via 'involuntary' thoughts, at others we attempt to recall instances and elements of our past. Walking can, therefore, be an 'exercise' in both 'reliving' the past in the imagination (with associated emotions and sensual references) and also in 'composition' – to make sense of the past–present relations. The walks returned us both to our 'roots' and 'routes': memories of place and time as formative parts of our past, having significant resonances for how we understand ourselves – what we have become, how we have grown to what we are, our 'life cycle'. In doing this recall we are tracing our 'roots' – asking questions and exploring the life 'route(s)' we have taken.

Life has its fascination for all of us – how did we get to the 'here', the 'now'? How did we take this route rather than that (Roberts 1999)? It is like a labyrinth or maze (see Chapter 8) in time that we seek to unravel, but the 'life panorama' – scenes, emotions, motives, choices in or for the past, present, future – we are part of is constantly changing. In prospection and retrospection, how is our 'walk of life' to be understood – as discontinuous moments, as post hoc narrative, or as islands of experience?

The accounts of childhood from Maggie and Brian bring to the fore the relationship between previous (childhood) experience and how it is understood through forms of memory – a key issue within the study of biographical accounts, including within WIBM. Two core themes from Walter Benjamin's (1992) work are relevant and are evidenced in our autobiographical walks above: the concept of experience as lived moments (Erlebnis), historical experience (Erfahrung), *and* the relationship of these (our histories, biographies, and lived moments) to memory and especially involuntary memory (see Chapters 3 and 7). When writing this account on her early years in Consett and remembering being at home with her Mam, Maggie could smell and almost taste the 'iron ore'. This is an example of involuntary memory sparked by remembering that place and time. Benjamin describes the past as being somewhere between 'the reach of the intellect, and unmistakably present in some material object (or in the sensation which such an object arouses in us), although we have no idea which one it is', and it is dependent upon chance whether we come across it (Benjamin 1992: 155). In *À la recherche du temps perdu* (*In search of lost time*), Proust's narrator, Marcel, says how poorly he remembered his childhood town of Combray until one day he tasted a madeleine and the experience 'transported him back to the past, whereas before then he had been limited to the promptings of memory which obeyed the call of attentiveness' (Proust, quoted in Benjamin 1992: 155). This sense impression is sparked by the taste and scent of the madeleine, the object.

In articulating his reflections on memory, Benjamin uses Proust (as well as Bergson, Freud, and Krauss) to explore the links between memory, place, and time. Proust is important for Benjamin specifically due to the relationship between 'memoire voluntaire', 'in the service of the intellect', and the way that 'the information it gives about the past retains no trace of it' and 'memoire involuntaire', which, sparked by an object, or a scent, transports one back to a place and time, a lived moment (Erlebnis) that lay buried, forgotten from consciousness (Benjamin 1992:154–5). Maggie's reflections on the walks she undertook in Consett, remembering the scent of the 'iron ore' gave her a sense of comfort, a sense of home that had been largely forgotten to her historical or voluntary memory, but had been retained in her body memory, her involuntary memory. In other words, only what has not explicitly entered consciousness, what has been left behind, can become part of the memoire involuntaire.

The relationship between those lived moments of experience (Erlebnis) that emerge into consciousness through the memoire involuntaire and the historical experience (Erfahrung) captured by the memoire voluntaire are layered into life stories, biographies as expressed above in the sections we share about walking in our home towns.

The analysis of biographical accounts is enhanced by the identification of forms of memory and how they interrelate in the 'composition' of events, feelings, senses, and relationships; in the 'telling' of experience. Involuntary memory, for example, as in Maggie's smell of 'iron ore' and in Brian's recent experience of a cemetery, and a bench under a tree – brings back former experiences into the mind, to then be joined with more voluntary 'recollection' and fuller 'reconstruction' of the 'past'. 'Memory', then, can take various forms of 'recurrence' – as 'spontaneous' (leading from the involuntary or spontaneous to other forms), as 'remembrance' and 'active' reminiscence, perhaps fostered by involuntary thoughts, and as 'return' where there is a 're-enactment' or 're-living' of the past. These forms work together in a to-and-fro movement in time as we form and re-form our past, present, and future (see Conclusion; see Roberts 2004). These accounts by Maggie and Brian demonstrate something of these movements in memory in 'recounting' their childhoods – the places and walks, associations, and in the descriptions of the physical 'returns' (visits) and walks they undertook, reflecting on their past lives.

In the walking interview biographical method, in the sharing of experience, the potential for the spark or breakthrough of involuntary memory into consciousness is ever-present, in the mobility from scene to scene, attunement to people, landscape, landmarks, and objects (as we have done here) when mapping a walk and using the memory of a walk to think back, to consciously (voluntarily) recollect and then as we consider and evaluate our previous lived experience. This recognition of types and operation of memory is, we argue, a central element in the conduct and interpretation of biographical research, as our auto-biographical 'walks' illustrate, specifically in relation to how individuals under-stand the 'workings' of everyday experience of social class, gender, and other social dimensions, temporally and in rural/urban spaces and places. We tell our biographies with reference to time and space/place. As Heddon (2008) argues, 'it is difficult to talk about a life or life story without bringing space into it – for we talk about mapping a life, life as a path or journey' and (following Lippard), place is 'space combined with memory' (Heddon 2008: 88, 93). Heddon declares, 'I am surely not alone in taking intimate lovers back to the places I once lived, as if that somehow will explain who I am' (Heddon 2008: 96).

In this text, we raise awareness of the researcher within the world – as a mov-ing, interacting, experiencing being; contribute a new approach in biographi-cal research – the Walking Interview as a Biographical Method (WIBM); and critically reflect upon theoretical, experiential, and imaginative use of walking in sociological and biographical research, often at the intersections of art and ethnography.

Taken together, the three sections of the book argue that the WIBM enables us (and other researchers) to: get in touch with our 'realities' that demand critical reflection through ways of *knowing and 'understanding'* through lived experience; value the importance of innovative ways of conducting biographical research as an organic approach to advancing dialogue by engaging the performative and sensing body; and reflect on walking as a creative and imaginative method – as embodied, relational, sensory, and multi-modal. Through the WIBM, we might access/say the unsayable and connect with our imagination and the role of the imaginary in inter-disciplinary social research.

References

Benjamin, W. (1992) *Illuminations*. (Tr. H. Zohn). London: Fontana Press.

Brockmeier, J. (2001) From the end to the beginning: Retrospective teleology in autobiography. In: J. Brockmeier and D. Carbaugh (eds.) *Narrative and Identity: Studies in Autobiography, Self and Culture*. Amsterdam: John Benjamins.

Bryson, B. (2015) *Notes from a Small Island*. London: Penguin Random House.

Bunker, N. (2011) *Making Haste from Babylon*. London: Pimlico.

Eliot, G. (1871–2) *Middlemarch*. London: Blackwood and Sons.

Germain, J. (1990) *Steel Works. Consett, from Steel to Tortilla Chips*. Why Not Publishing. Available at www.juliangermain.com/projects/steelworks.php (Accessed 23 September 2018).

Heddon, D. (2008) *Autobiography and Performance*. London: Palgrave Macmillan.

Lynch, R. (2014) Phileas Fogg snacks factories face closure in *the Independent*, Friday 5 September 2014. Available at www.independent.co.uk/news/business/news/phileas-fogg-snacks-factories-face-closure-9715199.html (Accessed 23 September 2018).

McElvoy, A. (1998) Comment: The North can't have jobs at any price. In: *The Independent*, Saturday 19 September 1998. Available at www.independent.co.uk/voices/comment-the-north-cant-have-jobs-at-any-price-1199540.html. (Accessed 23 September 2018).

Philbrick, N. (2007) *Mayflower*. London: Penguin.

Roberts, B. (1999) An auto/biographical account of educational experience. In: M. Erben (ed.) *Biography and Education*. Brighton: Falmer, 111–24.

Roberts, B. (2004) Health narratives, time perspectives and self-images, *Social Theory and Health*, 2(2): 170–183.

Roberts, B. (2011) Interpreting photographic portraits: Autobiography, time perspectives, and two school photographs, *Forum: Qualitative Sozialforschung/Forum: Qualitative Social Research*, 12(2): art. 25, http://dx.doi.org/10.17169/fqs-12.2.1687 (Accessed 24 April 2017).

EXERCISE THREE

Walking and imagining: Time/memory/making

This exercise explores how as we walk, we imagine – we exist within time and memory, we make our experiences and understandings within ongoing life events.

Is there a particular walk that you did in the past that you recall very clearly – possibly it is one that comes to mind every now and then? It could be one that you completed fairly recently, say within the last year or so.

Choose a walk that appeared to resonate with your 'senses' – gave a notion of wellbeing, a heightened awareness that had a 'meaningful' effect on your idea of self – a positive connection with others and your environment.

- What is staying in your memory? Why? It may be a walk on a holiday, or one from your school days, childhood, or a countryside walk.
- Have you undertaken that walk again or tried to re-create it elsewhere?

Often we attempt to find ('re-create') the same or similar feelings in walking, for example, holiday walks appear to have such particular resonance ('happy times', 'relaxing experiences' – or at least that is what we hope for and holiday brochures describe).

We often actively seek to remember events and experiences, often with the aid of photos, videos, mementos, or souvenirs – and recount experiences to friends and family when we return, and also re-create in choosing the next holiday trip.

- Visualise the walk and draw it out on paper.
- What initially comes to mind?

- Note down further memories and reflections in your fieldbook or notebook and/or annotate the map.
- You may also wish to find photographs from the walk and place them on the route map and then talk the route through with a partner; then working in pairs, you may wish to share experiences of such walks, memories, biographical details, and reflections on the method.

[Note: The conduct of the exercise must be done in accordance with relevant ethical and other professional, institutional procedures and legal requirements].

CONCLUSION

The future of the Walking Interview as a Biographical Method

In this concluding chapter we draw together the main points and themes of the book and offer some reflections for future biographical and inter-disciplinary research using the Walking Interview as a Biographical Method. In particular, we take account of our earlier discussions on digital 'data' (as sources, reportage and communication) as well as arts based materials and practices in biographical research. Biographical study, as conceived here as 'research on the move' in walking interviews, is not only set in the present, but connects to past experiences and future anticipations.

As we make clear in the Introduction and then throughout this book, biographical research within sociology and related fields has undergone a remarkable expansion within the last thirty or more years, in a number of steps – marked by prominent texts and international research committees, its application in numerous substantive research fields (e.g. health, migration), the growing 'dialogue' with artistic methods, and gradual broad 'acceptance' (but not without critique) within the gamut of sociological methodologies. In fact, biographical research has a long (if 'secondary') history within sociology, stemming back to the 1920s-1930s Chicagoan work (which in turn was influenced by late 19c and early 20c social exploration and investigation) and including its re-emergence within interactionist study of the 1960s, then linking with oral history in the 1980s and later with varieties of narrative research in the 1990s. It can also be placed as part of a wider 'movement' of rising social interest in the 'biographical', as shown in popular TV and film 'biopics', the developments in literary biography (and 'popular' biographies of celebrities and dramatic life stories of travails of illness, loss, etc.), the ubiquity of the CV, and online social media profiles - perhaps in some manner echoing the rise in multiple forms of 'social documentary' lives in the 1920s and 1930s (e.g. in journalism, reportage, film and literature) (see Stott 1973).

What is perhaps underlying the 'social quest' for the 'biographical' is that the meaning of the 'individual' has become more uncertain: not merely, it can be argued, due to increasing individual and social unease, doubt and anxiety both locally and globally on a number of fronts (political, environmental, etc.), but also through a number of social 'revolutions' including: - biological: through the rise of medical scanning, DNA sequencing, neuroscience developments, as we can know more about ourselves, behaviour, body and mind and our family ancestry; digital: through computing and digital devices we have greater, easier access to imagery, knowledge and communication about our lives, our social, material, natural world, with also the possibilities of participation in 'augmented', 'immersive' and 'virtual worlds'. The social-economic order is shifting too through globalised trade, banking and finance, political uncertainty (e.g. the rise of nationalism), global environmental challenges, and 'social acceleration' (Rosa 2013) and the development of 'metric power' (Beer 2016). These shifts give rise to a renewed social focus upon the making of the 'biographical self' and indeed the 'relational self' in a world increasingly 'on the move' – where the definitions of social boundaries and identities are in flux. The Walking Interview as a Biographical Method – a 'method on the move' - contributes to the advancement of biographical research in a time of uncertainty with its renewed interest in the social (re-)formation of the 'biographical' - the individual life within its social context.

Dimensions of the Walking Interview as a Biographical Method

In the book we have addressed a number of dimensions of the WIBM – areas of influence on the approach to the study of lives and some of its concerns, or fields where it has been applied:

Biography and the Arts – Biographical research has increasingly engaged in recent years with a whole range of artistic practices – film and video, performance, photographic genres (e.g. social documentary, street, portraits), creative artworks (e.g. by respondents), found materials, and historical and literary sources (diaries, biographies) (Heddon 2008; O'Neill et al. 2015; Stanley 2013). In the book we have examined, in particular, linkages between 'walking' artistic methodologies and biographical research, demonstrating the ways in which the former brings to the latter the 'living' dimensions of the senses, space, and creativity in the expression, documentation and understanding of lived experience.

Biography and Politics – The book has discussed the interrelation between biographical research and politics in a number of ways – through a focus upon arts and performance advocacy; migration and asylum; marching and protest; and also the micro-politics of the everyday, for example, by seeing the walking interview as a participatory practice, to enable aspects of the 'doing' of justice in the research process, as well as performing and articulating rights to citizenship, and to safety or asylum (O'Neill 2018; O'Neill and Stenning 2013). We have also demonstrated and theorised the relationship between the micro-politics of everyday life and broader social structures, processes and issues, both to articulate and explore the relationship between personal concerns and public questions (Mills 1970; Roberts 2006).

Biography and Digital Technology – The advent of the portable tape recorder brought new possibilities for recording the lives of individuals which was a particular spur to oral history work. Today, with the spread of hand-held digital devices and cameras the ability to record voices and other sounds, and video, photographs, and other data (e.g. locational) is readily possible for both researcher and the researched. This 'opening up' to recording and sharing online, creates ethical (including professional and potential legal) issues regarding gaining consent and who has access, which are already core aspects of research protocols; but the ease of data collection and sharing (e.g. in real time) requires careful consideration in gaining institutional support when formulating and carrying out projects (c.f. the ethical procedures or rules of institutional and professional bodies), and ensuring participants' consent (e.g. on access to materials) both during and in the dissemination of the research. The 'digital impact' on narrative/biographical methods is already considerable – and will increase as new developments (e.g. in sensitivity to the environment, mapping and positioning, recording of personal data, etc.) arise, leading to a deepening of methodological and interpretive issues (including the amount and inter-connection of data, analytical procedures to be used, dissemination and a range of participants/audiences – including their responses, privacy and consent).

Biography and Methodological Advances – The Walking Interview as a Biographical Method may employ a range of techniques or procedures. The walking interview itself may be recorded in various ways and in diverse surroundings. In addition, the research may draw upon a number of sociological and artistic research approaches and technologies. There is much discussion in social sciences around 'mixed methodologies'; while the 'mixing' of methods and materials is not new, the increase in reaching across disciplines and the growing interest in artistic practices, along with the arrival of digital resources, has brought some urgency to discussion. Here is required new conceptions of how 'data' – sound, text, image – are to be produced and interrelated, in layers, links: between image/voiced interviews; internet resources and communication; holographic, augmented, virtual video studio/scene realities; the sensual and emotional; produced artwork; and also 'found materials'. A project 'mix' of some of these methods and materials can form a 'mosaic' – which can be approached from various starting points – a non-linear or multi-linear, multi-time, 'constellational' approach, with data related in many possible ways. Synaesthesic sensitivity (to the interplay of the senses), for example, could well become an important part of methodological development with links to the inter-connectedness of spatial with temporal dimensions of knowledge and understanding.

New approaches and terms or concepts will be required, from within the social sciences and adapted from digital technologies and arts based practices – to not simply 'mix' methods but to interrogate the possibilities of 'inter-mixing' in the range of inter-connections of materials, that are becoming available. A key point to make here is that researchers should be cognisant of why particular methods, techniques, procedures and materials are used: to what purpose – how are they conceiving, what are they accessing in the social world and adding to the understanding of biography and biographical sociology?

Biography and Theoretical Advances – Biographical research has drawn on a wide range of perspectives – particularly from 'micro theories', such as inter-actionism and narrative approaches (Riessman 2008; Roberts 2002; Roberts 2006; Schütze 2005; Wengraf 2001). We have explored connections with critical theory, especially the work of Walter Benjamin, visual ethnography, discussion of emotions and the senses, the mobilities 'paradigm', Chicago Sociology, situationism and psychogeography, and a wide range of artistic work. Of particular importance in this enterprise is the complex inter-relationship between 'micrology', the small-scale everyday experiences, and broader social structures and processes: this is the 'promise' of biographical sociology, an understanding of the inter-connections between individual lives and lived experiences within wider socio-historical contexts (Mills 1970; Roberts 2006).

Biographical and ethnographic conceptions

The Walking Interview as a Biographical Method has both affinities to ethnography and to biographical research (Roberts 2002) – but in drawing on these it seeks to be open to the importance of sound and other 'scapes', and how we interact with/in 'scenes' that are socially and environmentally complex.

How we interpret and respond to our surroundings, the natural and built environment and the social relational world, is pre-shaped to varying degrees by certain conceptions, or frames of reference (and according to past experience, new circumstance, etc.); across the social sciences and arts writers and practitioners have explored and formed means of encapsulating their surroundings (the city, the crowd, social change) using a myriad of perspectives. Artists (in painting and drawing, performance, sculpture, video, etc.); documentary practitioners (written, audio/visual); poets, novelists and dramatists, have approached and responded to socio-cultural circumstances, social events, the natural world in a myriad of ways – but commonly through a number of organising perspectives: naturalistic, realistic, sensational, melodramatic, gothic, romantic, documentary, sur-realistic, and other 'ways of comprehending' (see Clifford 1981; Entin 2007; Stott 1973). These 'genres' are not clear-cut but shift and come together in their definition and application. Sociologists, ethnographers, social investigators, documentarians, or commentators have also had social conceptions or paradigms, sometimes overlapping with those of other practitioners (c.f. the varied 'mobilities' research) (Atkinson 1990; Bruyn 1966; Pink 2007; Pink 2008).

The question of the implications of an adopted 'perspective' is relevant to all research, including how the use WIBM 'forms' and 'represents' the social relations or setting of the research and its participants – so what are the assumptions that are being made, in general or in specific instances in examples of its research e.g. is to some extent a kind of 'romantic' or 'liberal' view being formed – as charged against the Chicago School, and much 1930s photo-documentary (Smith 1988; Stott 1973)? Is there a 'politics' or 'stance' (even if not explicit) in social viewpoint, if so, what is it and how is it being expressed by researcher, researched and in the 'finished' project (although 'projects' remain always open, subject to some re-interpretation and new materials, particularly due to the ease of digital representation and dissemination)? To be 'fully' reflexive on its practice, researchers should consider their ongoing experience and outlook of conducting a WIBM (i.e. including 'attunement' to others and surroundings, or 'immersion' in a life story, the relational aspects of research and the critical distance necessary for procedure and analysis).

Researching and writing has a strong biographical connection – linking to our identity, and self-expression (Roberts 2007: 90; Roberts 2013; Roberts 2016: 161). Conducting research brings questions of competence in written language but also issues of personal adequacy in communication concerning how the connections and coherence of the research process is being relayed. It can also bring a further anxiety relating manner or the extent to which the 'reality' of the 'world' researched is being 'represented' – does the 'text' 'portray' the subject area and what are the personal or social implications of such a view being given on participants (and the researcher). For example, Agee in the late 1930s early 1940s grappled with 'writing' about the world he saw in the classic social documentary *Let Us Now Praise Famous Men* (Agee and Evans 2006) by using multiple genres (philosophical confessional, poetic, description, etc.), and very unorthodox punctuation and book and sentence structure to try and 'capture' the life and situation of distressed farmers, with deep concern regarding as to how he was portraying those he studied. In showing his struggle, even anguish, in writing his reflective account, he reveals the workings not only of composition – in giving a view of the social world - but the operation of his consciousness (Stott 1973: 311). Biographical research, as in walking interviews, is auto/biographical – the study of the lives of others creates and applies individual and social understandings and impacts on the construction of our own life (Stanley and Morgan 1993).

Walking and biographical research

The walking interview method provides an opportunity for biographical research to add a more dynamic investigation into lives than a more formal interview – it gives a 'method on the move' – as in a mobile, relational, embodied process and practice; interacting with others and with the natural and social environment. In doing so, it builds upon ethnographic 'interviewing' which is often more based on informal conversations 'in the field'. Here, three areas are important to consider, (drawing together our earlier discussions in this book relating to 'movement') in order to further advance and explore the methodological approach: Time/Space/Place; Memory; and Composition for research 'on the move':

Time/Space/Place

Walking is undertaken through time and movement in near space (scene) and place (wider location) and often in co-presence with others (c.f. Goffman). We understand our lives by constructing accounts of experiences as within immediate and wider settings (and relations) – the grounding of events, relationships and material circumstance, and in social networks. But our understandings are not simply formed in a linear past-present-future manner; rather, we move forwards, backwards, even side-ways in time conceptions within past, present and future (e.g. as present-past; future-present; past-future) (see Roberts 2004).

Our intention in developing the Walking Interview as a Biographical Method is to provide for a more 'moving' - 'alive' – innovative sociological approach which attends to the more sensual, the 'passing' (movement through the socio-natural world), that is multi-modal in techniques and practices, using multiple perspectives while retaining the importance of socio-historical contexts, and has a recognition of the impact of new technologies on time-space perspectives – and, importantly, as part of a recognition that social research has to be re-imagined and reconfigured (c.f. Back and Puwar 2013; Roberts et al. 2016). In walking, we shift between time perspectives – concurrent past, present and future conceptions – due to individual movement across scenes and associated new sensations. We 'walk in time' – recording and sifting our re-collection of memories, associations in thought, unfolding experiences, and monitoring (conscious and unconscious) our walking actions, and have possible conversations with others, all interplaying with our reasons for a particular walk and anticipations of its aftermath. We also walk within our understandings of place/space: the organisation and meaning of space/place come into being through social relations which are 'theorised' through class, race and gender (or other) relations (Massey 1994).

Memory

Memory and re-membering are central to individual movement and social relations, which may be 'paced out' along the ground in walking (Ingold 2010). A walk is a 'passage' through time and space – at some moments on walks (or in retrospect) we may make a point of saying to ourselves 'This moment I will remember', 'tagging' it for future recall: some 'moments' it appears 'stick' in memory, and 'return' (are 're-membered') later. In this way walks can be part of our autobiographical structurings (see Chapter 10). The biography of a life can be conceived according to its history, the operation of memory, and the ways we connect life events – formed within our incomplete knowledge of our social situation. In making such life event connections, we not only produce interpretations (and projections) of our life, but also create self-images or 'typifications' of ourselves and others, that may give us some 'certainties' on our surroundings and relationships, and how we can respond to life's experiences (health, education, family), on our embodiments and material realities (Roberts 2004). In walking we replay and adjust such connections and typifications to understand our surrounding world.

Much of our voluntary and also involuntary memories are associated with space/place – when we try to bring an incident or an individual to mind we might associate them with a certain location, and then further details may well arise; objects can also be used to aid and stimulate memory. Rumsey argues that recall is a 'rebuilding process', as a memory is 'called up' for use it becomes stronger whether it is a factual (e.g. an event) or a 'somatic' (physical) (e.g. smell, sound, skill) memory – it is taken from the past, modified and placed in a context of present meaning (Rumsey 2016: 34–7). She adds that while the relation between memory and physical environment is not well understood, walking is of interest as it is not just a body travelling through space/place, it gives context and stimulation to the mind – as shown by many intellectuals (writers, scientists) and others using the physicality of a walk to release a blockage in thought – something, it seems, we can miss in ('stationary') online research (Rumsey 2016: 114: 38-9).

In walking we may reflect on our lives and as 'instances' in life 'recur' in memory we attempt to fit them – contextualise them: we muse on what is past, what is still present of the past, or on whether what is to come will be the same as now and in our past? In fitting elements of our lives (or relationships, health, education, work, leisure interests, etc.) together we employ a wide range of rhetorical or metaphorical devices – fortune, choice, coincidence, etc. and seek or note what was then our individual 'changing points'. In doing so, life it appears becomes a less linear entity, rather also a backwards and forwards movement in perception and understanding – so past events (e.g. an accident) may be viewed in various narrative ways (according to the present and also our perceived future) (Roberts 2004). We might call this 'constellational thinking' (O'Neill 2017). 'Remembering' something in the past can take place seemingly spontaneously, without warning, or we may 'retrieve' an event for renewed consideration – which itself may bring something not expected – and we may give it some modification. While walking, 'passing' through a 'scene' may bring these kinds of remembering and reworking – and associated emotions and sensations, into our consciousness (as illustrated in Chapter 10). Implicated here is the formation and reformation of the self as embodied, sensual and expressive: we may have particular 'reminiscences' of past walks which may raise these dimensions of experience and may be significant for the individual ongoing notions of self, identity and outlook.

Composition

Walking can be likened to the process of composing – again, many writers, poets, scientists have used walking to 'think' – form new ideas, 'chew' over issues, construct an argument, musical score, or poem, and so on. The 'rhythm' of walking and the mind are seemingly working together. 'Composing' can, therefore, be linked to the rhythm of walking; more broadly, for instance, Edensor describes a 'rhythmanalysis' (quoting Lefebvre) since as 'everywhere where there is interaction between a place, a time and an expenditure of energy, there is rhythm' (Edensor 2010: 69). The Walking Interview as a Biographical Method as a 'method on the move' attempts to reflect the participants 'rhythms' in the organisation of the cognitive, sensual and emotional experiencing of everyday situations.

Composition involves imagination and time – relating elements from past experience into our current situation and possible future life 'avenues'. As researchers we may well regard putting together thoughts relating to our work as a outwardly conscious, active, more or less straightforward process; but as with any other individuals, in walking we are also composing – 'editing', reworking our experience (perceptions, interpretations), giving them new meanings and relationships, in the everyday construction and reconstruction of relationships to others and our socio-natural environments. Research is embodied – it can be a physically and mentally demanding activity; a walking interview, as any walk, can be tiring on the body and mind whether in urban and non-urban environments.

Traditionally, both qualitative and quantitative research have relied, to a great extent, on writing texts in terms of organisational formal procedures and outputs. But, we must keep aware that 'writing' takes place throughout research, from grant application, through field note taking, to reports and publications. Again, writing involves 'composition' – the relating elements together in a coherent, flowing manner connected by an argument, examples and so on, to 'convince', 'satisfy' or ' 'interest' the reader according to a set of objectives, as well as purposes or methodological criteria. 'Text' production and use will obviously continue to be central to research as new technologies depend on 'words'. But, increasingly 'composition' will include the interrelation of text/image/sound (and interactively the range of senses) made possible by digital technologies and devices. For instance, ethnographers and walking artists (as we have seen) have used and combined diverse 'materials' and practices to form understanding of how we perceive, imagine and construct our 'reality', for example, Pink (2007) relates images and video in visual ethnography; Heddon (2008) connects performance, autobiography and walking, while O'Neill (O'Neill et al. 2001; O'Neill 2008) brings together art and ethnography (ethno-mimesis) and walking. How we experience, conceive and compose the social and natural world from our personal and wider oral, visual and other 'resources' – and how these interplay – is at the centre of the use of walking (and associated interview) as a biographical method.

Theorising, experiencing and imagining in biographical research

In this book, the Walking Interview as a Biographical Method (WIBM) has been offered as a contribution to biographical sociology, and has been outlined through three related sections, on theorising, experience and imagining. The methodological foundations of the WIBM have been contextualized, for instance, within the history of sociology and biographical research, including the Chicago School, C. W. Mills, critical theory (specifically Walter Benjamin), and the use of walking in arts practice. The 'rise' of walking research brings a focus on embodiment and movement; the senses and 'sensory sociality'; 'attunement'; the 'making of place'; and dialogic and participatory commitment – and on how these can be methodologically and interpretively interrelated (O'Neill 2015; Pink et al. 2010; Pink 2008). Biographical research itself is also undergoing rapid change:

> [T]he field is developing along a number of dimensions, in large part due to drawing from the arts and digital media; as being reflective, creative, imaginative and perceptive; as containing multi-methods, multi-media, and multi-sites; as multi-sensual, multi-temporal, multi-conscious; as critical, participatory and socially engaged; and as theoretical and theorizing – and reflecting the broadening of qualitative research.
>
> *(see Back and Puwar 2013; Roberts 2016: 164)*

Within biographical research there is a 'tradition' of guides to the field and practice (including topics, examples, methodological assumptions, procedures, ethics, etc.) which attempt to give an overview of what the field constitutes at a particular time; but such outlines can become problematic as research materials, procedures, interpretive schemes, etc. expand (Back and Puwar 2012; Denzin 1970; Denzin 1989; Dollard 1935; Edel 1978; Kazmierska 2018; Plummer 2001; Plummer 2013; Roberts 2002; Stanley and Morgan 1993). It has been not the intention in the book to stipulate 'requirements' for WIBM (or a 'manifesto' or programme – c.f. Danchev 2011); within biographical research it will remain a broad, even further extending, practice with old and new approaches to the collection and relating diverse materials, while drawing upon perspectives and practices across the social sciences, arts and other fields (e.g. the biological sciences). In the forthcoming section (after Exercise Four) we offer 'Principles and Practice: A Framework' – with the objective to give some guidance (but not a definitive statement) to researchers wanting to explore and take forward the Walking Interview as a Biographical Method – to study lived/living lives within their social worlds.

References

Agee, J. and Evans, W. (2006) *Let Us Now Praise Famous Men*. London: Penguin (orig. pub. Houghton Mifflin 1941).

Atkinson, P. (1990) *The Ethnographic Imagination*. London: Routledge.

Back, L. and Puwar, N. (2012) A manifesto for live methods: Provocations and capacities, *The Sociological Review*, Special Issue, 60(1_suppl): 6–17.

Back, L. and Puwar, N. (eds.) (2013) *Live Methods*. London: Wiley-Blackwell.

Beer, D. (2016) *Metric Power*. London: Palgrave Macmillan.

Bruyn, S. T. (1966) *The Humanistic Perspective in Sociology*. Englewood-Cliffs, NJ: Prentice-Hall.

Clifford, J. (1981) On ethnographic surrealism, *Comparative Studies in Society and History*, 23(4): 539–564.

Danchev, A. (2011) *Artists' Manifestos From the Futurists to the Stuckists*. Harmondsworth: Penguin.

Denzin, N. K. (1970) *Sociological Methods*. London: Butterworths.

Denzin, N. K. (1989) *Interpretive Biography*. London: Sage.

Dollard, J. (1935) *Criteria for the Life History*. New Haven: Yale University Press.

Edel, L. (1978) Biography: A manifesto, *Biography*, Winter, 1(1): 1–3.

Edensor, T. (2010) Walking in rhythms: Place, regulation, style and the flow of experience, *Visual Studies*, 25(1): 69–79.

Entin, J. B. (2007) *Sensational Modernism*. Chapel Hill, NA: The University of North Carolina Press.

Heddon, D. (2008) *Autobiography and Performance*. London: Palgrave Macmillan.

Ingold, T. (2010) Ways of mind-walking: reading, writing, painting, *Visual Studies*, 25(1): 15–23.

Kazmierska, K. (2018) Doing biographical research—Ethical concerns in changing social contexts, *Polish Sociological Review*, 3(203): 393–411.

Massey, D. (1994) *Space, Place and Gender*. Cambridge: Polity.

Mills, C. W. (1970) *The Sociological Imagination*. Harmondsworth: Penguin.

O'Neill, M. (2008) Transnational Refugees: The Transformative Role of Art? *Forum Qualitative Sozialforschung/Forum: Qualitative Social Research*, 9(2), Available at: <http://www.qualitative-research.net/index.php/fqs/article/view/403>. (Accessed 23rd October 2018).

O'Neill, M. (2015) Participatory biographies: Walking, sensing, belonging. In: M. O'Neill, B. Roberts, and A. Sparkes (eds.) *Advances in Biographical Methods*. Abingdon, Oxon: Routledge.

O'Neill, M. (2017) Studying the Marginalised with Mixed Methods. In: M. Hviid Jacobsen, and S. Walklate (eds.) *Liquid Criminology: Doing Imaginative Criminological Research*. Abingdon, Oxon: Routledge.

O'Neill, M. (2018) Walking, well-being and community: racialized mothers building cultural citizenship using participatory arts and participatory action research, *Ethnic and Racial Studies*, 41(1): 73–97.

O'Neill, M., in association with Giddens, S., Breatnach, P., Bagley, C., Bourne, D. and Judge, T. (2001) Renewed methodologies for social research: Ethno-mimesis as performative praxis, *The Sociological Review*, 50(1): 69–88.

O'Neill, M., Roberts, B. and Sparkes, A. (eds.) (2015) *Advances in Biographical Methods*. Abingdon, Oxon: Routledge.

O'Neill, M. and Stenning, P. (2013) Walking biographies and innovations in visual and participatory methods: Community, Politics and Resistance in Downtown East Side Vancouver. In: C. Heinz, and G. Hornung (eds.) *The Medialization of Auto/Biographies: Different Forms and Their Communicative Contexts* co-edited by Hamburg: UVK.

Pink, S. (2007) Walking with video, *Visual Studies*, 22(3): 240–252.

Pink, S. (2008) *Doing Sensory Ethnography*. London: Sage.

Pink, S., Hubbard, P., O'Neill, M. and Radley, A. (2010) Walking across disciplines: From ethnography to arts practice, *Visual Studies*, 25(1): 1–7.

Plummer, K. (2001) *Documents of Life 2*. London: Sage.

Plummer, K. (2013) Stories and storied lives: A manifesto. In: L. Stanley (ed.) *Documents of Life Revisited*. Aldershot: Ashgate.

Riessman, C. K. (2008) *Narrative Methods for the Human Sciences*. London: Sage.

Roberts, B. (2002) *Biographical Research*. Buckingham: OU.

Roberts, B. (2004) Health narratives, time perspectives and self-images, *Social Theory and Health*, 2(2): 170–183.

Roberts, B. (2006) *Micro Social Theory*. Basingstoke: Palgrave Macmillan.

Roberts, B. (2007) *Getting the Most Out of the Research Experience*. London: Sage.

Roberts, B. (2013) Imaginative inquiry and the lives of ideas. In: C. Fogel, E. Quinlan, and A. Quinlan (eds.) *Imaginative Inquiry*. Palo Alto: Academica Press.

Roberts, B. (2016) Reflections on a life in social science. In: M. Greiff, och R. Johansson (Redaktörer) *I ständing rörelse: Mellan Arbete, Kulture och Didaktik – En vanbok till Lars Berggren*. Malmo: Mezzo Media.

Roberts, S., Snee, H., Hine, C., Morey, Y. and Watson, H. (eds.) (2016) *Digital Methods for Social Science*. Basingstoke: Palgrave Macmillan.

Rosa, H. (2013) *Social Acceleration. A New Theory of Modernity*. New York: Columbia University Press.

Rumsey, A. S. (2016) *When We Are No More*. London: Bloomsbury.

Schütze, F. (2005) Cognitive figures of autobiographical extempore narration. In: R. Miller (ed.) *Biographical Research Methods*, vol. II. London: Sage.

Smith, D. (1988) *The Chicago School: A Liberal Critique of Capitalism*. Basingstoke: Macmillan.

Stanley, L. (ed.) (2013) *Documents If Life Revisited*. Abingdon: Routledge.

Stanley, L. and Morgan, D. (eds.) (1993) On auto/biography in sociology, *Sociology*, 27(1): 41–52.

Stott, W. (1973) *Documentary Expression and Thirties America*. Oxford: OUP.

Wengraf, T. (2001) *Qualitative Research Interviewing. Biographical Narrative and Semi-Structured Methods*. London: Sage.

EXERCISE FOUR

WIBM exercise: Observing, experiencing, imagining

This exercise brings together the key elements of the previous sections and exercises to undertake a WIBM.

There is no one single way of undertaking a WIBM. In this exercise, you will be invited to try out two possible ways of undertaking a WIBM – sharing a walk with a partner (as an 'interviewer') or you and a partner sharing each other's walk.

Take some time to both remember and re-imagine a favourite walk, or a walk that is important to you.

1. Draw the route of your walk – marking/mapping the landmarks that you can remember along the way.
2. At this point, you could talk your map/walk through with a partner (as an 'interviewer').
3. Take the walk, either alone or with a partner ('interviewer') – note down any thoughts/reflections in your notebook or sound recorder. Take photographs along the way to document your walk.
4. Consider the features you placed on your map as you go along. If other landmarks or objects in the landscape take your attention, then share these if with a partner, and also record these in your notebook/ sound recorder, including any memories, feelings that they invoke.
5. Alternatively, both you and a partner could both undertake 1, 2, and 3 – doing your own walks – to be compared later.

Print your photographs and add them or 'curate' them around your route map.

- Talk this through with your partner or interviewer.
- You may wish to take it in turns to do so.
- You may also wish to record your narratives/talk.

Listen to your sound file and/or read your notebook, listing key themes and quotations.

- You may wish to use a computer software programme for the analysis of qualitative data to sort and store your themes/analysis from the walk and sound recordings, as well as your images.

Whether your walk has been undertaken alone OR you and a partner have shared each other's walks, discuss the analysis, findings, and experiences with each other.

- Discuss the ethical process and implications of this exercise.

[Note: The conduct of the exercise must be done in accordance with relevant ethical and other professional, institutional procedures and legal requirements]

THE WALKING INTERVIEW AS A BIOGRAPHICAL METHOD

Principles and practice: A framework

Biographical research is a dynamic and increasingly popular field in sociology, supported by the formation of research centres, national associations, networks, and journals. The Walking Interview as a Biographical Method (WIBM), as part of biographical research, seeks to investigate individuals' daily life experiences and their past and future perspectives, using a variety of concepts, materials, and interpretive approaches, whilst walking, to provide a life account, a story of a life, or an aspect of a life 'on the move'.

The Walking Interview as a Biographical Method should have the intention to *evoke*, seek to *invoke*, and produce research that has *resonance* as it is constituted theoretically, experientially, and imaginatively. We hope you enjoy thinking, practising, and experiencing the WIBM.

Theoretical/epistemological underpinnings

We have been influenced by a range of theoretical and methodological perspectives from various fields within sociology and outside, including Chicago Sociology, urban sociology and mobilities research, visual ethnography, artistic practices, critical theory, and historical commentary.

The following Principles and practice: A framework can guide WIBM in relation to: concepts; creative interpretive imagination; procedures and analysis; ethics; and praxis.

Concepts

A set of concepts will be necessary to guide a piece of walking interview biographical research – for example:

Embodiment – how the body (in walking) is involved in experiencing the materiality of the environment within the mind/consciousness and sensuality.

Passing – the awareness of movement in space and time: a consideration of both embodiment in the physical experience of walking and the 'social world' as in flux.

Memory – how our recollections and introspections are implicated in the movement in consciousness between past, present, and future perspectives – as retrospection, 'spection', and prospection.

Mobility and rhythm – moving in time and through place and immediate space, according to a shifting pace.

Moments – the instances of experience, including 'small stories' and immediate dialogue between research participants.

Scene – the immediate vista seen from an individual's position and 'comprehended' through the senses.

Senses – to account for the senses, how they inform and are informed within an ongoing experience.

Sensibility – an approach to conducting biographical research that is 'attuned' (see below) both to sense and meaning-making in planning, doing, and analysing/writing up research with an 'ethnographic feel' or 'eye'.

Time – the dimensions of perceived time – 'time perspectives': our consciousness in differing conceptions of past, present, and future.

Timing – an awareness of 'moments', of 'time passing' in 'unfolding' experiences: consciousness as moving between perspectives of past, present, and future.

Creative interpretive imagination

The WIBM puts creativity and imagination at the centre of interpretation. A number of dimensions can be identified for understanding the experience of living/walking in the social world as we make and re-make our lives.

Acuity – an interpretive and conceptual sharpness and perceptiveness; observation.

Attunement – interconnecting with another – being on the same 'wavelength', mutual sharing of understandings – a 'tuning in', an 'appreciation' of the respondent's view and circumstances and our own participation – neither too close, nor too far.

Biographic understanding – lives as lived – understood and 'appreciated' in their social and environmental context – their social relations, in space/place.

Creativity – new ways of working/new connections between disparate material/visual elements: ideas, methods, representation – drawing on other disciplines, the arts, and other practices.

Emotionality – the awareness and impact of emotions that are being expressed by the interviewee (and the researcher) e.g., empathy.

Haptic involvement – active understanding space and objects in the surrounding environment.

Inference – to explore the possible connections between texts – inter-textuality.

Immersion – engrossment, insights gained through detailed knowledge (cf. attunement).

Reflexivity – monitoring of self, the processes of working – consideration of what has been done, how and why it has been done, and how to proceed. A reflective mode of monitoring of action.

Sensuality – a monitoring of the senses – 'sensory registers'; how they inform ongoing practice and relationships.

Procedures and analysis

Biographical research has applied a wide range of interpretive procedures and analysis – forms of thematic, discourse, narrative, grounded theory approaches, etc. Here, we draw attention to a number of techniques to realise imagination and practice for undertaking and analysing a WIBM. This is in addition to/alongside thematic, discourse, narrative, and grounded theory methods of analysis.

Assemblage – montage, collage, frottage, layers, and linking – the 'pinning', 'cutting', 'pasting', 'layering' of materials and analysis (e.g., text and images) to interrelate them in complex ways, for example, to 'curate'.

Constellational thinking and analysis – the relational understanding of experience and the complex circumstances of its articulation, emergence, and analysis.

Mapping – imagining, visualising a walk (which may be pre-drawn as a physical map) alerts us to how time, distance, place, direction are culturally and structurally (differentially) formed ('mapped') by public and private organisations, groups, and individuals. 'Mapping' is also a continuous, routine, mental process during a walk as we negotiate our environment – which may take a 'turn' (physically, in memory, etc.) that was not foreseen.

Multi-modal – means having multiple modes or modalities – a walk may be captured in sound, image, film, poetically, and the data curated or layered for analysis and dissemination in filmic work, performance, poetically, or all three (or more).

Valency – the nature and degree of connection between analytic elements from the social world.

Ethics

Ethics is a process, not an event – it is important to reflect upon what it means to undertake an ethical approach to the WIBM. The WIBM is a relational process, and so at the centre of good practice in research ethics is necessary awareness of this dimension.

There is detailed research guidance both from professional associations and research bodies, for instance, the International and European Sociological Associations, as well as in-country professional associations (e.g., the Irish Research Council). In the UK, there are a range of bodies: the British Sociological Association, The Social Research Association, and Research Councils (the Economic and Social Research Council, and the Arts and Humanities Research Council). University (Departmental and School) Ethics Committees' advice and ethical requirements have to be addressed, as well as those of non-academic institutions (cf. health organisations, law) where relevant. For instance, the ESRC (UK) gives a range of principles that cover the 'rights and dignity' of individuals and groups involved, 'risk and harm', the 'benefits' to individuals and society, the basis of participation (e.g., voluntary, informed), the definition of 'responsibility and accountability' of the researcher, the issue of the 'independence' of the research and possible 'conflicts of interest', and the 'integrity and transparency' of research.[1]

It is important that researchers reflect upon ethics and associated implications of their research throughout the whole process from design through to dissemination, reporting, archiving, and publications. The ESRC framework asks researchers to 'promote a culture of ethical reflection, debate and mutual learning' in the research process. There is the need, here, to explore and recognise differing cultural perspectives and to be aware of important ethical dimensions attached to the use of participatory and 'creative methods' (poetry, drama, visual materials, etc.)

Praxis

In working with life histories, biography, and the representation or reimagining of people's life stories in photographs or film, in visual and performative art forms, there is the ever present possibility for the research to be 'transformative' – a potential for individual and/or social change to take place for participant and/or researcher. A 'difference' may be made to biographical experience due to the impact of: new knowledge and understanding gained in process of narrating a life story, the circumstance of the telling, and/or the relations between the two.

By 'Praxis', we mean purposeful knowledge – knowledge that may be policy relevant. The participatory ways that we can work with 'co-researchers' or 'research participants' seek to ensure that an arena is created for their voices to be shared and heard, as well as understood. In this book (see Chapters 6 and 7), we have emphasised the importance of opening and keeping open a 'space' for critical discourse and analysis as a radical democratic imaginary.[2]

- We invite readers to reflect upon the way that knowledge produced through WIBM might create or inspire interventions in policy and practice.

Notes

1 See the ESRC Research Ethics Framework on the website for more information: https://esrc.ukri.org/funding/guidance-for-applicants/research-ethics/. See also the Toolkit for Participatory Theatre and Walking as Social Research Methods (PASAR) available at: http://eprints.ncrm.ac.uk/4120/1/2.%20Toolkit%20PASAR%20Fina l%2030%20Jan%2018.pdf. The NCRM has a very helpful series of three video casts by Dr Helen Kara on the theories, principles and practice of research ethics. Available at https://www.ncrm.ac.uk/resources/video/# (Accessed 13 August 2018). See also Kara (2018) who explores Euro-Western and Indigenous perspectives on research ethics and unpacks the ethical implications of using creative and participatory methods. This book highlights the need for researchers to have and learn cultural competence, as well as providing useful analysis of the ethical use of creative methods such as poetry, writing and performance. Kara, H. (2018) *Research Ethics in the Real World: Euro-Western and Indigenous Perspectives*. Bristol: Policy Press.
See also: Kazmierska, K. (2018) Doing Biographical Research—Ethical Concerns in Changing Social Contexts, *Polish Sociological Review*, 3 (203):393–411.
2 For example, in Chapter 7, the WIBM with *Open Clasp* and Faye the subsequent analysis and sharing of the walk, undertaken by Faye (not her real name) led to a research paper/publication (O'Neill and McHugh 2017) that was also given back to the Direct Access Hostel and informed practice, as well as a play/performance created from the voices and experiences of the women who took part in the workshop and walkshop. Thus, sharing the women's lives and input across the widest possible audience not only raises awareness, and supports better understanding, but changes hearts and minds and impacts on social policy.
O'Neill, M. and McHugh, C. (2017) Walking with Faye from a direct access hostel to her special place in the city: walking, body and image space. A visual essay. *Journal of Social Work Practice*, 31 (2): 207–23.

INDEX

Note: Page numbers in *italics* indicate figures.

Milton Keynes UK
Ingram Content Group UK Ltd.
UKHW022143070324
439135UK00004B/16